POETRY OF WITNESS

POETRY OF WITNESS

The Tradition in English, 1500–2001

EDITED BY

Carolyn Forché

AND

Duncan Wu

W. W. NORTON & COMPANY

NEW YORK · LONDON

For information about special discounts for bulk purchases,
please contact W. W. Norton Special Sales
at specialsales@wwnorton.com or 800-233-4830

Manufacturing by Courier Westford
Book design by Brooke Koven
Production manager: Devon Zahn

Library of Congress Cataloging-in-Publication Data

Poetry of Witness : the Tradition in English, 1500/2001 / edited by
Carolyn Forché and Duncan Wu. — First edition.
pages cm
Includes index.
ISBN 978-0-393-34042-6 (pbk.)
1. Poetry—Translations into English. 2. Witnesses—Poetry.
3. Political atrocities—Poetry. 4. Military history—Poetry.
I. Forché, Carolyn, editor of compilation.
II. Wu, Duncan, editor of compilation.
PN6101.P544 2014
808.81'9358—dc23
                                          2013035019

W. W. Norton & Company, Inc.
500 Fifth Avenue, New York, N.Y. 10110
www.wwnorton.com

W. W. Norton & Company Ltd.
Castle House, 75/76 Wells Street, London W1T 3QT

1 2 3 4 5 6 7 8 9 0

Contents

II • THE CIVIL WAR

III • THE AGE OF UNCERTAINTY   209

VI • THE AGE OF WORLD WAR   509

POETRY OF WITNESS

Introduction

by Duncan Wu

THIS BOOK IS the work of those marked by history. It contains poets whose lives were shaped by insurmountable forces, thrown off course, even—at worst—destroyed. Some of these poems were composed at an extreme of human endurance, on the brink of breakdown or death; all bear witness to historical event, and the irresistibility of its impact.

To William Meredith (see p. 592), the poet's engagement with the world is a matter of conscience, for "the imperfections of society . . . can *only* be responded to militantly, by poet and reader." As he saw it, the distinctive experience of life in the twentieth century, with its perils and pitfalls, obliged him to act as dissident: it was, he said, "the most *urgent* role at a time like ours."[1] Readers play their part in this process: Carolyn Forché argues for witness as "a mode of reading rather than of writing, of readerly encounter with the literature of that-which-happened, and its mode is evidentiary rather than representational—as evidentiary, in fact, as spilled blood."[2] If the function of the reader is to encounter "the literature of that-which-happened," that of the artist is to testify—one to which writers are compelled by their relation to words. Forché observes that "poetic language attempts a coming to terms with evil and its embodiments, and there are appeals for a shared sense of humanity and collective resistance."[3] These principles provide the basis for this book.

---

1. William Meredith, "Reasons for Poetry," *Quarterly Journal of the Library of Congress* 39.3 (1982) 184–93, p. 190.
2. see p. 21, below.
3. see p. 24, below.

Poetry of Witness has its roots in Forché's experience of El Salvador, the occupied West Bank, Lebanon, and South Africa, during the latter part of the last century: in those troubled places her sensibility was forged by what she has termed "the impress of extremity." Kindred spirits in that experience include Joseph Brodsky, Anna Akhmatova, Yannis Ritsos, Paul Celan, Federico García Lorca, and Nazim Hikmet—to all of whom the twentieth century delivered an abundance of unlooked-for encounters with forces that shaped their lives. In acknowledgment of that kinship she collected their works in a single volume of twentieth-century poetry, *Against Forgetting*, published by W. W. Norton in 1993.

Although the concept of witness is the product of the last century, and hitherto applied to writers of that time, this volume argues it is found elsewhere. Indeed, there is no lack of it in the canon. Why should that be? In part, it bears out Forché's contention in her introduction to *Against Forgetting*, that the concentration of contemporary poets on the realm of the personal, almost to the point of myopia, is peculiar to recent times. Prior to that, poets commonly discussed experiences shared by the larger community in which they lived.

There is another reason. The experiences that compel our poets are frequently beyond the containing power of language. Forché quotes Paul Celan: language "had to go through its own responselessness, go through horrible silences, go through the thousand darknesses of death-bringing speech" (see p. 22, below). The connection between the outside world and a work of art that testifies to its atrocities is unclear and, to a large extent, unknowable. Take for instance the poetry of Samuel Bamford, who was in St. Peter's Field on August 16, 1819, when the order was given for mounted cavalrymen to charge, sabers drawn, into a crowd of sixty thousand unarmed civilians, including women and children, leaving 14 dead and 654 injured. Those nonviolent protestors wanted better representation in a Parliament dominated by placemen and timeservers with no understanding of their sufferings. It would be fascinating to know how Bamford took that experience—one that was deeply personal, as he feared in its aftermath his wife to be among the injured—and converted it into a poem governed by the rules of meter, rhyme, and stanzaic form, "The Song of the Slaughter" (p. 354). Such creative discipline is all the more remarkable in someone incarcerated at Lincoln Jail.[4]

---

4. For more on Bamford and Peterloo, see pp. 350–52, below, as well as John Gardner, *Poetry and Popular Protest: Peterloo, Cato Street and the Queen Caroline Controversy* (Basingstoke, Hampshire, 2011), chapter 2; Robert Reid, *The Peterloo Massacre* (London, 1989); Robert Walmsley, *Peterloo: The Case Reopened* (New York, 1969); and Robert Poole, "The

Celan's point is that the initial response of the imagination is silence, and that language is inadequate to the task of articulating fully our reaction to the extremes of experience. It might be argued there is little new in this—and that, indeed, is our view. For poetry of witness as Forché defines it, despite its theoretical origins (which lie in the discourse of the twentieth and early twenty-first centuries), has always been the means by which the imagination has articulated its response to war, imprisonment, oppression, and enslavement. Like Celan, we argue that, of all genres, poetry is best suited to the task. We refer to its ability to accommodate the sublime, the ineffable, that of which we cannot speak. This is admittedly a Romantic argument and, perhaps for that reason, its application to poetry predating the French Revolution might be thought irrational. Yet preromantic poets come as close to discussing emotions beyond verbal formulation as their successors, not least in the case of Wyatt's "Sighs are my food," written during what he had every reason to expect would be his final imprisonment, or Surrey's "The storms are passed, these clouds are overblown," composed within days, perhaps hours, of his beheading (pp. 41, 49).

What, for that matter, was St. Thomas More doing when he composed the short verses that begin this volume (pp. 34–35), other than testifying to the emotions that accompanied his final days of imprisonment? Much the same might be said of Seymour's "Forgetting God" (p. 42) and Askew's "Ballad Written in Newgate" (p. 51), conceived as their authors approached (however reluctantly) their final moments. Their utterances raise the question of what might be the perspective of a writer who believes death to be minutes hence. Such feelings remain beyond words, other than through the idealizing construct of verse. St. Robert Southwell seems in some poems to be anticipating his own demise and preparing for it: in "Decease Release" (p. 75) he writes in the persona of the executed Mary Queen of Scots, and in "I Die Alive" (p. 76) that of the imprisoned Philip Howard, thirteenth Earl of Arundel, who waited in the Tower of London for an execution that would never come. That imaginative construct—of a man meditating his end—is as compelling a spiritual exercise as any in this volume. It comes from someone who knew he had limited time in which to pursue a mission the sole conclusion of which would be torture and death. He would have suspected he would be prevented from writing in confinement, as seems to have been the case. His surviving verse was composed during the six brief years in which he lived clandestinely in London, moving from one hiding place to the next, while he served the spiritual needs of those willing to take the ultimate risk for their beliefs. That the outcome was one to which he could testify only in advance serves as partial apology for his sometimes cryptic mode of expression. As he speaks for others, so he speaks for himself.

Forché defines extremity as "the product of the drive to expunge one category in the name of another, to sacrifice the individual on the altar of the communal and vice versa."[5] It underpins the poetry in this volume, and our first duty as editors has been to understand our authors' lives and engage with the world in which they lived and breathed. War, imprisonment, torture, expectation of imminent death, exile, or slavery, have pointed us in the right direction, while commitment to politically loaded causes, and (on occasion) involvement in espionage, are recurrent themes. As with all acts of historical reconstruction, our judgments have involved as much scrutiny of the biographical facts as interpretation of them.

In the case of John Wilmot, second Earl of Rochester—an enigmatic figure when considered in the context purely of his poetry—we place emphasis on his service in the Royal Navy, when he fought with distinction in the Second Anglo-Dutch War under the command of the Earl of Sandwich. Rochester was in the thick of a bombardment in Bergen Harbor on August 2, 1665, two friends standing immediately next to him being cut in half by a single cannonball. (According to Burnet, the projectile "carried away Mr. Mountague's belly, so that he died within an hour after."[6]) It was a bloody, arduous, lethal encounter in which the English suffered terrible losses—yet, according to Sandwich, Rochester "showed himself brave, industrious, and of useful parts," while Burnet reported he possessed "as brave and as resolute a courage as was possible."[7] What Rochester thought of the king's reward of 750 pounds and appointment of Gentleman of the Bedchamber (a post that entailed sleeping in the king's bedroom) we can only conjecture, but his wartime experiences can hardly have eased the return to court.

"I am homesick for war," Karl Shapiro was to write, nearly four centuries later;[8] perhaps that was Rochester's reaction, for he rejoined the British fleet

5. Carolyn Forché, introduction to *Against Forgetting: Twentieth-Century Poetry of Witness* (New York, 1993), p. 46.
6. Quoted by John Adlard, *The Debt to Pleasure* (Manchester, 1974), p. 37.
7. Ibid., p. 34.
8. Karl Shapiro, "Human Nature."

"without communicating his design to his closest relations"[9] (or indeed the king) on May 31, 1666, in time for the Four Days' Battle, which began on June 1st off North Foreland. This was another hellish display of which the toll of injuries and deaths tells the tale: ten English captains killed and eight wounded; nine English ships sunk; 1,500 men wounded and 1,800 killed. The roar of battle was audible to pleasure seekers in Hyde Park, eighty miles away. In its midst Rochester volunteered for a suicide mission—to carry a message from his commander, Sir Edward Spragge, in a small vessel, to another ship in the fleet. At first Spragge could not find anyone crazy enough to navigate his way through the blizzard of musket fire and cannonballs, but Rochester "went in a little boat through all the shot, and delivered his message, and returned back to Sir Edward, which was much commended by all that saw it."[10]

Rochester's first biographer, Gilbert Burnet, said he "thought it necessary to begin his life with these demonstrations of his courage in an element and way of fighting, which is acknowledged to be the greatest trial of clear and undaunted valour." Perhaps, but the more noteworthy observation is that no one undergoes such escapades without being profoundly altered by them. The editor of Rochester's correspondence says the poet was "deeply affected" by the Bergen incident,[11] and Rochester cannot have been less disturbed by the Four Days' Battle (a more intense encounter than Bergen, and of which Rochester was among the few volunteers to survive). Stories that he was intoxicated for five years on end, colluded in murder, got into fights, and "felt the devil inside him" upon arrival in London, suggest he found the transition to civilian life difficult.

This may explain why Rochester lived as if extinction was imminent. (It can be no accident that the debauchee of one of his late poems is like "some brave admiral, in former war"; see p. 229.) In his world the arbitrary, the random, and the meaningless dictate one's existence. His famed apostrophe finds "Nothing," traced to the monarch, to be the determining force in the universe. And what else is St. James's Park in Rochester's curse poem besides a theater of casual encounters void of significance? Squeamishness about language should not blind us to the truth—that his was the sensibility

---

9. Adlard, p. 38.

10. Quoted by James William Johnson, *A Profane Wit: The Life of John Wilmot, Earl of Rochester* (Rochester, NY, 2004), p. 85.

11. See *The Letters of John Wilmot, Earl of Rochester*, ed. Jeremy Treglown (Chicago, 1980), p. 45.

of a sensitive, and profoundly moral, man.[12] His view of humanity is nowhere more clear than in his "Satyr Against Reason and Mankind":

> For hunger or for love they fight and tear,
> Whilst wretched man is still in arms for fear.
> For fear he arms, and is of arms afraid,
> From fear, to fear successively betrayed;
> Base fear, the source whence his best passions came:
> His boasted honour, and his dear-bought fame . . .

It was not that Rochester was enslaved to fear; his conduct under fire disproves that. His argument is that humanity, driven by recognition of cosmic nothingness, throws itself into the arms of chimeras: honor, fame, and (most despised of all) a beneficent deity. Regardless of whether we agree, Rochester's vision exemplifies the unease with which former combatants harbor the insights of war in times of peace. Samuel Menashe cast the problem in suitably direct terms:

> Of course, as a survivor of an infantry company, I was marked by death for life when I was nineteen. In the first years after the war, I thought each day was the last day. I was amazed by the aplomb of those who spoke of what they would do next summer. Later, each day was the only day. Usually, I could give the day its due, live in the present, but I had no foresight for a future. Perhaps it is why I am still in the flat to which I moved when I was thirty-one years old.[13]

At the end of a single day's engagement during the Battle of the Bulge, a mere 29 out of the 190 men in Menashe's company remained alive and uncaptured—a small proportion of the 89,500 Americans listed as casualties. The hitherto unimaginable scale of destruction witnessed by those involved in the Second World War lends urgency to their poetic testimony; even those detained from the front line (such as Robert Creeley, p. 612) were changed irrevocably by it.

Not all our authors were combatants; the trials of civilian life at times of war

---

12. Some commentators doubt whether he was a rake at all; see for instance Germaine Greer, *John Wilmot, Earl of Rochester* (Devon, 2000), chapter 1, introduction.
13. Samuel Menashe, "Giving the Day its Due," foreword to *New and Selected Poems*, ed. Christopher Ricks (Tarset, Northumberland, 2010), p. xv.

are sufficient permanently to alter a writer's sensibility. It is no accident that more than half of Emily Dickinson's verse was written during the American Civil War,[14] a time when people she knew were slaughtered, and the world she had known was under threat. Her writings tell us that loss, suffering, and the daily expectation of catastrophe were burdens carried by the civilian consciousness at that period; so it was that, having heard of the Battle of Antietam at the end of 1862, the bloodiest single day in American military history, she wrote: "Sorrow seems more general than it did, and not the estate of a few persons, since the war began; and if the anguish of others helped one with one's own, now would be many medicines." Her poetry, she added, was "[sung] off charnel steps" (a charnel is a building containing bodies or bones).[15] The shock dealt by the death of Frazar Stearns, son of the president of Amherst College, at Newbern, North Carolina, is evident from Dickinson's letter of late March 1862, in which she describes "His big heart shot away by a 'minie ball,' " before recounting his death: "He fell by the side of Professor Clark, his superior officer—lived ten minutes in a soldier's arms, asked twice for water— murmured just 'My God!' and passed!"[16]

Poetry of Witness foregrounds the historical context inhabited by the author, obliging us to consider the manner in which it impinged on his or her vision. We have pondered at length the case of William Blake, witness to the riots of June 1780 when, over the course of nearly a week, tens of thousands of protestors stormed through London. The Gordon Riots, so-called after their instigator, the anti-Catholic agitator Lord George Gordon, began with destruction of the Catholic chapels of the Sardinian and Bavarian embassies. Rioters then besieged the residences of eminent Catholics. More than a hundred houses were destroyed; the mob took effective control of a number of roads (in the City, the Strand, Southwark, Shoreditch, and Spitalfields), and attacked London Bridge, the Sessions House at the Old Bailey, and the Bank of England.

Blake was walking toward Newgate at around 6:30 p.m. on the evening of Tuesday June 6 when he encountered a group of rioters on their way to the nearby prison to which several of their number had been committed over the weekend. He watched as they proceeded, in a methodical manner, to demol-

---

14. R. W. Franklin, Dickinson's editor, dates 937 poems to the war years.
15. Emily Dickinson to Louise and Frances Norcross, now dated to December 1862; see *The Letters of Emily Dickinson*, ed. Thomas H. Johnson (2 vols., Cambridge, MA, 1958), ii 436.
16. Ibid., ii 397.

ish the building with pickaxes and sledgehammers. Within an hour, more than three hundred inmates were free, but the jail was torched before all were out of their cells, and the frantic screams of those inside were heard as they roasted to death. Fragments of red-hot metal shot into the darkening sky as huge pieces of masonry collapsed to the ground. Some protestors clambered onto the structure, perching precariously on window ledges that had yet to crumble. Others caroused in the street, as they broke open wine and liquor found in cellars used by the prison governor, while blacksmiths removed fetters from the ankles of newly freed prisoners. Over the next two days, public houses, schools, and offices would be burned to the ground, as well as the Fleet Prison, Bridewell, the King's Bench, Southwark, and the Surrey House of Correction. Blake must have seen some of these events, as well as the eventual reinstatement of civil order on the Thursday.

As historians have long argued, the Gordon Riots were motivated less by religious bigotry than by inequalities of income and social class, and Blake was aware of that.[17] The protagonists were working people—small shopkeepers, pedlars, craftsmen, apprentices, discharged soldiers and sailors, waiters, and servants—whose actions were directed against the property of the wealthy (merchants, manufacturers, and other professionals), the most obvious example being Lord Mansfield's house in Bloomsbury, torched along with his "rich wardrobe," "superb" furniture, and library of over one thousand books. As one historian observes, the riots manifested "a groping desire to settle accounts with the rich, if only for a day, and to achieve some rough kind of social justice."[18] An additional motive was their opposition to the American war, now five years old (which explains the large number of sailors among them).

The only authoritative account we have of Blake's involvement emphasizes his disinclination to be there. In the first major biography of the poet, Alexander Gilchrist wrote: "Suddenly, he encountered the advancing wave of Blackguardism, and was forced (for from such a great surging mob there is no disentanglement) to go along in the very front rank, and witness the storm and burning of the fortress-like prison, and release of its three hun-

17. See for instance George Rudé, "The Gordon Riots: A Study of the Rioters and Their Victims," *Transactions of the Royal Historical Society*, 5th ser., 6 (1956) 93–114; R. J. White, *The Age of George III* (London, 1968), pp. 185–87. When Gordon attempted to suppress the riots, many of those involved had no idea who he was; see Christopher Hibbert, *King Mob* (Stroud, Gloucestershire, 2004), p. 100.
18. Rudé, p. 111.

dred inmates."[19] Every biography is a product of its historical moment, and Gilchrist's is no exception. By the early 1860s, when he was writing, radical causes were in temporary retreat, Chartism having been crushed out of existence as decisively as the campaign for Parliamentary reform four decades before. Regardless of the evidence, Gilchrist could not allow it to be thought that Blake had been party to the collapse of civil law in central London.

While it is most unlikely Blake would ever have fought alongside an anti-Catholic mob, it is conceivable he sympathized with at least some of their actions. The destruction of an ancient prison in the heart of London, horrific though it may have been, must have stirred the man who would write, "Prisons are built with stones of Law, Brothels with bricks of Religion,"[20] and declare fellow feeling for "the captive in chains & the poor in the prison."[21] Blake was of the same generation as many rioters, having completed his own apprenticeship less than a year before. He must have understood their grievances: if so, he was not alone.[22] The army refused to fire on them, aware of sailors among the crowds. Urged by John Wilkes to raise the *posse comitatus*, the Lord Mayor declined.[23] Nor would the Court of Aldermen lift a finger to suppress them.

Whatever his feelings about what he witnessed, we can be sure Blake would never forget the sights and sounds of that evening, which brought him as close as he would ever get to full-scale revolution—a subject that recurs throughout his writings. G. E. Bentley Jr. observes that

> images of "burning", "fire", "flames", and "rage" in his poetry and in his picture of "Fire" are likely to be related to the scenes he saw during the Gordon riots, and from them one may construct a description of the riots: "all rush together in the night in wrath and raging fire", "a mighty multitude rage furious" "in flames of red wrath burning"; "Albions mountains

---

19. Alexander Gilchrist, as quoted by G. E. Bentley Jr., *The Stranger from Paradise: A Biography of William Blake* (New Haven, 2001), p. 57.
20. Blake, *The Marriage of Heaven and Hell*, plate 8.
21. Blake, *Vala* Night the Second, p. 36, l. 10.
22. Experts remain divided. For conflicting views, see David V. Erdman, *Blake: Prophet Against Empire* (3rd ed., Princeton, NJ, 1977), pp. 8–10 and Jerome J. McGann, "Did Blake Betray the French Revolution?," in *Presenting Poetry: Composition, Publication, Reception: Essays in Honour of Ian Jack*, ed. Howard Erskine-Hill and Richard A. McCabe (Cambridge, 1995), 117–37, p. 128.
23. See Arthur H. Cash, *John Wilkes: The Scandalous Father of Civil Liberty* (New Haven, 2006), p. 362.

run with blood, the cries of war & of tumult", "Above the rest the howl was heard from Westminster louder & louder", and "Around Saint James's glow the fires"; from Westminster "Eastward & Southward & Northward are incircled with flaming fires", "In thunder smoke & sullen flames & howlings & fury & blood", "in dungeons circled with ceaseless fires"; "All is confusion, all is tumult". Blake's visions of apocalypse come partly from personal experiences.[24]

Bentley's observation underlines the value of Forché's ideas to the way in which we think about writers and their work. In recent decades, Blake has been appropriated by those who would encounter him as mythmaker or cryptographer, with the result that his art is rendered cerebral, the plaything of intellectuals. Poetry of witness reminds us that Blake's art grew out of his life. It argues that, at the point at which the artist confronts extremity—whether imprisonment, torture, or warfare—his vision is altered irrevocably, turning utterance into testimony. Blake was not the same after his encounter with the Gordon Rioters. Perhaps he reveled in the spectacle of Newgate in flames and followed the mob over successive days, watching as one institution after another was reduced to ashes. It taught him what anarchy and destruction looked like. He knew the terror and excitement that came from watching the world burn down—and, as Bentley argues, those feelings pass into the mainstream of his work.

Throughout the chronological period we have surveyed, women writers are exceptional, in more senses than one. Cultural norms prior to the Second World War were so uncongenial that their existence is a minor miracle. Deprived of an education equal to that of male counterparts, most females were considered suitable as housekeepers and mothers, but not writers, and definitely not intellectuals.[25] Society decreed that a woman who read books—other than romantic novels, that is—had abrogated her correct purpose of being airheaded, beautiful, and (if she was lucky) marriageable. Worse still, one who wrote poetry was a freak, fit for display but not other purposes; Jane Austen published her novels anonymously for good reason. Those who did publish verse were expected to paraphrase pas-

---

24. G. E. Bentley Jr., *The Stranger from Paradise: A Biography of William Blake* (New Haven, 2001), p. 57.

25. It was in acknowledgment of his society's low valuation of women, rather than his own, that Samuel Johnson is reported to have told Boswell that a woman preacher was "like a dog on hind legs; it is not done well, but it is surprising that it is done at all."

sages of the Bible or address abstract deities such as Hope or Charity. They were not expected to discuss contemporary figures in any context other than commemorations of, for example, the king's birthday, far less to analyze contemporary politics. It is hardly surprising, therefore, that many in the eighteenth century believed women had no business commenting on slavery; the act of opposing it was unacceptable, and that of criticizing it *in a poem* contemptible. Women poets who contravened such taboos did so at risk, aware they were vulnerable to accusations that their engagement with politics left them "unsexed,"[26] stripped of femininity. This was a male construct, and perhaps only a male reviewer would have ridiculed an author to the extent of making potential readers ashamed of being seen with a copy of her work; of calling on publishers to boycott her; and, at his most ruthless, of denouncing her as a prostitute, as happened to Mary Wollstonecraft and Helen Maria Williams.[27]

Anna Laetitia Barbauld was aware of the likely penalty when in 1792 she wrote, "Yes, injured woman, rise, assert thy right!," in response to Wollstonecraft's *Vindication of the Rights of Woman* (see p. 262); only that could explain why she decided not to publish her poem when it was written. Caution bought her reprieve, but could not save her. Literary London knew scant restraint in its chauvinism, and when in 1812 Barbauld published verses in which the state of the nation was analyzed in terms that gave no comfort to Spencer Perceval's Tory administration, she drew enough bad press to discourage her from ever uttering another word in print. The ferocity of male reviewers (particularly John Wilson Croker, who would deliver withering accounts of other liberal writers including Keats) attests to the scale of the perceived threat. For this reason we regard those women courageous enough to have engaged in political debate through poetry as activists. A heroic couplet may indeed comprise an act, a deed, a blow struck for a cause—sufficient to turn its author into a target. Whether we speak of martyrs (Anne Askew), bluestockings (Hannah More), or Communists (Sylvia Townsend Warner),

---

26. The allusion is to Lady Macbeth, but also to Richard Polwhele's *The Unsexed Females* (1798), an attack on (among others) Mary Wollstonecraft, Anna Laetitia Barbauld, Charlotte Smith, Helen Maria Williams, and Ann Yearsley.

27. Wollstonecraft's biography was described by one reviewer as a "manual of speculative debauchery" by which young women might be guided into "the notorious receptacles of patrician prostitution"; Williams was described by one critic as "an intemperate advocate for Gallic licentiousness." See Don Locke, *A Fantasy of Reason* (London, 1980), p. 135 and Richard Polwhele, *The Unsexed Females* (London, 1798), p. 19.

many of the women in these pages were motivated by their willingness to denounce religious or political injustice, an act for which there is always a price to be paid.

Hindsight inclines us to underrate risk; our knowledge of ultimate victory inclines us to think those on the Allied side in the Second World War confident of victory from the start. That could not be more wrong. The outcome of the war, or of any conflict, is never certain. By the same token, we should consider those involved in the fight against slavery as in constant peril. The law being on the side of those inclined to resist change, campaigners were under scrutiny, their liberty often conditional. In late 1700s and early 1800s England they knew only that they faced a lucrative industry established since the late fifteenth century. Plantation owners had a powerful lobby in Parliament, arguing slaves were essential to commerce with Africa, and that the trade was patriotic, as slave ships provided manpower for the Royal Navy during wartime (the Napoleonic Wars continued until 1815). Even to the enlightened, such views commanded attention. Physical force was used against dissidents. There were threats against the life of Thomas Clarkson, as well as assassination attempts, while the "Clapham Sect" (the name given to founders of the antislavery society in England) was a term of ridicule applied by enemies, of whom there were many. By publishing poems in support of the abolitionist cause, More and Yearsley exposed themselves to the ridicule not merely of peers but of those who sought to silence them: to the *European Magazine*, More's poem was "feebly executed,"[28] while the *Critical Review* found Yearsley's poem "rather turgid."[29] In America, abolitionists were equally vulnerable. Frederick Douglass was permanently injured by mobs when he toured the country lecturing on the evils of slavery. Lydia Maria Child's *Appeal in Favor of that Class of Americans Called Africans* (1833), a well-informed history of America's dependence on slaves, calling for their immediate emancipation and the abolition of all racial discrimination, resulted in its author's casting out by social and literary circles. Old friends cut her dead in the street. Her library revoked her membership.[30] The *Juvenile Miscellany*, which she edited, lost its subscribers and folded within the year. In the South, where the *Appeal* was banned, there were burnings of her books.

Blacklisting has often been the response to women resistant to preju-

---

28. *European Magazine* 13 (1788), p. 166.
29. *Critical Review* 65 (1788), p. 314.
30. See John Greenleaf Whittier's biographical introduction to *Letters of Lydia Maria Child* (Boston, 1882), pp. ix–x.

dice and moral cowardice: when Eliza Hamilton Dunlop published "The Aboriginal Mother," a condemnation of the Myall Creek Massacre, in *The Australian* in 1838, she created enemies who would attack subsequent publications on grounds of principle (p. 391), and when Elizabeth Barrett Browning published "A Curse for a Nation" in London in 1860 (see p. 414), aware it might be interpreted as an attack on her homeland for failing to aid Italian revolutionaries, reviewers condemned her "terrible assumption of vainglory," "hysterical antipathy to England" and "delirium of imbecile one-sidedness." *Blackwood's Edinburgh Magazine* was outraged that women were allowed "to interfere with politics."[31] As if this were not enough, she was abandoned by British publishers and criticized for her views after death even by obituarists. James Thomson, the only poet to write a memorial poem about her, had every reason to compare her death with that of a soldier on a battlefield.[32]

Those fighting for their rights in late eighteenth- and early nineteenth-century Britain were equally embattled. For a long time the authorities met protest with ruthless suppression, as when striking soldiers sought redress in Sheffield in 1795 and were fired on for their trouble (see p. 256). Nor was the government above inciting riots with the assistance of *agents provocateurs* as a means of discrediting peaceful demonstrators and their cause. The uprising in Pentrich in 1817, which posed no threat to the government, was suppressed with the help of "Oliver the spy" (W. J. Richards), and its organizers executed as traitors. Later in the century Ernest Jones and Thomas Cooper, agitating for similar causes, were detained in conditions of considerable hardship (see pp. 433, 397); they cannot have known their cause would, ultimately, enjoy success (though it might be admitted that contemporary Britain continues to lack the full complement of rights for which they agitated).

The poems in this book are acts of resistance. Some of our authors defy injustice to the extent of incurring the wrath of those willing to impose the ultimate sanction of death; some face risks, whether on the battlefield or in the forum of public debate, with the outcome not in an afterlife but in the here and now; all testify to the impress of extremity. Our reading of their work carries its own responsibility—not solely that of understanding the world from which it came, nor of comprehending how dearly such utter-

---

31. *The Athenaeum* (March 17, 1860), pp. 371–72; *Saturday Review*, March 31, 1860, pp. 402–4; *Blackwood's Edinburgh Magazine* 87 (March 1860), p. 494.
32. For this detail and other insights into Browning, I am grateful to Leonid M. Arinstein, "A Curse for a Nation: A Controversial Episode in Elizabeth Barrett Browning's Political Poetry," *Review of English Studies* 20 (1969), pp. 33–42.

ances are bought, but also that of being receptive to its burden. As William Meredith puts it:

> Whatever a poem is up to, it requires our trust along with our consent to let it try to change our way of thinking and feeling. Nothing without this risk. I expect hang-gliding must be like poetry. Once you get used to it, you can't imagine not wanting the scare of it. But it's more serious than hang-gliding. Poetry is the safest known mode of human risk. You risk only staying alive.[33]

VARIOUS CATEGORIES of poem and writer are not eligible for inclusion in this volume. Works by anonymous authors are automatically excluded, as each case is argued from the writer's life; where nothing (or very little) is known, the case cannot be made. It is not known, for instance, whether the authors of *Beowulf*, "The Battle of Maldon," or any other Anglo-Saxon poem about war, had battlefield experience, making it impossible to argue for them.

That the poet bear witness to extremity is the requirement by which we have measured our judgments. By "extreme," we refer to experiences that are the result of societal injustice, the depredations of the state, or sins of omission—specifically war, imprisonment, torture, and political oppression of various kinds. We do not include mental breakdown, which explains our omission of Thomas Hoccleve (who would otherwise have been our earliest poet), William Cowper, and Christopher Smart, to name a few. However, physical illness on an epidemic scale constitutes a form of extremity borne collectively, on which basis we include George Wither, Ben Jonson (witnesses to plague), and Thom Gunn (AIDS).

There are many writers whose work we have considered on more than one occasion, up to the conclusion of our labors; these include Alexander Brome, Byron, Burns, Thomas Moore, Southey, William Cullen Bryant, Sidney Keyes, David Gascoyne, Henry Reed, and T. S. Eliot. Our decision to exclude was reached only after close scrutiny of the poetry and the biographical facts. Our aim has been to impose consistency on the contents of this book, regardless of affection for the writer and their work.

Poets of witness alive at the time of publication are so numerous as to

---

33. William Meredith, "Reasons for Poetry," *Quarterly Journal of the Library of Congress* 39.3 (1982) 184–93, p. 193.

render fruitless attempts to do them justice here. The decision to omit them was made in the hope that at some point in the future we can appoint them subjects of a separate collection, as they deserve. In the meantime, compensation may be found in Forché's *Against Forgetting: Twentieth-Century Poetry of Witness* (1993), which includes poems in English and translation by authors still active at the time of this writing (2013).

It was decided at an early stage of work that this volume complement *Against Forgetting*. We therefore decided not to duplicate works or writers included there, and to select only poetry composed in English. For that reason there are fewer women writers than we would have wished in the section dealing with the twentieth century. Again, we refer the reader to *Against Forgetting* for those who, but for their appearance there, would have been selected in these pages, or who (being writers in another tongue) do not qualify for inclusion.

These poems offer a perspective on the literary canon not previously seen. Not only are well-known writers represented by untypical works, they are surrounded by figures sometimes omitted from profiles of their times, or from critical discussion. The theoretical background to this study is outlined in detail by Carolyn Forché in "Reading the Living Archives," which follows this introduction, but the fundamental argument of the volume is simply and clearly articulated: each poet earns his or her place in "dialectical opposition to the extremity that has made witness necessary."[34] Such sensibilities are not the product only of recent times, but a perennial feature of human history—for the imagination has always been on trial. *Poetry of Witness* presents the finest works to emerge from that tradition, arguing they rank alongside the greatest in the language.

Georgetown University, March 2013

---

34. Carolyn Forché, introduction to *Against Forgetting: Twentieth-Century Poetry of Witness* (New York, 1993), p. 46.

Reading the Living Archives:
The Witness of Literary Art

by Carolyn Forché

T HE LETTER ARRIVED on a series of plain postcards in Joseph Brodsky's penciled cursive, mailed separately from his newly imposed exile in Ann Arbor, Michigan, very near the township of my childhood. They contained his advice to a young poet brash enough to send her youthful efforts to him. "You should consider including in your poems more of your own, well, philosophy," he wrote. And on another card: "It is also a pity that you do not read Russian, but I think you should try to read Anna Akhmatova."

It was, I believe, two years earlier that I had read excerpts from the transcript of Brodsky's trial in the former Soviet Union, condemning him to forced labor. When asked on what authority he pronounced himself a poet, he had answered that the vocation came from God. Now he was advising me to read Akhmatova, and so that winter I went into the stacks of the Library of Congress and found a volume of her poems, translated by Stanley Kunitz and Max Hayward. Kneeling on the floor between the shelves, I read the following passage:

> In the terrible years of the Yezhov terror I spent seventeen months waiting in line outside the prison in Leningrad. One day somebody in the crowd identified me. Standing behind me was a woman, with lips blue from the cold, who had, of course, never heard me called by name before. Now she started out of the torpor common to us all and asked me in a whisper (everyone whispered there):
> > "Can you describe this?"
> > And I said, "I can."

> Then something like a smile passed fleetingly over what had
> once been her face.[1]

Akhmatova referred to this passage as *Vmesto predisoviia* ("Instead of a Preface"), adding it as prologue to her great poem, "Requiem," written during the years of her son Lev Gumilev's imprisonment. The poem was her *podvig*, her spiritual accomplishment of "remembering injustice and suffering" as experienced within herself and as collectively borne. Anna's friend, Lidiya Chukovskaya, remembers her subsisting on black bread and tea. According to the research of Amanda Haight:

> She was extremely thin and frequently ill. She would get up from bed to go and stand, sometimes in freezing weather, in the long lines of people waiting outside the prisons, hoping against hope to be able to see her son or at least pass over a parcel. . . . The poems of "Requiem," composed at this time, were learned by heart by Lidiya Chukovskaya, Nadezhda Mandelstam, and several other friends who did not know who else was preserving them. Sometimes Akhmatova showed them a poem on a piece of paper which she burned as soon as she was sure it had been committed to memory. . . . In a time when a poem on a scrap of paper could mean a death sentence, to continue to write, to commit one's work to faithful friends who were prepared to learn poems by heart and thus preserve them, was only possible if one was convinced of the absolute importance and necessity of poetry.[2]

As I was still in my early twenties and educated in the United States, I hadn't thought of poetry in these terms. I had not yet encountered evil in anything resembling this form, and had not yet, therefore, imagined the impress of extremity upon the poetic imagination, nor conceived of our relation to others as one of infinite obligation: to stand with them in the hour of need, even abject and destitute, in supplication and without need of response. If it were so—if description were possible, of the world and its sufferings, then the response would be that smile, or rather something resembling it, passing over *what had once been her face.*

"Requiem" meditated on the fate of Russia in her torment, marking the stages of suffering, as one would visit the stations of Christ's passion.

---

1. *Poems of Akhmatova* translated and introduced by Stanley Kunitz with Max Hayward (Boston, 1973), p. 99.
2. Amanda Haight, *Anna Akhmatova: A Poetic Pilgrimage* (Oxford, 1976), p. 99.

Akhmatova wrote it in the cry of a woman who had become all women. In the poem's progression, Akhmatova takes leave of herself and becomes vigilant beyond all wakefulness. By turns she accepts and disowns her pain, survives, forsakes the tribute of remembrance, and consigns her monument to a prison wall.

I was as yet unaware that *most* prominent twentieth-century poets beyond the English-speaking countries (and even some within them) had endured such experiences during their lives, and those blessed to survive wrote their poetry not after such experiences but in their *aftermath*—in languages that had also passed through these sufferings; languages that also continued to bear wounds, legible in the line breaks, in constellations of imagery, in ruptures of utterance, in silences and fissures of written speech.

Aftermath is a temporal debris field, where historical remains are strewn (of large events as well as those peripheral or lost); where that-which-happened remains present, including the consciousness in which such events arose. This is writing to be apprehended "in the light of conscience," as another Russian poet, Marina Tsvetaeva, once wrote.[3] As such, it calls upon the reader, who is the *other* of this work, to be in turn marked by what such language makes present before her, what it holds open and begets in the reader.

In his *Ethics and Infinity*, Emmanuel Lévinas writes:

> The witness witnesses to what is said by him (through him, or as him). For he has said "Here I am!" before the other one; and from the fact that before the one other he recognizes the responsibility which is incumbent upon him, he finds himself having manifested what the face of the other one has meant for him. The glory of the Infinite reveals itself by what it is capable of doing in the witness.[4]

This witness is a call to the *other* (perhaps in both senses, as the other within the poet, and the one other whom the text addresses), very much as in the face-to-face encounter of Martin Buber's *I and Thou*, later elaborated and extended by Lévinas as:

> an awakening that is neither reflection upon oneself nor universalization. An awakening signifying a responsibility for the other, the other

---

3. Marina Tsvetaeva, *Art in the Light of Conscience* translated by Angela Livingston (Cambridge, MA, 1992).

4. Emmanuel Lévinas, *Ethique et Infini: Dialogues avec Philippe Nemo* (Paris, 1982), p. 105. Extract translated by Carolyn Forché.

who must be fed and clothed—my substitution for the other, my expiation for the suffering, and no doubt for the wrongdoing of the other. An expiation assigned to me without any possible avoidance, and by which my uniqueness as myself, instead of being alienated, is intensified by my irreplaceability.[5]

This awakening is also a readerly coming to awareness before the *saying* of poetry that calls the reader to her irrevocable and inexhaustible responsibility for the other as present in the testamentary utterance. A poem is lyric art, but Lévinas claims that a poetic work is at the same time a document, and the art that went into its making is at once a use of discourse. This discourse deals with objects that are also spoken in the newspapers, posters, memoirs, and letters of every passing age—though in the case of poetry's strictly poetic expression these objects merely furnish a favorable occasion and serve as pretexts. It is of the essence of art to signify only between the lines—in the intervals of time, between times—like a footprint that would precede the step, or an echo preceding the sound of a voice.

This voice is the saying of the witness, which is not a translation of experience into poetry but is itself experience.

Philippe Lacoue-Labarthe, writing on the work of Celan, proposes

to call what [the poem] translates "experience," provided that we both understand the word in its strict sense—the Latin *ex-periri*, a crossing through danger—and especially that we avoid associating it with what is "lived," the stuff of anecdotes.[6]

But a poem, in its witnessing, "arises out of experience that is not perceived as it occurs, is not registered in the first person 'precisely since it ruined this first person, reduced it to a ghostlike status, to being a "me without me."'" So the poem's witness is not a recounting, is not mimetic narrative, is not political confessionalism, and "it is not simply an act of memory. It bears witness, as Jacques Derrida suggests, in the manner of an ethical or political act."

· · ·

---

5. Emmanuel Lévinas, *Proper Names* translated by Michael B. Smith (Stanford, CA, 1996), p. 6.
6. Philippe Lacoue-Labarthe, *Poetry as Experience* translated by Andrea Tarnowsky (Stanford, CA, 1999), p. 18.

THE "POETRY of witness," as a term of literary art, had not yet had its genesis, but soon after learning of Brodsky and Akhmatova I began an epistolary friendship with the late Terrence Des Pres, author of *The Survivor: An Anatomy of Life in the Death Camps*, in which he cites Akhmatova's preface to "Requiem" as epigraph to a chapter on the survivor's will to bear witness. Within months of meeting Des Pres in the summer of 1977, I traveled to Spain to translate Claribel Alegría, herself a poet in exile, and in January of 1978 was welcomed by one of her relatives to El Salvador, where I was to work as a documenter of human rights abuses in the period immediately preceding a twelve-year civil war (working closely with associates of Monsignor Oscar Romero, then archbishop of San Salvador, and with my contact in the International Secretariat of Amnesty International).

If asked when I returned from El Salvador for the last time in those years, I have said March 16, 1980, a week before the assassination of Monsignor Romero. After thirty years, I now understand that I did not return on that date, that the woman who traveled to El Salvador—the young poet I had been—did not come back. The woman who *did* return wrote, in those years, seven poems marked by the El Salvador experience, and also an essay, published in the summer of 1981 in *The American Poetry Review*, in which this returning poet states: "It is my feeling that the twentieth-century human condition demands a poetry of witness." Two years later, Czesław Miłosz would publish his monograph, *The Witness of Poetry*, and a phrase, "poetry of witness," entered the lexicon of literary terms, regarded skeptically by some as a euphemism for "political poetry," or as political poetry by other means. "Witness" would come to refer, much of the time, to the person of the poet, much as it refers to a man or woman testifying under oath in a court of law. "Poets of witness" were considered by some to be engaged in writing documentary literature, or poetic reportage, and in the mode of political confessionalism.

As compelling as many such "witness" poems are, "poetry of witness" originated in a very different constellation of thought, in which it was not regarded as constituting a poet's identity, nor prescribing a new *littérature engagée*. "Poetry of witness," a term descending from the literature of the Shoah and complicated by philosophical, religious, linguistic, and psychoanalytic understandings of "witness," remains to be set forth. In my sense of this term, it is a mode of reading rather than of writing, of readerly encounter with the literature of that-which-happened, and its mode is evidentiary rather than representational—as evidentiary, in fact, as spilled blood.

· · ·

WHILE THE solitude and tranquility thought to be the condition of literary production were absent for many twentieth- and twenty-first century poets, even in the aftermath of their survival, writers *have* survived and written despite all that has happened, and against all odds. They have created exemplary literary art with language that has also passed through catastrophe. The body of thought that informs the "poetry of witness" suggests, moreover, that language can itself be damaged. This idea of "damaged language" appears in George Steiner's *Language and Silence*, when he considers the German language "being used to run hell, getting the habits of hell into its syntax":

> Languages have great reserves of life. They can absorb masses of hysteria, illiteracy, and cheapness. . . . But there comes a breaking point. Use a language to conceive, organize, and justify Belsen; use it to make out specifications for gas ovens; use it to dehumanize man during twelve years of calculated bestiality. Something will happen to it. . . . Something of the lies and sadism will settle in the marrow of the language. Imperceptibly at first, like the poisons of radiation sifting silently into the bone. But the cancer will begin, and the deep-set destruction. The language will no longer grow and freshen. It will no longer perform, quite as well as it used to, its two principal functions: the conveyance of humane order which we call law, and the communication of the quick of the human spirit which we call grace.[7]

The damage need not be regarded, however, as always irreparable. In the words of Paul Celan in his speech at Bremen:

> One thing remained attainable, close and unlost amid all the losses: language. Language was not lost, in spite of all that happened. But it had to go through its own responselessness, go through horrible silences, go through the thousand darknesses of death-bringing speech.[8]

It was this language, this poetry that had passed through death-bringing speech, that I set out to find and gather in my anthology, *Against Forgetting*

---

7. George Steiner, *Language and Silence: Essays on Language, Literature, and the Inhuman* (New York, NY, 1977), p. 101.
8. Paul Celan, "Speech on the Occasion of receiving the Literature Prize of the Free Hanseatic City of Bremen," translated by John Felsteiner, *Selected Poems and Prose of Paul Celan* (New York, NY, 2001), p. 395.

(1993). I hoped to discover the trace of extremity that might remain legible in these poems. Common among them is an explicit will to bear witness. Here is Wisława Szymborska:

> Write it. Write. In ordinary ink
> on ordinary paper: they were given no food,
> they all died of hunger. "All. How many?
> It's a big meadow. How much grass
> for each one?" Write: I don't know.
> History counts its skeletons in round numbers.[9]

There are inventories of losses, as in Akhmatova's "Requiem":

> Nothing I counted mine, out of my life,
> is mine to take:
>
> not my son's terrible eyes,
> not the elaborate stone flower
> of grief, not the day of the storm,
> not the trial of the visiting hour,
>
> not the dear coolness of his hands,
> not the lime trees' agitated shade,
> not the thin cricket-sound
> of consolation's parting word.[10]

The difficulties of forgetting and remembering are marked. Vahan Tekeyan:

> Forgetting. Yes. I will forget it all.
> One after the other. The roads I crossed.
> The roads I did not. Everything that happened.
> And everything that did not.[11]

Guillaume Apollinaire:

---

9. Wisława Szymborska, "Hunger Camp at Jasło," in *Against Forgetting*, ed. Carolyn Forché (New York, 1993), p. 459.
10. Anna Akhmatova, "Requiem," ibid., p. 106.
11. Vahan Tekeyan, "Forgetting," ibid., p. 59.

Memories composing now a single memory
As a hundred furs make only one coat
As those thousands of wounds make only one newspaper article.[12]

Of the self's fragmentation, we read in Angel Cuadra:

The common man I might have been
reproaches me now,
blaming me for his ostracism
his solitary shadow,
his silent exile.[13]

Early in the twentieth century, there is evidence of faith and prayer in poetry, and of belief in the sacred. Toward the middle of the century, there is a discernible shift toward alienation from the deity. Celan:

They dug and they dug, so their day
went by for them, their night. And they did not praise God,
who, so they heard, wanted all this,
who, so they heard, knew all this.[14]

The temporal sense seems changed. In Velimir Khlebnikov's "Suppose I make a timepiece of humanity," we read this:

I tell you, the universe is the scratch
Of a match on the face of the calculus,
And my thoughts are a picklock at work
On a door, and behind it someone is dying . . .[15]

There are many other shared qualities, such as the experience of consciousness itself as fragmented and altered, and for the first time, soldier poets write of the extremity of the battlefield explicitly in terms of its horrors. Poetic language attempts a coming to terms with evil and its embodiments, and there are appeals for a shared sense of humanity and collective resistance. There are many poems of address: to war as figural, to death and evil, memory and hunger as figural, and of course to the world to come:

12. Guillaume Apollinaire, "Shadow," ibid., p. 67.
13. Angel Cuadra, "In Brief," ibid., p. 593.
14. Paul Celan, "There was earth inside them, and they dug," ibid., p. 382.
15. Velimir Khlebnikov, "Suppose I make a timepiece of humanity," ibid., pp. 100–101.

We speak loudly but no one understands us.

But we are not surprised

For we are speaking the language

That will be spoken tomorrow.[16]

IN CONDITIONS of extremity (war, suffering, struggle), the witness is *in relation*, and cannot remove him or herself. Relation is proximity, and this closeness subjects the witness to the possibility of being wounded. No special protection can be sought and no outcome intended. The witness who writes out of extremity writes his or her wound, as if such writing were making an incision. Consciousness itself is cut open. At the site of the wound, language breaks, becomes tentative, interrogational, kaleidoscopic. The form of this language bears the trace of extremity, and may be comprised of fragments: questions, aphorisms, broken passages of lyric prose or poetry, quotations, dialogue, brief and lucid passages that may or may not resemble what previously had been written.

The word "extremity" (*extremus*) is the superlative correlative of the word "exterior" (*exterus*). Extremity suggests "utmost," "exceedingly great," and also "outermost," "farthest," implying intense suffering and even world death; a suffering without knowledge of its own end. Ethical reading of such works does not inhere in assessing their truth value or efficacy as "representation," but rather in recognizing their evidentiary nature: here language is a life-form, marked by human experience, and is also itself material evidence of *that-which-occurred*. This evidence continues to mark human consciousness. The *aftermath* is a region of devastated consciousness of barbarism and the human capacity for cruelty and complicity with evil. In this aftermath, we are able to read—in the scarred landscape of battlefields, in bomb craters and unreconstructed ruins, in oral and written testimony *and* its extension in literary art—the mark or trace of extremity.

In the work of witness, of writing out of extremity, the poem does not become a means to an extraliterary end: the poet, according to Maurice Blanchot:

is excluded from the facile, humanistic hope that by writing, or "creating," he would transform his dark experience into greater consciousness. On the contrary: dismissed, excluded from what is written—unable even

---

16. Horst Bienek, "Resistance," ibid., p. 471.

to be present by virtue of the non-presence of his very death—he has to renounce all conceivable relations of a self (either living or dying) to the poem which henceforth belongs to the other.[17]

Terrence Des Pres would not have relinquished the "humanistic hope" of transformation, but Blanchot's reading of the poet's renunciation, of the poem as address to the other to whom it henceforth belongs, corresponds radiantly for me to formulations in the ethics of Levinas, and also to the thought of Derrida (after his ethical turn). "This will be about bearing witness," Derrida writes in an essay on Celan, "and about poetics as bearing witness. . . . A poem can 'bear witness' to a poetics. It can promise it, it can be a response to it, as to a testamentary promise." Derrida imagines the poem as a singularity, marked in its date, "that, in the reference that carries it beyond itself toward the other or toward the world, opens the verbal body to things other than itself."[18] What the poem lays open to the other is an unending address, a call to the other, which manifests *that-which-happened*.

Witness, then, is neither martyrdom nor the saying of a juridical truth, but the owning of one's infinite responsibility for the *other one* (*l'autri*). It is not to be mistaken for politicized confessionalism. The confessional is the mode of the subjective, and the representational that of the objective, and it is necessary to move beyond both and place ourselves *under* and *before* the other in an ethical relation that precedes ontology (Lévinas), an understanding that humans come into being through relation. In the aftermath of Auschwitz, we begin with a heteronymous self and understand Descartes' subject/object construction as a two-century-old denial of the primacy of the other and of relation. We abandon this denial to enter an intersubjective sphere of lived immediacy. In the poetry of witness, the poem makes present to us the experience of the other, the poem *is* the experience, rather than a symbolic representation. When we read the poem as witness, we are marked by it and become ourselves witnesses to what it has made present before us. Language incises the page, wounding it with testimonial presence, and the reader is marked by encounter with that presence. Witness begets witness. The text we read becomes a living archive.

17. Maurice Blanchot, *The Writing of the Disaster* translated by Ann Smock (Lincoln, Nebraska, 1995), p. 135).
18. Jacques Derrida, *Sovereignties in Question: the Poetics of Paul Celan* ed. Thomas Dutoit and Outi Pasanen (New York, NY, 2005), pp. 65–66.

A Note on Texts

TEXTS IN THIS volume are edited with the needs of the modern reader in mind. With few exceptions, works written prior to 1900 are derived from early printed sources. Orthography, punctuation, capitalization, and other features are brought into line with twenty-first century standards, though we have based our editorial decisions at all times on the evidence of our copy text. Capital letters are thus used only where there is some rationale for them, such as personification. Orthography, often the work of the printer rather than the author, is normalized, as is punctuation. We have modified the propensity for exclamation marks, elliptical apostrophes, and overuse of semicolons, colons, and the like, so as to bring texts closer to the kind of pointing a modern reader might reasonably expect. Semicolons have sometimes been turned into commas, and colons have occasionally been turned into semicolons—the objective being to ensure that a manner of punctuation that, two or more centuries ago, seemed appropriate, does not come between the reader and the work. At all events, we are guided by the original text, even where we have toned down its pointing. In the cases of all writers, we have observed the decisions of scholars with gratitude to their labors. Texts in section 6 (that is to say, works composed from the latter part of the nineteenth century onward) are reproduced from the most authoritative source with minimal editorial intervention. Each text is followed by date of composition, where we are able to ascertain it, and date of first publication.

Acknowledgments

WE ARE THE beneficiaries of the labors of many writers and scholars who have shaped our understanding of the writers in this volume. John Buchtel, Charles E. Robinson, John Gardner, and David Norbrook directed us to textual sources that would otherwise have been either inaccessible or unknown to us. For assistance and advice of various kinds, we are pleased to acknowledge: Robert A. Brinkley, Penelope Creeley, Kwame Dawes, Jeremy Dimmick, Cian Duffy, Bronwyn Duncan, Colin Dwyer, James Fitzmaurice, David Gewanter, Claire Harman, William McCarthy, John O'Leary, Lena Cowen Orlin, Robin Robertson, Jason Rosenblatt, Daniel Shore, Bart Van Es, Elizabeth Webby, Marcus Wood, and the staff of the Houghton Library, Harvard. We are grateful also to Jill Bialosky, our editor at W. W. Norton; her editorial assistant, Rebecca Schultz; our copy editor David Stanford Burr, and our respective literary representatives—Bill Clegg in New York (Carolyn Forché) and Charlie Viney in London (Duncan Wu). Both editors owe a debt to Penn Szittya, a true friend, who recruited us to the English Department at Georgetown and made possible our happy collaboration. For assistance, guidance, and fortification during work on this book, Carolyn Forché thanks Harry Mattison, and Duncan Wu thanks Catherine Payling.

I

The Age of Tyranny

ᛟ

A S MONARCH, HENRY VIII was directly responsible for formulating policy, and involved on a daily basis in government affairs. Compared with those of the present monarch, his powers were far reaching. He could forge alliances, declare wars, appoint and dismiss ministers. What made him a tyrant was the arbitrary extension of his powers to include, for instance, the ability to execute political opponents. By invoking the power of attainder, he was able to deprive those accused of treason of the right of trial or any means of legal defense. And as soon as he acceded to the throne, he used these powers to get rid of two men who advised his father but for whom he had no use, Edmund Dudley and Sir Richard Empson.

Once Henry knew he could get away with this, he resorted to it often. It had the effect of making those who had the king's ear highly dangerous, for they had only to cast rivals in a treasonous light to persuade him to sign death warrants. Which explains why the poetry of Wyatt and Surrey is suffused with the knowledge of life's transience. His principal ministers were as vulnerable as anyone: Sir Thomas More and Sir Thomas Cromwell are the obvious examples, to whom might be added Cardinal Wolsey, hunted to his grave. Henry was no less ruthless with dynastic rivals such as sixty-eight-year-old Margaret Pole, Countess of Salisbury, wholly innocent of treason but hacked to death in the Tower nonetheless. And then there is Henry's unsentimental attitude to his wives, particularly Anne Boleyn (married January 1533, executed May 19, 1536, along with her brother and four others) and Katherine Howard (married July 28, 1540, executed February 13, 1541).

Henry did not come to power intending to change the national religion; the driving force of what was to be the Reformation was the need to divorce Catherine of Aragon so he could marry Anne Boleyn. Progress toward a breach with Rome was slow, but things developed more quickly after Archbishop Cranmer declared Henry's first marriage invalid in May 1533. A week later, Anne was crowned, and on July 11 Henry was excommunicated by the pope. The following year he declared himself "the only Supreme Head on earth of the Church of England." He then dissolved the monasteries, appropriating their lands and riches—a revolution in landownership to rival that precipitated by the Norman Conquest.

Such thoroughgoing change was bound to lead to violence, localized rebellions, and vigorous disputes, as many people preferred the old religion to the new. The repercussions would last for centuries. It was as if the country could not decide what it wanted—and, in fact, the state religion changed three times between 1547 and 1558, giving rise to violent opposition either to the Protestantizing impulses of those advising Edward VI, or to the Catholicizing influence of Mary I. Under Elizabeth I, opinion became further polarized with the emergence of Puritan ideologues who demanded further reformation.

The reign of Elizabeth I has often been reimagined on film and stage, and for good reason. She was a strong ruler. During the reign of her sister Mary Tudor (1553–1558), her life had been in the balance, for she was always the more popular of the two, and became the focus of various rebellions, notably that of Sir Thomas Wyatt the younger (son of the poet included at p. 36). After accession to the throne she passed the Act of Supremacy, declaring herself governor of the Church of England. For the time being, she remained tolerant toward Catholicism, which her sister had done her best to reestablish. That changed after Pope Pius V excommunicated her in 1570, before the start of a mission designed to reconvert English Protestants. Elizabeth's response, in 1571, was a bill enforcing Protestant observances; then, after the Jesuit mission began in 1580, she made it a capital offence merely to be a Catholic priest on British soil, or to conceal one: at least sixty-four were executed over the next seven years. As with all traitors, their punishment was to be hanged, cut down while still breathing, castrated, eviscerated, hacked into quarters, and to have their heads placed on pikes. In order to find them, Elizabeth established an intelligence network under Sir Francis Walsingham, and authorized an interrogator, Richard Topcliffe. Topcliffe had torture facilities in his own home, and devised new methods of inflicting pain on his victims, the best-known of whom is St. Robert Southwell, SJ (see p. 72).

Catholics in England found relief from the stringency of Elizabeth's rule under that of her successor, James I—who (as he was already King James VI of Scotland) declared himself King of Great Britain in 1604. He reduced fines for recusancy and resisted the invitation to use the Gunpowder Plot as pretext for another round of religious persecution, despite the entreaties of his senior advisor Robert Cecil, of whom Catholics had reason to be apprehensive. In fact, James's reign produced a mere 25 executions of Catholics as compared to 189 between 1570 and 1603.

However, James (like his predecessors) adhered to the belief that he was divinely appointed, and was the author of several tracts justifying what now seems the craziest of ideas both in theory and practice. But he was nothing like Henry VIII, lacking the insecurity that would make him put to the sword those who disagreed. Instead his instincts inclined him to culture and matters intellectual. Why else would Ben Jonson who, under Elizabethan law, had appeared before the consistory court for recusancy, have become his friend and ultimately enjoy his patronage as poet laureate?

> How, best of kings, dost thou a sceptre bear!
>   How, best of poets, dost thou laurel wear!
> But two things rare the Fates had in their store,
>   And gave thee both, to show they could no more;
> For such a poet, while thy days were green,
>   Thou wert, as chief of them are said t' have been;
> And such a prince thou art we daily see,
>   As chief of those still promise they will be.
> Whom should my muse then fly to, but the best
>   Of kings for grace; of poets for my test?
>
> (BEN JONSON, "TO KING JAMES")

St. Thomas More (1478–1535)

THIS BOOK BEGINS with an author contemplating his own death, which he knew would take place within weeks, possibly days, of the time at which he composed the poems we present here. Thomas More was born into a wealthy family with connections at court, and after studying rhetoric at Oxford began his career as a lawyer at Lincoln's Inn (where he met Erasmus, who was to become a friend). He was a prolific writer, being responsible for (among other things) *Utopia* (1516), a humanist satire that remains in print to this day. His elevation to the king's council was followed by appointment as Speaker of the House of Commons and, in October 1529, Lord Chancellor, when he replaced his patron, Cardinal Wolsey. For a time he was one of the most powerful men in the land, but he was compelled to resign in May 1532 for declining to support Henry VIII's union with Anne Boleyn. Having refused to swear to the Act of Succession on April 12, 1534, because it rejected papal jurisdiction, he was confined to the Tower of London five days later. From then it was only a matter of time before his execution. Tried on July 1, 1535, for refusing to acknowledge the king's new title of Supreme Head of the Church, More was found guilty, the usual sentence (to be hung, drawn, and quartered) commuted to beheading out of respect for his former office. The two poems presented here were composed during his final days. "Lewis the Lost Lover" was written shortly after Thomas Cromwell (the king's principal minister) had visited More's cell at the behest of the king, where he "pretended much friendship towards him, and for his comfort told him that the King's Highness was his good and gracious Lord, and minded not with any matter wherein he should have any cause of scruple." After Cromwell was gone, More composed the poem with a piece of coal, as he had no writing implements; "Davy the Dicer" was written shortly after. More was executed at the Tower on July 6, 1535. In 1935 he was canonized and in 2000 made patron saint of politicians by Pope John Paul II.

Lewis the Lost Lover[1]

Eye-flattering fortune, look thou never so fair,
Nor never so pleasauntly begin to smile
As though thou wouldst my ruin all repair—
During my life thou shalt not me beguile.
Trust shall I God, to enter in a while
His haven of heaven ever sure and uniform: *consistent*
Ever after thy caulm, look I for a storm.   *calm*

Written between May 4 and July 1, 1535, published 1557

Davy the Dicer

Long was I, Lady Luck, your serving-man,
And now have I lost again all that I gat;
Wherefore when I think on you now and then,
And in my mind remember this and that,
You may not blame me though I beshrew your cat,[1]
But, in faith, I bless you again a thousand times
For lending me now some leisure to make rhymes.

Written between May 4 and July 1, 1535, published 1557

---

1. Apparently written after a visit to More's cell from Thomas Cromwell, who Henry VIII had sent to soften him up. More's reaction was to compose a poem that rejects the possibility of being beguiled, preferring instead to place his trust in God.
DAVY THE DICER
1. I beshrew your cat] I curse whatever plans you have in store for me.

Sir Thomas Wyatt (c. 1503–1542)

For a time, Wyatt was one of Henry VIII's most trusted diplomats, who in 1532 accompanied the king and Anne Boleyn to meet François I of France; "Sometime I fled the fire that me brent" probably concerns this trip. But Henry was capricious, and susceptible to lobbying: persuaded that Wyatt had seduced Boleyn, he imprisoned him in the Tower of London on May 5, 1536, shortly after detaining four other men suspected of having committed adultery with her, whose executions Wyatt is likely to have witnessed from his cell on May 17, two days before that of Boleyn. He eluded the axe thanks to Thomas Cromwell, Henry VIII's principal secretary and chief minister, who was spearheading the Reformation. After Wyatt's release from the Tower in mid-June, he was made steward of Conisborough Castle and assisted in the suppression of the uprising in the north. In March 1537 he was made ambassador to the Court of Emperor Charles V (in Spain), and for the next two and a half years was abroad; among other things, he became embroiled in a plot to assassinate papal legate Cardinal Pole. Shortly after Wyatt's return to England in 1540, Cromwell was arrested, the victim of political foes who persuaded Henry he was guilty of treason. After a botched execution, what was left of his head was impaled on a pike on London Bridge; "The pillar perished is whereto I leant" refers to this loss. His enemies then engineered a charge of treason against Wyatt, delivered January 17, 1541; back in the Tower, he composed "The flaming sighs that boil within my breast," among other works. For two months he remained in prison, expecting each day to be his last, but on March 19 Katherine Howard interceded on his behalf, and he was released, receiving a pardon from the king at the end of the month. Wyatt went on to become vice admiral of the fleet against France and was sent on a diplomatic mission to Falmouth. On his return, he contracted a fever and died, October 11, 1542. He was thirty-nine.

Sometime I fled the fire that me brent[1]

Sometime I fled the fire that me brent	*burned*
By sea, by land, by water and by wind;	
And now I follow the coals that be quent	*quenched*
From Dover to Calais against my mind.	*with reluctance*
Lo, how desire is both sprung and spent!	*excited*
And he may see that whilom was so blind,	*once*
And all his labour now he laugh to scorn,	
Meshed in the briars that erst was all to-torn.	*torn to shreds*

Written c. October 1532, published 1559

Who list his wealth and ease retain[1]

Who list his wealth and ease retain,
Himself let him unknown contain;[2]
Press not too fast in at that gate
Where the return stands by disdain:[3]
For sure, *circa Regna tonat*.[4]

The high mountains are blasted oft
When the low valley is mild and soft;
Fortune with health stands at debate;
The fall is grievous from aloft—
And sure, *circa Regna tonat*.

---

1. This poem was written when Wyatt accompanied Henry VIII and Anne Boleyn to France in October 1532. It may concern his changed feelings for Anne.

WHO LIST HIS WEALTH AND EASE RETAIN

1. Composed during Wyatt's imprisonment in May 1536 in the Tower of London for having allegedly committed adultery with Anne Boleyn, whose execution took place on May 19.

2. Who list . . . contain] Let the person who wishes to preserve his wealth and well-being remain unknown to the world.

3. Where the return stands by disdain] Where, forced to exit, you experience others' disdain.

4. *circa Regna tonat*] Thunder roars around the throne.

These bloody days have broken my heart;
My lust, my youth did them depart,
And blind desire of estate;
Who hastes to climb seeks to revert:[5]
Of truth, *circa Regna tonat.*

The bell tower showed me such sight[6]
That in my head sticks day and night;
There did I learn out of a grate,
For all favor, glory or might,[7]
That yet *circa Regna tonat.*

By proof, I say, there did I learn,
Wit helpeth not defence too yerne,   *eagerly*
Of innocency to plead or prate;[8]
Bear low, therefore, give God the stern,[9]
For sure, *circa Regna tonat.*

Written c. May 19, 1536, published 1961

In court to serve, decked with fresh array[1]

In court to serve, decked with fresh array,
    Of sugared meats feeling the sweet repast,
The life in banquets and sundry kinds of play
    Amid the press of lordly looks to waste,
        Hath with it joined ofttimes such bitter taste

---

5. Who hastes to climb seeks to revert] He who hastens to climb up the ladder is looking for a fall.
6. such sight] i.e. that of Anne Boleyn's execution, May 19, 1536.
7. For all favor . . . might] Regardless of one's favor, glory or might.
8. Wit helpeth . . . or prate] Intelligence (wit) is of no help when trying to plead one's innocence.
9. Bear low . . . the stern] Remain of a lowly station, and allow God to steer your course.

IN COURT TO SERVE, DECKED WITH FRESH ARRAY
1. When first published, this poem was entitled "The Courtier's Life."

That whoso joins such kind of life to hold
    In prison joys,[2] fettered with chains of gold.

Published 1557

The pillar perished is whereto I leant[1]

The pillar perished is whereto I leant—
The strongest stay of mine unquiet mind;
The like of it no man again can find,
From east to west still seeking though he went—
To mine unhap, for hap away hath rent
Of all my joy the very bark and rind;
And I, alas, by chance am thus assigned
Dearly to mourn till death do it relent.[2]
But since that thus it is by destiny,
What can I more but have a woeful heart?—
My pen in plaint, my voice in woeful cry,
My mind in woe, my body full of smart,
And I myself myself always to hate—
Till dreadful death do cease my doleful state?

Written shortly after July 28, 1540, published 1557

---

2. In prison joys] i.e., feels joy in prison.

THE PILLAR PERISHED IS WHERETO I LEANT
1. Thomas Cromwell, Wyatt's protector, was arrested and executed on July 28, 1540. After a brutal execution, Cromwell's mutilated head was placed on a pike on London Bridge as a warning to others. This left Wyatt cruelly exposed; a trumped-up charge of treason was delivered against him on January 17, 1541.
2. till death do it relent] till death brings my misfortune to an end.

The flaming sighs that boil within my breast[1]

The flaming sighs that boil within my breast
Sometime break forth, and they can well declare
The heart's unrest, and how that it doth fare—
The pain thereof, the grief, and all the rest.
The watered eyes from whence the tears do fall
Do feel some force, or else they would be dry;
The wasted flesh of colour dead can try,   *understand*
And sometime tell what sweetness is in gall;
And he that list to see, and to discern
How care can force within a wearied mind,   *can be of consequence*
Come he to me, I am that place assigned.
But for all this, no force, it doth no harm.   *no matter*
The wound, alas, hap in some other place
From whence no tool away the scar can raze.

But you that of such like have had your part   *have also been imprisoned*
Can best be judge. Wherefore, my friend so dear,
I thought it good my state should now appear
To you, and that there is no great desert.[2]
And whereas you, in weighty matters great,
Of fortune saw the shadow that you know,
For trifling things I now am stricken so
That, though I feel my heart doth wound and beat,
I sit alone, save on the second day   *every other day*
My fever comes, with whom I spend my time
In burning heat, while that she list assign.
And who hath health and liberty alway,
Let him thank God, and let him not provoke
To have the like of this my painful stroke.

Probably written between January 17 and March 19, 1541,
published 1557

1. This poem was written during Wyatt's imprisonment on a charge of treason in the Tower of London, 17 January to March 19, 1541; at the time of writing it was almost certain he would be executed.
2. there is no great desert] I have done nothing to deserve imprisonment.

Sighs are my food, drink are my tears[1]

Sighs are my food, drink are my tears;
Clinking of fetters such music would crave.
Stink and close air away my life wears;
Innocency is all the hope I have.
Rain, wind, or weather I judge by mine ears:
Malice assaulted that righteousness should save.[2]
Sure I am, Bryan, this wound shall heal again,
But yet, alas, the scar shall still remain.

Written between January 17 and March 19, 1541, published 1557

Thomas Seymour,
Baron Seymour of Sudeley
(b. in or before 1509, d. 1549)

THE RISE OF the handsome, dashing Thomas Seymour, Baron Seymour of Sudeley, coincided with that of his sister Jane, third wife of Henry VIII. He was involved in diplomatic missions to France in 1538 and to Austria in 1542, and was sent as resident ambassador to Mary of Hungary, regent of the Low Countries, in 1543. That summer, he served as marshal of the English army in the Low Countries, and in September 1544 took part in the capture of Boulogne. His downfall was precipitated by the reign of Edward VI. The new king was nine years old, and his decisions were made by his uncle, the Protector of the Realm, Edward Seymour, Earl of Hertford—Thomas's brother. In a more harmonious family that might have been advantageous,

---

1. This poem was written during Wyatt's imprisonment on a charge of treason in the Tower of London, January 17 to March 19, 1541; at the time of writing it was almost certain he would be executed. It was apparently addressed to Sir Francis Bryan, a poet, diplomat, and courtier known as the "Vicar of Hell."
2. Malice . . . should save] Malice (in the shape of Bryan) attacked the person (Wyatt) who deserves to be saved by righteousness.

but competitiveness and jealousy soured relations between the siblings, and, after much plotting, Thomas was arrested. Charges were brought against him by the Privy Council, some of them justified, such as his attempts to conspire against the Protector. A bill of attainder was introduced into Parliament in February 1549, and Seymour was executed on March 20. In his final days he composed "Forgetting God," which should be read alongside the elegy of his friend and colleague, John Harington, on page 43.

Forgetting God

Forgetting God to love a king
Hath been my rod; or else nothing
In this frail life, being a blast
Of care and strife, till it be past.
Yet God did call me in my pride
Lest I should fall and from him slide;
For whom he loves he must correct,
That they may be of his elect—
Then Death, haste thee! thou shalt me gain
Immortally with God to reign.
Lord, send the king like years as Noè   *Noah*
In governing this realm in joy;
And after this frail life, such grace
That in thy bliss he may find place.

Written between March 5 and 20, 1549, published 1769

John Harington (c. 1517–1582)

HARINGTON BEGAN HIS career as courtier to Henry VIII, whose natural daughter, Ethelreda, he married in 1547. He had entered the service of Sir Thomas Seymour in 1546, and the next few years of his life were affected by Seymour's spectacular fall from grace during the reign of Edward VI (see p. 41). Seymour's arrest in January 1549 led to Harington's incarceration in the Tower of London, where he remained until the spring of 1550. Seymour was executed on Tower Hill on March 20, 1549, and it may have been on that day, or soon after, that Harington composed the sonnet included here. Harington was released but arrested again in 1554 for suspected involvement in the Wyatt rebellion against Mary Tudor; he attended Princess Elizabeth during her confinement to the Tower (for suspected collusion in the rebellion), March to May 1554. With Elizabeth's accession to the throne in 1558, Harington's fortunes improved; he was given two exchequer posts and a number of land grants, and would represent Old Sarum in the Parliament of 1559.

A Sonnet Written Upon My Lord Admiral Seymour[1]

Of person rare, strong limbs, and manly shape;
Of nature, framed to serve on sea or land;
Of friendship firm, in good state and ill hap;
In peace, headwise; in war, skill great, bold hand;
On horse, on foot, in peril or in play
None could excel, though many did assay;
A subject true to King, and servant great;

---

1. Seymour was executed on Tower Hill on March 20, and it may have been on that day, or soon after, that Harington composed this sonnet. Although Harington was wrong to regard Seymour as innocent of the accusations made against him, his poem is no less heartfelt on that account.

Friend to God's truth, enemy to Rome's deceit;
Sumptuous abroad, for honour of the land;
Temperate at home, yet kept great state with stay   *strength*
And noble house, and gave more mouths more meat
Than some advanced on higher steps to stand—
Yet against nature, reason, and just laws
His blood was spilt, guiltless, without just cause.

Written on or shortly after March 20, 1549, published 1769

Henry Howard, Earl of Surrey
(1516/1517–1547)

BORN INTO ONE of the most influential and wealthiest families in England, Howard was an aristocrat and lived his life accordingly. In October 1532, he accompanied Henry VIII and Anne Boleyn to Calais for their meeting with François I of France; his friend Sir Thomas Wyatt (p. 36) was also on that trip. In the summer and early autumn of 1537, Howard was confined first to the Tower of London and then to Windsor Castle under suspicion of having sided with those involved in an uprising against the king; while at Windsor he composed "So cruel a prison." He was released in time to witness the trial and execution of his cousin Katherine Howard in February 1542, and the death of Wyatt in October. Though heavily involved in Henry VIII's invasion of France in June 1544, he was recalled to face charges of treason and mismanagement—which, though false, were difficult to answer. It was probably at this time he composed "Th' Assyrians' King, in peace with foul desire." During final imprisonment in the Tower of London he worked on paraphrases of the Psalms in which he reflected on betrayal and abandonment; evidence against him came principally from his friends, who were offered inducements of various kinds. After an unsuccessful attempt to escape by crawling down the privy leading to the Thames, he was beheaded on January 19, 1547. Surrey occupies an important place in literary history for having introduced blank verse (unrhymed iambic pentameter) into English poetry.

So cruel a prison how could betide, alas[1]

So cruel a prison how could betide, alas,
As proud Windsor?—where I in lust and joy,   *pleasure*
With a king's son, my childish[2] years did pass,
In greater feast than Priam's sons of Troy;

Where each sweet place returns a taste full sour—
The large green courts, where we were wont to hove, *linger*
With eyes cast up unto the maidens' tower[3]
And easy sighs, such as folk draw in love;

The stately seats, the ladies bright of hue,
The dances short, long tales of great delight
With words and looks that tigers could but rue,
Where each of us did plead the other's right;

The palm play[4] where, despoiled for the game,
With dazed eyes oft we by gleams of love
Have missed the ball and got sight of our dame,
To bait[5] her eyes which kept the leads above;

The gravel ground, with sleeves tied on the helm,[6]
On foaming horse, with swords and friendly hearts,
With cheer, as though one should another whelm,
Where we have fought, and chased oft with darts;

---

1. This poem was written during Howard's imprisonment at Windsor Castle, for his fight with Sir Edward Seymour over his alleged sympathies with the Lincolnshire rebellion against the king. Surrey's confinement lasted only a few weeks. His recollections of Windsor are of time spent with the king's natural son, Henry Fitzroy, who died of consumption on July 22, 1536.
2. childish] youthful.
3. the maidens' tower] the part of the castle where the ladies were quartered.
4. palm play] *jeu de paume*, an indoor form of tennis played without racquets.
5. bait] attract. The players are distracted from the game by their attempts to impress the ladies who look down from the leaded galleries of the tennis court.
6. sleeves tied on the helm] A lady's colors would be tied to a knight's helmet when jousting.

With silver drops the meads yet spread for ruth
In active games of nimbleness and strength,
Where we did strain, trailed by swarms of youth
Our tender limbs, that yet shot up in length;

The secret groves which oft we made resound
Of pleasant plaint and of our ladies' praise,   *song*
Recording oft what grace each one had found—
What hope of speed, what dread of long delays;

The wild forest, the clothed holts[7] with green,
With reins availed and swift y-breathed horse,
With cry of hounds and merry blasts between,
Where we did chase the fearful hart a force;[8]

The wide vales eke, that harbored us each night,   *too*
Wherewith, alas, reviveth in my breast
The sweet accord, such sleeps as yet delight
The pleasant dreams, the quiet bed of rest;

The secret thoughts imparted with such trust,
The wanton talk, the diverse change of play,
The friendship sworn, each promise kept so just,
Wherewith we passed the winter nights away.

And with this thought the blood forsakes my face,
The tears berain my cheeks of deadly hue,
The which, as soon as sobbing sighs, alas,
Up-supped have, thus I my plaint renew:

"Oh place of bliss, renewer of my woes,
Give me accompt, where is my noble fere[9]
Whom in thy walls thou didst each night enclose,
To other lief, but unto me most dear?"   *beloved*

---

7. holts] woods.
8. a force] the hart was run down to exhaustion.
9. my noble fere] a reference to Henry Fitzroy, Duke of Richmond, with whom Howard
was brought up.

Echo, alas, that doth my sorrow rue,
Returns thereto a hollow sound of plaint.   *sorrow*
Thus I alone, where all my freedom grew,
In prison pine with bondage and restraint;

And with remembrance of the greater grief,
To banish the less I find my chief relief.

Written summer/autumn 1537, published 1557

Th' Assyrians' King, in peace with foul desire[1]

Th' Assyrians' King, in peace with foul desire,
And filthy lust that stained his regal heart,
In war that should set princely hearts afire
Vanquished did yield for want of martial art.
The dent of swords from kisses seemed strange,
And harder than his lady's side his targe;   *shield*
From glutton feasts to soldier's fare a change;
His helmet far above a garland's charge.   *weight*
Who scarce the name of manhood did retain,
Drenched in sloth and womanish delight,
Feeble of spirit, unpatient of pain,
When he had lost his honour and his right
        (Proud time of wealth,[2] in storms appalled with dread),
        Murdered himself to show some manful deed.

Perhaps written c. 1544, published 1557

---

1. Ostensibly about Sardanapalus, who lived in hedonistic luxury then burned himself and his court to the ground while being besieged by the Medes, this poem is often taken to be a critique of Henry VIII.
2. Proud time of wealth] proud in times of plenty.

Psalm 55[1]

Give ear to my suit, Lord! fromward hide not thy face;   *away*
Behold! hearken, in grief, lamenting how I pray.
My foes that bray so loud, and eke threpe on so fast,   *contend*
Buckled to do me scath, so is their malice bent.   *harm*
Care pierceth my entrails, and travaileth my spirit;
The grisly fear of death environeth my breast;   *surrounds*
A trembling cold of dread clean overwhelmeth my heart.
"Oh!" think I, "had I wings like to the simple dove,
This peril might I fly, and seek some place of rest
In wilder woods, where I might dwell far from these cares."
What speedy way of wing my plaints should they lay on,   *sorrows*
To 'scape the stormy blast that threatened is to me?
Rein those unbridled tongues! Break that conjured league!
For I deciphered have amid our town the strife;
Guile and wrong keep the walls, they ward both day and night,
And mischief joined with care doth keep the marketstead   *marketplace*
Whilst wickedness with crafts in heaps swarm through the street.
Ne my declared foe wrought me all this reproach;[2]
By harm so looked for, it weigheth half the less.
For though mine enemy's hap had been for to prevail,
I could have hid my face from venom of his eye.
It was a friendly foe, by shadow of goodwill,
Mine old fere, and dear friend, my guide that trapped me;   *companion*
Where I was wont to fetch the cure of all my care,
And in his bosom hide my secret zeal to God.
Such sudden surprise quick may him hell devour,
Whilst I invoke the Lord, whose power shall me defend.
My prayer shall not cease from that the sun ascends,
Till he his alture win, and hide them in the sea.   *height*
With words of hot effect, that moveth from heart contrite,
Such humble suit, oh Lord, doth pierce thy patient ear!
It was the Lord that brake the bloody compacts of those

---

1. This paraphrase of Psalm 55 was composed during Howard's final imprisonment prior to his execution at Tower Hill. In it, he reflects on the irony that it was his former friends, to whom he confided his beliefs, secrets, and ambitions, who had destroyed him.
2. Ne my declared foe wrought me all this reproach] It isn't only my declared foe who has engineered this disgrace.

That pricked on with ire, to slaughter me and mine.
The everlasting God whose kingdom hath no end,
Whom by no tale to dread he could divert from sin,
The conscience unquiet he strikes with heavy hand,
And proves their force in faith, whom he swore to defend.
Butter falls not so soft as doth his patience long,
And overpasseth fine oil running not half so smooth.
But when his sufferance finds that bridled wrath provokes,
His threatened wrath he whets more sharp than tool can file.
Friar, whose harm and tongue presents the wicked sort
Of those false wolves, with coats which do their
    ravin hide;   *predatoriness*
That swear to me by heaven, the footstool of the Lord,
Though force had hurt my fame, they did not touch my life.
Such patching care I loathe, as feeds the wealth with lies;[3]
But in the other Psalm of David find I ease.
Jacta curam tuam super Dominum, et ipse te enutriet.[4]

Written shortly before January 19, 1547, published 1815

The storms are passed, these clouds are overblown[1]

The storms are passed, these clouds are overblown,
And humble cheer great rigor hath repressed.
For the default is set a pain foreknown,
And patience graft in a determined breast.
And in the heart where heaps of grief were grown,
The sweet revenge[2] hath planted mirth and rest;
No company so pleasant as mine own.
. . . [This line is missing.]
Thraldom at large hath made this prison free;
Danger well passed, remembered, works delight.

---

3. Such patching care I loathe, as feeds the wealth with lies] I detest such deceitful, careful words, designed to fill me with a false sense of security.
4. Cast thy care upon the Lord, and He shall sustain thee.
THE STORMS ARE PASSED, THESE CLOUDS ARE OVERBLOWN
1. According to his son, this was the last poem Surrey was to write.
2. The sweet revenge] of his "cheer," which has turned imprisonment into freedom.

Of lingering doubts such hope is sprung pardie,   *without doubt*
That nought I find displeasant in my sight;
But when my glass presenteth unto me
The cureless wound that bleedeth day and night,
To think, alas, such hap should granted be   *fate*
Unto a wretch that hath no heart to fight,
To spill that blood that hath so oft been shed
For Britain's sake, alas, and now is dead.

Written shortly before January 19, 1547, published 1557

Anne Askew (c. 1521–1546)

ASKEW WAS OF a good family: her father, who owned land in Lincoln-shire and Nottinghamshire, was knighted in 1513, and appointed high sheriff of Lincolnshire in 1521. He arranged her marriage, against her will, to the Catholic Thomas Kyme, shortly after which she converted to Protestantism. Cast out by her husband, she sought divorce from him in London, only to be arrested for distributing banned Protestant pamphlets. It was her misfortune that this was the last year of Henry VIII's reign, during which warring factions were struggling for dominance in expectation of the time when his heir, a minor, ascended the throne; in particular, conservative elements at court were pushing hard for the persecution of those who, like Askew, denied transubstantiation. Such views rendered the priest unnecessary as mediator between God and the faithful and so, not surprisingly, aroused the opposition of clerics: Edmund Bonner, bishop of London, and Stephen Gardiner, bishop of Winchester, were among those who sought her arrest and imprisonment. In March 1545, she was interrogated about her religious beliefs for two weeks. Her alleged association with reformist circles in the court of Katharine Parr was a particular provocation, and on that matter she was questioned closely. On June 13, 1545, she was arraigned for heresy at the Guildhall, but released for lack of evidence. Then, on June 28, 1546, she was arraigned again, and this time condemned "without any trial of a jury," in contravention of lawful process. Incarcerated at the Tower of London she was subjected to torture by those who demanded the names of noblewomen who sympathized with her. When she declined to answer, Privy Councilors Sir Richard Rich and Sir Thomas Wriothesley fastened her to the rack and turned the wheel themselves, even though the law did not allow the use of torture on condemned prisoners. Despite threats, she declined to recant and was transferred to Newgate to wait for execution, "in extremity of sickness." Aged twenty-five, she was burned at the stake at Smithfield on July 16, 1546. Later that year her account of her ordeal was published in Germany by the Protestant agitator, John Bale.

Ballad Written in Newgate

Like as the armed knight
Appointed to the field,
With this world will I fight
And Faith shall be my shield.

Faith is that weapon strong
Which will not fail at need;
My foes, therefore, among
Therewith[1] will I proceed.

As it is had in strength
And force of Christ's way,
It will prevail at length
Though all the devils say nay.

Faith in the fathers old
Obtained rightwisness[2]
Which make me very bold
To fear no world's distress.

I now rejoice in heart
And Hope bid me do so,
For Christ will take my part
And ease me of my woe.

---

1. Therewith] With faith . . .
2. rightwisness] righteousness.

Thou say'st, Lord, who so knock,
To them wilt thou attend;
Undo, therefore, the lock
And thy strong power send.

More enemies now I have
Than hairs upon my head;
Let them not me deprave
But fight thou in my stead.

On thee my care I cast;
For all their cruel spite
I set not by their haste,
For thou art my delight.

I am not she that list
My anchor to let fall
For every drizzling mist
My ship substantial.

Not oft use I to write
In prose nor yet in rhyme,
Yet will I show one sight
That I saw in my time.

I saw a royal throne
Where Justice should have sit,
But in her stead was one
Of moody cruel wit;

Absorbed³ was rightwisness   *righteousness*
As of the raging flood;
Satan in his excess
Sucked up the guiltless blood.

---

3. Absorbed] swallowed up.

Then thought I, "Jesus Lord,
When thou shalt judge us all,
Hard is it to record
On these men what will fall.

Yet Lord, I thee desire
For that they do to me,
Let them not taste the hire
Of their iniquity."

Written by July 16, 1546, published 1547

Elizabeth I (1533–1603)

THESE POEMS COME from a period during the reign of Elizabeth's Catholic half sister Mary Tudor (from 1553 to 1558) when the young Princess Elizabeth was under constant suspicion and her life in peril. Calls to execute her increased in number after the failed rebellion of Thomas Wyatt the younger (1521–1554), son of the poet included at page 36, above, intended to dethrone Mary. Elizabeth may indeed have been culpable, as she had been in contact with the conspirators. And, regardless of her actual involvement, she would always remain the focus of discontent with Mary. She was incarcerated in the Tower of London on March 17, 1554, an ominous sign that appeared to foreshadow a traitor's death; certainly, few prisoners left the Tower alive. During her imprisonment she was examined by the Privy Council, a move that could have led to charges being laid against her, but there was no evidence on which her enemies could act. The principal rebel, Wyatt, took care to exonerate her from blame when questioned, repeating his claim on the scaffold immediately before execution on April 11. She was still fearful for her life when, on May 19, she was taken from the Tower of London to house arrest at the Oxfordshire palace of Woodstock, where she would remain for just under a year (until May 1555). During that time she was guarded by up to sixty soldiers day and night, and her movements were closely monitored. The books she read were scrutinized, and writing materials given to her when she requested them, were reclaimed afterward. No one was permitted to visit her other than by permission, and then with a chaperone. She remained aware of the possibility she could be summarily executed—one that would persist for some time after her release. The poems she composed at Woodstock speak of the unease she must have felt, and the fragility of her continuing existence. Things could not remain this way forever, nor would they. After a few years, Mary died, and Elizabeth would ascend the throne to become one of the most celebrated of British monarchs. Her experience of incarceration in London and Oxfordshire has been described as "the ordeal of her life," and she would recall it in letters, speeches, and prayers written throughout her reign.

Writ With Charcoal on a Shutter at Woodstock

Oh Fortune, thy wresting, wavering state
Hath fraught with cares my troubled wit
Whose witness this present prison late
Could bear, where once was joy flown quite.
Thou causedst the guilty to be loosed
From lands where innocents were enclosed,
And caused the guiltless to be reserved,
And freed those that death had well deserved.
But all herein can be naught wrought,
So God grant to my foes as they have thought.

Written 1554, published 1612

Written With a Diamond on a Window at Woodstock[1]

Much suspected by me:
Nothing proved can be.
               Quoth Elizabeth prisoner.

Written May 1555, published 1583

---

1. This brief verse was composed shortly before Elizabeth's departure from Woodstock.

Sir Edmund Spenser (1552–1599)

SPENSER SPENT ALMOST all his creative adult life in Ireland (then a British colony), becoming a permanent resident there in 1580, when appointed private secretary to Arthur, Lord Grey de Wilton, Lord Deputy from July onward. On October 6 that year he joined Grey's force of nearly one thousand men bound for Fort Del Oro, three hundred miles from Dublin, where Spanish troops had landed, reinforcements for an Irish rebellion brewing in Munster. Grey drove his army hard, through cold, torrential rains, executing several sergeants and a score of private soldiers for unauthorized foraging. For the first time, Spenser saw the Irish countryside, devastated after years of warfare: roads overgrown, bridges destroyed, corpses littering the fields and ditches, peasants starved and terrified. The "Spanish" force, in fact an ill-trained collection of Italian and Basque soldiers, was already exhausted when Grey reached them, and after some perfunctory skirmishes they sued for surrender. Despite their repeated pleas for mercy, Grey's response was to massacre the six hundred or so men who remained within the fort. Even at the time, this was controversial, and generated criticism at home; Spenser defended it, arguing that had Grey spared the "Spanish" troops, they would certainly have assisted in a rebellion, that their massacre was a warning to others, and that "there was no other way but to make that short end of them which was made." (Such atrocities were justified by the fact that, like many other Englishmen, Spenser believed the Irish to be lawless barbarians descended from blood-drinking Scythians.) Spenser joined Grey's other military expeditions including that against the O'Connors in Connaught, and in subsequent years probably witnessed (and may have been involved in) violent campaigns against the O'Mores, O'Tooles, O'Byrnes, and Kavanaghs, some of whose confiscated land he soon owned; by 1588 he was proprietor of the ruined Norman castle of Kilcolman and its estate of over three thousand acres, taken during suppression of the Desmond rebellion. Spenser's recent biographer, Andrew Hadfield, writes that *The Faerie Queene*, Book V "argues that only if justice is imposed in Ireland can the British Isles flourish in peace and prosperity." In Spenser's allegory, Irena (peace) is freed from the clutches of tyranny by Artegall, the Knight of Justice.

The Faerie Queene
BOOK 5, CONTAINING
THE LEGEND OF ARTEGALL OR OF JUSTICE

CANTO 12 (EXTRACT)

> *Artegall doth Sir Burbon aid,*
> *And blames for changing shield:*
> *He with the great Grantorto fights,*
> *And slayeth him in field.*

1

Oh sacred hunger of ambitious minds
    And impotent desire of men to reign,
    Whom neither dread of God, that devils binds,
    Nor laws of men, that commonweals contain,
    Nor bands of nature, that wild beasts restrain,
    Can keep from outrage and from doing wrong,
    Where they may hope a kingdom to obtain.
    No faith so firm, no trust can be so strong,
No love so lasting then, that may enduren long.

2

Witness may Burbon be, whom all the bands
    Which may a Knight assure, had surely bound,
    Until the love of Lordship and of lands
    Made him become most faithless and unsound:
    And witness be Gerioneo found,
    Who for like cause faire Belge did oppress,
    And right and wrong most cruelly confound:
    And so be now Grantorto who no less
Than all the rest burst out to all outrageousness.

3

Gainst whom Sir Artegall, long having since
    Taken in hand th' exploit, being thereto
    Appointed by that mighty Fairy Prince,
    Great Gloriane, that tyrant to fordo,

kill

Through other great adventures hitherto
Had it forslacked. But now time drawing nigh, *neglected*
To him assigned, her high behest to do,
To the sea shore he gan his way apply,
To weet if shipping ready he mote there descry.

4
Though when they came to the sea-coast, they found
A ship all ready (as good fortune fell)
To put to sea, with whom they did compound, *make terms*
To pass them over, where them list to tell:
The wind and weather served them so well,
That in one day they with the coast did fall;[1]
Whereas they ready found them to repel,
Great hosts of men in order martial,
Which them forbade to land, and footing did forestall.

5
But nathemore would they from land refrain, *never the more*
But when as nigh unto the shore they drew,
That foot of man might sound the bottom plain,
Talus into the sea did forth issue,
Though darts from shore and stones they at him threw;
And wading through the waves with steadfast sway, *force*
Maugre the might of all those troops in view, *In spite of*
Did win the shore, whence he them chased away,
And made to fly, like doves, whom the eagle doth affray. *frighten*

6
The whiles Sir Artegall, with that old knight[2]
Did forth descend, there being none them near,
And forward marched to a town in sight.
By this came tidings to the tyrant's ear
By those which erst did fly away for fear
Of their arrival: wherewith troubled sore,

---

1. they with the coast did fall] they landed.
2. that old knight] Sir Sergis.

He all his forces straight to him did rear,   *gather*
 And forth issuing with his scouts afore,
Meant them to have encountered ere they left the shore.

7

But ere he marched far, he with them met,
 And fiercely charged them with all his force;
 But Talus sternly did upon them set,   *cruelly*
 And brushed and battered them without remorse, *thrashed*
 That on the ground he left full many a corse;
 Ne any able was him to withstand,
 But he them overthrew both man and horse,
 That they lay scattred over all the land,
As thick as doth the seed after the sower's hand.[3]

8

Till Artegall him seeing so to rage,
 Willed him to stay, and sign of truce did make,
 To which all harkning did a while assuage
 Their forces' fury, and their terror slake;
 Till he an herald called and to him spake,
 Willing him wend unto the tyrant straight,
 And tell him that not for such slaughters' sake
 He thither came, but for to try the right
Of fair Irena's cause with him in single fight.

9

And willed him for to reclaim with speed   *recall*
 His scattered people, ere they all were slain,
 And time and place convenient to areed,[4]
 In which they two the combat might darraine. *engage*
 Which message when Grantorto heard, full fain
 And glad he was the slaughter so to stay,

---

3. It is almost unknown for Spenser to describe mass slaughter in this way, and the only explanation for it is that he is recalling sights witnessed while with Grey in Ireland. There is no attempt either to condemn the bloodshed, or to excuse it; a dispenser of justice with divine omniscience, Talus acts "without remorse."
4. convenient to areed] fitting to determine.

And pointed for the combat twixt them twain   *appointed*
   The morrow next, ne gave him longer day.
So sounded the retreat, and drew his folk away.

10

That night Sir Artegall did cause his tent
   There to be pitched on the open plain;
   For he[5] had given straight commandement
   That none should dare him once to entertain,
   Which none durst break, though many would right fain
   For fair Irena, whom they loved dear.
   But yet old Sergis did so well him pain,[6]
   That from close friends, that dared not to appear,
He all things did purvey, which for them needful were.   *provide*

11

The morrow next, that was the dismal day[7]
   Appointed for Irena's death before,
   So soon as it did to the world display
   His cheerful face, and light to men restore,
   The heavy maid,[8] to whom none tidings bore
   Of Artegall's arrival, her to free,
   Looked up with eyes full sad and heart full sore;
   Weening her life's last hour then near to be,   *Knowing*
Sith no redemption nigh she did nor hear nor see.

12

Then up she rose, and on herself did dight   *dress*
   Most squalid garments, fit for such a day,
   And with dull countenance, and with doleful sprite,
   She forth was brought in sorrowful dismay,
   For to receive the doom of her decay.   *punishment of death*
   But coming to the place, and finding there
   Sir Artegall, in battailous array   *warlike*

---

5. he] Grantorto.
6. him pain] took trouble on his behalf.
7. the dismal day] evil day.
8. maid] Irena.

Waiting his foe, it did her dead heart cheer
And new life to her lent, in midst of deadly fear.

13

Like as a tender rose in open plain
    That with untimely drought nigh withered was,
    And hung the head, soon as few drops of rain
    Thereon distil, and dew her dainty face,
    Gins to look up, and with fresh wonted grace
    Dispreads the glory of her leaves gay;   *opens out*
    Such was Irena's countenance, such her case,   *condition*
    When Artegall she saw in that array,
There waiting for the tyrant, till it was far day.   *late in the day*

14

Who came at length, with proud presumptuous gait
    Into the field, as if he fearless were,
    All armed in a coat of iron plate
    Of great defence to ward the deadly fear,[9]
    And on his head a steel cap he did wear
    Of colour rusty brown, but sure and strong;
    And in his hand an huge pole-axe did bear,   *battle-axe*
    Whose steel was iron studded, but not long,   *handle*
With which he wont to fight, to justify his wrong.[10]

15

Of stature huge and hideous he was,   *immense*
    Like to a giant for his monstrous height,
    And did in strength most sorts of men surpass,
    Ne ever any found his match in might;
    Thereto he had great skill in single fight:
    His face was ugly and his countenance stern
    That could have frayed one with the very sight,   *frightened*
    And gaped like a gulf when he did gerne,   *snarl*
That whether man or monster one could scarce discern.

---

9. ward the deadly fear] repel the fear of death.
10. The description of Grantorto indicates he is dressed like an Irish foot soldier.

16

Soon as he did within the lists appear,   *area of battle*
    With dreadful look he Artegall beheld
    As if he would have daunted him with fear,
    And grinning grisly, did against him wield
    His deadly weapon, which in hand he held.
    But th' elfin swain, that oft had seen like sight,   *knightly man*
    Was with his ghastly count'nance nothing quelled,
    But gan him straight to buckle to the fight,
And cast his shield about, to be in ready plight.

17

The trumpets sound and they together go,
    With dreadful terror and with fell intent;   *fierce*
    And their huge strokes full dangerously bestow,
    To do most damage, where as most they meant.
    But with such force and fury violent,
    The tyrant thundered his thick blows so fast,
    That through the iron walls their way they rent,
    And even to the vital parts they passed,
Ne ought could them endure, but all they cleft or brast.   *burst*

18

Which cruel outrage when as Artegall
    Did well avize, thenceforth with wary heed   *perceive*
    He shunned his strokes wherever they did fall,
    And way did give unto their graceless speed;   *cruel*
    As when a skilful mariner doth reed   *see*
    A storm approaching that doth peril threat—
    He will not bide the danger of such dread,
    But strikes his sails, and vereth his mainsheet,[11]
And lends unto it leave the empty air to beat.

---

11. strikes his sails . . . mainsheet] shortens his sails and raises the rope that secures the mainsail in order to reduce the amount of wind behind the ship.

19

So did the Fairy Knight himself abear,   *conduct*
    And stooped oft his head from shame[12] to shield;
    No shame to stoop, one's head more high to rear,
    And much to gain, a little for to yield;
    So stoutest knights doen oftentimes in field.
    But still the tyrant sternly at him laid,
    And did his iron axe so nimbly wield
    That many wounds into his flesh it made,
And with his burdenous blows him sore did overlade.   *press hard*

20

Yet when as fit advantage he did spy,
    The whiles the cursed felon high did rear   *villain*
    His cruel hand, to smite him mortally,
    Under his stroke he to him stepping near,
    Right in the flank him strooke with deadly drear[13]
    That the gore blood thence gushing grievously,
    Did underneath him like a pond appear,
    And all his armor did with purple dye—
Thereat he brayed loud, and yelled dreadfully.   *Because of which*

21

Yet the huge stroke, which he before intended,
    Kept on his course, as he did it direct,
    And with such monstrous poise adowne descended,
    That seemed nought could him from death protect:
    But he it well did ward with wise respect,   *care*
    And twixt him and the blow his shield did cast,
    Which thereon seizing, took no great effect,
    But biting deep therein did stick so fast,
That by no means it back again he forth could wrast.   *pull away*

22

Long while he tugged and strove to get it out,
    And all his power applied thereunto,

---

12. shame] shameful injury.
13. deadly drear] the pain and sorrow of death.

That he therewith the knight drew all about:
Nathless, for all that ever he could do, *Nevertheless*
His axe he could not from his shield undo,
Which Artegall perceiving, strooke no more,
But loosing soon his shield, did it forgo, *let go*
And whiles he combred was therewith so sore, *encumbered*
He gan at him let drive more fiercely than afore.

23

So well he him pursued, that at the last *attacked*
He struck him with Chrysaor[14] on the head,
That with the souse[15] thereof full sore aghast,
He staggered to and fro in doubtful stead.
Again whiles he him saw so ill bested, *beset*
He did him smite with all his might and main,
That falling on his mother earth he fed:
Whom when he saw prostrated on the plain,
He lightly reft his head, to ease him of his pain. *chopped off*

24

Which when the people round about him saw,
They shouted all for joy of his success,
Glad to be quit from that proud tyrant's awe, *terror*
Which with strong power did them long time oppress;
And running all with greedy joyfulness
To faire Irena, at her feet did fall,
And her adored with due humbleness,
As their true Liege and Princess natural;
And eke her champion's glory sounded over all.

25

Who straight her leading with meet majesty
Unto the palace, where their kings did reign,
Did her therein establish peaceably,
And to her Kingdom's seat restore again;
And all such persons as did late maintain

---

14. Chrysaor] Artegal's sword.
15. souse] heavy downward blow.

That tyrant's part, with close or open aid,
He sorely punished with heavy pain;
That in short space, whiles there with her he stayed,
Not one was left, that durst her once have disobeyed.

26

During which time, that he did there remain,
His study was true Justice how to deal,
And day and night employed his busy pain
How to reform that ragged commonweal:
And that same iron man which could reveal
All hidden crimes, through all that realm he sent,
To search out those, that used to rob and steal,
Or did rebel gainst lawful government;
On whom he did inflict most grievous punishment.

Probably composed 1595–1596, published January 1596

Sir Walter Ralegh (1554–1618)

SIX FEET IN height, Ralegh was taller than most men of his time and appears to have exercised a powerful attraction for many women including his queen, who regarded him as "a kind of oracle." He remained a court favorite for a decade but his fall from grace, when it came, was spectacular. In late 1591 he clandestinely married one of the Queen's maids of honor, Bess Throckmorton, with whom he had a child in March 1592. This could not remain secret for long, and was strongly disapproved of; when it became public knowledge the family was split up, placed in custody, and imprisoned in the Tower of London. The edict by which they were locked up was arbitrary (that is, not subject to legal process): Ralegh lost all contact with his family, and probably saw the baby only once. During this period he composed the first two poems included here. Known as the "Cynthia" poems, they were discovered in manuscript at Hatfield House in the mid-nineteenth century. Ralegh probably gave the manuscript to Robert Cecil, the Queen's secretary of state and a newly appointed Privy Councilor, to pass on to her. Judging the poems unhelpful to Ralegh's cause, Cecil placed them in his archive where they remained for the next three centuries. They are the elaborate, haunting testimony of a man who was, in effect, a political prisoner. Ralegh did not remain in detention for long, and his quest for the legendary El Dorado, and subsequent service against the Spanish Armada, eventually redeemed him in the eyes of the Queen. Toward the end of her reign, however, he lost favor with Cecil—a serious matter, because Cecil had influence with James VI of Scotland, Elizabeth's successor. When Elizabeth I died on March 24, 1603, Ralegh's existence came to depend on the whim of a monarch with whom he had no credit. Within months he was at the receiving end of a trumped-up charge of treason, placed under house arrest, and on July 20 imprisoned in the Tower. A week later, he attempted unsuccessfully, in a gesture regarded as both theatrical and unchristian, to commit suicide. At the show trial that followed, he was found guilty. He became the focus of much public sympathy, which may explain why James I reprieved him from execution on the scaffold, condemning him instead to imprisonment. For twelve years Ralegh set up a laboratory in his rooms in the Bloody Tower where he conducted scientific experiments and wrote his epic *History of the World*, the theme of which is the tyranny, injustice, and wickedness of monarchs. In 1616 he was released to undertake a final expedition to El Dorado: it was a disaster. There were skirmishes with the Spaniards, his son was killed, and no gold was found. James imprisoned Ralegh again, on charges of attempting to foment war with Spain (effectively an act of treason). Condemned to execution on the morning of October 29, Ralegh spent his last night writing the last of the poems in this selection. Nearly four centuries after his death, he remains a focus of legend, myths, and adventure tales (the claim that he introduced tobacco and potatoes to England is probably untrue).

My body in the walls captived

My body in the walls captived
Feels not the wounds of spiteful envy,
But my thralled mind, of liberty deprived,   *imprisoned*
Fast fettered in her ancient memory,
Doth nought behold but sorrow's dying face;

Such prison erst was so delightful   *formerly*
As it desired no other dwelling place,
But time's effects, and destinies despiteful,
Have changed both my keeper and my fare.
Love's fire and beauty's light I then had store,
But now close kept, as captives wonted are,
That food, that heat, that light I find no more;
    Despair bolts up my doors, and I alone
    Speak to dead walls, but those hear not my moan.

Written 1592/1593, published 1870

The End of the Books of the Ocean's Love to Cynthia, and the Beginning of the 22nd Book, Entreating of Sorrow

My day's delights, my springtime joys fordone,
Which in the dawn and rising sun of youth
Had their creation, and were first begun,

Do in the evening, and the winter sad
Present my mind, which takes my time's accompt
The grief remaining of the joy it had.

My times that then ran o'er themselves in this
And now run out in others' happiness
Bring unto those new joys and newborn days;

So could she not, if she were not the sun
Which sees the birth and burial of all else,
And holds that power with which she first begun,

Leaving each withered body to be torn
By fortune, and by times tempestuous,
Which by her virtue, once fair fruit have borne,

Knowing she can renew, and can create
Green from the ground, and flowers even out of stone
By virtue lasting over time and date,

Leaving us only woe, which like the moss
Having compassion of unburied bones,
Cleaves to mischance, and unrepaired loss,

For tender stalks. . . .

Written 1592/1593, published 1870

What Is Our Life?

What is our life? A play of passion,
Our mirth the music of division;
Our mother's wombs the tiring-houses be,   *dressing-rooms*
Where we are dressed for this short comedy;
Heaven the judicious sharp spectator is,
That sits and marks still who doth act amiss;
Our graves that hide us from the searching sun
Are like drawn curtains when the play is done.
Thus march we, playing, to our latest rest;
Only we die in earnest—that's no jest.

Published 1612

Even such is time, which takes in trust

Even such is time, which takes in trust
Our youth, our joys, and all we have,
And pays us but with age and dust;
Who in the dark and silent grave,
When we have wandered all our ways

Shuts up the story of our days;
And from which earth and grave and dust
The Lord shall raise me up I trust.

Written October 28, 1618, published 1618

Chidiock Tichborne (1558–1586)

TICHBORNE WAS A priest from an old Catholic family at a time when to practice the old religion was extremely dangerous. Although he was allowed to practice his religion during the early part of his life, subsequent developments made this unlawful. In 1570, Elizabeth I was excommunicated by the pope, and in response she made Catholicism illegal and outlawed its priests, who were subject to capital punishment if discovered. The authorities had long had their eye on the Tichbornes: Chidiock and his father were arrested for using "popish relics" in 1583, and three years later the entire family was accused of "popish practices." In 1586 Tichborne became one of six men to join a conspiracy organized by another Catholic, Anthony Babington, to assassinate Elizabeth and replace her with the Catholic Mary Queen of Scots. The conspirators expected this to trigger an invasion by the combined armies of Philip II of Spain and the Catholic League in France, who would turn England back into a Catholic country. From an early stage, they were infiltrated by Robert Poley, an agent of Francis Walsingham, Queen Elizabeth's personal spymaster, who monitored the plotters' discussions and eventually ordered their arrest in August 1586. Having been found guilty of conspiracy to murder the Queen, Tichborne was condemned to a traitor's death—to be hanged, cut down before his neck broke, castrated, disemboweled, quartered, and finally beheaded. On his last night on earth, he wrote to his wife, Agnes, enclosing the poem included here. Immediately prior to his death, Tichborne addressed the assembled crowds at length, "and moved great pity towards him." Aged only twenty-eight, he was executed on September 20, 1586 in St. Giles-in-the-Fields.

My prime of youth is but a frost of cares

My prime of youth is but a frost of cares;
My feast of joy is but a dish of pain;
My crop of corn is but a field of tares;   *weeds*
And all my good is but vain hope of gain.
The day is fled and I saw no sun,
And now I live and now my life is done.

The spring is past and yet it hath not sprung;
The fruit is dead and yet the leaves be green;
My youth is gone and yet I am but young;
I saw the world and yet I was not seen.
My thread is cut, and now my thread is spun,
And now I live and now my life is done.

I sought my death and found it in my womb;
I looked for life and saw it was a shade;
I trod the earth and knew it was mine tomb;
And now I die and now I am but made.
The glass is full and now the glass is run,
And now I live and now my life is done.

Written by September 19, 1586, published 1586

Sir John Harington (bap. 1560, d. 1612)

SON OF THE poet at p. 43 above, Harington's godparents were Elizabeth I and William Herbert, Earl of Pembroke. Educated at Eton and Cambridge, he studied the law at Lincoln's Inn but was forced to leave at his father's death. He served as justice of the peace in Ireland in the 1580s, during which time he worked on the first English translation of Ariosto's epic romance, *Orlando Furioso* (1591). In his *New Discourse of a Stale Subject* (1596), Harington presented his design for a water closet, an early version of which he installed at Richmond palace. During his second tour of duty in Ireland, in 1599, he was one of seventeen thousand men under the command of Robert Devereux, second Earl of Essex, sent to suppress the rebellion of Hugh O'Neill, second Earl of Tyrone, during the Nine Years' War; on July 30 he was among those knighted for their part in the campaign. He was present on August 15 when the English army, a force of over two thousand, was ambushed, attacked, and put to flight by eight hundred Irish guerrillas in the Curlew Mountains, later described by Sir Robert Cecil as "a monstrous dishonour to this nation as ever happened." Harington subsequently met O'Neill with Sir William Warren, and presented him with a copy of his *Orlando*. He returned to England to face the barrage of criticism that attached to Essex for military failure in Ireland, but was restored to favor soon after. He continued to write and publish for the rest of his life, and remains one of the most enduringly fascinating characters of the period.

Of the Wars in Ireland

I praise the speech,[1] but cannot now abide it,
That war is sweet to those that have not tried it;
For I have proved it now, and plainly see 't,
It is so sweet, it maketh all things sweet.
At home Canary wines and Greek grow loathsome;
Here milk is nectar, water tasteth toothsome.
There without baked, roast, boiled, it is no cheer;
Biscuit we like, and bonny clabo here.   *sour buttermilk*
There we complain of one rare-roasted chick;
Here viler meat, worse cooked, ne'er makes me sick.
At home in silken sparvers, beds of down,   *canopies*
We scant can rest, but still toss up and down;
Here I can sleep, a saddle to my pillow,
A hedge the curtain, canopy a willow.
There is a child but cry, oh what a spite!
Here we can brook three larums in one night.   *calls to arm*
There homely rooms must be perfumed with roses;
Here match and powder ne'er offends our noses.

1. the speech] Harington refers to Pindar's adage, made famous by Erasmus, "Dulce bellum inexpertis" (war is sweet to those who have not experienced it).

There from a storm of rain we run like pullets;   *chickens*
Here we stand fast against a shower of bullets.
Lo then how greatly their opinions err
That think there is no great delight in war.
>   But yet for this, sweet war, I'll be thy debtor:
>   I shall forever love my home the better.

Written shortly after August 1599, published 1615

Of Treason

Treason doth never prosper? What's the reason?
For if it prosper, none dare call it treason.

Published 1615

A Groom of the Chamber's Religion in Henry VIII's Time[1]

One of King Henry's favorites began
To move the King one day to take a man
Whom of his chamber he might make a Groom.[2]
"Soft," said the King, "before I grant that room,
It is a question not to be neglected,
How he in his religion stands affected."
"For his religion," answered then the minion,
"I do not certain know what's his opinion;
>   But sure he may, talking with men of learning,
>   Conform himself in less than ten days' warning."

Published 1618

---

1. Harington's father (see p. 43) was courtier to Henry VIII, and had probably told his son many stories of the long-deceased monarch.
2. A Groom of the Chamber occupied a position of trust within the King's Household, performing various domestic duties relating directly to the monarch.

St. Robert Southwell, SJ (1561–1595)

SOUTHWELL'S VOCATION AS a Jesuit priest was to minister to Catholics. That made him an outlaw, for in 1580 Elizabeth I made it treasonous for anyone to practice anything besides the state religion established by her father, Henry VIII. In 1586, the year Southwell began his mission, a priest's chances of survival were one in three; he was lucky, for he survived six years. Even then, he was captured only after being lured to a house at Uxenden, near Harrow, to celebrate Mass with a family, one of whom was a government informant. Unfortunately, Southwell was taken directly to the home of Richard Topcliffe, a professional interrogator answerable exclusively to the Queen, where (according to Topcliffe's own testimony) Southwell was manacled at the wrists with "his feet standing upon the ground and his hands but as high as he can reach against the wall," and subjected to a form of torture by which internal injury was inflicted without causing outward marks on the body. Southwell was almost dead when cut down, vomiting copious quantities of blood. He spent the next two and a half years in solitary confinement at the Tower of London and then at Newgate. At his trial in February 1595 he said he had been tortured on no less than ten occasions. Found guilty of being a priest (something he had never concealed), he was punished by being "drawn to Tyburn upon a hurdle, there to be hanged and cut down alive; his bowels to be burned before his face; his head to be stricken off; his body to be quartered and disposed at her majesty's pleasure." This took place the day after his trial, February 21, 1595. Southwell was canonized as one of forty English martyrs in 1970. For more on Southwell's life and poetry, see p. 3, above.

The Burning Babe

As I in hoary winter's night
Stood shivering in the snow,

Surprised I was with sudden heat
Which made my heart to glow;

And lifting up a fearful eye
To view what fire was near,
A pretty babe all burning bright
Did in the air appear;

Who scorched with excessive heat
Such floods of tears did shed
As though his floods should quench his flames
Which with his tears were fed.

"Alas!" quoth he, "but newly born,
In fiery heats I fry,
Yet none approach to warm their hearts
Or feel my fire but I;

My faultless breast the furnace is,
The fuel wounding thorns;
Love is the fire and sighs the smoke,
The ashes, shame and scorns;

The fuel Justice layeth on,
And Mercy blows the coals,
The metal in this furnace wrought
Are men's defiled souls—

For which, as now on fire I am
To work them to their good,
So will I melt into a bath
To wash them in my blood."

With this he vanished out of sight
And swiftly shrunk away,
And straight I called unto mind
That it was Christmas Day.

Written between 1586 and 1592, published 1602

Times Go by Turns

The lopped tree in time may grow again—
Most naked plants renew both fruit and flower;
The sorriest wight may find release of pain,   *person*
The driest soil suck in some moist'ning shower:
Times go by turns, and chances change by course,
From foul to fair, from better hap to worse.   *chance*

The sea of fortune doth not ever flow,
She draws her favors to the lowest ebb;
Her tides hath equal times to come and go,
Her loom doth weave the fine and coarsest web:
No joy so great but runneth to an end,
No hap so hard but may in fine[1] amend.

Not always fall of leaf, nor ever spring,
No endless night, yet not eternal day;
The saddest birds a season find to sing,
The roughest storm a calm may soon allay:
Thus with succeeding turns God tempereth all
That man may hope to rise, yet fear to fall.

A chance may win that by mischance was lost;
The net that holds no great, takes little fish;
In some things all, in all things none are crossed;
Few all they need, but none have all they wish:
Unmeddled joys here to no man befall—   *unmixed*
Who least, hath some; who most, hath never all.

Written between 1586 and 1592, published 1595

---

1. in fine] at last.

Decease Release[1]

Dum morior orior[2]

The pounded spice both taste and scent doth please,
In fading smoke the force doth incense show;
The perished kernel springeth with increase,
The loppèd tree doth best and soonest grow.

God's spice I was, and pounding was my due,
In fading breath my incense savored best;
Death was the mean my kernel to renew;
By lopping, shot I up to heavenly rest.

Some things more perfect are in their decay,
Like spark that going out gives clearest light;
Such was my hap whose doleful dying day   *fortune, lot*
Began my joy and termèd fortune's spite.   *ended*

Alive a Queen, now dead I am a Saint—
Once Mary called, my name now Martyr is;
From earthly reign debarrèd by restraint,
In lieu whereof I reign in heavenly bliss.

My life my grief, my death hath wrought my joy,
My friends my foil, my foes my weal procured;
My speedy death hath shortened long annoy,   *vexation*
And loss of life an endless life assured.

My scaffold was the bed where ease I found,
The block a pillow of eternal rest;
My headman cast me in a blissful swound—
His axe cut off my cares from cumbered breast.

---

1. This poem is a celebration of Mary Stuart, Queen of Scots, executed by order of Elizabeth on February 8, 1587, after years of imprisonment. It articulates the thoughts of the martyred queen from beyond the grave.
2. Dying I rise.

Rue not my death, rejoice at my repose;
It was no death to me but to my woe;
The bud was opened to let out the rose,
The chains unloosed to let the captive go.

A prince by birth, a prisoner by mishap;
From crown to cross, from throne to thrall I fell;   *imprisonment*
My right my ruth, my titles wrought my trap,
My weal my woe, my worldly heaven my hell.

By death from prisoner to a prince enhanced,
From cross to crown, from thrall to throne again;
My ruth my right, my trap my style advanced;   *status*
From woe to weal, from hell to heavenly reign.

Written after February 8, 1587, published 1817

I Die Alive[1]

Oh life, what lets thee from a quick decease?   *detains*
Oh death, what draws thee from a present prey?
My feast is done, my soul would be at ease,
My grace is said—oh death, come take away!

I live but such a life as ever dies,
I die but such a death as never ends;
My death to end my dying life denies,
And life my living death no whit amends.

Thus still I die yet still I do revive,
My living death by dying life is fed;

---

1. This poem is composed in the persona of the imprisoned Philip Howard, thirteenth Earl of Arundel, the foremost nobleman in England, arraigned for his Catholic faith, who waited in the Tower of London for an execution that never came (he died in his cell, having been poisoned). Southwell did not know the earl personally but ministered to him by correspondence, secreting letters among legal documents.

Grace more than nature keeps my heart alive
Whose idle hopes and vain desires are dead.

Not where I breathe but where I love I live,
Not where I love but where I am I die;
The life I wish must future glory give,
The deaths I feel, in present dangers lie.

Written 1589, published 1595

I Die Without Desert[1]

If orphan child enwrapped in swathing bands
Doth move to mercy when forlorn it lies;
If none without remorse of love withstands
The piteous noise of infant's silly cries—   *defenseless*
Then hope, my helpless heart, some tender ears
Will rue thy orphan state and feeble tears.

Relinquished lamb in solitary wood
With dying bleat doth move the toughest mind;
The grasping pangs of new engendered brood,
Base though they be, compassion use to find:
Why should I then of pity doubt to speed,
Whose hap would force the hardest heart to bleed?   *fate*

Left orphan-like in helpless state I rue,
With only sighs and tears I plead my case;
My dying plaints I daily do renew
And fill with heavy noise a desert place;
Some tender heart will weep to hear me moan—
Men pity may, but help me God alone!

---

1. The manuscript identifies this poem's speaker as "Arthur Earle of Britain murthered by his uncle King John."

Rain down, ye heavens, your tears this case requires;
Man's eyes unable are enough to shed;
If sorrow could have place in heavenly choirs,
A juster ground the world hath seldom bred—
For right is wronged and virtue waged with blood,
The bad are blissed, God murdered in the good.

A gracious plant for fruit, for leaf and flower,
A peerless gem for virtue, proof and price,
A noble peer for prowess, wit and power,
A friend to truth, a foe I was to vice;
And lo, alas, now innocent I die—
A case that might even make the stones to cry.

Thus fortune's favors still are bent to flight;
Thus worldly bliss in final bale doth end;
Thus virtue still pursued is with spite—
But let my fall, though rueful, none offend.
God doth sometimes first crop the sweetest flower
And leaves the weed till time do it devour.

Written 1589, published 1595

William Shakespeare (1564–1616)

SHAKESPEARE WAS SIX years old when the pope excommunicated the Queen, an act that precipitated decades of sectarian turmoil. Catholic on both sides, his family registered with acute sensitivity the increasingly fugitive status of the old religion. Not only was Shakespeare the nephew of Edward Arden, whose mansion, Park Hall, was a hotbed of counterreformation activity in the midlands, he was also a distant relative of Robert Southwell, SJ (see p. 72). His father, John Shakespeare, apparently signed a Spiritual Testament vowing fidelity to the Catholic Church in 1580, probably at the urging of Edmund Campion. And Shakespeare must have known that his schoolteacher between the ages of seven and eleven, Simon Hunt, fled England in 1575 to become a Jesuit priest on the Continent. As an adolescent, Shakespeare may have been employed as tutor to the children of the wealthy Catholic Alexander Hoghton at Hoghton Tower in Lancashire; if so, he was there at the same time as Campion and another Jesuit, Robert Parsons. In October 1583, John Somerville of Edstone, five miles north of Stratford, a relative of Shakespeare's mother, set out for London with the intention of shooting the Queen, "and hoped to see her head on a pole, for that she was a serpent and a viper." Apprehended at Oxford, he was convicted of high treason and found strangled in his cell at Newgate Prison; his head was impaled on a pike and placed on Tower Bridge. His father-in-law, Edward Arden, was also convicted, despite being innocent of wrongdoing; he was hanged, drawn and quartered, and his head displayed on London Bridge. This triggered investigations into Stratford "papists" by the Queen's hard-line Protestant henchman, and local justice of the peace, Sir Thomas Lucy. There may have been house-to-house searches before this (as there were afterward), in which the local sheriff and his men tore apart homes of suspected Catholics. As relations of Somerville, the Shakespeare family is unlikely to have escaped Lucy's attention. Perhaps in defiance, the youthful Will is said to have poached deer and rabbit on Lucy's estate, for which Lucy "had him oft whipped and sometimes imprisoned and at last made him fly his native country." Scholars including Richard Wilson and Stephen Greenblatt argue persuasively that Shakespeare was raised within a faith that had been criminalized by the government, and although the playwright's beliefs were not "securely bound either by the Catholic Church or by the Church of England," elements of Catholicism occur throughout the plays and poems. How else to explain the holy water that consecrates the lovers' beds at the end of *A Midsummer Night's Dream* or the saints mentioned throughout the plays? Murdered without having taken the last rites, the Ghost of Hamlet's Father is condemned to purgatory, a concept rejected by Protestants. *Hamlet* may be affected by worldly turmoil in other ways; if composed in early 1601, as has been argued, it could be shaped in part by the arrest of the Earl of Essex (executed for treason on February 25, 1601) and of Shakespeare's patron, the Earl of Southampton, imprisoned from February 1601 to April 1603. (Both were sympathetic to Catholicism and offered hope of religious toleration; Shakespeare would have followed their fortunes closely.) In addition to an extract from *Hamlet* we include Sonnet 107, which celebrates the succession of James I, who promptly ended the conflicts in Spain and Ireland, and moderated the government's hard line against Catholics ("And peace proclaims olives of endless age").

Hamlet

ACT I, SCENE V (EXTRACT)

HAMLET
Whither wilt thou lead me? Speak, I'll go no further.

GHOST
Mark me.

HAMLET
      I will.

GHOST
              My hour is almost come
When I to sulphurous and tormenting flames
Must render up myself.

HAMLET
                  Alas, poor ghost!

GHOST
Pity me not, but lend thy serious hearing
To what I shall unfold.

HAMLET
                   Speak! I am bound to hear.

GHOST
So art thou to revenge, when thou shalt hear.

HAMLET
What?

GHOST
           I am thy father's spirit,
Doomed for a certain term to walk the night
And for the day confined to fast in fires,
Till the foul crimes done in my days of nature

Are burned and purged away. But that I am forbid
To tell the secrets of my prison house,[1]
I could a tale unfold whose lightest word
Would harrow up thy soul, freeze thy young blood,
Make thy two eyes like stars start from their spheres,
Thy knotty and combined locks to part
And each particular hair to stand on end
Like quills upon the fearful porpentine.   *frightened porcupine*
But this eternal blazon must not be
To ears of flesh and blood. List, list, oh list!
If thou didst ever thy dear father love—

HAMLET
Oh God!

GHOST
Revenge his foul and most unnatural murder.

HAMLET
Murder?

GHOST
Murder most foul, as in the best it is,
But this most foul, strange, and unnatural.

HAMLET
Haste me to know't, that I with wings as swift
As meditation, or the thoughts of love,
May sweep to my revenge.

GHOST
                              I find thee apt.
And duller shouldst thou be than the fat weed
That roots itself in ease on Lethe wharf,
Wouldst thou not stir in this. Now, Hamlet, hear.
'Tis given out that, sleeping in my orchard,

---

1. I am forbid . . . prison house] Stephen Greenblatt points out that Shakespeare would
not have been able explicitly to say that the Ghost is in purgatory.

A serpent stung me—so the whole ear of Denmark
Is by a forged process of my death
Rankly abused—but know, thou noble youth,
The serpent that did sting thy father's life
Now wears his crown.

HAMLET
Oh my prophetic soul! My uncle?

GHOST
Aye, that incestuous, that adulterate beast,
With witchcraft of his wit, with traitorous gifts—
Oh wicked wit, and gifts that have the power
So to seduce!—won to his shameful lust
The will of my most seeming-virtuous queen.
Oh Hamlet, what a falling off was there,
From me, whose love was of that dignity
That it went hand in hand even with the vow
I made to her in marriage, and to decline
Upon a wretch whose natural gifts were poor
To those of mine.
But virtue, as it never will be moved,
Though lewdness court it in a shape of heaven,
So lust, though to a radiant angel linked,
Will sate itself in a celestial bed
And prey on garbage.
But soft, methinks I scent the morning air:
Brief let me be. Sleeping within my orchard,
My custom always of the afternoon,
Upon my secure hour thy uncle stole
With juice of cursed hebenon in a vial,   *poison*
And in the porches of my ears did pour
The leperous distilment, whose effect
Holds such an enmity with blood of man
That swift as quicksilver it courses through
The natural gates and alleys of the body,
And with a sudden vigor it doth posset
And curd, like eager droppings into milk,
The thin and wholesome blood. So did it mine,

And a most instant tetter barked about,   *rash*
Most lazar like, with vile and loathsome crust
All my smooth body.
Thus was I, sleeping, by a brother's hand
Of life, of crown, of queen at once dispatched,
Cut off even in the blossoms of my sin,
Unhouseled, disappointed, unaneled,[2]
No reck'ning made, but sent to my account
With all my imperfections on my head.
Oh horrible! Oh horrible! most horrible!
If thou has nature in thee, bear it not,
Let not the royal bed of Denmark be
A couch for luxury and damned incest.
But howsoever thou pursuest this act,
Taint not thy mind nor let thy soul contrive
Against thy mother aught. Leave her to heaven,
And to those thorns that in her bosom lodge
To prick and sting her. Fare thee well at once:
The glowworm shows the matin to be near
And gins to pale his uneffectual fire.
Adieu, adieu, adieu. Remember me.

Written 1600–1601; "bad quarto" published 1603,
"good quarto" published 1604

Sonnet 107

Not mine own fears, nor the prophetic soul
Of the wide world, dreaming on things to come,
Can yet the lease of my true love control,
Supposed as forfeit to a confined doom.[1]

---

2. Unhouseled, disappointed, unaneled] a reference to the last rites of the Catholic Church. The "housel" is the eucharist; "anel" means to anoint with holy oil. The Ghost is "disappointed" because he had not made proper "appointment" (or preparation) for death.
SONNET 107
1. forfeit to a confined doom] subject to limited duration.

The mortal moon[2] hath her eclipse endured,
And the sad augurs mock their own presage;[3]
Uncertainties now crown themselves assured,[4]
And peace proclaims olives of endless age.[5]
Now with the drops of this most balmy time
My love looks fresh, and Death to me subscribes,   *surrenders*
Since, spite of him, I'll live in this poor rhyme,
While he insults o'er dull and speechless tribes;
    And thou in this shalt find thy monument,
    When tyrants' crests and tombs of brass are spent.

Probably written 1603, published 1609

Christopher Marlowe (bap. 1564, d. 1593)

WHILE A CAMBRIDGE undergraduate, Marlowe was recruited by Sir Francis Walsingham (Elizabeth I's spymaster) as a government agent—a curious choice, as Marlowe was no shrinking violet. He was militantly atheistic, flamboyantly homosexual, and chronically fight prone. All the same, he seems to have carried out missions in France, and may have investigated the Catholic seminary at Rheims. Success as a playwright came with *Tamburlaine the Great*, written for the Lord Admiral's Men in autumn 1587, the first drama to exploit the dramatic potential of blank verse; between 1588 and 1592 Marlowe would write *Doctor Faustus*, *The Jew of Malta*, *The Massacre at Paris*, and *Edward II*. In September 1589 he fought William Bradley, son of the landlord of the Bishop Inn on the Gray's Inn Road, with sword and dagger, killing him. This was an offense for which there would usually be serious consequences, but after less than two weeks in Newgate he was

---

2. mortal moon] a reference to Elizabeth I.
3. sad augurs mock their own presage] the astrologers are sad because their own predictions, which they once stated, are now shown to be worthy of mockery.
4. Incertainties now crown themselves assured] events once regarded as uncertain are now inevitable.
5. And peace proclaims olives of endless age] this is a period of perpetual peace.

free. In January 1592 he went on another mission, this time to Flushing in the Low Countries where he was betrayed by an associate and convicted of forging metal coins. This was a crime that carried a capital penalty, yet Marlowe was at liberty by May, partly because he claimed acquaintance with Henry Percy, ninth Earl of Northumberland, and Ferdinando Stanley, Lord Strange. When he returned to London he had two further brushes with the law involving fights. They seemed no more to warrant detention than did his atheistic views: he claimed religion was a device "only to keep men in awe"; the sacrament best "administered in a tobacco pipe"; "Christ was a bastard and his mother dishonest"; and (most outrageously of all) that Christ and St. John the Baptist were gay lovers—though the Privy Council did summon him for questioning on May 18, 1593 and ordered him to report daily until further notice. On the evening of Wednesday May 30, he was involved in a brawl at a house in Deptford Strand, near London, allegedly over an unpaid bill. Stabbed above the right eye, Marlowe died from intracranial bleeding. He was twenty-nine. A number of circumstances, including the presence among his companions of Robert Poley, another Walsingham agent, continue to raise suspicions over his untimely demise.

Edward II (extract)[1]

SCENE: THE DUNGEON

EDWARD
Who's there? What light is that? Wherefore comes thou?

LIGHTBORNE
To comfort you and bring you joyful news.

EDWARD
Small comfort finds poor Edward in thy looks:
Villain, I know thou com'st to murder me.

---

1. *Edward II* was Marlowe's last play; this extract is from the scene in which King Edward is murdered in his prison cell. Lightborne, the assassin, is a psychotic murderer who is Marlowe's addition to the historical facts.

LIGHTBORNE

To murder you, my most gracious lord?
Far is it from my heart to do you harm!
The queen sent me to see how you were used,
For she relents at this your misery.
And what eyes can refrain from shedding tears
To see a king in this most piteous state?

EDWARD

Weep'st thou already? List awhile to me,
And then thy heart, were it as Gurney's is,
Or as Matrevis', hewn from the Caucasus,
Yet will it melt ere I have done my tale.
This dungeon where they keep me is the sink
Wherein the filth of all the castle falls.

LIGHTBORNE

Oh, villains!

EDWARD

And there in mire and puddle have I stood
This ten days' space and, lest that I should sleep,
One plays continually upon a drum.
They give me bread and water, being a king,
So that for want of sleep and sustenance
My mind's distempered and my body's numbed,
And whether I have limbs or no I know not.
Oh would my blood dropped out from every vein
As doth this water from my tattered robes!
Tell Isabel the queen I looked not thus
When for her sake I ran at tilt in France,
And there unhorsed the Duke of Cleremont.

LIGHTBORNE

Oh, speak no more, my lord! This breaks my heart.
Lie on this bed and rest yourself awhile.

EDWARD

These looks of thine can harbor nought but death;
I see my tragedy written in thy brows.
Yet stay awhile, forbear thy bloody hand,
And let me see the stroke before it comes
That, even then when I shall lose my life,
My mind may be more steadfast on my God.

LIGHTBORNE

What means your highness to mistrust me thus?

EDWARD

What means thou to dissemble with me thus?

LIGHTBORNE

These hands were never stained with innocent blood,
Nor shall they now be tainted with a king's.

EDWARD

Forgive my thought for having such a thought.
One jewel have I left; receive thou this.
(*He gives a jewel.*)
Still fear I, and I know not what's the cause,
But every joint shakes as I give it thee.
Oh, if thou harbor'st murder in thy heart,
Let this gift change thy mind and save thy soul.
Know that I am a king—oh, at that name
I feel a hell of grief. Where is my crown?
Gone, gone, and do I remain alive?

LIGHTBORNE

You're overwatched, my lord; lie down and rest.

EDWARD

But that grief keeps me waking, I should sleep,
For not these ten days have these eyes' lids closed;
Now as I speak they fall—and yet with fear
Open again.

(LIGHTBORNE *sits on the bed.*)
                          Oh, wherefore sitst thou here?

LIGHTBORNE
If you mistrust me, I'll be gone, my lord.

EDWARD
No, no, for if thou mean'st to murder me
Thou wilt return again, and therefore stay.

LIGHTBORNE
He sleeps.

EDWARD
Oh, let me not die yet! Stay, oh stay a while!

LIGHTBORNE
How now, my lord?

EDWARD
Something still buzzeth in mine ears
And tells me if I sleep I never wake;
This fear is that which makes me tremble thus.
And therefore tell me, wherefore art thou come?

LIGHTBORNE
To rid thee of thy life. Matrevis, come!
(*Enter* MATREVIS *and* GURNEY.)

EDWARD
I am too weak and feeble to resist.
Assist me, sweet God, and receive my soul!

LIGHTBORNE
Run for the table.

EDWARD
Oh spare me, or dispatch me in a trice!
(MATREVIS *and* GURNEY *bring in a table and a red-hot spit.*)

LIGHTBORNE

So lay the table down, and stamp on it,
But not too hard, lest that you bruise his body.
(*As* EDWARD *is trapped under a table,* LIGHTBORNE *pushes the spit up his anus.* EDWARD *dies.*)

MATREVIS

I fear me that this cry will raise the town,
And therefore let us take horse and away.

LIGHTBORNE

Tell me, sirs, was it not bravely done?

GURNEY

Excellent well. Take this for thy reward.
(*Then* GURNEY *stabs* LIGHTBORNE.)
Come, let us cast the body in the moat,
And bear the King's to Mortimer, our lord.
Away!

Written c. 1591–1592, published 1594

Hero and Leander (extract)[1]

On Hellespont, guilty of true love's blood,
In view and opposite two cities stood,
Sea-borderers, disjoined by Neptune's might;
The one Abydos, the other Sestos hight.   *called*
At Sestos Hero dwelt—Hero the fair,
Whom young Apollo courted for her hair,
And offered as a dower his burning throne,
Where she should sit for men to gaze upon.
The outside of her garments were of lawn,   *fine linen*
The lining purple silk, with gilt stars drawn;
Her wide sleeves green, and bordered with a grove,   *embroidered*

---

1. This is the opening of Marlowe's last poem, unfinished at the time of his death.

Where Venus in her naked glory strove
To please the careless and disdainful eyes
Of proud Adonis that before her lies.
Her kirtle blue, whereon was many a stain,   *skirt*
Made with the blood of wretched lovers slain.
Upon her head she wore a myrtle wreath,
From whence her veil reached to the ground beneath;
Her veil was artificial flowers and leaves,
Whose workmanship both man and beast deceives;
Many would praise the sweet smell as she passed,
When 'twas the odor which her breath forth cast—
And there for honey, bees have sought in vain,
And beat from thence, have lighted there again.
About her neck hung chains of pebblestone,
Which lightened by her neck, like diamonds shone.
She wore no gloves, for neither sun nor wind
Would burn or parch her hands, but to her mind,
Or warm or cool them, for they took delight
To play upon those hands, they were so white.
Buskins of shells, all silvered, used she,   *boots*
And branched[2] with blushing coral to the knee;
Where sparrows perched, of hollow pearl and gold,
Such as the world would wonder to behold:
Those with sweet water oft her handmaid fills,
Which as she went would chirrup through the bills.
Some say, for her the fairest Cupid pined,
And looking in her face, was strooken blind.
But this is true, so like was one the other,
As he imagined Hero was his mother;
And oftentimes into her bosom flew,
About her naked neck his bare arms threw,
And laid his childish head upon her breast,
And with still panting rocked, there took his rest.
So lovely fair was Hero, Venus' nun,
As Nature wept, thinking she was undone,
Because she took more from her than she left,
And of such wondrous beauty her bereft:

---

2. branched] embroidered with shapes like branches.

Therefore in sign her treasure suffered wrack,
Since Hero's time hath half the world been black.
    Amorous Leander, beautiful and young
(Whose tragedy divine Musaeus sung),
Dwelt at Abydos; since him dwelt there none
For whom succeeding times make greater moan.
His dangling tresses that were never shorn,
Had they been cut, and unto Colchos borne,
Would have allured the venturous youth of Greece   *adventurous*
To hazard more than for the golden fleece.
Fair Cynthia wished his arms might be her sphere;
Grief makes her pale, because she moves not there.
His body was as straight as Circe's wand;
Jove might have sipped out nectar from his hand.
Even as delicious meat is to the taste,
So was his neck in touching, and surpassed
The white of Pelops' shoulder.³ I could tell ye
How smooth his breast was, and how white his belly,
And whose immortal fingers did imprint
That heavenly path with many a curious dint
That runs along his back, but my rude pen
Can hardly blazon forth the loves of men,
Much less of powerful gods: let it suffice
That my slack muse sings of Leander's eyes,
Those orient cheeks and lips, exceeding his⁴   *shining*
That leaped into the water for a kiss
Of his own shadow and, despising many,
Died ere he could enjoy the love of any.
Had wild Hippolytus Leander seen,
Enamored of his beauty had he been.
His presence made the rudest peasant melt,
That in the vast uplandish country dwelt;   *remote*
The barbarous Thracian soldier, moved with nought,

---

3. Pelops was dismembered by his father, Tantalus, who served his flesh to an assembly of the gods. Only Demeter failed to recognize what had happened, and ate the shoulder before she could be stopped. The gods resurrected Pelops, giving him a prosthetic shoulder made of ivory.
4. his] a reference to Narcissus, whose love of his own reflected image led him to jump into a river in which he drowned.

Was moved with him, and for his favor sought.
Some swore he was a maid in man's attire,
For in his looks were all that men desire:
A pleasant smiling cheek, a speaking eye,   *expressive*
A brow for love to banquet royally.
And such as knew he was a man would say,
"Leander, thou art made for amorous play!
Why art thou not in love, and loved of all?
Though thou be fair, yet be not thine own thrall."

Written probably 1593, published early 1598

Sir Henry Wotton (1568–1639)

WOTTON WAS A courtier and soldier whose fate depended on his politi-
cal alliances. With his friend John Donne (whom he had known at Oxford
University), Wotton was among thousands assembled for an assault on the
Spanish mainland in June 1596; it met with limited success. The following
year, Wotton followed Robert Devereux, second Earl of Essex, to the Azores,
to fight the Spanish. After this mission failed, Essex fell out with the Queen;
later, Essex having withdrawn from court, Donne and Wotton exchanged
verse letters. Donne began with "Here's no more news than virtue" (on July
20, 1598) (see p. 96), inspiring Wotton's response, "'Tis not a coat of gray," to
which Donne answered with "Sir, more than kisses" (see p. 97). These poems
merit inclusion here for their observations on the insecurity of the courtier.
Wotton left Essex's service and became advisor to the new king, James I,
whose disfavor he managed to incur in 1612. He was eventually rehabilitated,
and dispatched on an embassy to the Hague. Wotton later became Provost of
Eton College, where he died in December 1639.

To Mr. John Donne[1]

Worthy sir,
'Tis not a coat of gray or shepherd's life,
'Tis not in fields or woods remote to live
That adds or takes from one that peace or strife
Which to our days such good or ill doth give;
   It is the mind that makes the man's estate
   Forever happy or unfortunate.

Then first the mind of passions must be free
Of him that would to happiness aspire,
Whether in princes' palaces he be
Or whether to his cottage he retire;
   For our desires, that on extremes are bent,
   Are friends to care and traitors to content.

Nor should we blame our friends (though false they be),
Since there are thousands false for one that's true,
But our own blindness that we cannot see
To choose the best although they be but few;
   For he that every feignèd friend will trust
   Proves true to friend but to himself unjust.

The faults we have are they that make our woe;
Our virtues are the motives of our joy;
Then is it vain if we to deserts go
To seek our bliss or shroud us from annoy: *trouble*
   Our place need not be changèd but our will
   For everywhere we may do good or ill.

But this I do not dedicate to thee
As one that holds himself fit to advise,
Or that my lines to him should precepts be

---

1. Wotton and Donne were old friends who had known each other at Oxford and served together under the Earl of Essex. This poem is part of a series of verse letters on the evils of court life, beginning with Donne's "Here's no more news than virtue" on page 96, to which it is a response. In turn, Donne would respond with "Sir, more than kisses," on page 97.

That is less ill than I, and much more wise;
   Yet 'tis no harm morality to preach,
   For men do often learn when they do teach.

Written late July/early August 1598, published 1911

Upon the Sudden Restraint of the Earl of Somerset, Then Falling From Favor[1]

Dazzled thus, with height of place,
Whilst our hopes our wits beguile,
No man marks the narrow space
'Twixt a prison and a smile.

Then, since Fortune's favors fade,
You, that in her arms do sleep,
Learn to swim and not to wade
For the hearts of kings are deep.

But if greatness be so blind
As to trust in towers of air,
Let it be with goodness lined
That at least the fall be fair.

Then, though darkened, you shall say,
When friends fail and princes frown,
Virtue is the roughest way
But proves at night a bed of down.

Probably written shortly after October 17, 1615, published 1651

---

1. Robert Carr, Earl of Somerset (1585/1586?–1645) was already a Groom of the Bedchamber when, in 1607, he became a "favorite" of James I. The king's affection was unmistakeable, the reward of which was money, land, and prestige: Carr became Viscount Rochester in 1611 and a member of the Privy Council in 1612; he married Frances Howard in 1613. His involvement in the murder of Sir Thomas Overbury (by means of a poisoned enema) led to imprisonment in October 1615 and trial in May 1616, which culminated in a death sentence. The king had no intention of carrying out the sentence and the Carrs were released in 1622 and pardoned two years later.

John Donne (1572–1631)

DONNE WAS BROUGHT up in one of the most prominent Catholic families in Britain, counting among his relatives several who had endured persecution and torture for their faith: his mother was the daughter of the niece of Sir Thomas More (see p. 34); two of his uncles were Jesuits, and one of them, Jasper Heywood, was apprehended for treason, tortured, and tried, though he would be spared the death sentence (Donne was among those who visited him in prison); Donne's brother Henry was arrested and tortured for harboring a Catholic priest in his lodgings, and died in Newgate in 1593. In 1596, after studying at Oxford (where he met Henry Wotton), Donne became a soldier in the service of Robert Devereux, second Earl of Essex, in time to board one of the sixteen galleons of the Royal Navy that were successfully to raid Cadiz harbor on June 21. "The fight was very terrible," one witness recalled, "and most hideous to the beholder by the continual discharging of those roaring and thundering great pieces on all sides." The following year, Donne sailed with Sir Walter Ralegh (p. 64) to the Azores on a mission to intercept the Spanish fleet laden with silver. On return to England, he witnessed Essex's momentous falling-out with Queen Elizabeth; Essex left London, taking his secretary Henry Wotton with him. "Here's no more news than virtue," Donne wrote to Wotton a few weeks later, in a biting commentary on court life. Wotton responded with "'Tis not a coat of gray" (see p. 93), which produced a further letter from Donne, "Sir, more than kisses." Both men knew the risks and punishments associated with their profession, which were worse for a Catholic. The pressure to conform was intense, not least because professional advancement was otherwise impossible. By 1598, when Donne was employed by Sir Thomas Egerton, Lord Keeper of the Great Seal, a prominent figure in government circles, he knew that, were he to make his way in the world, he must abandon the faith into which he had been born. Feelings of guilt might help explain why his devotional poetry emphasizes corrective affliction: in one sonnet his heart must be "battered," God bidden to "break, blow, burn," while elsewhere God must "burn off" his sinful "rusts." In subsequent years he would be ordained dean at St. Paul's Cathedral, in which role he attacked Catholic missions to England as a threat to the security of the state, and defended James I against accusations of popery.

To Mr. Henry Wotton[1]

Here's no more news than virtue. I may as well
Tell you Cales[2] or St Michael's tale for news, as tell
That vice doth here habitually dwell.

Yet as to get stomachs[3] we walk up and down,
And toil to sweeten rest, so, may God frown
If but to loathe both I haunt court or Town.[4]

For here no one is from th' extremity
Of vice by any other reason free
But that the next to him still is worse than he.

In this world's warfare they whom rugged Fate   *harsh*
(God's commissary) doth so thoroughly hate
As in the court's squadron to marshal their state,

If they stand armed with silly honesty,   *simple*
With wishing prayers and neat integrity,
Like Indians 'gainst Spanish hosts they be.

Suspicious boldness[5] to this place belongs,
And to have as many ears as all have tongues;
Tender to know, tough to acknowledge wrongs.

---

1. Donne was at court, located at Greenwich, where he was secretary to the Lord Keeper. A few weeks before writing to Wotton he had seen the Earl of Essex threaten Queen Elizabeth, an act resulting in his expulsion from court.
2. Cales] Cadiz; Wotton and Donne joined Essex's assault on the Spanish port in June 1596.
3. to get stomachs] to work up our appetites.
4. Town] London.
5. Suspicious boldness] readiness to see hostility.

Believe me, sir, in my youth's giddiest days,
When to be like the court, was a play's praise,
Plays were not so like courts, as courts are like plays.

Then let us at these mimic antics jest,
Whose deepest projects and egregious gests   *outstanding deeds*
Are but dull morals of a game at chests.   *chess*

But now 'tis incongruity to smile:
Therefore I end and bid farewell awhile
At court—though *from* court were the better style.

Written July 20, 1598, published 1633.

To Mr. Henry Wotton [1]

Sir, more than kisses, letters mingle souls;
For thus friends absent speak. This ease controls
The tediousness of my life: but for these
I could ideate nothing which could please,   *imagine*
But I should wither in one day, and pass
To a bottle of hay, that am a lock of grass.   *bundle*
          Life is a voyage, and in our life's ways
Countries, courts, towns are rocks or remoras;   *obstacles*
They break or stop all ships, yet our state's such
That though than pitch they stain worse, we must touch.
          If in the furnace of the even line, [2]
Or under the adverse icy Poles thou pine,
Thou know'st two temperate regions girded in,
Dwell there, but oh, what refuge canst thou win
Parched in the court, and in the country frozen?
Shall cities built of both extremes be chosen?
Can dung and garlic be a perfume? Or can

---

1. This poem is a response to Wotton's verse letter to Donne on page 93 above.
2. even line] equator.

A scorpion and torpedo[3] cure a man?
Cities are worst of all three; of all three
(Oh knotty riddle!), each is worst equally.
    Cities are sepulchers; they who dwell there
Are carcasses as if no such they were.
And courts are theaters where some men play
Princes, some slaves, all to one end, and of one clay.
The country is a desert where no good
Gained as habits, not born, is understood.
There men become beasts, and prone to more evils;
In cities, blocks; and in a lewd court, devils.
    As in the first Chaos, confusedly,
Each element's qualities were in the other three;
So pride, lust, covetise, being several
To these three places,[4] yet all are in all,
And mingled thus, their issue incestuous.
Falsehood is denizened.[5] Virtue's barbarous.
Let no man say there, "Virtue's flinty wall
Shall lock vice in me. I'll do none, but know all."   *confine*
Men are sponges which to pour out receive,[6]
Who know false play, rather then lose, deceive.
For in best understandings sin began:
Angels sinned first, then devils, and then man.
Only (perchance) beasts sin not; wretched we
Are beasts in all, but white integrity.
I think if men, which in these places live
Durst look in themselves, and themselves retrieve,
They would like strangers greet themselves, seeing then
Utopian youth grown old Italian.
    Be then thine own home, and in thyself dwell;
Inn[7] anywhere: continuance maketh hell.
And seeing the snail, which everywhere doth roam,

---

3. A scorpion and torpedo] combined stimulant and sedative.
4. So pride . . . places] i.e., pride belongs to the court; lust to the country; and covetous-
ness to the city.
5. Falsehood resides in all three places (court, country, and city).
6. Men are like sponges in that they receive only in order to pour out.
7. Inn] used as a verb meaning "to stay on a temporary basis."

Carrying his own house still, still is at home—
Follow (for he is easy-paced) this snail;
Be thine own palace, or the world's thy jail.
And in the world's sea, do not (like cork) sleep
Upon the waters' face, nor in the deep
Sink like a lead without a line; but as
Fishes glide, leaving no print where they pass
Nor making sound, so closely thy course go:
Let men dispute whether thou breathe or no.
Only in this one thing, be no Galenist.[8] To make
Court's hot ambitions wholesome, do not take
A dram of country's dullness, do not add
Correctives, but, as chymics, purge the bad.
    But sir, I advise not you, I rather do
Say o'er those lessons, which I learned of you
Whom, free from German schisms,[9] and lightness   *fickleness*
Of France, and fair Italy's faithlessness,
Having from these sucked all they had of worth,
And brought home that faith which you carried forth,
I throughly love. But if myself I've won
To know my rules, I have—and you have—
                           Donne.

Written August 1598, published 1633

The Anniversary

      All kings and all their favorites,
      All glory of honours, beauties, wits,
  The sun itself, which makes times, as they pass,
  Is elder by a year now than it was

---

8. Followers of the Greek philosopher and physician believed in correcting excess of heat, cold, moisture, and dryness by supplying its opposite. In defiance of that, Donne sides with "chymics" (or advocates of chemical remedies) who would advise Wotton to purge evil rather than balance it.

9. The princes of Germany were constantly fighting over religious or political questions.

When thou and I first one another saw.
All other things to their destruction draw:
    Only our love hath no decay.
This, no tomorrow hath, nor yesterday;
Running, it never runs from us away,
But truly keeps his first, last, everlasting day.

    Two graves must hide thine and my corse:
    If one might, death were no divorce.
Alas, as well as other princes, we
(Who prince enough in one another be)
Must leave at last in death these eyes and ears
Oft fed with true oaths, and with sweet-salt tears;
    But souls where nothing dwells but love
(All other thoughts being inmates¹) then shall prove   *experience*
This, or a love increased, there above,
When bodies to their graves, souls from their graves² remove.

    And then we shall be throughly blessed,
    But we no more than all the rest.
Here upon earth we're kings, and none but we
Can be such kings, nor of such subjects be:³
Who is so safe as we, where none can do
Treason to us, except one of us two?
    True and false fears let us refrain: *restrain*
Let us love nobly, and live, and add again
Years and years unto years, till we attain
To write threescore. This is the second of our reign.

Perhaps written 1599, published 1633

---

1. inmates] temporary dwellers, lodgers.
2. souls from their graves] i.e., souls from bodies.
3. nor of such subjects be] nor be subjects of such kings.

Batter my heart, three-personed God

Batter my heart, three-personed God, for you
As yet but knock, breathe, shine, and seek to mend;
That I may rise and stand, o'erthrow me and bend
Your force to break, blow, burn, and make me new.
I, like an usurped town, to another due,[1]
Labor to admit you—but oh, to no end,
Reason your viceroy in me, me should defend,
But is captived, and proves weak or untrue;
Yet dearly I love you, and would be loved fain,[2]
But am betrothed unto your enemy:
Divorce me, untie, or break that knot again,
Take me to you, imprison me, for I
Except you enthral me, never shall be free,   *imprison*
Nor ever chaste, except you ravish me.

Probably written between 1609 and 1611, published 1633

Good Friday, 1613. Riding Westward.

Let man's soul be a sphere, and then, in this,
The intelligence that moves, devotion is;
And as the other spheres, by being grown
Subject to foreign motions, lose their own,
And being by others hurried every day,
Scarce in a year their natural form obey:
Pleasure or business, so, our souls admit
For their first mover, and are whirled by it.
Hence is 't that I am carried towards the west
This day, when my soul's form bends towards the east.
There I should see a sun, by rising set,
And by that setting endless day beget;

---

1. to another due] owing loyalty to someone else.
2. and would be loved fain] and eagerly wish to be loved in return.

But that Christ on this cross did rise and fall,
Sin had eternally benighted all.
Yet dare I almost be glad, I do not see
That spectacle of too much weight for me.
Who sees God's face, that is self life, must die;
What a death were it then to see God die?
It made his own lieutenant, Nature, shrink;
It made his footstool crack, and the sun wink.
Could I behold those hands, which span the poles
And tune all spheres at once, pierced with those holes?
Could I behold that endless height, which is
Zenith to us, and to our antipodes,
Humbled below us? Or that blood, which is
The seat of all our souls, if not of his,
Made dirt of dust, or that flesh which was worn
By God for his apparel, ragged and torn?
If on these things I durst not look, durst I
Upon his miserable mother cast mine eye,
Who was God's partner here, and furnished thus
Half of that sacrifice which ransomed us?
Though these things, as I ride, be from mine eye,
They are present yet unto my memory,
For that looks towards them; and thou look'st towards me,
Oh Savior, as thou hang'st upon the tree.
I turn my back to thee but to receive
Corrections till thy mercies bid thee leave.
Oh think me worth thine anger—punish me,
Burn off my rusts, and my deformity,
Restore thine image, so much, by thy grace,
That thou mayst know me, and I'll turn my face.

Written c. April 3, 1613, published 1633

Ben Jonson (1572–1637)

By TEMPERAMENT, JONSON was disinclined to settle for a quiet life: after starting out as a bricklayer he became a soldier with the English army in the Netherlands, where he "had in the face of both the camps killed one man," apparently for sport. His second play, *The Isle of Dogs*, was a satire on the court of Elizabeth I, the performance of which in July 1597 triggered the shutting down of all theaters in metropolitan London, and the arrest and imprisonment of its author, by order of the Queen's sadistic interrogator Richard Topcliffe. In September 1598 Jonson fought a duel with an actor, Gabriel Spencer, whom he killed with a rapier; after confessing to manslaughter, he pleaded benefit of clergy, a loophole that enabled him, by the narrowest of margins, to avoid the gallows. During his brief spell in Newgate, Jonson converted to Catholicism, thanks probably to Thomas Wright, SJ, himself in semidetention; Jonson remained Catholic for the next twelve years. Before leaving prison, he was branded on the thumb, marking him a convicted felon, which served only as further inducement for public and personal defiance: he ridiculed the court of Elizabeth I in *Cynthia's Revels* (1600); beat up fellow playwright John Marston and "took his pistol from him"; attacked Marston verbally in *Poetaster* (1601), precipitating a complaint to Chief Justice Popham; was ejected by Lord Chamberlain Suffolk from a performance of a masque at Hampton Court in 1604 (probably for declaring his opinion of it too raucously); and a year later imprisoned for coauthoring *Eastward Ho!* which mocked James I's sale of knighthoods to Scottish followers. His faith rendered him vulnerable to attack, as when in 1603 the first production of *Sejanus* led to accusations of "popery and treason" from Henry Howard, first Earl of Northampton (younger son of the poet Surrey, p. 44), inciting an unseemly "brawl" with one of the earl's hangers-on, which in turn prompted investigation by the Privy Council. Given how much trouble he was in, it was hardly politic for Jonson to have dined with Robert Catesby and Thomas Winter (among others), two of the Gunpowder Plotters, less than a month before they planned to blow up the Houses of Parliament. Perhaps he did so as a government agent, for on November 7 he was ordered by the Privy Council to find a Catholic priest it wanted to interrogate about the plot. Though he failed in that mission, Jonson declared loyalty to the Crown, and wrote a patriotic epigram to Lord Monteagle, the Catholic peer who brought the conspiracy to light (p. 108). Jonson remained in London during the outbreak of bubonic plague in early 1606, nursing in his arms his friend Sir John Roe. Throughout these years, Jonson remained true to his adopted faith: in 1606 he appeared three times before the Consistory Court for recusancy, accused of failing to take communion in the Church of England and of being "a seducer of youth to the Popish religion." Further tightening of anti-Catholic legislation led him to return to the Church of England in 1610. In 1616 publication of the first edition of his collected works led to appointment (in fact if not name) as Britain's first poet laureate. Jonson is here represented by, among other things, the opening scene of *Volpone*, composed shortly after the foiling of the Gunpowder Plot and staged in February or March 1606, in which Richard Dutton detects an attack on Robert Cecil, head of the Privy Council and enemy to Catholicism, whose nickname was "the fox." Volpone's worship of gold points to Cecil, argues Dutton, as "he used his positions under the crown vastly to increase his personal wealth, at the expense of anyone and everyone else." The play's admirers included Lord Aubigny, Jonson's Catholic patron, and John Donne (see p. 95).

Volpone

ACT I, SCENE I (EXTRACT)
VOLPONE'S HOUSE. VOLPONE IN A LARGE BED. ENTER MOSCA. VOLPONE AWAKES.

VOLPONE
Good morning to the day—and next, my gold!
Open the shrine, that I may see my saint.
(MOSCA *draws a curtain, revealing piles of gold.*)
Hail, the world's soul—and mine! More glad than is
The teeming earth to see the longed-for sun
Peep through the horns of the celestial ram
Am I, to view thy splendor, darkening his;

That lying here, among my other hoards,
Show'st like a flame by night, or like the day
Struck out of chaos, when all darkness fled
Unto the center. Oh, thou son of Sol
(But brighter than thy father), let me kiss
With adoration thee, and every relic
Of sacred treasure in this blessed room!
Well did wise poets by thy glorious name
Title that age which they would have the best
(Thou being the best of things), and far transcending
All style of joy in children, parents, friends,
Or any other waking dream on earth.
Thy looks when they to Venus did ascribe,
They should have given her twenty thousand cupids,
Such are thy beauties and our loves! Dear saint,
Riches, the dumb god that giv'st all men tongues,
That canst do nought, and yet mak'st men do all things;
The price of souls; even hell, with thee to boot,
Is made worth heaven! Thou art virtue, fame,
Honour, and all things else. Who can get thee,
He shall be noble, valiant, honest, wise—

MOSCA

And what he will, sir. Riches are in fortune
A greater good than wisdom is in nature.

VOLPONE

True, my beloved Mosca. Yet I glory
More in the cunning purchase of my wealth   *acquisition*
Than in the glad possession, since I gain
No common way. I use no trade, no venture;
I wound no earth with ploughshares; fat no beasts
To feed the shambles; have no mills for iron,   *slaughterhouse*
Oil, corn, or men, to grind 'em into powder;
I blow no subtle glass; expose no ships
To threat'nings of the furrow-facèd sea;
I turn no moneys in the public bank,
Nor usure private—

MOSCA

                     No sir, nor devour
Soft prodigals. You shall ha' some will swallow
A melting heir as glibly as your Dutch
Will pills of butter, and ne'er purge for 't;
Tear forth the fathers of poor families
Out of their beds, and coffin them alive
In some kind, clasping prison where their bones
May be forthcoming when the flesh is rotten.
But your sweet nature doth abhor these courses;
You loathe the widow's or the orphan's tears
Should wash your pavements, or their piteous cries
Ring in your roofs and beat the air for vengeance—

VOLPONE

Right, Mosca, I do loathe it!

MOSCA

                          And besides, sir,
You are not like the thresher that doth stand
With a huge flail, watching a heap of corn,
And, hungry, dares not taste the smallest grain
But feeds on mallows and such bitter herbs;
Nor like the merchant who hath filled his vaults
With Romagnia and rich Candian wines
Yet drinks the lees of Lombard's vinegar.
You will not lie in straw, whilst moths and worms
Feed on your sumptuous hangings and soft beds.
You know the use of riches and dare give, now,
From that bright heap, to me, your poor observer,
Or to your dwarf, or your hermaphrodite,
Your eunuch, or what other household trifle
Your pleasure allows maint'nance—

VOLPONE

                          Hold thee, Mosca,
(*Gives him money.*)
Take of my hand; thou strik'st on truth in all,

And they are envious term thee parasite.
Call forth my dwarf, my eunuch, and my fool,
And let 'em make me sport.
(*Exit* MOSCA.)

                    What should I do
But cocker up my genius and live free
To all delights my fortune calls me to?
I have no wife, no parent, child, ally,
To give my substance to; but whom I make
Must be my heir, and this makes men observe me.
This draws new clients, daily, to my house,
Women and men of every sex and age
That bring me presents, send me plate, coin, jewels,
With hope that when I die (which they expect
Each greedy minute) it shall then return
Tenfold upon them; whilst some, covetous
Above the rest, seek to engross me, whole,
And counter-work the one unto the other,
Contend in gifts, as they would seem in love.
All which I suffer, playing with their hopes,
And am content to coin 'em into profit,
And look upon their kindness, and take more,
And look on that; still bearing them in hand,
Letting the cherry knock against their lips,
And draw it by their mouths, and back again. How now!

                              Written early 1606, published 1607

On Sir John Roe[1]

I'll not offend thee with a vain tear more,
Glad-mentioned Roe: thou art but gone before,
Whither the world must follow. And I, now,

---

1. Sir John Roe was Jonson's closest friend, though nine years his junior. He died of bubonic plague on January 17, 1606, in Jonson's arms; Jonson paid his funeral expenses.

Breathe to expect my when, and make my how;
Which, if most gracious heaven grant like thine,
Who wets my grave can be no friend of mine.

Written shortly after January 17, 1606, published 1616

To William, Lord Monteagle[1]

Lo, what my country should have done (have raised
An obelisk or column to thy name,
Or, if she would but modestly have praised
Thy fact, in brass or marble writ the same),
I, that am glad of thy great chance, here do!
And, proud my work shall outlast common deeds,
Durst think it great, and worthy wonder too—
But thine, for which I do't, so much exceeds!
My country's parents I have many known,
But saver of my country—thee alone.

Probably written shortly after January 23, 1606, published 1616

Inviting a Friend to Supper

Tonight, grave sir, both my poor house and I
Do equally desire your company;
Not that we think us worthy such a guest,
But that your worth will dignify our feast
With those that come, whose grace may make that seem

---

1. William Parker, thirteenth Baron Morley and fifth Baron Monteagle, discovered the Gunpowder Plot and revealed it to the Privy Council, in return for which he received public praise, lands worth £200 a year, and an annual pension of £500. When in 1606 Parliament passed a bill of thanksgiving, Monteagle was excluded from the list of those credited with having thwarted the plot; it may have been on that occasion Jonson wrote this epigram.

Something, which else could hope for no esteem.
It is the fair acceptance, sir, creates
The entertainment perfect, not the cates.   *food*
Yet shall you have, to rectify your palate,
An olive, capers, or some better salad
Ushering the mutton; with a short-legged hen,
If we can get her, full of eggs, and then
Lemons, and wine for sauce; to these a cony   *rabbit*
Is not to be despaired of, for our money;
And, though fowl now be scarce, yet there are clerks,
The sky not falling, think we may have larks.
I'll tell you of more, and lie, so you will come:
Of partridge, pheasant, woodcock, of which some
May yet be there, and godwit, if we can;   *marsh birds*
Knat, rail, and ruff too. Howsoe'er, my man
Shall read a piece of Virgil, Tacitus,
Livy, or of some better book to us,
Of which we'll speak our minds amid our meat;
And I'll profess no verses to repeat.
To this, if aught appear which I not know of,
That will the pastry, not my paper, show of.
Digestive cheese and fruit there sure will be;
But that which most doth take my muse and me,
Is a pure cup of rich Canary wine,
Which is the Mermaid's[1] now, but shall be mine;
Of which had Horace, or Anacreon tasted,
Their lives, as so their lines, till now had lasted.
Tobacco, nectar, or the Thespian spring,
Are all but Luther's beer[2] to this I sing.
Of this we will sup free, but moderately,
And we will have no Poley or Parrot by,[3]
Nor shall our cups make any guilty men;

---

1. The Mermaid Tavern was Jonson's hostelry of choice.
2. Luther's beer] German beer was in Jonson's time regarded as weaker than English beer.
3. And we will have no Poley or Parrot by] Robert Poley and Henry Parrot were government spies employed by Sir Francis Walsingham, Chief Interrogator of Elizabeth I, by whom Jonson was arrested years before. Poley was present at the murder of Christopher Marlowe, and had been instrumental in the uncovering of the Babington plot (see p. 68).

But, at our parting, we will be as when
We innocently met. No simple word
That shall be uttered at our mirthful board,
Shall make us sad next morning, or affright
The liberty that we'll enjoy tonight.

Written between 1607 and 1612, published 1616

On Something That Walks Somewhere

At court I met it, in clothes brave enough
To be a courtier, and looks grave enough
To seem a statesman. As I near it came,
It made me a great face; I asked the name.
"A Lord!" it cried, "buried in flesh and blood,
And such from whom let no man hope least good,
For I will do none; and as little ill,
For I will dare none." Good Lord, walk dead still.

Published 1616

On Spies

Spies, you are lights in state, but of base stuff,
Who, when you have burned yourselves down to the snuff,
Stink, and are thrown away. End fair enough.

Published 1616

II

The Civil War

𐂷

CHARLES I's ACCIDENT-PRONE tendencies were clear from the moment he ascended the throne in spring 1625. One of his first acts was to marry the fifteen-year-old French Princess Henrietta Maria, in return for secretly promised concessions to Catholics in England. Rumors about those concessions, and fears the marriage would inaugurate a Catholic dynasty, created immediate distrust between him and Parliament. (Charles may have forgotten that MPs' grandfathers could recall Catholic conspiracies against Queen Elizabeth, while their fathers remembered a plot to blow up the Houses of Parliament.) At war with Spain, he was in constant need of funds and found Parliament reluctant to grant them, so that within the first year of his reign he was reduced to visiting the Jewel House to find out which of the crown jewels could be pawned; however, he did not take such drastic action until the start of the Civil War.

Having raised only a fraction of what he needed from Parliament, he soon found himself under additional pressure when he declared war on France, the most significant part of that conflict being the expedition to relieve the Huguenots of La Rochelle in June 1627. Thanks in part to poor financing, the entire enterprise turned into a nightmare. The British never reached La Rochelle, and those who did not die from starvation and disease were killed in battle. Of the eight thousand men who set out, only three thousand would return. Undeterred, Charles was keen to mount another expedition, but efforts to extract funds from MPs produced squabbles rather than revenue, and he dissolved Parliament in 1629. The high-handedness of this gesture was never forgotten, but he was under no obligation to convene Parliament, and for years was happy to suspend foreign policy if it saved him from having to parley with the Commons.

It was a huge error on his part to attempt to impose his High Anglican views on the Scots, who responded with a full-scale invasion of northeast England including Newcastle. Charles decided in 1640 to recall Parliament twice, believing that English antipathy toward the Scots would lead to him being granted the resources needed to repel them. He could hardly have been more wrong. Indignant at being regarded as a cash dispenser—to be ignored by a king it regarded as a Catholic stooge until he required financial assistance—the Long Parliament of November 1640 responded to his demands with a bill denying him the right to dissolve Parliament without its consent, and another obliging it to reconvene every three years, regardless of the monarch's will. It then set about removal of his political allies who, one by one, went to the scaffold, their fates sealed by Henry VIII's weapon of choice—the bill of attainder.

As usual, luck was not on Charles's side, nor was his political judgment. It was not a good idea to attempt to arrest five members of the Commons and one of the Lords on grounds of high treason, as Charles did on January 4, 1642. All of the miscreants slipped away before they could be apprehended, and the Speaker refused to say where they had gone. No monarch since has entered the Commons by force. Charles soon fled London (a Parliamentary stronghold) and began campaigning for support in the country. He raised the royal standard (hastily patched together) at Nottingham on August 22, 1642, calling upon loyal subjects to support his attempts to retake London.

No one was untouched by the Civil War. During its first phase, there were separate conflicts in England, Scotland, and Ireland. The cost was enormous—and not just in financial terms. From war-related disease alone, England would lose 3.7 percent of its population; Scotland 6 percent; and Ireland 41 percent. Many poets of this period served on one side or the other—Vaughan, Bunyan, Wither, Herrick, L'Estrange, Graham, Fairfax—and their writings testify to what they witnessed. To be wounded by musket shot, even superficially, was a serious matter in an age when medical science was still dominated by the theories of the Roman philosopher, Galen: the usual treatment, were any deemed viable, was amputation. Poets who risked their lives, or saw their friends do so, speak of the human cost in ways that foreshadow writers of World War I (see, for instance, pp. 121–22). Yet it is fascinating how such

Cavalier lyrists as Waller, Lovelace, and Suckling sublimated their experience in songs addressed to women, preferring to speak of love rather than of war. It is as if such aesthetic decisions were in themselves an act of defiance, declaring their authors' implied contempt for the messianic high seriousness of Wither and Winstanley.

It is almost impossible to conceive the trauma (not so much for the king as his people) of the execution of Charles I on January 30, 1649: it percolates through the poetry of Marvell, Graham, Fairfax, and Philips. Two years later it seemed likely that Henry, Duke of Gloucester, youngest brother of Charles II, would be crowned, with Oliver Cromwell as Regent—monarchical government, in other words, conducted under Parliamentary supervision. However, the duke was disinclined, having been warned by his late father, and in December 1653 Cromwell was installed as Lord Protector, ruling with the assistance of a council of state consisting of between thirteen and twenty-one members, reverting from June 1657 to a form of kingship in all but name. Some poets in these pages were exultant—Wither, for instance, who detested the two Stuarts under whose rule he had suffered, and Republicans such as Milton, who would serve as Cromwell's Secretary for Foreign Tongues (translating state documents into Latin, the language of international diplomacy). But the new form of government could not last. Cromwell's son Richard lacked the confidence of the army and was forced to resign in May 1659.

When Charles II entered London in triumph on May 29, 1660, it was as a monarch whose powers were more circumscribed than ever by the overseeing agency of Parliament—a force he would come to resent, and with which he was in frequent conflict, his instinctive loyalties drawing him closer to Catholic interests on the Continent than to those of his subjects. The England to which he returned was scarred not solely by having executed God's vice-regent upon earth, but by years of Civil War and the privations that followed. The country was "grown old with woes," as Katherine Philips would write, yet there were many besides her who welcomed Charles's return—not just on political grounds but because it represented restitution of a cosmic order.

> 'Twixt kings and subjects there's this mighty odds:
> Subjects are taught by men; kings by the gods.
>
> (ROBERT HERRICK, 1648,
> "THE DIFFERENCE BETWIXT KINGS AND SUBJECTS")

Edward Herbert, first Baron Herbert of Cherbury and first Baron Herbert of Castle Island (1582?–1648)

HERBERT BECAME A linguist at Oxford; he traveled the Continent and in 1610 took part in the siege of Juliers, being among the first to enter the town when it fell. Four years later he joined the Dutch army and fought the Spanish. James I appointed him ambassador to France in 1619; he returned to England five years later. During the events leading up to Civil War, he sided with Charles I and was imprisoned in the Tower of London for arguing in the House of Lords that the king could be held to have broken his coronation oath only if he made war against Parliament "without cause." After apologizing to the House he was released and retired to his castle in Montgomeryshire, Wales. His sons were involved in the Civil War on the Royalist side, but he endeavored to remain outside the conflict, pleading ill health. The war caught up with him nonetheless: on September 3, 1644, Sir Thomas Middleton's Parliamentary forces arrived at his castle and demanded its surrender. Herbert handed it over and moved to London (the castle would be destroyed by Parliamentary soldiers after the war ended). In declining health, he continued his studies and died on August 20, 1648.

14 October 1644

Enraging griefs, though you most diverse be
In your first causes, you may yet agree
    To take an equal share within my heart,
      Since if each grief strive for the greatest part
You needs must vex yourselves as well as me.

For your own sakes and mine then make an end;
In vain you do about a heart contend
    Which, though it seem in greatness to dilate,
    Is but a tumor, which in this its state
The choicest remedies would but offend.

Then storm it at once, I neither feel constraint
Scorning your worst, nor suffer any taint
    Dying by multitudes—though, if you strive,
    I fear my heart may thus be kept alive
Until it under its own burden faint.

What is it not done? Why then, my God, I find,
Would have me use you to reform my mind,
    Since through his help I may from you extract
    An essence pure, so spriteful and compact
As it will be from grosser parts refined—

Which being again converted by his Grace
To godly sorrow, I may both efface
    Those sins first caused you, and together have
    Your power to kill turned to a power to save,
And bring my soul to its desired place.

Written October 14, 1644, published 1665

George Wither (1588–1667)

POSSESSOR OF AN irrepressible messianic streak, Wither spent much of his life castigating those in power, threatening them with the ire of God; hardly surprising, then, to find him among the most frequently imprisoned poets in this volume. He was an established writer by the time plague struck London in 1625, the severest attack thus far during the century. While those around him disappeared, Wither made notes for an eight-canto epic, *Britain's*

Remembrancer (1628), a vivid portrayal of the capital and its few remaining inhabitants at an extraordinary moment in history. A trenchant critic of the "tyranny" of kingship, Wither welcomed the Civil War in which he captained a troop of cavalrymen on the Parliamentarian side; he was a combatant at the Battle of Turnham Green in November 1642. The following September he fought at the siege of Gloucester under Colonel John Middleton, recording the experience in *Campo-Musae* (1643) (field musings), a remarkable sonnet sequence containing one of the few eyewitness accounts of the Civil War in verse, written within days of the events it describes. Wither's description of "Men sprawling in their blood" is virtually reportage. He had a long career ahead of him: after Charles I's execution Wither was among those charged with dispersal of the king's estate, giving rise to anecdotes of him strutting about in the coronation robes. Having supported the Protectorate, Wither was vulnerable to charges of disloyalty to the Stuarts. Sure enough, he was placed under surveillance and imprisoned in Newgate in spring 1661, by a new king whose grandfather he had known (and by whom he had also been imprisoned) many years before. On March 24, 1662, he was examined before the House of Commons on a charge of seditious libel, convicted, and sent to the Tower; he was seventy-five when released in July 1663. He would continue to publish pamphlets deemed seditious by the government until the end of his life.

Britain's Remembrancer[1]

CANTO 2 (EXTRACT)

For with a doubled and redoubled stroke
The plague went on, and in among us broke

---

1. This is Wither's record of the plague of 1625. Out of a population of some three hundred thousand, over forty thousand would die, mostly during the summer months. King and court left, the law term ended prematurely, public officials fled, shops closed, houses were shuttered, and anarchy reigned. This was not the City's first encounter with the pestilence; periodic bouts had occurred over the preceding hundred years, the most recent in 1603. But it was a legitimate source of terror: no one knew its cause nor what might prevent or cure it. It could strike without warning and torment victims with a painful, lingering death.

With such unequalled fury and such rage
As Britain never felt in any age.
With some at every turning she did meet
Of every alley—every lane and street
She got possession—and we had no way
Or passage but she there in ambush lay.
Through nooks and corners she pursued the chase;
There was no barring her from any place,
For in the public fields in wait she laid
And into private gardens was conveyed.
Sometime she did among our garments hide
And so disperse among us unespied
Her strong infections; otherwhile unseen
A servant, friend or child betrayed hath been
To bring it home, and men were fearful grown
To tarry or converse among their own.
Friends fled each other, kinsmen stood aloof;
The son to come within his father's roof
Presumed not; the mother was constrained
To let her child depart unentertained;
The love betwixt the husband and the wife
Was oft neglected for the love of life;
And many a one their promise falsified
Who vowed that nought but death should them divide.
Some to frequent the markets were afraid,
And some to feed on what was thence purveyed—
For on young pigs such purple spots were seen
As marks of death on plague-sick men have been,
And it appeared that our suburb-hogs
Were little better than our cats and dogs.
Men knew not whither they might safely come,
Nor where to make appointments, nor with whom;
Nay, many shunned God's house, and much did fear
So far to trust him, as to meet him there.
In brief, the plague did such destruction threat,
And fears and perils were become so great
That most men's hearts did fail, and they to flight
Betook themselves with all the speed they might—

Not only they who private persons were
But such as did the public titles bear.

CANTO 4 (EXTRACT)

Here, one man staggered by with visage pale,
There leaned another, grunting on a stall;
A third half dead lay gasping for his grave;
A fourth did out at window call and rave;
Yon came the bearers, sweating from the pit,
To fetch more bodies to replenish it;
A little further off, one sits and shows
The spots which he death's tokens doth suppose. . . .

        I fixed mine eyes
On many a private man's calamities,
And saw the streets (wherein a while ago
We scarce could pass, the people filled them so)
Appear nigh desolate; yea, quite forlorn
And for their wonted visitants to mourn.
     Much-peopled Westminster, where late I saw
So many reverend Judges of the law
With clients and with suitors hemmed round,
Where courts and palaces did so abound
With businesses, and where together met
Our thrones of justice and our mercy seat—
That place was then frequented, as you see
Some villages on holidays will be
When half the township and the hamlets nigh
Are met to revel at some parish by.
Perhaps the wronging of the orphans' cause,
Denying or perverting of the laws
There practised, did set this plague a-breeding
And sent the term from Westminster to Reading.
Her goodly church and chapel did appear
Like some poor minster which hath twice a year
Four visitants; and her great hall (wherein
So great a rendezvous had lately been)
Did look like those old structures where long since,

Men say, King Arthur kept his residence.
The Parliament had left her to go see
If they could learn at Oxford to agree,
Or if that air were better for the health
And safety of our English Commonwealth.
But there some did so counsel and so urge
The body politic to take a purge,
To purify the parts that seemed foul;
Some others did that motion so control
And plead so much for cordials, and for that
Which strengthen might the sinews of the State,
That all the time, the labour and the cost,
Which had bestowed been, was wholly lost.
And here the empty House of Parliament
Did look as if it had been discontent,
Or grieved methought that Oxford should not be
More prosperous yet; nor could I any see
Resort to comfort her. But there did I
Behold two traitors' heads which, perching high,
Did show their teeth as if they had been grinning
At those afflictions which are now beginning;
Yea, their wide eyeholes stared methought as though
They looked to see that House now overthrow
Itself, which they with powder up had blown
Had God, their snares, and them, not overthrown.

      Whitehall, where not three months before I spied
Great Britain in the height of all her pride,
And France with her contending, which could most
Outbrave old Rome and Persia, in their cost   *surpass*
On robes and feasts—even that lay solitary
As doth a quite-forsaken monastery
In some lone forest, and we could not pass
To many places, but through weeds and grass.
Perhaps the sins of late committed there
Occasions of such desolation were;
Pray God, there be not others in the State
That will make all at last be desolate!

      The Strand, that goodly thoroughfare between
The Court and City (and where I have seen

Well nigh a million passing in one day)
Is now almost an unfrequented way;
And peradventure, for those impudencies,
Those riots, and those other foul offences
Which in that place were frequent, when it had
So great resort, it is now justly made
To stand unvisited. God grant it may
Repent, lest longer and another way
It stand unpeopled, or some others use
Those blessings which the owners now abuse.

     The City houses of our English Peers
Now smoked as seldom as in other years
Their country palaces, and they perchance
Much better know than doth my ignorance
Why so it came to pass. But wish I shall
That they their ways to mind would better call,
Lest both their country and their city piles
Be smoking seen, and burning, many miles.

     The Inns of Court I entered, and I saw
Each room so desolate, as if the law
Had outlawed all her students, or that there
Some feared arrestings where no Sergeants were.
Most dream that this great fright was thither sent
Not purposely, but came by accident;
And so but little use is taken from
God's judgments to amend the times to come.

Written 1625, published 1628

Campo-Musae (extracts)[1]

Behold, the plough by whom we are all fed
Is thrown into the ditch; our herds decay;

---

1. This sonnet sequence records Wither's firsthand experience of the Civil War, particularly his participation at the siege of Gloucester between August 3 and September 5, 1643 under the command of Colonel John Middleton. Gloucester was held by the parliamentarians, on whose side Wither fought.

Our shepherds and our husbandmen are fled;
Artificers may shut up shop and play;
The labourer must either starve or fight;
The gownman must a swordman learn to be;
Nor magistrate nor laws can do us right;
The creditor and debtor may agree;
The glutton must be glad of homely fare;
The drunkard must drink water or be dry;
Old lousy rags Pride must be fain to wear;
Our idle dames in vain for bread shall cry;
 And they who late in finest linen lay
 Shall scarce have leave to lodge in straw and hay.

How are our goodly buildings overthrown!
How are our pleasant arbors hacked and hewed!
How bare and rude are those neat places grown
Where fruitful orchards and fair groves we viewed!
Through walks and fields, which I have visited
With peaceful mates, and free from fear of harms—
Yea, there, where oft fair ladies I have led,
I now lead on a troop of men in arms.
In meadows, where our sports were wont to be,
And where we playing wantonly have lain,
Men sprawling in their blood we now do see—
Grim postures of the dying and the slain;
 And where sweet music hath refreshed the ear,
 Sad groans of ghosts departing now we hear.

In ev'ry field, in ev'ry lane and street,
In ev'ry house, almost in ev'ry place,
With cries and tears and loud complaints we meet,
And each one thinks his own the saddest case.
But what are private losses, while we view
Three famous kingdoms, woefully exposed
To miserable ruin, and so few
Lament that plague wherewith we are enclosed?
Myself and my estate I shall contemn

Till we, in freedom, sing our Syon songs,[2]
Till we have peace, in our Jerusalem,
And Church and State have what to them belongs;
    For what, to these, are oxen, sheep and kine,
    Or any loss, that is but yours or mine?

    *

Whilst thus I mused, behold, the foe came on
And to possess the bordering hills began!
My Colonel, experienced Middleton[3]
(A valiant Scot), that day led up the van;
A troop that flanked him on the left I led.
The word was ordered forth, the soldier shouted,
Our martial music them encouraged,
And, each from other, fears of danger flouted!
Our forces joined in clouds of fiery smoke,
Whence many whizzing thunderbolts were shot;
Our glittering swords, like flashing lightnings, struck
Each others' eyes, and bloody showers begot:
    Enough whereby our courage might be tried,
    And yet with no great loss on either side.

For lest (while of each part the forlorn hopes
Together strove) our side might seek to take
A narrow pass (which might have made some stops,
To their great hazard, in retreating back),
They wheeled about, as if to gain some ground
Of more advantage. So, before the place
We rightly knew, or their intention found,
Instead of a recharge, we gave them chase—
Which, being finished, and my warmed blood
Grown colder, by our adversary's flight,

---

2. Till we . . . Syon songs] Wither alludes to Psalm 137, in which the slave master orders his captives to "Sing us one of the songs of Zion!" Wither envisages a time when the British people will no longer be enslaved to a monarch.
3. Wither defended Gloucester with the parliamentarians under Colonel John Middleton (c. 1608–1674), from Kincardineshire. He had begun his military career as a pikeman in France some time after 1631.

Another foe, which long my peace withstood,
A challenge brought me for another fight:
    And in the dark, when that day's march was done,
    A second furious battle we begun.

Written September to November 1643, published December 1643

Robert Herrick (bap. 1591, d. 1674)

NO ONE COULD doubt the power of his *Hesperides* (1648), one of the greatest poetry collections of the age. Herrick was educated at Cambridge, where Oliver Cromwell was among his contemporaries. After taking his BA and MA, he was ordained deacon in 1623. In July 1627 Herrick was chaplain to George Villiers, Duke of Buckingham, on an expedition to capture the Île de Ré and relieve the Huguenots at the port and fortress of La Rochelle. The venture was a disaster. The siege dragged on until late October and five thousand out of eight thousand men died in combat or succumbed to disease; to the end, the French Royalist forces prevented the British reaching La Rochelle. Of their final attempt, a French eyewitness observed: "our ears were deafened with the thunder of the cannon, and the sea was covered with a dense black cloud of smoke which was riven by gun-flashes." In its midst, Herrick must have known his life to be in peril, and would have seen much suffering. As the British retreated, the French slaughtered over a thousand soldiers in a single day. Two years later, back in England, Charles I presented him to the vicarage of Dean Prior. Always a Royalist, he sided with the king from the outset of the Civil Wars, and may have witnessed conflict close to home, for the southwest was the site of a number of important battles; Cromwell defeated the Royalists on Bovey Heath, in January 1646, ten miles from Dean Prior. In March, Herrick was relieved from his living and replaced by a Presbyterian minister. Forced into refuge, he fled ultimately to London in 1647. Though not a combatant, Herrick suffered the privations of war as much as anyone, penniless in England's capital city: those experiences leave their mark on many of the nearly fourteen hundred poems in *Hesperides*, from which this selection is drawn. At the Restoration, Herrick was reinstated to Dean Prior, where he served until retirement in 1671.

Farewell the Frost, or Welcome the Spring

Fled are the frosts, and now the fields appear
Reclothed in fresh and verdant diaper;   *decoration*
Thawed are the snows, and now the lusty spring
Gives to each mead a neat enameling;
The palms put forth their gems, and every tree
Now swaggers in her leavy gallantry;   *display*
The while the Daulian minstrel[1] sweetly sings
With warbling notes her Tyrrean sufferings.
What gentle winds perspire? As if here   *blow gently*
Never had been the northern plunderer
To strip the trees and fields to their distress,
Leaving them to a pitied nakedness.
And look how, when a frantic storm doth tear
A stubborn oak or holm (long growing there)
But lulled to calmness, then succeeds a breeze
That scarcely stirs the nodding leaves of trees.
So when this war (which tempest like doth spoil
Our salt, our corn, our honey, wine, and oil)
Falls to a temper and doth mildly cast   *equilibrium*
His inconsiderate frenzy off at last,
The gentle dove may, when these turmoils cease,
Bring in her bill once more, the branch of Peace.

Written 1642/1643, published early 1648

His Cavalier

Give me that man that dares bestride
The active seahorse, and with pride
Through that huge field of waters ride;
Who with his looks too, can appease
The ruffling winds and raging seas,
In midst of all their outrages.

---

1. Daulian minstrel] nightingale.

This, this a virtuous man can do:
Sail against rocks, and split them too—
Aye, and a world of pikes pass through!

Written c. 1644, published early 1648

To the King Upon His Coming With His Army Into the West[1]

Welcome, most welcome to our vows and us,
Most great and universal Genius!
The drooping west, which hitherto has stood
As one in long-lamented widowhood,
Looks like a bride now, or a bed of flowers
Newly refreshed both by the sun and showers.
War, which before was horrid, now appears
Lovely in you, brave Prince of cavaliers!
A deal of courage in each bosom springs
By your access—oh you, the best of kings,
Ride on with all white omens, so that where
Your standard's up, we fix a conquest there.

Written c. July 1644, published early 1648

The Bad Season Makes the Poet Sad

Dull to myself, and almost dead to these
My many fresh and fragrant mistresses;
Lost to all music now, since everything
Puts on the semblance here of sorrowing:
Sick is the land to the heart, and doth endure
More dangerous faintings by her desperate cure.
But if that golden age would come again
And Charles here rule as he before did reign;

---

1. Charles I was in Exeter by July 1644.

If smooth and unperplexed the seasons were
As when the sweet Maria lived here[2]—
I should delight to have my curls half drowned
In Tyrian dews,[3] and head with roses crowned,
And once more yet (ere I am laid out dead)
Knock at a star with my exalted head.

Written 1644/1645, published early 1648

To the King, Upon His Taking of Leicester[1]

This day is yours, great Charles, and in this War
Your fate and ours alike victorious are!
In her white stole now Victory does rest
Ensphered with palm on your triumphant crest.
Fortune is now your captive—other kings
Hold but her hands; you hold both hands and wings!

Written early June 1645, published early 1648

Upon Mr. William Lawes, the Rare Musician[1]

Should I not put on blacks, when each one here
Comes with his cypress, and devotes a tear?
Should I not grieve, my Lawes, when every lute,
Viol and voice is by thy loss struck mute?—

---

2. Queen Henrietta Maria left England for France in the summer of 1644.
3. Tyrian dews] the purple dye made in ancient days at Tyre would have been favored by a Royalist, purple being the color worn by the king.
To the King, Upon His Taking of Leicester
1. The Royalist army under Prince Rupert took Leicester on May 31, 1645.
Upon Mr. William Lawes, the Rare Musician
1. William Lawes (1602–1645) was an instrumentalist and composer who fought on the Royalist side in the Civil War. He was killed at the Battle of Rowton Heath, September 24, 1645.

Thy loss, brave man, whose numbers have been hurled,
And no less praised, then spread throughout the world!
Some have thee called Amphion; some of us
Named thee Terpander or sweet Orpheus;
Some this, some that—but all in this agree:
Music had both her birth and death with thee.

Written soon after September 24, 1645, published early 1648

His Loss

All has been plundered from me but my wit;
Fortune herself can lay no claim to it.

Written sometime after March 25, 1646, published early 1648

His Return to London

From the dull confines of the drooping west,
To see the dayspring from the pregnant east,
Ravished in spirit I come—nay more, I fly
To thee, blest place of my nativity!
Thus, thus, with hallowed foot I touch the ground,
With thousand blessings by thy fortune crowned.
Oh fruitful genius that bestowest here
An everlasting plenty, year by year!
Oh place, oh people, manners framed to please
All nations, customs, kindreds, languages!
I am a freeborn Roman; suffer, then,
That I among you live a citizen.
London my home is, though by hard fate sent
Into a long and irksome banishment,
Yet since called back; henceforward let me be,
Oh native country, repossessed by thee!

For rather than I'll to the west return,
I'll beg of thee first here to have mine urn.
Weak I am grown, and must in short time fall;
Give thou my sacred relics burial.

Written 1647, published early 1648

Francis Quarles (1592–1644)

QUARLES WAS BORN into a well-to-do Puritan family and educated at Christ's College, Cambridge, then at Lincoln's Inn. He settled in London on a private income, devoting himself to literary and scholarly interests. In 1625 he became secretary to James Ussher, newly appointed archbishop of Armagh, taking his young family out to Drogheda. Both men shared a Royalist, anti-Catholic, yet moderate Protestant outlook; Quarles was all his life a believer in the divine right of kings. He returned to London in around 1630, and five years later published *Emblems*, containing the poems that would bring him fame. He moved to the Essex village of Terling during the Civil War. Surrounded by Puritan fanatics, he fled to the king's court at Oxford in 1643 or 1644. The poem we include dates from this period, and enjoyed popularity when published anonymously in Oxford. It satirizes the radicalism of those who had driven Quarles from Terling, placing in their mouths sentiments he despised. He died a pauper, either in Terling or London, in September 1644.

Know then, my brethren, heaven is clear[1]

Know then, my brethren, heaven is clear
    And all the clouds are gone;
The righteous now shall flourish and

---

1. This poem first appeared in *The Shepherd's Oracle* (1644); it ridicules the fanaticism that drove Quarles from his home in Terling.

Good days are coming on;
Come then, my brethren, and be glad
        And eke rejoice with me:
Lawn sleeves and rochets[2] shall go down
        And hey, then up go we!

We'll break the windows which the Whore
        Of Babylon[3] hath painted,
And when the Popish Saints are down
        Then Barrow[4] shall be sainted;
There's neither cross nor crucifix
        Shall stand for men to see—
Rome's trash and trumperies shall go down
        And hey, then up go we!

Whate'er the Popish hands have built
        Our hammers shall undo;
We'll break their pipes[5] and burn their copes
        And pull down churches too;
We'll exercise within the groves
        And teach beneath a tree;
We'll make a pulpit of a cart—
        And hey, then up go we!

We'll down with all the varsities[6]
        Where "larning" is professed
Because they practice and maintain
        The language of the beast;[7]
We'll drive the doctors out of doors,
        And Arts (whate'er they be);

---

2. Lawn sleeves and rochets] lawn sleeves were worn by senior Anglican clergy; rochet is a type of linen surplice worn by bishops.
3. Whore / Of Babylon] The Catholic Church.
4. Henry Barrow (1550–1593) was a radical separatist who regarded existing church governance as misguided and antichristian; he was imprisoned and executed.
5. pipes] organ pipes.
6. varsities] universities.
7. The language of the beast] Latin, used by both the Catholic and Anglican churches.

We'll cry both Arts and larning down—
        And hey, then up go we!

We'll down with Deans and Prebends too,
        But I rejoice to tell ye,
How then we will eat pig our fill
        And capon by the belly;
We'll burn the fathers' witty tomes[8]
        And make the schoolmen[9] flee;
We'll down with all that smells of wit,
        And hey, then up go we!

If once that antichristian crew
        Be crushed and overthrown,
We'll teach the nobles how to crouch
        And keep the gentry down;
Good manners have an evil report
        And turns to pride we see,
We'll therefore cry good manners down
        And hey, then up go we!

The name of Lord shall be abhorred
        For every man's a brother,
No reason why in Church or State
        One man should rule another;
But when the change of government
        Shall set our fingers free,
We'll make the wanton sisters stoop
        And hey, then up go we!

Our cobblers shall translate their souls
        From caves obscure and shady,
We'll make Tom Turd as good as my Lord,
        And Joan as good as my Lady!
We'll crush and fling the marriage ring
        In the Roman See;

8. the fathers' witty tomes] books written by early Christian scholars.
9. schoolmen] medieval theologians.

We'll ask no bands, but even clap hands
　　And hey, then up go we!

Written c. 1643–44, published 1644

Mildmay Fane, second Earl of Westmorland (1602–1666)

BORN INTO A titled family with a castle in Kent, Fane was possessor of a number of lucrative offices; in the years prior to Civil War he became commissioner for the compositions for knighthood, and served as justice of the peace and deputy lieutenant in Northamptonshire. In August 1642, he attempted to muster troops in Oundle to fight for the Royalists, but was captured by the Parliamentary army before the job was completed. The House of Lords decided to confine him to the Tower of London, though successive easements of the sentence allowed him first to reside at his house in Bartholomew Close in London, and then to ride within five miles of the City. Nonetheless, he was compelled to pledge loyalty to the Commonwealth and subscribe to the solemn league and covenant before commissioners of the Great Seal on April 22, 1645. From then until 1660 he withdrew from public life, returning as lord lieutenant of Northamptonshire after the Restoration. His best-known volume, *Otia Sacra*, appeared in 1648. He was friendly with another Royalist poet, Robert Herrick (p. 123), who encouraged him to publish.

To Prince Charles[1]

So doth the early plum, the pear, the cherry
Commit a rape and make nice females merry
When longing-ripe—as your return will bless

---

1. This poem was written after the future Charles II had left British shores in summer 1646. The most likely time is spring 1648, when the Scottish Parliament was preparing to invite the Prince of Wales to lead an invasion of England.

The British Islands with new cheerfulness;
Be pleased no longer therefore, sir, to tarry,
Lest a whole gleek² of kingdoms should miscarry;
But you that are the blossom of all hope,
Dispel the mists from off this horoscope;
And in the stead of jealousy and fears,
Let there be harmony throughout your spheres.
There needs no other midwifery to these
As wished-for truth and now-desired peace,
But your fair hand to bring the same to pass
And place your royal father where he was.
This be your noble issue, whilst all those
Abortive prove, that so seemed to oppose;
And while they'd bring to birth, and yet want strength,
Teach them to know themselves and you at length.

Written probably spring 1648, published 1648

To the People of England¹

Whither, oh wicked brood, d'ye run?
Is't not enough, what was begun
In a mad fury, but d'ye still
Invent new feuds and how to kill?
Must sword be drawn again t'appease,
As if on land and on the seas
Of English blood there had not been
Enough yet spent or malice seen?
Must war prevail o'er peace and truth,
Whilst every London 'prentice youth
Is taught to scorn and trample down

---

2. gleek] a threesome—England, Wales, and Ireland.
To the People of England
1. This poem was written shortly after the resignation of Richard Cromwell in May 1659, when the Royalists were organizing an uprising, giving cause for fears of another Civil War.

The clergy's rights and lawman's gown?
And that which to our enemies we
Might wish, as that they not agree,
By home dissension we prefer
To be our own executioner.
        Thus do not wolves nor lions rage
Less 'gainst some other parentage?
Are we more fell than beasts? Doth power
And force incite us to devour
Each other? Is not fury blind
To cause us to rush on our own kind?
Or is our sin so great? No fate
Save this may serve to expiate,
Bereft at once of speech and sense,
What may be read or gathered thence,
But that for Remus' blood once spilt
Posterity should feel the guilt.

Written June 5, 1659, published 2001

Edmund Waller (1606–1687)

WALLER'S POETRY IS urbane, a product of the circle of wits and writers who gathered at Great Tew in Oxfordshire, country seat of his friend Lucius Cary, Viscount Falkland. Yet Waller's many poems in praise of the great and talented are themselves evidence of an insecurity understandable in a highly factionalized society governed by political loyalty. He began as a Royalist and from 1624 had a seat in the Commons where he was foremost among those who supported Charles I. Found guilty of involvement in a plot to allow the king's army unfettered access to London, he was interrogated and remained in prison for a year and a half without trial, uncertain of his fate. In November 1644 he was fined ten thousand pounds and exiled to France. He returned to England after the war and in 1655 was appointed commissioner for trade by Cromwell, to whom he was second cousin by marriage. Waller was thus capable of writing a "panegyrick" to Cromwell, and later addressing one to Charles II "Upon His Majesty's Happy Return" in 1660. He continued to write poems in praise of the royal family, and played an active role in Parliament. "To Chloris" refers to the Civil War ("growing mischiefs") and submerges its author's anxieties beneath a cynical comment on love.

To Chloris

Chloris, since first our calm of peace
Was frighted hence, this good we find:
Your favors with your fears increase
And growing mischiefs make you kind.
So the fair tree which still preserves
Her fruit and state whilst no wind blows,
In storms from that uprightness swerves,
And the glad earth about her strews
With treasure from her yielding boughs.

Written after 1642, published 1645

Go, lovely rose!

Go, lovely rose!
Tell her that wastes her time and me
That now she knows,
When I resemble her to thee,
How sweet and fair she seems to be.

Tell her that's young,
And shuns to have her graces spied,
That hadst thou sprung
In deserts where no men abide,
Thou must have uncommended died.

Small is the worth
Of beauty from the light retired;
Bid her come forth,
Suffer herself to be desired
And not blush so to be admired.

Then die! that she
The common fate of all things rare
May read in thee;
How small a part of time they share
That are so wondrous sweet and fair!

Published 1645

John Milton (1608–1674)

HAD HE NOT written the greatest blank verse epic in the language, Milton would be remembered as a polemicist who argued, often at risk to himself, against censorship; for more lenient divorce laws; for the execution of bishops and others who used the Church to amass personal wealth; and (most dangerously) for regicide. In short, the author of *Paradise Lost* was the kind of writer who today would be described as a "controversialist"—unafraid of speaking plainly, regardless of whose feathers he ruffled. His first marriage in 1642, which resulted almost immediately in separation, led him to argue in print that divorce be made available to anyone whose union was spiritually and emotionally barren. This was sufficiently radical for him to be summoned by the House of Lords for "examination," along with his printer, before Parliament passed a law stipulating that all books be submitted to censorship prior to publication, a measure Milton would oppose in *Areopagitica* (1644). During the trial of Charles I, Milton wrote a pamphlet saying on its title page that "it is lawful . . . for any who have the power, to call to account a tyrant or wicked king and, after due conviction, to depose and put him to death." Within weeks, Milton had been invited by the council of state to be secretary of foreign tongues, responsible for translating official correspondence into Latin, the language of international diplomacy. Charles's execution sent shock waves across the Continent, and precipitated repeated attacks on Milton by Royalist pamphleteers at home and abroad. His publication of a tract defending republicanism a month prior to the restoration of Charles II was impolitic, to say the least, but he was already much hated by Royalists, and would probably have been hunted down regardless. As soon as Charles was back on English soil, Milton went into hiding. On August 27, 1660 all known copies of his books were incinerated at the Old Bailey. He was liable to execution until the Act of Free and General Pardon received the royal assent at the end of August. Nonetheless, he was apprehended and spent his fifty-second birthday in the Tower of London—where, but for the intervention of friends (including Marvell), he might have been executed. He was pardoned and released on December 17, 1660, and would go on to complete *Paradise Lost* in 1663. The years following his imprisonment and release were anxious ones. He lived in political ignominy, fearful of rearrest, and in the invocation of *Paradise Lost*, Book 7, described himself as

> fallen on evil days,
> On evil days though fallen, and evil tongues;
> In darkness, and with dangers compassed round,
> And solitude . . .

When the Assault Was Intended to the City[1]

Captain or colonel, or knight in arms,
Whose chance on these defenceless doors may seize,
If deed of honour did thee ever please,
Guard them, and him within protect from harms.
He can requite thee, for he knows the charms

---

1. The manuscript title of "Captain or colonel, or knight in arms" reveals its precise context: "On his door when the City expected an assault." This is a Civil War poem written at a moment when Charles I's Royalist forces were besieging what is now west London. In his imagination, Milton addresses an officer of the Crown, requesting that his house be spared in return for the "fame" of being thanked in poetry. If its title is to be believed, the poem was pinned to the front door of Milton's house in Aldersgate Street after its author had gone into hiding.

That call fame on such gentle acts as these,
And he can spread thy name o'er lands and seas,
Whatever clime the sun's bright circle warms.
Lift not thy spear against the muses' bower!
The great Emathian conqueror bid spare
The house of Pindarus,[2] when temple and tower
Went to the ground; and the repeated air
Of sad Electra's poet had the power
To save the Athenian walls from ruin bare.[3]

Written by or before November 13, 1642, published 1645

On the Detraction Which Followed Upon My Writing Certain Treatises[1]

I did but prompt the age to quit their clogs
By the known rules of ancient liberty,
When straight a barbarous noise environs me   *surrounds*
Of owls and cuckoos, asses, apes and dogs;
As when those hinds that were transformed to frogs
Railed at Latona's twin-born progeny[2]
Which after held the sun and moon in fee.
But this is got by casting pearl to hogs
That bawl for freedom in their senseless mood
And still revolt when truth would set them free—
Licence they mean when they cry "Liberty!"

---

2. Alexander ("The great Emathian conqueror") spared the house once occupied by the Greek lyric poet Pindar.
3. Athens was spared when, in 404 BC, a man was heard singing the first chorus from Euripedes' *Electra*.

ON THE DETRACTION WHICH FOLLOWED UPON MY WRITING CERTAIN TREATISES
1. Milton argued for easier access to divorce in tracts published in 1643 and 1644, eliciting enraged responses. Calls for their suppression led to his being examined by the House of Lords.
2. Latona and her baby twins Apollo and Diana (deities of sun and moon) wanted to drink at a pool but were prevented by Lycian peasants who stirred it up and muddied it. As punishment, Jove turned the peasants into frogs.

For who loves that, must first be wise and good;
But from that mark how far they rove we see,
For all this waste of wealth and loss of blood.

Written 1646, published 1673

On the Lord General Fairfax at the Siege of Colchester[1]

Fairfax, whose name in arms through Europe rings
And filling each mouth with envy or with praise,
And all her jealous monarchs with amaze,
And rumors loud that daunt remotest kings—
Thy firm unshaken valour ever brings
Victory home, though new rebellions raise
Their hydra heads, and the false north[2] displays
Her broken league to imp her serpent wings.
Oh yet a nobler task awaits thy hand,
For what can war but endless war still breed
Till truth and right from violence be freed,
And public faith cleared from the shameful brand
Of public fraud—in vain doth valour bleed
While avarice and rapine share the land.

Written between July 8 and August 17, 1648, published 1694

---

1. Fairfax (also a poet—see p. 148) was one of the greatest soldiers of the Parliamentary army. He successfully laid siege to Colchester, the town surrendering to him on August 27, 1648.
2. the false north] Scotland, which invaded England in breach of the Solemn League and Covenant.

To the Lord General Cromwell[1]

Cromwell, our chief of men, who through a cloud
Not of war only, but detractions rude,
Guided by faith and matchless fortitude
To peace and truth thy glorious way hath ploughed,
And on the neck of crowned fortune proud
Hast reared God's trophies and his work pursued,
While Darwen[2] stream with blood of Scots imbrued,
And Dunbar field[3] resounds thy praises loud,
And Worcester's laureate wreath;[4] yet much remains
To conquer still; peace hath her victories
No less renowned than war, new foes arise
Threatening to bind our souls with secular chains:
Help us to save free conscience from the paw
Of hireling wolves whose gospel is their maw.

Written May 1652, published 1694

To Sir Henry Vane the Younger[1]

Vane, young in years, but in sage counsel old,
Than whom a better senator ne'er held
The helm of Rome, when gowns not arms repelled

---

1. This sonnet was written at a time when Parliament was considering religious liberty, the cause advocated by Cromwell being that of complete liberty of dissent, in opposition to those who wanted an established church with clergy employed by the state.
2. Cromwell routed the Scots close to the River Darwen in Lancashire, August 1648.
3. Cromwell routed the Scots at Dunbar, September 3, 1650.
4. Cromwell defeated the Scottish army raised by the future Charles II at Worcester, September 3, 1651.

To Sir Henry Vane the Younger
1. "To Sir Henry Vane the Younger" is addressed to Milton's younger friend and colleague on the Council of State, one of the leading Republicans in Britain. It praises Vane for his service to the government not least in reorganizing the British navy and then persuading the council to wage war with the Dutch. Vane would be beheaded in 1662 for treason, the expected punishment for a defiant regicide.

The fierce Epirot[2] and the African bold.[3]
Whether to settle peace, or to unfold
The drift of hollow states,[4] hard to be spelled;
Then to advise how war may best, upheld,
Move by her two main nerves, iron and gold,
In all her equipage; besides to know
Both spiritual power and civil, what each means,
What severs each, thou hast learned, which few have done.
The bounds of either sword to thee we owe;
Therefore on thy right hand religion leans
In peace, and reckons thee her eldest son.

Written July 3, 1652, published 1662

On the Late Massacre in Piedmont[1]

Avenge, oh Lord, thy slaughtered saints whose bones
Lie scattered on the Alpine mountains cold;
Even them who kept thy truth so pure of old
When all our fathers worshipped stocks and stones,
Forget not. In thy book record their groans
Who were thy sheep and in their ancient fold
Slain by the bloody Piedmontese, that rolled
Mother with infant down the rocks. Their moans
The vales redoubled to the hills, and they
To heaven. Their martyred blood and ashes sow
O'er all the Italian fields where still doth sway

---

2. Epirot] Pyrrhus, King of Epirus.
3. the African bold] Hannibal.
4. hollow states] insincere countries.
ON THE LATE MASSACRE IN PIEDMONT
1. Inspired by the slaughter of seventeen hundred members of the Vaudois, an early Protestant sect in Alpine villages on the borders of France and Italy, by an army led by the Marquis of Pianezza. Cromwell was sympathetic to the Vaudois, and on his behalf Milton wrote letters of protest to European heads of state. That this was no mere chore is revealed by this poem, which begins by calling for divine retribution.

The triple tyrant,[2] that from these may grow
A hundredfold who, having learned thy way,
Early may fly the Babylonian woe.

Written late June 1655, published 1673

Sir John Suckling (bap. 1609, d. 1641?)

IN JULY 1627 Suckling served in the Duke of Buckingham's expedition to the
Île de Ré (for which Robert Herrick was chaplain), to relieve La Rochelle from
rebelling French Huguenots; went on to serve at the Siege of 's-Hertogenbosch
in 1629, an action of the Eighty Years' War, alongside the Dutch Republi-
can army; and less than a month later joined Lord Wimbledon's regiment in
the Dutch service. Charles I knighted him in September 1630, when he was
twenty-one. In 1631, he assisted Sir Henry Vane in negotiations for the recon-
quest and restoration of the Palatinate; frequently in peril, he witnessed what
was to become the Thirty Years' War. Experience of such violent conflict had
a profound effect on him, and on arrival in London in April 1632, he devoted
himself to writing, womanizing, and gambling—including cribbage, of which
he was the inventor. In 1638 he returned to active service on behalf of the king,
involving himself in two failed invasions of Scotland. Apprehended while try-
ing to release one of the king's supporters recently imprisoned in the Tower of
London, he had no option but to flee to Paris where he perished, possibly by
his own hand. He was thirty-two years old.

Against Fruition

Stay here, fond youth, and ask no more, be wise—
Knowing too much long since lost Paradise;
The virtuous joys thou hast, thou wouldst should still

---

2. The triple tyrant] a reference to the three-tiered crown of the pope.

Last in their pride, and wouldst not take it ill
If rudely from sweet dreams (and for a toy)
Thou wert waked? He wakes himself that does enjoy.

Fruition adds no new wealth, but destroys,
And, while it pleaseth much the palate, cloys;
Who thinks he shall be happier for that
As reasonably might hope he might grow fat
By eating to a surfeit: this once past,
What relishes? Even kisses lose their taste.

Urge not 'tis necessary, alas! We know
The homeliest thing which mankind does is so;
The world is of a vast extent we see,
And must be peopled; children there must be;
So must bread too; but since there are enough
Born to the drudgery, what need we plough?

Women enjoyed (whate'er before t' have been)
Are like romances read or sights once seen:
Fruition's dull, and spoils the play much more
Than if one read and knew the plot before;
'Tis expectation makes a blessing dear:
Heaven were not heaven, if we knew what it were.

And as in prospects we are there pleased most
Where something keeps the eye from being lost
And leaves us room to guess, so here restraint
Holds up delight, that with excess would faint.
They who know all the wealth they have, are poor—
He's only rich that cannot tell his store.   *count*

Written between 1632 and 1637, published 1646

'Tis now since I sat down before

'Tis now since I sat down before
    That foolish fort, a heart,
(Time strangely spent) a year and more,
    And still I did my part;

Made my approaches—from her hand
    Unto her lip did rise,
And did already understand
    The language of her eyes;

Proceeded on with no less art,
    My tongue was engineer:
I thought to undermine the heart
    By whispering in the ear.

When this did nothing, I brought down
    Great canon-oaths, and shot
A thousand thousand to the town
    And still it yielded not.

I then resolved to starve the place
    By cutting off all kisses,
Praising and gazing on her face,
    And all such little blisses.

To draw her out, and from her strength,
    I drew all batteries in,
And brought myself to lie at length
    As if no siege had been.

When I had done what man could do
    And thought the place mine own,
The enemy lay quiet too,
    And smiled at all was done.

I sent to know from whence and where
    These hopes and this relief?
A spy informed Honour was there,
    And did command in chief.

"March, march," quoth I, "The word straight give,
    Let's lose no time, but leave her:
That giant upon air will live,
    And hold it out forever."

To such a place our camp remove
    As will no siege abide;
I hate a fool that starves her love
    Only to feed her pride.

Written between 1632 and 1637, published 1646

The Invocation

Ye juster powers of love and fate,
Give me the reason why
    A lover crossed
    And all hopes lost
May not have leave to die?

It is but just, and love needs must
Confess it is his part,
    When she doth spy
    One wounded lie
To pierce the other's heart.

But yet if he so cruel be
To have one breast to hate,
    If I must live
    And thus survive,
How far more cruel's fate?

In this same state I find too late
I am, and here's the grief:
    Cupid can cure,
    Death heal I'm sure,
  Yet neither sends relief.

To live or die, beg only I,
Just powers, some end me give;
    And traitor like
    Thus force me not
  Without a heart to live.

Written between 1632 and 1637, published 1646

Gerrard Winstanley (bap. 1609, d. 1676)

OF ALL CIVIL War lives, that of Gerrard Winstanley best exemplifies the extremity of the times. Born to a family of humble origins, he trained as a tailor but the war led to loss of his business. Further financial woes led him to begin transcribing prophetic utterances in 1647; then, on Sunday April 1, 1649, Winstanley led a group of followers onto common land on St. George's Hill in Walton to sow vegetables. Following his lead, other settlements sprang up at Iver, Wellingborough, and Coxhall. In the manifesto published shortly after, Winstanley demanded common ownership of land, abolition of its buying and selling, a communal practice of agriculture, and abolition of the payment of rent. He also demanded an end to the legal system and the established church. Though nonviolent, the Diggers suffered constant harassment, including physical intimidation and burning of their houses, which led to collapse of the venture in 1650. Visionary in his aims, Winstanley provided a glimpse of an egalitarian society to which idealists have returned ever since. "The Diggers' Song" is still recorded and sung by musicians of our own time.

The Diggers' Song

You noble Diggers all, stand up now, stand up now!
    You noble Diggers all, stand up now,
The waste land to maintain, seeing cavaliers by name
Your digging does disdain and persons all defame—
    Stand up now, stand up now!

Your houses they pull down, stand up now, stand up now;
    Your houses they pull down, stand up now!
Your houses they pull down to fright poor men in town,
But the gentry must come down, and the poor shall wear the crown!
    Stand up now, Diggers all.

With spades and hoes and ploughs, stand up now, stand up now;
    With spades and hoes and ploughs, stand up now,
Your freedom to uphold, seeing cavaliers are bold
To kill you if they could, and rights from you to hold—
    Stand up now, Diggers all.

Their self-will is their law, stand up now, stand up now,
    Their self-will is their law, stand up now.
Since tyranny came in, they count it now no sin
To make a jail a gin, to starve poor men therein—   *trap*
    Stand up now, Diggers all.

The gentry are all round, stand up now, stand up now,
    The gentry are all round, stand up now;
The gentry are all round, on each side they are found,
Their wisdom's so profound, to cheat us of our ground—
    Stand up now, stand up now.

The lawyers they conjoin, stand up now, stand up now,
    The lawyers they conjoin, stand up now;
To arrest you they advise, such fury they devise,
The devil in them lies and hath blinded both their eyes—
    Stand up now, stand up now.

The clergy they come in, stand up now, stand up now,
    The clergy they come in, stand up now;
The clergy they come in, and say it is a sin
That we should now begin our freedom for to win—
      Stand up now, Diggers all.

The tithes they yet will have, stand up now, stand up now;
    The tithes they yet will have, stand up now!
The tithes they yet will have, and lawyers their fees crave,
And this they say is brave, to make the poor their slave—
      Stand up now, Diggers all.

'Gainst lawyers and 'gainst priests, stand up now, stand up now,
    'Gainst lawyers and 'gainst priests stand up now!
For tyrants they are both, even flat against their oath,
To grant us they are loath, free meat and drink and cloth—
      Stand up now, Diggers all.

The club is all their law, stand up now, stand up now;
    The club is all their law, stand up now!
The club is all their law to keep poor men in awe,
But they no vision saw to maintain such a law—
      Stand up now, Diggers all.

The cavaliers are foes, stand up now, stand up now,
    The cavaliers are foes, stand up now!
The cavaliers are foes, themselves they do disclose
By verses not in prose, to please the singing boys—
      Stand up now, Diggers all.

To conquer them by love, come in now, come in now;
    To conquer them by love, come in now;
To conquer them by love, as it does you behove,
For he is King above, no power is like to love—
      Glory here, Diggers all!

Written 1649, published 1894

The winter's past, the springtime now appears[1]

The winter's past, the springtime now appears:
> Begone, thou kingly tyrant, with all thy cavaliers!
Thy day is past, and sure thou dost appear
> To be the bondsman's son, and not the freeborn heir.

Published 1652

Thomas Fairfax, third Lord Fairfax of Cameron (1612–1671)

A PROFESSIONAL SOLDIER who learned his trade in France and the Low Countries, Fairfax fought for Charles I in the Bishops' Wars against the Scots and was knighted for his service in January 1641. But when Civil War was declared in 1642 he changed sides, joining the Parliamentarian forces in Yorkshire: as principal commander he was responsible for their most resounding victories. Despite having a smaller army than the Royalists, Fairfax drove Charles's men from Leeds and led a daring attack on Wakefield. He engineered the destruction of Royalist power in the north, culminating with victory at Marston Moor in July 1644. At the age of thirty-two, he was appointed commander in chief of the New Model Army, in which capacity he was responsible for victory at Naseby in June 1645. In May 1648 he led the Parliamentary forces against Royalists in the south, pursuing them to Colchester where he laid siege to the city over seventy-five days, during which time Milton addressed a sonnet to him (see p. 138). Fairfax opposed execution of the king, and attempted to persuade his colleagues to abandon or delay it—efforts he continued until the moment of Charles's beheading.

---

1. When Winstanley first published this poem, it was preceded by the following comment: "And many other oppressions did the kingly government bring upon the people, as you may read at large in Samuel." Winstanley then proceeds to promote commonwealth government on the grounds that it avoids "buying and selling; and thereby becomes a man of peace, and the restorer of ancient peace and freedom" (*The Law of Freedom* 1652, p. 29).

His lament for the "fatal day" of January 30, 1649, is deeply felt. Afterward he took responsibility for suppressing Leveler mutinies in the army, executing all ringleaders. Refusing to invade Scotland, he retired in June 1650 to Nun Appleton in Yorkshire with his family, engaging Andrew Marvell (p. 181) as tutor to his twelve-year-old daughter Mary.

On the Fatal Day, 30 January 1649

Oh let that day from time be blotted quite
And let belief of 't in next age be waived   *abandoned*
In deepest silence th' act concealed might,
So that the kingdom's credit might be saved;
But if the power divine permitted this,
His will's the law, and ours must acquiesce.

Curae loquuntur leves; ingentes stupent.[1]

Written January 30, 1649, published 1909

Upon the New Building at Appleton

Think not, oh man that dwells herein,
This house a stay, but as an inn
Which for convenience fitly stands
In way to one not made with hands;
But if a time here thou take rest,
Yet think eternity's the best.

Written 1650, published 1909

---

1. Slight griefs make us talk, great ones make us dumb.

Shortness of Life

In rosy morn I saw Aurora red,
But when the sun his beams had fully spread
She vanished; I saw a frost and then dew
Twixt time so short as scarce a time I knew.
This stranger seemed when in more raised thought
I saw Death come—how soon a life he'd caught!—
Where, in the turning of an eye, he'd done
Far speedier execution than the sun.

Published 1909

James Graham, first Marquess of Montrose (1612–1650)

INTREPID, RECKLESS, DETERMINED—such adjectives hardly do justice to one of the most resourceful and swashbuckling of Charles's Cavaliers. He was educated at the University of St. Andrews and after meeting Charles I in 1636 turned against him, joining the Covenanter opposition for which he commanded forces in northeast Scotland. In July 1639 he met Charles again, this time as part of a delegation sent to negotiate at Berwick, and at that point changed allegiance, entering into a secret correspondence with him. He thereafter spied for Charles, only to be caught and imprisoned in June 1641. On release, he joined the king in England and in February 1644 was appointed lieutenant general. Created marquess in May, he returned to Scotland in charge of his own army, which won major victories against forces larger than his own until it seemed he had won Scotland for the king. In May 1645 he informed Charles (now on the verge of defeat in England) he could find refuge in Scotland, but it was not to be: Graham's army was soon routed. After the king's execution, Graham attempted to engineer restoration of the exiled Charles II, who appointed him Lord High Admiral of Scotland. Graham found support in Norway, occupied the Orkneys, and traveled south, but his army was attacked and he was taken prisoner. He was carted through the streets of Edinburgh, hanged for three hours, his head displayed on the Old Tolbooth, and his limbs hacked off and displayed in towns across Scotland.

On the Faithlessness and Venality of the Times

Unhappy is the man
    In whose breast is confined
The sorrows and distresses all
    Of an afflicted mind.

The extremity is great,
    He dies if he conceal,
The world's so void of secret friends,
    Betrayed if he reveal.

Then break, afflicted hearts,
    And live not in these days;
When all prove merchants of their faith,
    None trusts what other says.

For when the sun doth shine,
    Then shadows do appear;
But when the sun doth hide his face
    They with the sun retire.

Some friends as shadows are,
    And fortune as the sun;
They never proffer any help
    Till fortune first begin.

But if in any case
    Fortune shall first decay,
Then they, as shadows of the sun,
    With fortune run away.

Published 1706

Can little beasts with lions roar

Can little beasts with lions roar
And little birds with eagles soar?
Can shallow streams command the seas
And little ants the humming bees?
No, no, no, no, it is not meet
The head should stoop unto the feet.

Written possibly 1642, published 1848

Upon the Death of Charles I[1]

Great, good and just! could I but rate   *compare the extent of*
My griefs to thy too-rigid fate,
I'd weep the world in such a strain
As it would once deluge again!
But since thy loud-tongued blood demands supplies
More from Briareus' hands than Argus' eyes,[2]
I'll tune thy elegies to trumpet sounds
And write thy epitaph in blood and wounds.

Written c. February 1649, published 1650

On Hearing What Was His Sentence[1]

Let them bestow on every airth[2] a limb,
Open all my veins that I may swim

---

1. Early texts report that Montrose wrote this poem with the point of his sword.
2. Briareus was a creature in Greek myth with fifty heads and one hundred hands; Argus was a giant with one hundred eyes.

On Hearing What Was His Sentence
1. Editorial titles for this poem include "Verses wrote by the Marquis of Montrose with the point of a diamond upon the glass window of his prison after receiving his sentence."
2. airth] point of the compass.

To thee, my savior, in that crimson lake;
Then place my parboiled head upon a stake—
Scatter my ashes, throw them in the air!
Lord (since thou know'st where all these atoms are),
I'm hopeful, once thou'lt recollect my dust,   *reassemble*
And confident thou'lt raise me with the just.

Written 20 May 1650, published 1711

Anne Bradstreet (1612/1613–1672)

ONE GLANCE AT the poets who surround Anne Bradstreet in this volume should be sufficient to indicate what she and her husband, Simon, were fleeing when they set sail from Southampton on John Winthrop's flagship, the *Arabella*, for New England, in March 1630. The Bradstreets came from Puritan families and were driven abroad by tensions generated by the Catholicizing influence of a king who had married a Catholic Princess (Henrietta Maria)—tensions that led to Civil War. The price of exile was high: many died on the voyage, and others died of disease in America. But the Bradstreets were lucky; they raised eight children, and Simon was successful in business. Bradstreet's "A Dialogue Between Old England and New" offers her analysis of the times, though the poem is untypical. Her life in seventeenth-century Massachusetts revolved around domestic concerns, the principal subject of her verse. When she published *The Tenth Muse Lately Sprung Up in America* (1650), she became the first woman and New Englander to publish an original collection of poems. She died of consumption in Andover, Massachusetts, on September 16, 1672.

A Dialogue Between Old England and New (extracts)

NEW ENGLAND

Alas, dear mother, fairest Queen and best,
With honor, wealth, and peace, happy and blessed,
What ails thee? Hang thy head and cross thine arms,
And sit in the dust to sigh these sad alarms?
What deluge of new woes thus overwhelm
The glories of thy ever-famous realm?
What means this wailing tone, this mournful guise?
Ah, tell thy daughter, she may sympathize. . . .

OLD ENGLAND

Before I tell the effect, I'll show the cause
Which are my sins—the breach of sacred laws:
Idolatory supplanter of a nation
With foolish superstitious adoration
Are liked and countenanced by men of might;
The Gospel trodden down and hath no right;
Church Offices were sold and bought for gain
(That pope had hope to find Rome here again);
For oaths and blasphemies, did ever ear
From Beelzebub himself such language hear?
What scorning of the saints of the most high?
What injuries did daily on them lie?
What false reports, what nicknames did they take,
Not for their own but for their master's sake?
And thou, poor soul, wert jeered among the rest,
Thy flying for the truth was made a jest;   *reaching*
For Sabbath breaking, and for drunkenness,
Did ever land profaneness more express?
From crying blood yet cleansed am not I—
Martyrs and others, dying causelessly. . . .
Well, to the matter then, there's grown of late
'Twixt King and Peers a question of state:
Which is the chief—the law or else the king?

One said, "It's he"; the other, "No such thing!"
'Tis said, my better part in Parliament
To ease my groaning land, showed their intent
To crush the proud and right to each man deal,
To help the Church and stay the commonweal. . . .
Next the militia, they urged sore—
This was denied (I need not say wherefore).
The King displeased at York,[1] himself absents,
They humbly beg return, show their intents;
The writing, printing, posting to and fro
Shows all was done, I'll therefore let it go.
But now I come to speak of my disaster:
Contention grown 'twixt subjects and their master.
 They worded it so long they fell to blows,[2]
That thousands lay on heaps—here bleeds my woes:
I that no wars so many years have known
Am now destroyed and slaughtered by mine own;
But could the field alone this strife decide,
One battle two or three I might abide;
But these may be beginnings of more woe—
Who knows, but this may be my overthrow!
Oh, pity me in this sad perturbation,
My plundered towns, my houses' devastation,
My weeping virgins and my young men slain,
My wealthy trading fallen, my dearth of grain,
The seedtimes come, but ploughman hath no hope
Because he knows not who shall in[3] his crop;
The poor they want their pay, their children bread,
Their woeful mothers' tears unpitied.
If any pity in thy heart remain,
Or any childlike love thou dost retain,
For my relief, do what there lies in thee,
And recompense that good I've done to thee.

---

1. Charles I moved his court to York in April 1642.
2. Bradstreet may be referring to the Battle of Edgehill, the first of the Civil War in October 1642.
3. in] harvest, reap (verb).

NEW ENGLAND

Dear mother, cease complaints and wipe your eyes,
Shake off your dust—cheer up and now arise;
You are my mother, nurse, and I your flesh,
Your sunken bowels gladly would refresh;
Your griefs I pity but soon hope to see
Out of your troubles much good fruit to be:
To see those latter days of hoped-for good,
Though now beclouded all with tears and blood.
After dark popery the day did clear,
But now the Sun in's brightness shall appear. . . .
These are the days the Church's foes to crush,
To root out popelings[4] head, tail, branch and rush;
Let's bring Baal's vestments[5] forth to make a fire—
Their miters, surplices, and all their tire,   *accoutrements*
Copes, rochets,[6] croziers, and such empty trash,
And let their names consume, but let the flash
Light Christendom, and all the world to see
We hate Rome's whore, with all her trumpery!

Written 1642, published 1650

Sir Roger L'Estrange (1616–1704)

THOUGH NOT THE best-known author of this period, L'Estrange was one of
the most prolific, having published over six million words during the Resto-
ration period alone. He came of age in time to fight in the first Bishops' War
against the Scots, and then on the Royalist side at Newark and Edgehill. In
August 1643 he took part in the seizure of King's Lynn, held by the Royal-

---

4. popelings] Roman Catholics.
5. Baal's vestments] garments worn by Catholic priests.
6. rochets] ecclesiastical vestments.

ists until September 19. Determined to regain the town one way or another, L'Estrange was authorized by the king to use bribery, but was betrayed by an accomplice, arrested in a tavern while in his slippers, and thrown into jail. Uncertain of his fate, he composed "Loyalty Confined," which declares its author's commitment to the king. On December 28, 1644, a court-martial in London sentenced L'Estrange to death for spying, a judgment challenged by Charles I, Prince Rupert, and the House of Lords. He spent the next three years in Newgate Prison, fearing his reprieve to be provisional, believing execution might come at any moment. In fact, he would live another six decades. He absconded from Newgate early in 1648, in time to take part in the Kentish uprising in May. When that failed, he fled to the Continent, returning to London in 1653. After the Restoration he became a press regulator, monitoring publications for seditious material and controlling a network of spies and informants to hunt down regicides. He also discovered his vocation as journalist, translator, and pamphleteer, writing eloquently in *The Observator* (1681–1687), the most powerful organ of Tory propaganda at the time. His fortunes changed again with the Glorious Revolution, when he was jailed as a known Jacobite. It had been a colorful career: who else of this period could claim to be renowned as a composer and player of the bass viol; to have denounced Milton as a "villainous leading incendiary," and been condemned by Bunyan as "Mr Filth"?

Loyalty Confined[1]

Beat on, proud billows, Boreas[2] blow!
    Swell, curled waves, high as Jove's roof!
   Your incivility doth show
    That innocence is tempest-proof;
Though surly Nereus[3] frown, my thoughts are calm;
Then strike, affliction, for thy wounds are balm!

---

1. The original title of this poem is "The Liberty of the Imprisoned Royalist"; it was composed in the prison at King's Lynn.
2. Boreas] the north wind.
3. Nereus] the sea.

That which the world miscalls a jail
    A private closet is to me,
  Whilst a good conscience is my bail
    And innocence my liberty:
Locks, bars, and solitude, together met,
Make me no prisoner but an anchorite.[4]

I, while I wished to be retired,
    Into this private room was turned,
  As if their wisdoms had conspired
    The salamander should be burned;
Or, like those sophists who would drown a fish,
So I am condemned to suffer what I wish.

The cynic hugs his poverty,[5]
    The pelican her wilderness,[6]
  And 'tis the Indian's pride to be
    Naked on frozen Caucasus;
Contentment cannot smart, stoics we see
Make torments easy to their apathy.[7]

These manacles upon my arm
    I, as my mistress's favors, wear;
  And for to keep my ankles warm
    I have some iron shackles there;
These walls are but my garrison; this cell
(Which men call jail) doth prove my citadel.

So he that struck at Jason's life,
    Thinking he had his purpose sure,
  By a malicious, friendly knife
    Did only wound him to a cure;

---

4. anchorite] hermit.
5. The cynic hugs his poverty] In ancient Greece, the cynics were a philosophical sect famed for their dislike of wealth and worldly comforts.
6. The pelican her wilderness] a reference to Psalm 102:6: "I am like a pelican of the wilderness."
7. stoics . . . easy to their apathy] i.e., stoicism makes us insensible to physical discomfort.

Malice I see wants wit, for what is meant
Mischief ofttimes proves favor by the event.

I'm in this cabinet locked up
    Like some high-prized margarite,[8]
  Or like the great mogul or pope
    Am cloistered up from public sight:
Retirement is a piece of majesty,
And thus, proud sultan, I'm as great as thee.

Here sin for want of food must starve
    Where tempting objects are not seen,
  And these strong walls do only serve
    To keep vice out and keep me in;
Malice of late's grown charitable sure—
I'm not committed but I'm kept secure.

When once my prince affliction hath,
    Prosperity doth treason seem,
  And for to smooth so rough a path
    I can learn patience from him;
Now not to suffer shows no loyal heart—
When kings want ease, subjects must learn to smart.

Have you not seen the nightingale,
    A pilgrim cooped into a cage?
  How doth she chant her wonted tale
    In that, her narrow hermitage?
Even then her charming melody doth prove
That all her bars are trees, her cage a grove.

My soul is free as the ambient air
    Although my baser part's immured,
  Whilst loyal thoughts do still repair
    To accompany my solitude;

---

8. margarite] precious stone.

And though immured, yet I can chirp and sing:
Disgrace to rebels is glory to my king.

What though I cannot see my king
    Either in his person or his coin,
  Yet contemplation is a thing
    That renders what I have not, mine:
My king from me what adamant can part,
Whom I do wear engraven on my heart?

I am that bird whom they combine
    Thus to deprive of liberty,
  But though they do my corpse confine,
    Yet maugre hate, my soul is free: *in spite of*
Although rebellion does my body bind,
My king can only captivate my mind.

Written December 1644, published 1647

Richard Lovelace (1617–1657)

BORN INTO A military family, Lovelace took his MA at Oxford where he composed his first play and encountered Charles I and Henrietta Maria; at that period he was, wrote one witness, "the most amiable and beautiful person that eye ever beheld." Lovelace fought in the two Bishops' Wars of 1639–40 between England and Scotland, and loyalty to the king prompted him to take the helm in an enterprise that was to spark the Civil War: in April 1642 he led sympathizers in Kent on a march to London to deliver a Royalist petition to Parliament. This led to a seven-week spell in prison where Lovelace probably wrote the first two poems included here. By the time of his release, the Civil War had begun. Though he took no active part, he was imprisoned in 1648, to detain him from protests relating to the king's impending execution (on January 30, 1649). During confinement he prepared *Lucasta* for the press, containing poems composed during the war, published in June 1649. By the time of his release, the king was dead, and his own fortunes were in tatters. Depressed, ill, and penniless, he died in lodgings in Gunpowder Alley, Shoe Lane, London, in 1657.

To Althea From Prison

When Love with unconfinéd wings
    Hovers within my gates,
And my divine Althea brings
    To whisper at the grates;
When I lie tangled in her hair
    And fettered to her eye,
The gods that wanton in the air
    Know no such liberty.

When flowing cups run swiftly round
    With no allaying Thames,   *diluting*
Our careless heads with roses bound,
    Our hearts with loyal flames;
When thirsty grief in wine we steep,   *soak*
    When healths and draughts go free,
Fishes that tipple in the deep
    Know no such liberty.

When like committed linnets I   *imprisoned*
    With shriller throat shall sing
The sweetness, mercy, majesty
    And glories of my King;
When I shall voice aloud how good
    He is, how great should be,
Enlargéd winds that curl the flood   *liberated*
    Know no such liberty.

Stone walls do not a prison make
    Nor iron bars a cage;
Minds innocent and quiet take

That for an hermitage;
   If I have freedom in my love
      And in my soul am free,
   Angels alone, that soar above,
      Enjoy such liberty.

Written c. 1642, published June 1649

To Lucasta From Prison

Long in thy shackles, Liberty,
   I ask not from these walls, but thee;
Left for a while another's bride
   To fancy all the world beside.

Yet ere I do begin to love,
   See how I all my objects prove;
Then my free soul to that confine,
   'Twere possible I might call mine.

First I would be in love with Peace,
   And her rich swelling breasts increase;
But how, alas, how may that be,
   Despising Earth, she will love me?

Fain would I be in love with War,
   As my dear just avenging star;
But War is loved so everywhere,
   Even he disdains a lodging here.

Thee and thy wounds I would bemoan,
   Fair thorough-shot Religion;
But he lives only that kills thee,
   And whoso binds thy hands is free.

I would love a Parliament
    As a main prop from Heaven sent;
But ah, who's he that would be wedded
    To the fairest body that's beheaded?

Next would I court my Liberty
    And then my birthright, Property;
But can that be, when it is known
    There's nothing you can call your own?

A Reformation I would have,
    As for our griefs a sovereign salve—
That is, a cleansing of each wheel
    Of state, that yet some rust doth feel.

But not a Reformation so,
    As to reform were to o'erthrow;
Like watches by unskilful men
    Disjointed and set ill again.

The public faith I would adore
    But she is bankrupt of her store;
Nor how to trust her can I see,
    For she that cozens all, must me.

Since then none of these can be
    Fit objects for my love and me;
What then remains but the only spring
    Of all our loves and joys?—the KING.

He who being the whole ball
    Of day[1] on earth, lends it to all;
When seeking to eclipse his right,
    Blinded, we stand in our own light.

---

1. ball / Of day] the sun.

And now an universal mist
    Of error is spread o'er each breast
With such a fury edged as is
    Not found in the inward of the abyss.

Oh, from thy glorious starry wain
    Dispense on me one sacred beam
To light me where I soon may see
    How to serve you, and you trust me!

Published June 1649

To Lucasta, Going to the Wars

Tell me not, sweet, I am unkind,
    That from the nunnery
Of thy chaste breast and quiet mind
    To war and arms I fly.

True, a new mistress now I chase,
    The first foe in the field;
And with a stronger faith embrace
    A sword, a horse, a shield.

Yet this inconstancy is such
    As you too shall adore;
I could not love thee, dear, so much,
    Loved I not honour more.

Published June 1649

Sing out, pent souls, sing cheerfully!

I
Sing out, pent souls, sing cheerfully!
Care shackles you in liberty;
Mirth frees you in captivity:
   Would you double fetters add?
    Else why so sad?

Chorus
Besides your pinioned arms you'll find
Grief too can manacle the mind.

II
Live then prisoners uncontrolled;
Drink o' th' strong, the rich, the old
Till wine too hath your wits in hold;
   Then if still your jollity
    And throats are free,

Chorus
Triumph in your bonds and pains
And dance to the music of your chains!

      Written c. 1648, published June 1649

Sonnet

Depose your finger of that ring
 And crown mine with't awhile
Now I restor't. Pray, does it bring
 Back with it more of soil,
Or shines it not as innocent,
As honest, as before 'twas lent?

So then enrich me with that treasure,
   'Twill but increase your store,
And please me, fair one, with that pleasure
   Must please you still the more:
Not to save others is a curse
The blackest, when y'are ne'er the worse.

Published June 1649

Abraham Cowley (1618–1667)

BOTANIST, STUDENT OF medicine, pamphleteer, spy, and dramatist, Cowley was famous enough in his own time to be given a monument next to Chaucer and Spenser in Westminster Abbey, and his poems remained a staple of the canon well into the nineteenth century. When Civil War began he left Cambridge for Oxford (a Royalist stronghold), where he hoped to write an epic on Charles's victory over the Parliamentarians; it was not to be. The Royalist defeat at Newbury in September 1643 brought news of the death in battle of his friend Lucius Cary, Viscount Falkland. It was a blow—on a personal level and a creative one. Cowley struggled to continue but by the time he reached a commemoration of Falkland, he found it hard to maintain the optimism with which he had begun, and his tone shifted from the heroic manner of earlier passages to that of elegy. He put the manuscript aside and made no attempt to publish it during his lifetime. Exiled to France with the court of Henrietta Maria, Cowley worked as secret agent, carrying messages between members of the Royalist party. He returned to England in 1654 and was arrested the following year. While in prison he prepared his *Poems* (1656) for publication; on release he retired to Oxford to pursue his study of botany.

The Civil War

BOOK III[1] (EXTRACTS)

The cannon next their message 'gan to say—
On came the dreadful business of the day.
Here with sharp neighs the spriteful horses sound
And with proud tramplings beat the putrid ground.   *crumbling*
The drums' grave voice and sullen noise of guns
With the shrill trumpets' brighter accent runs
(A dismal consort!) through the trembling air
Whilst groans of wounded men the burden bear.
Through dust and smoke (that day's untimely night)
The powder's nimble flames and restless light
Of glittering swords amaze and fright the eyes,
So through black storms the winged lightning flies!
Death in all shapes and in all habits dressed
(Such was his sportful rage) the field possessed.
Could nought on earth at once afford the sight,
Variety so great without delight:
No place but saw some unexpected wound,
No part of man but some wild bullet found,
Uncertain fate o'er all the field did range—
Here strange deaths seen, and there escapes as strange.
More equally no fight did ere dispense
The acts of fortune or of providence.
At last bright victory over Charles his head
Thrust forth some beams—the clouds before it fled.
We forced the enclosures and the hill we won;
Ah, how much sweat and blood did down it run! . . .

Good God! What other kind of men were those
Heaven for itself from out our army chose?
Placed above these by virtue higher far
Than they above the beasts by nature are.

---

1. This is the final part of the poem, describing the Battle of Newbury on September 20, 1643.

Fielding and Morgan[2]—these were men indeed!
Ye earthless spirits who for your country bleed,
This small reward of your vast merits take
And would my verse were nobler for your sake!
Nor did the rash and heedless cannon there
Thy youth, birth, fortune and much virtue spare,
Excellent Spencer,[3] in thy bloom of day,
From all the joys of life thou art snatched away.
No more must thou behold the sun's dear light,
No more thy brighter wife must bless thy sight,
No more must mankind thine high virtues see—
Thy very tomb is robbed of part of thee!
So a young beauteous palm or cedar lies
Struck by bruit thunder from the parted skies;
With one loud blow by heaven's artillery given,
The root's plucked up and trunk deformedly riven.
Much to be wept by all the nymphs around,
Blasted it lies and torn on mother ground.
The great Carnarvon[4] too, that soul of might
(See how around the soldiers weep and fight)
Mortally wounded on the plain does lie:
His friends stand weeping, and Death smiling by. . . .
An eastern wind from Newbury rushing came:
It sighed, methought, it sighed out Falkland's name;[5]
Falkland, methought, the hills all echoed round,
Falkland, methought, each bird did sadly sound.
A muse stood by me and just then I writ

2. Colonel Edward Fielding and Colonel Thomas Morgan, Royalist officers killed at Newbury.
3. Henry Spencer, Earl of Sunderland, was buried on the battlefield, perhaps because his body was so badly mangled, his heart having been cut out and taken for burial in the family vault at Althorp.
4. Robert Dormer, Earl of Carnarvon, was run through with a sword at Newbury and died an hour later.
5. Lucius Cary, Viscount Falkland, was killed by a stray bullet early in the battle.

My King's great acts in verses not unfit.
The troubled muse fell shapeless into air—
Instead of ink dropped from my pen a tear.
Oh, 'tis a deadly truth: Falkland is slain!
His noble blood all dyes the accursed plain.

      Had Essex and his whole ungodly host,
Had all the Puritan name that day been lost
Yet would our loss too, rightly understood,
Cost us as much in tears as them in blood.
Men of all vices, all mixed sins we slew,
But they the man in whom all virtues grew.
They're gainers then, for in these frantic days
They may with ease armies as wicked raise,
But something like a miracle must be shown
If ever we recruit his loss alone.
We slew a rout which nature framed so ill
That they had nothing of a soul but will;
They killed a man whose knowledge did contain
All that the apple promised us in vain.
The farthest lands of art did he invade
And widestretched nature was his triumph made—
What unjust weights into this scale were hurled?
We gained a field, and lost in him a world. . . .

Written September/October 1643, published 1973

Lucy Hutchinson (1620–1681)

Lucy Apsley was born in the Tower of London, where her father was lieutenant of the Tower. She was precociously intellectual, reading and listening to sermons by the age of four, eventually gaining competence at Latin, Greek, Hebrew, and French. In 1638 she married John Hutchinson, a student of theology with an estate in Owthorpe, Nottinghamshire, to which they moved in October 1641. At the outbreak of war he enlisted on the Parliamentary side, and was appointed governor of Nottingham and its castle in 1643. Three years later he assumed a seat in the Long Parliament and after the war was one of the judges who presided over trial of the king. During the Interregnum the Hutchinsons retired from public life, refusing to cooperate with the Protectorate; instead they remodeled their estate and house. At the Restoration, Hutchinson was hunted down as a regicide, his being one of the signatures on Charles I's death warrant, but was spared a martyr's death thanks to a letter of repentance forged by his wife and sent to the Speaker of the House of Commons. Upon his release, Lucy urged him to flee the country but he refused; in 1663 he was rearrested for alleged involvement in a republican conspiracy and imprisoned in Sandown Castle, where he died on September 11 the following year. His death was a shattering experience for Lucy, and her grief produced a series of remarkable elegies, of which two are presented here. David Norbrook, the foremost of Hutchinson's editors, describes the first of them, composed as an epitaph, as "an astonishingly bold piece of oppositional verse"; "Upon two pictures" condemns those beneficiaries of Hutchinson's mercy who later betrayed him. Lucy subsequently wrote her husband's biography, which remains one of the most readable and engaging histories of the Civil War; she describes Charles I as having "nothing of faith or truth, justice or generosity in him; he was the most obstinate person in his self-will that ever was, and so bent upon being an absolute uncontrollable sovereign that he was resolved either to be such a king or none." She is equally skeptical of Henrietta Maria, for her Catholic loyalties: "This lady being by her own priests affected with the meritoriousness of advancing her own religion, whose principle it is to subvert all other, applied that way her great wit and parts." In later years, Hutchinson became a student of Calvinism (as her late husband had been), and criticized the atheism made fashionable by the Earl of Rochester (see p. 228), son of her cousin, Anne Wilmot. She died at Owthorpe in October 1681. Over the last two decades she has become one of the best-known women writers of her time, more widely studied than ever.

Epitaph on Colonel John Hutchinson

Ye sons of England, whose unquenched flame
Of pious love may yet that title claim,

Let not your rash feet on that marble tread
Before you have its sad inscription read:
Behold, it weeps! Do not these tears presage
Descending showers on this prodigious age,
Where only rocks for innocent bloodshed mourn,
While human hearts to flinty quarries turn?
Now read: this stone doth close up the dark cave
Where Liberty sleeps in her champion's grave.

Written shortly after September 1664, published 1997

Upon Two Pictures: One, a Gallant Man Dressed up in Armor; the Other, the Same Honorable Person Looking Through a Prison Grate and Leaning on a Bible[1]

The table you here see presents
A true-born prince's lineaments.
No vulgar hands set on his crown,
Nor could they cast his empire down
Whose soul stooped not to servile things,
But triumphed over foiled kings.
Such arms he had, but his defence
Firm courage was, and innocence;
Such killing weapons too he wore—
Not to destroy but to restore;
Which done, he threw the sword away,
Embracing those who prostrate lay.
      But oh, ungrateful, treacherous age!
Those whom he saved from tyrant's rage
To tyrant's rage abandoned him
That did their liberties redeem.
The foes he to protection took,
Him, when he needed it, forsook
And basely hunted to the grave

---

1. Both pictures, assuming they existed, depicted Colonel John Hutchinson.

Whose crime was that he them did save.
But lest your weak soul be dismayed
At virtue hunted and betrayed,
See him in prison ne'er so great
As when his false aides did retreat;
His courage then most brightly shone
When it was left to conquer all alone,
Who crushed his foes by his brave fall
And triumphed in his funeral.

Written after September 1664, published 1997

Henry Vaughan (1621–1695)

VAUGHAN WAS BORN in Newton by Usk, Brecknockshire, Wales, to a family that honored Church and King—loyalties to which he always remained true. After Jesus College, Oxford, he was sent to London to pursue the law. Shortly after his arrival there in 1640, Parliament set about the task of executing the king's political friends, including the Earl of Stafford and Archbishop Laud. Vaughan must have been a horrified observer of these events; by the time Charles I raised the royal standard at Nottingham and called upon loyal subjects for support, Vaughan was twenty-one. For the first few years of the Civil War he worked as clerk to Judge Sir Marmaduke Lloyd, but his energies were soon required on the battlefield. He was a combatant at the Battle of Rowton Heath on September 24, 1645, alongside his twin brother Thomas, who was taken prisoner by the Parliamentary forces under Sydnam Poyntz. Henry was among those who managed to evade capture, withdrawing to Beeston Castle in Cheshire, where the Royalists were under siege. They held out until November, but were forced to surrender for lack of supplies. Royalist resistance collapsed in Wales with the taking of Raglan Castle in February 1646, and Vaughan retired from active service. After the Royalist defeat, he was pained by the eviction from their livings of clergymen who were friends— Matthew Herbert (his former schoolmaster), Thomas Powell of Cantref, and Thomas Lewes, rector of Llanfigan. He may have seen the Second Civil War in Wales during the spring and summer of 1648, led by an alliance of Royalists, Presbyterians, and disgruntled Parliamentarians, as a second chance, but was deeply grieved by the death of his younger brother William, a casualty of the war, in July, and the execution of Charles I the following year. The cumulative effect of these successive losses is filtered through his postwar masterpiece, *Silex Scintillans* (1650, enlarged edition 1655), which contains, as Alan Rudrum observes, "a good deal of evidence . . . that the public events of the Second Civil War and its aftermath were traumatic for [Vaughan]." Vaughan began to practice as a medical doctor in the 1650s, and that seems to have remained his livelihood in subsequent years. Though he would publish no poetry after the second edition of *Silex*, he is now ranked among the foremost of the "metaphysical poets," the best of whose work anticipates that of the Romantics some 150 years later.

An Elegy on the Death of Mr. RW, Slain in the Late Unfortunate Differences at Rowton Heath, Near Chester, 1645[1]

I am confirmed, and so much wing is given
To my wild thoughts that they dare strike at heaven.
A full year's grief I struggled with, and stood
Still on my sandy hopes' uncertain good;
So loath was I to yield to all those fears,
I still opposed thee and denied my tears.
But thou art gone, and the untimely loss,
Like that one day, hath made all others cross.
Have you seen on some river's flowery brow
A well-built elm or stately cedar grow,
Whose curled tops gilt with the morning ray
Beckoned the sun and whispered to the day?—
When, unexpected from the angry north,
A fatal sullen whirlwind sallies forth

---

1. As the poem begins, a year after the battle, Vaughan accepts that his friend must be dead, though he had hoped that, in the chaos, RW had survived. The battle of Rowton Heath took place on September 24, 1645. Vaughan fought on the Royalist side of which six hundred men were killed and nine hundred injured; the identity of Mr. RW is unknown.

And with a full-mouthed blast rends from the ground
The shady twins[2] which, rushing, scatter round
Their sighing leaves whilst, overborne with strength,
Their trembling heads bow to a prostrate length:
So forced fell he; so immaturely death   *prematurely*
Stifled his able heart and active breath.
The world scarce knew him yet, his early soul
Had but new-broke her day and rather stole
A sight than gave one, as if subtly she[3]
Would learn our stock, but hide his treasury.
His years (should time lay both his wings and glass
Unto his charge) could not be summed (alas!)
To a full score; though in so short a span
His riper thoughts had purchased more of man
Than all those worthless livers which yet quick
Have quite outgone their own arithmetic.
He seized perfections, and without a dull
And mossy gray possessed a solid skull[4]—
No crooked knowledge neither, nor did he
Wear the friend's name for ends and policy
And then lay it by, as those lost youths of the stage
Who only flourished for the play's short age
And then retired; like jewels in each part
He wore his friends, but chiefly at his heart.
          Nor was it only in this he did excel;
His equal valour could as much, as well.
He knew no fear but of his God, yet durst
No injury nor (as some have) e'er pursed
The sweat and tears of others, yet would be
More forward in a royal gallantry   *display*
Than all those vast pretenders,[5] which of late
Swelled in the ruins of their King and State.
He weaved not self-ends and the public good
Into one piece, nor with the people's blood

---

2. The shady twins] i.e., an elm and a cedar.
3. she] i.e., his soul.
4. skull] intelligence.
5. pretenders] probably Parliamentarians.

Filled his own veins; in all the doubtful way
Conscience and Honour ruled him. Oh, that day
When like the fathers in the fire and cloud
I missed thy face! I might in every crowd
See arms like thine, and men advance, but none
So near to lightning moved, nor so fell on.
      Have you observed how soon the nimble eye
Brings the object to conceit,[6] and doth so vie
Performance with the soul, that you would swear
The act and apprehension both lodged there?
Just so moved he: like shot his active hand
Drew blood ere well the foe could understand.
But here I lost him. Whether the last turn
Of thy few sands called on thy hasty urn,
Or some fierce rapid fate (hid from the eye)
Hath hurled thee prisoner to some distant sky[7]
I cannot tell, but that I do believe
Thy courage such as scorned a base reprieve.
Whatever 'twas, whether that day thy breath
Suffered a civil or the common death
(Which I do most suspect), and that I have
Failed in the glories of so known a grave,
Though thy loved ashes miss me, and mine eyes   *elude*
Had no acquaintance with thy exequies,   *funeral rites*
Nor at the last farewell, torn from thy sight
On the cold sheet have fixed a sad delight,
Yet whate'er pious hand (instead of mine)
Hath done this office to that dust of thine,
And till thou rise again from thy low bed
Lent a cheap pillow to thy quiet head,
Though but a private turf, it can do more
To keep thy name and memory in store
Than all those lordly fools which lock their bones
In the dumb piles of chested brass and stones.
Thou art rich in thy own fame, and needest not

---

6. Brings the object to conceit] comprehends the thing it perceives.
7. some distant sky] some far distant region of the country.

These marble frailties nor the gilded blot
Of posthume honours; there is not one sand
Sleeps o'er thy grave but can outbid that hand
And pencil too, so that of force we must
Confess their heaps show lesser than thy dust.
　　　　And, blessed soul, though this my sorrow can
Add nought to thy perfections, yet as man
Subject to envy, and the common fate,
It may redeem thee to a fairer date;
As some blind dial, when the day is done,
Can tell us at midnight there was a sun,
So these, perhaps, though much beneath thy fame,
May keep some weak remembrance of thy name,
And to the faith of better times commend
Thy loyal upright life, and gallant end.

　　　Nomen et arma locum servant, te, amice, nequivi
　　　Conspicere . . .[8]

　　　　　　　　　Written September 1646, published April 28, 1651

Misery[1]

Lord, bind me up, and let me lie
A prisoner to my liberty,
If such a state at all can be
As an impris'ment serving thee;
The wind, though gathered in thy fist,
Yet doth it blow still where it list,
And yet shouldst thou let go thy hold

---

8. Virgil, *Aeneid*, VI, 507–8: "Thy name and arms guard the place; thee, my friend, I could not see."
MISERY
1. This poem appeared in the first volume of Vaughan's *Silex Scintillans* (1650). The reference to "Action and blood" suggests it was composed during the Second Civil War in Wales, 1648.

Those gusts might quarrel and grow bold.
     As waters here, headlong and loose
The lower grounds still chase and choose,
Where spreading all the way they seek
And search out every hole and creek;
So my spilt thoughts winding from thee
Take the down-road to vanity
Where they all stray and strive, which shall
Find out the first and steepest fall;
I cheer their flow, giving supply
To what's already grown too high,
And having thus performed that part
Feed on those vomits of my heart.
I break the fence my own hands made
Then lay that trespass in the shade,
Some fig leaves still I do devise
As if thou hadst nor ears nor eyes.
Excess of friends, of words and wine
Take up my day, while thou dost shine
All unregarded, and thy book
Hath not so much as one poor look.
If thou steal in amid the mirth
And kindly tell me, "I am Earth,"
I shut thee out and let that slip,
Such music spoils good fellowship.
     Thus wretched I, and most unkind,
Exclude my dear God from my mind,
Exclude him thence, who of that cell
Would make a court, should he there dwell.
He goes, he yields, and troubled sore
His holy spirit grieves therefore,
The mighty God, the eternal King
Doth grieve for dust, and dust doth sing.
But I go on, haste to divest
Myself of reason, till oppressed
And buried in my surfeits I
Prove my own shame and misery.
Next day I call and cry for thee

Who shouldst not then come near to me,
But now it is thy servant's pleasure
Thou must (and dost) give him his measure.
      Thou dost, thou com'st, and in a shower
Of healing sweets thyself dost pour
Into my wounds, and now thy grace
(I know it well) fills all the place;
I sit with thee by this new light
And for that hour thou art my delight,
No man can more the world despise
Or thy great mercies better prize.
I school my eyes and strictly dwell
Within the circle of my cell,
That calm and silence are my joys
Which to thy peace are but mere noise.
At length I feel my head to ache,
My fingers itch and burn to take
Some new employment, I begin
To swell and foam and fret within.
    "The age, the present times are not
    To snudge in² and embrace a cot: *cottage*
    Action and blood now get the game;
    Disdain treads on the peaceful name.
    Who sits at home too bears a load
    Greater than those that gad abroad."³
Thus do I make thy gifts given me
The only quarrelers with thee:
I'd loose those knots thy hands did tie,
Then would go travel, fight or die.
Thousands of wild and waste infusions   *insinuations*
Like waves beat on my resolutions,
As flames about their fuel run
And work and wind till all be done;
So my fierce soul bustles about

2. *To snudge in*] to remain snug and quiet.
3. The italicized lines refer to the Second Civil War in Wales, which began with Royalist uprisings in March 1648. Vaughan's younger brother William was killed in July, probably from war wounds.

And never rests till all be out.
Thus wilded by a peevish heart   *maddened*
Which in thy music bears no part
I storm at thee, calling my peace
A lethargy, and mere disease;
Nay, those bright beams shot from thy eyes
To calm me in these mutinies
I style mere tempers which take place
At some set times, but are thy grace.

     Such is man's life, and such is mine
The worst of men, and yet still thine,
Still thine thou know'st, and if not so
Then give me over to my foe.
Yet since as easy 'tis for thee
To make man good, as bid him be,
And with one glance (could he that gain)
To look him out of all his pain,
Oh, send me from thy holy hill
So much of strength, as may fulfil
All thy delights (whate'er they be)
And sacred institutes in me;   *purposes*
Open my rocky heart, and fill
It with obedience to thy will,
Then seal it up, that as none see,
So none may enter there but thee.

     Oh hear, my God! Hear him, whose blood
Speaks more and better for my good!
Oh, let my cry come to thy throne!
My cry not poured with tears alone
(For tears alone are often foul)
But with the blood of all my soul,
With spirit-sighs and earnest groans,
Faithful and most repenting moans:
With these I cry and crying pine
Till thou both mend and make me thine.

Written 1648, published March 28, 1650

The Retreat

Happy those early days, when I
Shined in my angel-infancy!
Before I understood this place
Appointed for my second race,
Or taught my soul to fancy aught
But a white, celestial thought;
When yet I had not walked above
A mile or two from my first love,
And looking back, at that short space,
Could see a glimpse of his bright face;
When on some gilded cloud or flower
My gazing soul would dwell an hour,
And in those weaker glories spy
Some shadows of eternity;
Before I taught my tongue to wound
My conscience with a sinful sound,
Or had the black art to dispense
A several sin to every sense,
But felt through all this fleshly dress
Bright shoots of everlastingness.
    Oh, how I long to travel back,
And tread again that ancient track!
That I might once more reach that plain
Where first I left my glorious train;
From whence the enlightened spirit sees
That shady city of palm trees—
But ah, my soul with too much stay
Is drunk, and staggers in the way!
Some men a forward motion love,
But I by backward steps would move,
And when this dust falls to the urn,
In that state I came, return.

Published March 28, 1650

Andrew Marvell (1621–1678)

IT WAS A remarkable achievement for a man to make a successful career under Cromwell (which Marvell did, as Latin Secretary)—and then gain the trust of the newly restored Charles II, sufficient to claim the post of Russian ambassador and peace negotiator at conclusion of the Third Anglo-Dutch War. Marvell's swift-footedness is illustrated by his conduct when charged by the restored king with the task of hunting down former regicides: having directed official attention to a few token scapegoats, he managed to save the lives of many exiled Republicans and Protectorate officials. Had he been in the country during the Civil War, he would have fought on the Royalist side, but he was touring the Continent and did not return until 1647—in time to witness the strong anti-Parliamentarian ferment brewing in London and the Second Civil War that broke out in summer 1648. He was among those who elegized one of its Cavalier victims, Lord Francis Villiers; at this time, he also wrote a verse letter to another Cavalier, Richard Lovelace (see p. 160). Given Marvell's allegiances, the execution of Charles I would have been traumatic and, as Nigel Smith has argued, intense emotions inform "The Nymph Complaining for the Death of her Fawn": "Its veiled references to Parliamentary or Scottish soldiers who carry blood-guilt for the fawn's murder associate the poem with a strain of Royalist pastoral verse in which Charles I's martyrdom is painfully lamented." By 1650 Marvell was enough of a Parliamentarian to hail Cromwell's triumphant return from Ireland (where the populations of Drogheda and Wexford had been put to the sword) in the greatest political poem in the language, at the same time portraying the former king as a martyr (see p. 187 below). At around the time he finished the "Ode," Marvell moved to Nun Appleton in Yorkshire, having been engaged as tutor by Thomas Fairfax (see p. 148) for his twelve-year-old daughter, Mary; there in the summer of 1651 he composed *Upon Appleton House*, a meditation on the turmoil of recent years, which contains (besides much else) what sound like memories of the war: "the plain / Lies quilted o'er with bodies slain"—though it is worth remembering the entire English field army was gathered near Nun Appleton at Ripon as Marvell wrote, preparing to repel a Scottish invasion.

The turbulence of the times may explain why he is also author of one of the greatest retirement poems in English, "The Garden" (p. 200).

The Nymph Complaining for the Death of Her Fawn[1]

The wanton troopers riding by
Have shot my fawn and it will die.
Ungentle men! They cannot thrive
To kill thee. Thou ne'er didst alive
Them any harm; alas, nor could
Thy death yet do them any good.
I'm sure I never wished them ill,
Nor do I for all this, nor will.
But if my simple prayers may yet
Prevail with heaven to forget
Thy murder, I will join my tears
Rather than fail. But oh, my fears!
It cannot die so. Heaven's King
Keeps register of everything,
And nothing may we use in vain:
Even beasts must be with justice slain,
Else men are made their deodands.[2]
Though they should wash their guilty hands
In this warm lifeblood, which doth part
From thine, and wound me to the heart,
Yet could they not be clean: their stain   *guilt*
Is dyed in such a purple grain.
There is not such another in
The world to offer for their sin.
    Unconstant Sylvio (when yet   *unfaithful*
I had not found him counterfeit),
One morning (I remember well),
Tied in this silver chain and bell,

---

1. Nigel Smith conjectures this poem was composed shortly after the execution of Charles I in early 1649.
2. deodands] things to be forfeited or given to God.

Gave it to me: nay, and I know
What he said then, I'm sure I do;
Said he, "Look how your huntsman here
Hath taught a fawn to hunt his dear!"
But Sylvio soon had me beguiled.
This waxed tame, while he grew wild   *grew*
And quite regardless of my smart—
Left me his fawn, but took his heart.

     Thenceforth I set myself to play
My solitary time away
With this, and very well content,
Could so mine idle life have spent.
For it was full of sport, and light
Of foot and heart; and did invite
Me to its game. It seemed to bless
Itself in me. How could I less
Than love it? Oh, I cannot be
Unkind to a beast that loveth me.

     Had it lived long, I do not know
Whether it too might have done so
As Sylvio did; his gifts might be
Perhaps as false or more than he.
But I am sure, for aught that I
Could in so short a time espy,
Thy love was far more better than
The love of false and cruel men.

     With sweetest milk and sugar first
I it at mine own fingers nursed,
And as it grew, so every day
It waxed more white and sweet than they.
It had so sweet a breath! And oft
I blushed to see its foot more soft
And white—shall I say than my hand?—
Nay, any lady's of the land.

     It is a wondrous thing how fleet
'Twas on those little silver feet;
With what a pretty skipping grace
It oft would challenge me the race;
And when it had left me far away,

'Twould stay, and run again, and stay.
For it was nimbler much than hinds,
And trod as on the four winds.
        I have a garden of my own,
But so with roses overgrown
And lilies, that you would it guess
To be a little wilderness.
And all the springtime of the year
It only loved to be there.
Among the beds of lilies I
Have sought it oft, where it should lie—
Yet could not, till itself would rise,
Find it, although before mine eyes;
For in the flaxen lilies' shade
It like a bank of lilies laid.
Upon the roses it would feed
Until its lips ev'n seemed to bleed
And then to me 'twould boldly trip
And print those roses on my lip.
But all its chief delight was still
On roses thus itself to fill,
And its pure virgin limbs to fold
In whitest sheets of lilies cold.
Had it lived long, it would have been
Lilies without, roses within.
        Oh help, oh help! I see it faint,
And die as calmly as a saint.
See how it weeps! The tears do come
Sad, slowly dropping like a gum:
So weeps the wounded balsam; so
The holy frankincense doth flow.
The brotherless Heliades[3]
Melt in such amber tears as these.
        I in a golden vial will
Keep these two crystal tears and fill
It till it do o'erflow with mine,

---

3. The brotherless Heliades] The daughters of Helios (the sun) grieved at the death of their brother, Phaethon; the gods turned them into poplars and their tears into amber.

Then place it in Diana's shrine.
    Now my sweet fawn is vanished to
Whither the swans and turtles[4] go,
In fair Elysium to endure
With milk-white lambs and ermines pure.
Oh, do not run too fast, for I
Will but bespeak thy grave and die.
    First my unhappy statue shall
Be cut in marble, and withal
Let it be weeping too, but there
The engraver sure his art may spare,
For I so truly thee bemoan
That I shall weep though I be stone
Until my tears, still dropping, wear
My breast, themselves engraving there.
There at my feet shalt thou be laid,
Of purest alabaster made:
For I would have thine image be
White as I can, though not as thee.

Written early 1649, published January 1681

An Horatian Ode Upon Cromwell's Return From Ireland[1]

The forward youth that would appear
Must now forsake his muses dear,
    Nor in the shadows sing
    His numbers languishing.

---

4. turtles] turtledoves.

AN HORATIAN ODE UPON CROMWELL'S RETURN FROM IRELAND
1. After the execution of Charles I, during the summer of 1649, Cromwell led the New Model Army on a campaign in Ireland where he was victorious over the Catholic and Royalist alliance at the battle of Drogheda and Wexford (the entire populations of both towns being massacred in the process). He returned to a hero's welcome in London during which time he prepared for an invasion of Scotland in July. This poem was written during that period. Blair Worden has noted that it "records, as nothing else written during the puritan revolution does, the fundamental shift in English civilization which, when every reservation has been made, the middle of the seventeenth century brought about."

'Tis time to leave the books in dust
And oil the unused armor's rust,
    Removing from the wall
    The corslet² of the hall.

So restless Cromwell could not cease
In the inglorious arts of peace,
    But through adventurous war
    Urged his active star.

And like the three-forked lightning, first
Breaking the clouds where it was nursed,
    Did thorough his own side
    His fiery way divide.

(For 'tis all one to courage high,
The emulous or enemy;
    And with such to enclose
    Is more than to oppose.)

Then burning through the air he went
And palaces and temples rent;
    And Caesar's head at last
    Did through his laurels blast.

'Tis madness to resist or blame
The force of angry heaven's flame;
    And if we would speak true,
    Much to the man is due

Who, from his private gardens, where
He lived reserved and austere,
    As if his highest plot
    To plant the bergamot,

---

2. corslet] piece of armor protecting the body.

Could by industrious valour climb
To ruin the great work of time,
   And cast the kingdoms old
   Into another mould.

Though Justice against Fate complain
And plead the ancient rights in vain;
   But those do hold or break
   As men are strong or weak.

Nature, that hateth emptiness,
Allows of penetration less,
   And therefore must make room
   Where greater spirits come.

What field of all the Civil Wars
Where his were not the deepest scars?
   And Hampton[3] shows what part
   He had of wiser art,

Where, twining subtle fears with hope,
He wove a net of such a scope
   That Charles himself might chase
   To Carisbrooke's narrow case,

That thence the royal actor born
The tragic scaffold might adorn,
   While round the armed bands
   Did clap their bloody hands.

He nothing common did, or mean,
Upon that memorable scene,
   But with his keener eye
   The axe's edge did try;   *test*

---

3. Charles I stayed at Hampton Court Palace until he fled to Carisbrooke Castle on the Isle of Wight on November 11, 1647.

Nor called the gods with vulgar spite
To vindicate his helpless right,
    But bowed his comely head
    Down, as upon a bed.

This was that memorable hour
Which first assured the forced power.
    So when they did design
    The Capitol's first line,

A bleeding head where they begun
Did fright the architects to run;[4]
    And yet in that the State
    Foresaw its happy fate.

And now the Irish are ashamed
To see themselves in one year tamed:
    So much one man can do
    That does both act and know.

They can affirm his praises best,
And have, though overcome, confessed
    How good he is, how just,
    And fit for highest trust.

Nor yet grown stiffer with command,
But still in the Republic's hand—
    How fit he is to sway
    That can so well obey!

He to the Commons' feet presents
A kingdom for his first year's rents,
    And (what he may[5]) forbears
    His fame, to make it theirs;

---

4. Historians record how, when the Romans first built the Capitol, architects found a decapitated head.
5. what he may] insofar as he can.

And has his sword and spoils ungirt
To lay them at the public's skirt:
    So, when the falcon high
    Falls heavy from the sky,

She, having killed, no more doth search
But on the next green bough to perch
    Where, when he first does lure,
    The falconer has her sure.

What may not then our isle presume
While victory his crest does plume?
    What may not others fear
    If thus he crowns each year?

A Caesar he, erelong to Gaul,
To Italy an Hannibal,[6]
    And to all states not free
    Shall climacteric be.

The Pict no shelter now shall find   *Scot*
Within his parti-coloured mind,
    But from this valour sad
    Shrink underneath the plaid;

Happy, if in the tufted brake
The English hunter him mistake,
    Nor lay his hounds in near
    The Caledonian deer.

But thou, the war's and fortune's son,
March indefatigably on,
    And for the last effect
    Still keep the sword erect:

---

6. Hannibal invaded Italy in 218 BC.

Besides the force it has to fright
The spirits of the shady night,
   The same arts that did gain
   A power must it maintain.

Written June–July 1650, published January 1681

Upon Appleton House (extracts)

41

Oh thou, that dear and happy isle,
The garden of the world erewhile,
   Thou paradise of four seas
   Which Heaven planted us to please,
But, to exclude the world, did guard
With watery (if not flaming) sword;
What luckless apple did we taste
To make us mortal, and thee waste?

42

Unhappy! shall we never more
That sweet militia restore,
   When gardens only had their towers
   And all the garrisons were flowers;
When roses only arms might bear
And men did rosy garlands wear?
Tulips in several colours barred
Were then the Switzers of our guard.[1]

43

The gardener had the soldier's place
And his more gentle forts did trace;
   The nursery of all things green

---

1. Switzers of our guard] a reference to the black, yellow, and red uniform of the Swiss Guard, best known from those stationed at the Vatican since 1506.

Was then the only magazine;
The winter quarters were the stoves,
Where he the tender plants removes;
But war all this doth overgrow—
We ordnance plant and powder sow.   *artillery*

44

And yet there walks one² on the sod
Who, had it pleased him and God,
Might once have made our gardens spring
Fresh as his own and flourishing.
But he preferred to the Cinque Ports³
These five imaginary forts,
And in those half-dry trenches spanned
Power which the ocean might command.

45

For he did, with his utmost skill,
Ambition weed, but conscience till—
Conscience, that Heaven-nursed plant
Which most our earthly gardens want.
A prickling leaf it bears, and such
As that which shrinks at every touch,
But flowers eternal and divine
That in the crowns of saints do shine.

46

The sight does from these bastions ply,
The invisible artillery,
And at proud Cawood Castle⁴ seems

---

2. one] a reference to Thomas Fairfax, Marvell's employer, the greatest of the Civil War commanders on the Parliamentary side, who withdrew from public service when asked to invade Scotland.
3. Cinque Ports] the confederation of five ports and two ancient towns along the Kent and Sussex coastline, probably dating back to the eleventh century.
4. Even in Marvell's day, Cawood Castle was beginning to show its age. Two miles from Nun Appleton, it had been the palace of the archbishop of York but was dismantled after the Civil War. Today the only part of the original castle that survives is the gatehouse.

To point the battery of its beams,
As if it quarreled in the seat
The ambition of its prelate great;
But o'er the meads below it plays,
Or innocently seems to gaze.

47
And now to the abyss I pass
Of that unfathomable grass
Where men like grasshoppers appear
(But grasshoppers are giants there):
They, in their squeaking laugh, contemn
Us as we walk more low than them,
And, from the precipices tall
Of the green spires, to us do call.

48
To see men through this meadow dive,
We wonder how they rise alive
As, underwater, none does know
Whether he fall through it or go;
But as the mariners that sound
And show upon their lead the ground,
They bring up flowers so to be seen,
And prove they've at the bottom been.

49
No scene that turns with engines strange
Does oftener than these meadows change,
For when the sun the grass hath vexed,
The tawny mowers enter next
Who seem like Israelites to be,
Walking on foot through a green sea.
To them the grassy deeps divide,
And crowd a lane to either side.

50
With whistling scythe and elbow strong,
These massacre the grass along,

While one, unknowing, carves the rail⁵
Whose yet unfeathered quills her fail.
The edge all bloody from its breast
He draws, and does his stroke detest,
Fearing the flesh untimely mowed—
To him a fate as black forebode.

51

But bloody Thestylis that waits   *female peasant*
To bring the mowing camp their cates,   *food*
Greedy as kites has trussed it up
And forthwith means on it to sup,
When on another quick she lights
And cries, "He called us Israelites!
But now, to make his saying true,
Rails rain for quails, for manna, dew."

52

Unhappy birds! what does it boot
To build below the grass's root
When lowness is unsafe as height,
And chance o'ertakes what 'scapeth spite?
And now your orphan parents call
Sounds your untimely funeral;
Death-trumpets creak in such a note,
And 'tis the sourdine⁶ in their throat.

53

Or sooner hatch or higher build;
The mower now commands the field
In whose new traverse seemeth wrought
A camp of battle newly fought
Where, as the meads with hay, the plain
Lies quilted o'er with bodies slain;
The women that with forks it fling
Do represent the pillaging.

---

5. rail] a bird—the landrail or corncrake, which nests in a hollow in grassy land.
6. sourdine] muted trumpet.

54

And now the careless victors play,
Dancing the triumphs of the hay,
Where every mower's wholesome heat
Smells like an Alexander's sweat,
Their females fragrant as the mead
Which they in fairy circles tread.
When at their dance's end they kiss,
Their new-made hay not sweeter is.

55

When after this 'tis piled in cocks,
Like a calm sea it shows the rocks,
We wondering in the river near
How boats among them safely steer;
Or like the desert Memphis[7] sand
Short pyramids of hay do stand,
And such the Roman camps do rise
In hills for soldiers' obsequies.

56

This scene again withdrawing brings
A new and empty face of things;
A leveled space, as smooth and plain
As clothes for Lely[8] stretched to stain.
The world when first created sure
Was such a table rase and pure,
Or rather such is the Toril[9]
Ere the bulls enter at Madril.[10]

57

For to this naked equal flat
(Which Levelers[11] take pattern at),

---

7. Memphis] ancient city in Egypt, a World Heritage Site since 1979.
8. Sir Peter Lely (1618–1680) was the most prominent and successful of the artists who painted Charles II.
9. Toril] bullpen.
10. Madril] Madrid.
11. The Levelers believed in equality before the law and religious toleration; in summer

The villagers in common chase
Their cattle, which it closer raze;
And what below the scythe increased
Is pinched yet nearer by the beast
(Such in the painted world appeared
Davenant with the universal herd).[12]

58

They seem within the polished grass
A landscape drawn in looking-glass,
And shrunk in the huge pasture show
As spots, so shaped, on faces do—
Such fleas, ere they approach the eye,
In multiplying glasses lie.
They feed so wide, so slowly move,
As constellations do above. . . .

71

Thus I, easy philosopher,
Among the birds and trees confer,
And little now to make me, wants
Or of the fowls or of the plants;
Give me but wings as they, and I
Straight floating on the air shall fly,
Or turn me but, and you shall see
I was but an inverted tree.

72

Already I begin to call
In their most learned original;
And where I language want, my signs
The bird upon the bough divines;
And more attentive there doth sit
Than if she were with lime-twigs knit.

1651 their leaders were organizing to the east of the Nun Appleton estate.
12. Marvell refers to Sir William Davenant's *Gondibert* (1651), which describes a herd of
animals in a painting of the creation.

No leaf does tremble in the wind
Which I returning cannot find.

73
Out of these scattered sibyl's leaves
Strange prophecies my fancy weaves,
And in one history consumes,
Like Mexique paintings, all the plumes;[13]
What Rome, Greece, Palestine, ere said
I in this light mosaic read:
Thrice happy he who, not mistook,
Hath read in Nature's mystic book.

74
And see how Chance's better wit
Could with a mask my studies hit!
The oak leaves me embroider all
Between which caterpillars crawl,
And ivy with familiar trails
Me licks, and clasps, and curls, and hales.
Under this antic cope I move
Like some great prelate of the grove.

75
Then languishing with ease, I toss
On pallets swoll'n of velvet moss,
While the wind, cooling through the boughs,
Flatters with air my panting brows.
Thanks for my rest, ye mossy banks,
And unto you cool zephyrs thanks,
Who (as my hair) my thoughts too shed
And winnow from the chaff my head.

---

13. Marvell refers to *arte plumaria*, the pre-Conquest Mexican art of painting with different colored feathers.

76

How safe, methinks, and strong, behind
These trees have I encamped my mind;
Where Beauty, aiming at the heart,
Bends in some tree its useless dart;
And where the world no certain shot
Can make, or me it toucheth not.
But I on it securely play,
And gall its horsemen all the day.

77

Bind me, ye woodbines, in your twines,
Curl me about, ye gadding vines!
And oh so close your circles lace
That I may never leave this place;
But lest your fetters prove too weak,
Ere I your silken bondage break,
Do you, oh brambles, chain me too,
And courteous briars nail me through.

78

Here in the morning tie my chain,
Where the two woods have made a lane,
While, like a guard on either side,
The trees before their lord divide;
This, like a long and equal thread,
Betwixt two labyrinths does lead.
But where the floods did lately drown,
There at the evening stake me down.

79

For now the waves are fallen and dried,
And now the meadow's fresher dyed
Whose grass, with moister colour dashed,
Seems as green silks but newly washed.
No serpent new nor crocodile
Remains behind our little Nile,
Unless itself you will mistake
Among these meads the only snake.

80

See in what wanton harmless folds
It everywhere the meadow holds;
And its yet muddy back doth lick,
Till as a crystal mirror slick
Where all things gaze themselves, and doubt
If they be in it or without.
And for his shade which therein shines,
Narcissus-like, the sun too pines.

81

Oh, what a pleasure 'tis to hedge
My temples here with heavy sedge,
Abandoning my lazy side,
Stretched as a bank unto the tide;
Or to suspend my sliding foot
On the osier's undermined root,
And in its branches tough to hang,
While at my lines the fishes twang!

82

But now away, my hooks, my quills[14]
And angles (idle utensils!);   *fishing tackle*
The young Maria walks tonight:
Hide, trifling youth, thy pleasures slight.
'Twere shame that such judicious eyes
Should with such toys a man surprise;
She that already is the law
Of all her sex, her age's awe.

83

See how loose Nature, in respect
To her, itself doth recollect;
And everything so whished and fine   *hushed*
Starts forthwith to its bonne mine.   *good appearance*
The sun himself, of her aware,
Seems to descend with greater care;

---

14. quills] narrow tubular floats, made by anglers with a feather quill.

And lest she see him go to bed,
In blushing clouds conceals his head.

84

So when the shadows laid asleep
From underneath these banks do creep,
And on the river as it flows
With ebon shuts[15] begin to close,
The modest halcyon comes in sight   *kingfisher*
Flying betwixt the day and night,
And such an horror calm and dumb,
Admiring Nature does benumb.

85

The viscous air, wheresoe'er she fly,
Follows and sucks her azure dye;
The jellying stream compacts below,
If it might fix her shadow so;
The stupid fishes hang, as plain   *stupefied*
As flies in crystal overta'en,
And men the silent scene assist,
Charmed with the sapphire-winged mist.

86

Maria such, and so doth hush
The world, and through the evening rush.
No newborn comet such a train
Draws through the sky, nor star new-slain.
For straight those giddy rockets fail,
Which from the putrid earth exhale,
But by her flames, in heaven tried,
Nature is wholly vitrified.

87

'Tis she that to these gardens gave
That wondrous beauty which they have;
She straightness on the woods bestows;

---

15. ebon shuts] black shutters.

To her the meadow sweetness owes;
Nothing could make the river be
So crystal pure but only she;
She yet more pure, sweet, straight and fair,
Than gardens, woods, meads, rivers are.

Written between late June and mid–August 1651, published January 1681

The Garden

How vainly men themselves amaze   *perplex*
To win the palm, the oak, or bays,[1]
And their uncessant labours see
Crowned from some single herb or tree
Whose short and narrow-vergéd shade
Does prudently their toils upbraid;
While all the flowers and trees do close   *unite*
To weave the garlands of repose.

Fair Quiet, have I found thee here,
And Innocence, thy sister dear!
Mistaken long, I sought you then
In busy companies of men.
Your sacred plants, if here below,
Only among the plants will grow;
Society is all but rude
To this delicious solitude.

No white nor red was ever seen
So amorous as this lovely green.
Fond lovers, cruel as their flame,
Cut in these trees their mistress' name:
Little, alas, they know or heed
How far these beauties hers exceed!

1. the palm, the oak, or bays] for military, civic, or poetic honors.

Fair trees, wheres'e'er your barks I wound,
No name shall but your own be found.

When we have run our passions' heat
Love hither makes his best retreat.
The gods, that mortal beauty chase,
Still in a tree did end their race;
Apollo hunted Daphne so
Only that she might laurel grow;
And Pan did after Syrinx speed
Not as a nymph, but for a reed.

What wondrous life is this I lead!
Ripe apples drop about my head;
The luscious clusters of the vine
Upon my mouth do crush their wine;
The nectarine and curious peach
Into my hands themselves do reach;
Stumbling on melons, as I pass,
Ensnared with flowers, I fall on grass.

Meanwhile the mind, from pleasures less,
Withdraws into its happiness—
The mind, that ocean where each kind
Does straight its own resemblance find;
Yet it creates, transcending these,
Far other worlds and other seas,
Annihilating all that's made
To a green thought in a green shade.

Here at the fountain's sliding foot
Or at some fruit-tree's mossy root,
Casting the body's vest aside,
My soul into the boughs does glide;
There like a bird it sits and sings,
Then whets and combs its silver wings,
And, till prepared for longer flight,
Waves in its plumes the various light.

Such was that happy garden-state
While man there walked without a mate;
After a place so pure and sweet,
What other help could yet be meet?
But 'twas beyond a mortal's share
To wander solitary there:
Two paradises 'twere in one
To live in Paradise alone.

How well the skilful gardener drew
Of flowers and herbs this dial new,
Where from above the milder sun
Does through a fragrant zodiac run;
And, as it works, th' industrious bee
Computes its time as well as we.
How could such sweet and wholesome hours
Be reckoned, but with herbs and flowers!

Written 1668, published January 1681

Margaret Cavendish, Duchess of Newcastle Upon Tyne (1623?–1673)

CAVENDISH WAS BORN into a Royalist family near Colchester, Essex, and privately educated at home. When Civil War threatened, she left home and went to Oxford where she became maid of honor to Henrietta Maria, accompanying the court to France in 1644. There she met her husband, William Cavendish, Marquess of Newcastle upon Tyne, former Royalist commander at Marston Moor, whom she married in November or December 1645. The war exacted much from her as it did from everyone else: in August 1648 her brother Sir Charles Lucas was executed after the siege of Colchester. In *Sociable Letters* she would write: "Vices increase in a Civil War, by reason civil government is in disorder, civil magistrates corrupted, civil laws abolished, civil manners and decent customs banished, and in all their places is rapine, robbing, stabbing, treachery and falsehood. All the evil passions and debauched appetites are let loose to take their liberty. . . . I have suffered so much in it, as the loss of some of my nearest and dearest friends, and the ruin of those that did remain, that I may desire to forget it." During the Interregnum she moved to the house of Peter Paul Rubens in Antwerp, which her husband turned into a riding school. They were under considerable financial pressure, and she was compelled to return to London to petition the authorities for the proceeds from her husband's sequestered properties. The request was turned down on the grounds that William was "the greatest traitor to the state." She began to publish in 1653, the first woman openly to style herself as an author. She would be responsible for some thirteen titles in a range of genres including poetry, science fiction, drama, and philosophy. At the Restoration the Cavendishes returned to England and retired to Welbeck Abbey, Nottinghamshire, and Bolsover Castle, Derbyshire, both of which were plundered during the war, and which they set about repairing. Her pleasure in wearing flamboyant outfits of her own design, together with literary renown, made her a celebrity, and when she visited London in the spring of 1667 crowds flocked to see her. She became the first woman to be invited to the Royal Society to witness scientific demonstrations by Robert Boyle and Robert Hooke; Samuel Pepys, who admired her "naked" neck, found her "a very comely woman" and compared her with Princess Kristina of Sweden, a cross-dresser. She died at Welbeck on December 15, 1673 and was buried in Westminster Abbey. "A Description of Civil Wars" comes from *Nature's Pictures* (1656), written and published during Cavendish's exile on the Continent. Its various tales draw on her own experience of recent atrocities, one describing the execution of a young soldier "murthered in cold blood" by enemy forces. Its particulars tally with accounts of the death of Cavendish's older brother, Sir Charles Lucas:

> For they, as soon as had him in their power,
> Like greedy vultures did his life devour;
> He stood their rage, his courage knew no fear,
> Nor on grim death with terror did he stare,
> But did embrace him with a generous mind,
> With noble thoughts, and kisses that were kind:
> Volleys of shot did all his body tear;
> Where his blood's spilt, the earth no grass will bear.

A Description of Civil Wars

A kingdom which long time had lived in peace,
Her people rich with plenty, fat with ease,
With pride were haughty grown: pride envy bred;
From envy factions grew, then mischief spread
And libels everywhere were strewed about
Which after soon a Civil War broke out.
Some for the Commons fought, some for the King,
And great disorder was 'mongst everything;
Battles were lost and won on either side,
Where fortune ebbed and flowed, like to a tide.
At last the Commons won and then astride
Fierce Tyranny on noble necks did ride:
All monuments pulled down that stood long time
And ornaments were then thought a great crime.
No law did plead, unless the martial law—
The sword did rule and keep them all in awe;
No prayers offered to the gods on high,
All ceremony in the dust did lie;
Nothing was done in order, truth, and right;
Nought governed then but malice, spleen and spite.
      But mark how justly gods do punish men
To make them humble and to bow to them:
Though they had plenty, and thereof did eat,
They relished not that good and savory meat;
Because their conscience did them so torment,
For all their plenty they were discontent.
They took no rest, cares so oppressed their mind,
No joy nor comfort in the world could find;
When drowsy sleep upon their eyes did set,
Then fearful visions in their dreams they met;
In life no pleasure take, yet fear to die—
No mercy can they hope from gods on high.
Oh, serve the gods, and then the mind will be
Always in peace and sweet tranquility.

Published 1656

John Bunyan (bap. 1628, d. 1688)

THE SON OF a tinker, Bunyan was sixteen when, on November 30, 1644, he was drafted into the New Model Army. Unfortunately for him, his garrison at Newport Pagnell was ill-equipped and inadequately funded, and soldiers were forced to pawn clothes and other possessions to feed themselves. Trained to use a musket, march in formation, and use a handgun and sword, Bunyan served with his regiment at the siege of Oxford (1645) where he was nearly killed: "when I was a soldier, I with others were drawn out to go to such a place to besiege it, but when I was just ready to go, one of the company desired to go in my room, to which, when I had consented, he took my place; and coming to the siege, as he stood sentinel, he was shot into the head with a musket and died." After discharge from the army he underwent an intense nine-year psycho-spiritual crisis—"great guilt and fearful despair," as he described it—during which he preached and wrote religious pamphlets declaring a Calvinist belief in eternal punishment. Unlicensed to preach, he was arrested on November 12, 1660. Rather than promise not to break the law (which would have spared him the ordeal that followed), Bunyan insisted on the right to speak God's truth, and was sentenced to three months in prison, a sentence repeatedly extended for fear he would organize an uprising. In 1663 he published *Prison Meditations*, which articulated growing despair and the conviction he would die behind bars. While in jail, he wrote *Grace Abounding to the Chief of Sinners* (1666), his spiritual autobiography, and *The Pilgrim's Progress* (1678, 1684). Bunyan was finally released in May 1672. Since then, *The Pilgrim's Progress* has been translated into more than two hundred languages and by 1938 had gone through at least thirteen hundred editions.

The Pilgrim's Progress, Part I

THE AUTHOR'S APOLOGY FOR HIS BOOK (EXTRACT)

Wouldst thou divert thyself from melancholy?
Wouldst thou be pleasant, yet be far from folly?
Wouldst thou read riddles and their explanation
Or else be drownded in thy contemplation?
Dost thou love picking meat, or wouldst thou see
A man in the clouds and hear him speak to thee?
Wouldst thou be in a dream and yet not sleep?
Or wouldst thou in a moment laugh and weep?
Wouldst thou lose thyself, and catch no harm
And find thyself again without a charm?
Wouldst read thyself and read thou knowst not what
And yet know whether thou art blessed or not
By reading the same lines? Oh then come hither
And lay my book, thy head and heart together.

Written by autumn 1669, published 1678

The Pilgrim's Progress, Part II (extract)

APPLES WERE THEY WITH WHICH WE WERE BEGUILED

Apples were they with which we were beguiled,
Yet sin not apples hath our souls defiled;
Apples forbid, if eat, corrupts the blood;
To eat such when commanded does us good.
Drink of his flagons, then, thou church, his dove,
And eat his apples who art sick of love.

Written by early 1671, published 1684

HE THAT IS DOWN NEEDS FEAR NO FALL

He that is down needs fear no fall,
He that is low, no pride;
He that is humble ever shall
Have God to be his guide.

I am content with what I have,
Little be it or much;
And Lord, contentment still I crave
Because thou savest such.

Fullness to such a burden is
That go on pilgrimage;
Here little, and hereafter bliss,
Is best from age to age.

Written by early 1671, published 1684

WHO WOULD TRUE VALOUR SEE

Who would true valour see,
Let him come hither;
One here will constant be,
Come wind, come weather;
There's no discouragement
Shall make him once relent
His first avowed intent
To be a pilgrim.

Who so beset him round
With dismal stories
Do but themselves confound—
His strength the more is.
No lion can him fright,
He'll with a giant fight,
But he will have a right
To be a pilgrim.

Hobgoblin nor foul fiend
Can daunt his spirit;
He knows he at the end
Shall life inherit.
Then fancies flee away,
He'll fear not what men say,
He'll labour night and day
To be a pilgrim.

Written by early 1671, published 1684

III

The Age of Uncertainty

H OW CAN IT have been to live through the reign of a king who claimed to rule by divine right, then a bloody Civil War that resulted in that king's beheading, followed by a period in which a soldier ruled the country, and, finally, the coronation of the son of the king executed years before? Such turmoil dealt a blow to the body politic and the country at large, but that was as nothing compared with what was to come.

Charles II ascended the throne on a promise to devote himself to the Protestant faith, but turned out to be less committed than his father. From the outset, he was suspected of being a closet papist, a belief strengthened by his marriage on April 23, 1662 to Catherine of Braganza, a Catholic Princess. In December he threw fuel on the fire with a declaration of indulgence, proposing greater tolerance of Catholic worship, which produced uproar at court and in Parliament, and was duly withdrawn.

Suspicions as to Charles's religious affiliations never really died down. In 1668, James (the king's brother) converted to Catholicism and gained Charles's promise that he, too, would do so, initiating a series of acts culminating in the secret treaty with Louis XIV in 1670, by which Charles would receive yearly payments in return for a promise to assist the French in their battles against the Dutch (who were Protestant). This was the direct cause of the Third Anglo-Dutch War (1672–1674), the beginning of which coincided with another declaration of indulgence, abolishing legal restrictions on Catholics. In 1673, James's marriage to Mary of Modena (a French client state) opened up the prospect of a Catholic dynasty, something that generated tremendous alarm. To many, these tendencies were summed up in the persons of Charles's favorite mistresses, Louise Renée de Penancoët de Kéroualle, mother of his natural son Charles Lennox, and Barbara Palmer, Countess of Castlemaine (by whom Charles had no less than three sons), both of whom were Catholic.

The stage was set for religious hysteria, ignited during the summer of 1678 when a renegade priest, Titus Oates, alleged a vast conspiracy involving 541 Jesuits was poised to assassinate Charles, precipitate James's succession, put London to the flame, and massacre Protestants. He told also of potential Scottish, English, and Irish rebellions, and a Europe-wide papist conspiracy. It was nonsense, but an audience fanned by years of anti-Catholic propaganda granted it enough plausibility to sanction the trial and execution of thirty-five guiltless men. When Parliament reconvened in October there were attempts to exclude James from the succession by political means, instigated largely by Anthony Ashley Cooper, first Earl of Shaftesbury and leader of the Whig Party. Shaftesbury instead promoted the claims of Charles's illegitimate son, James Scott, Duke of Monmouth (a Protestant), and in November 1680 a bill was passed in the Commons preventing a Catholic succession, placing Monmouth next in line to the throne. When the House met to discuss a further bill in March 1681, Shaftesbury invited Charles to confirm Monmouth's right to succeed him; incensed, Charles dissolved Parliament and had Shaftesbury arrested on charges of treason. Monmouth led an armed rebellion against his father during June and July 1685, which ended at the Battle of Sedgmoor when his forces were routed. He was later captured and executed as a traitor.

The instability of Charles's reign was aggravated by the factionalism of his court, and the manner in which it was run: characterized by conspicuous consumption and unbridled promiscuity, it was a constant drain on the royal purse. The king's mistresses were the theme of common gossip, and not surprisingly: Castlemaine gave Charles a child every year between 1661 and 1665. (It made little difference that the king married in 1662, and became infatuated with Frances Stewart in 1663.) The king's closest friends tended to be those who shared his taste for ribaldry, ridicule, and excess.

Though Charles hardly needed the additional distraction of war, his reign was punctuated by conflict with the Dutch, produced by the desire to seize business from them in America, southeast Asia, and Africa. The War of 1665–1667 (in which the Earl of Rochester was a participant) bankrupted the government and ended in humiliation when the Dutch sailed up the Medway, set fire to much of the navy, and made off with the HMS *Royal Charles*, flagship of the British fleet. The Dutch War of 1672–74 (the result of Charles's treaty with France) had the effect of generating suspicion that Charles was promoting popery and arbitrary government; the Commons brought it to an end by denying him funds.

None of this affected those who, like Katherine Philips and Anne Finch, would always remain loyal, but it had a destabilizing effect on society at large. Rochester's portrait of Restoration London in "A Ramble in St. James's Park" is that of a hedonistic free-for-all in which trust and fidelity mean nothing. His recourse is satirical, as was Dryden's when he composed *Absalom and Achitophel*, a tale of underhand politics and filial treachery—and the king seems to have connived in their outrageousness. He certainly read Rochester's most pungent works in manuscript, and may have commissioned Dryden's poem. Yet in the care with which they portray a lack of moral compass on a grand scale, both poets critique—if only by implication—the ruler by whom it was licensed.

It was not hedonism that precipitated the end of the Stuart dynasty, but religion. James II's avowed intention was to return the kingdom to Catholicism. He crushed two rebellions, both of which aimed to reassert the claims of Protestantism as the state religion, and in his success perceived the hand of God. Emboldened, he imposed Catholic placemen as heads of house in Oxford and Cambridge Colleges, giving rise to fears they would become seminaries, then threatened to make Catholic appointments to vacant archbishoprics. The combination of popery and absolutism was too much, and his people welcomed to the throne his Protestant son-in-law, William of Orange (a Netherlander), when he landed on British soil on November 5, 1788; the Battle of the Boyne decided the matter on July 1, 1789.

William III was a different monarch from his predecessors: he had no interest in destroying political enemies, making clear he would work with whomever would help him govern effectively. At the same time, he ceded a number of prerogative powers to Parliament, such as control of royal expenditure and the size of the army, and the right to call and dissolve Parliament at will, making possible the evolution of a Parliamentary democracy. To a kingdom wearied by insurrection and Civil War, he brought stability. It was his greatest legacy. He enjoyed thirteen years of rule before misfortune brought his reign to an end: he was thrown by his horse and broke his collarbone, dying two weeks later of an inflammation of the lungs. One of his first acts had been to dismiss as poet laureate John Dryden who, being a Catholic convert, could not take the oath of allegiance, and to appoint in his place Thomas Shadwell. Dryden had already bested Shadwell in *Macflecknoe* (1676), the opening couplet of which the new king might have done well to remember:

> All human things are subject to decay,
> And when fate summons, monarchs must obey.

John Dryden (1631–1700)

WHAT DOES ONE say of a man who, two years after publishing an enco-
mium to Oliver Cromwell, could compose another to Charles II? In a less
turbulent world such adaptability might have seemed disreputable, but the
times in which Dryden lived were unreceptive to consistency, especially
for those who were ambitious. He knew both rulers personally, having served
Cromwell as secretary of the Latin and French tongues, and the restored king
as poet laureate and historiographer royal. Today he is remembered princi-
pally for his poems, including *Annus Mirabilis* (1667), *Absalom and Achitophel*
(1681) and *Religio Laici* (1682), all of which comment on public affairs. He
was reared a Puritan and spent the Civil War at Westminster School, which
had a strong Royalist bias. During the Interregnum, Dryden was an under-
graduate at Cambridge, receiving his BA in 1654. Three years later he was
working alongside Milton and Marvell as one of Cromwell's "secretaries of
the French and Latin tongues," preparing diplomatic documents, and would
accompany them as part of Cromwell's funeral cortege. The panegyrics he
composed to the new regime of Charles II led ultimately to his appointment as
poet laureate in 1668. *Absalom and Achitophel* (from which we present extracts)
remains his satirical masterpiece. It uses a biblical source to speak frankly
of the moral shortcomings of Charles II's court and the problems entailed
in the succession, arising from the popularity of Charles's illegitimate son
James Scott, who had emerged as a political threat (see p. 210). Satire was a
dangerous business in those days. Suspected of having authored a poem in
which the king's numerous mistresses were described as "False, foolish, old,
ill-natured and ill-bred," Dryden was beaten senseless as he walked home
through Covent Garden on December 18, 1679, and permanently injured as
a result. The culprit was never found, though some scholars propose John
Wilmot, Earl of Rochester (p. 228), as a candidate, who once threatened to
have Dryden cudgeled, and was no stranger to violence. Dryden converted
to Catholicism in 1685, and remained true to his newfound faith even when it
became a political liability. Unable to swear allegiance to William and Mary,

he lost the laureateship, saw it handed to a lesser poet (Shadwell), and made up the shortfall in his income by writing plays and translating Latin poetry.

Absalom and Achitophel[1] (extracts)

In pious times, ere priestcraft did begin,
Before polygamy was made a sin;
When man on many multiplied his kind,
Ere one to one was cursedly confined;
When nature prompted (and no law denied)
Promiscuous use of concubine and bride;
Then Israel's monarch[2] after heaven's own heart,
His vigorous warmth did variously impart
To wives and slaves; and, wide as his command,
Scattered his maker's image through the land.
Michal,[3] of royal blood, the crown did wear,
A soil ungrateful to the tiller's care:[4]
Not so the rest, for several mothers bore
To godlike David, several sons before;
But since like slaves his bed they did ascend,
No true succession could their seed attend.
   Of all this numerous progeny was none
So beautiful, so brave, as Absolon;[5]
Whether inspired by some diviner lust,
His father got him with a greater gust;
Or that his conscious destiny made way,
By manly beauty, to imperial sway.   *power*
Early in foreign fields he won renown

---

1. Charles II may have requested Dryden to write this poem, which uses biblical parallels as a way of discussing contemporary events, most obviously the exclusion crisis of 1681 (see headnote, p. 210 above).
2. Israel's monarch] a reference to Charles II.
3. Michal] Catherine of Braganza married Charles II in 1662.
4. None of Catherine's children survived infancy.
5. Absolon] James Scott, Duke of Monmouth and first Duke of Buccleugh (1649–1685) was the illegitimate Protestant son of Charles II.

With kings and states allied to Israel's crown;
In peace the thoughts of war he could remove,
And seemed as he were only born for love.
Whate'er he did was done with so much ease,
In him alone 'twas natural to please;
His motions all accompanied with grace,
And paradise was opened in his face.
With secret joy, indulgent David viewed
His youthful image in his son renewed;
To all his wishes nothing he denied
And made the charming Annabel[6] his bride.
What faults he had (for who from faults is free?),
His father could not or he would not see.
Some warm excesses which the law forbore
Were construed youth that purged by boiling o'er;
And Ammon's murder, by a specious name,
Was called a just revenge for injured fame.
    Thus praised and loved the noble youth remained
While David undisturbed in Sion reigned.
But life can never be sincerely blest:
Heaven punishes the bad and proves the best. . . .

Of these the false Achitophel[7] was first—
A name to all succeeding ages cursed;
For close designs and crooked counsels fit;
Sagacious, bold, and turbulent of wit;
Restless, unfixed in principles and place;
In power unpleased, impatient of disgrace;
A fiery soul which, working out its way,
Fretted the pygmy body to decay
And o'er-informed the tenement of clay.
A daring pilot in extremity;
Pleased with the danger when the waves went high

6. Annabel] Anna Scott, countess of Buccleugh, to whom Scott was married in April 1663.
7. Achitophel] Anthony Ashley Cooper, first Earl of Shaftesbury, foremost among the political opponents of Charles II.

He sought the storms; but, for a calm unfit,
Would steer too nigh the sands, to boast his wit.
Great wits are sure to madness near allied,
And thin partitions do their bounds divide;
Else why should he, with wealth and honour blest,
Refuse his age the needful hours of rest?
Punish a body which he could not please,
Bankrupt of life yet prodigal of ease?
And all to leave what with his toil he won,
To that unfeathered two-legged thing, a son—
Got while his soul did huddled notions try
And born a shapeless lump, like anarchy.
In friendship false, implacable in hate;
Resolved to ruin or to rule the state.
To compass this, the triple bond[8] he broke:
The pillars of the public safety shook
And fitted Israel for a foreign yoke.
Then seized with fear yet still affecting fame,
Usurped a patriot's all-atoning name.
So easy still it proves in factious times,
With public zeal to cancel private crimes:
How safe is treason, and how sacred ill,
Where none can sin against the people's will!
Where crowds can wink, and no offence be known,
Since in another's guilt they find their own?
Yet fame deserved no enemy can grudge;
The statesman we abhor but praise the judge.
In Israel's courts ne'er sat an abbethdin[9]
With more discerning eyes or hands more clean;
Unbribed, unsought, the wretched to redress,
Swift of dispatch and easy of access.
Oh, had he been content to serve the crown
With virtues only proper to the gown,
Or had the rankness of the soil been freed
From cockle that oppressed the noble seed,

---

8. triple bond] England formed a triple alliance with Sweden and the Netherlands against France in 1668.
9. abbethdin] judge.

David for him his tuneful harp had strung,
And heaven had wanted one immortal song.
But wild ambition loves to slide, not stand,
And fortune's ice prefers to virtue's land.
Achitophel, grown weary to possess
A lawful fame and lazy happiness,
Disdained the golden fruit to gather free,
And lent the crowd his arm to shake the tree.

Written summer 1681, published November 17, 1681

Katherine Philips (1632–1664)

PHILIPS CAME FROM a well-to-do Puritan family and was educated first at home then at boarding school in Hackney. At age sixteen she was married to James Philips, a colonel in the Parliamentary army known for the brutality with which he had suppressed Royalist rebellions, later a moderate MP in successive Parliaments under both Cromwell and Charles II. She lived with him at the priory in the small Welsh town of Cardigan, close to the River Teifi, for most of their married life. Despite her husband's views, Philips's sympathies were always Royalist. Her poetry of retirement (written under the name "Orinda") is highly ideological, for it values friendship as a countercultural force in opposition to the Protectorate. The retreat to a world of female friendship was an understandable response to the terrible losses of the Civil War. Her lament at the defeat at Worcester of the future Charles II was heartfelt ("Unhappy kings, who cannot keep a throne"), as was her condemnation of the Welsh Republican, Vavasor Powell, for his claim that Charles I had broken the Ten Commandments. After the Restoration, she became a friend of Sir Charles Cotterell, Charles II's Master of Ceremonies, who had fought on the Royalist side in the Civil War and spent the Interregnum in exile with the royal family. Thanks partly to him, she enjoyed success with her translation of Corneille's *Pompey* (1663), copies of which were presented to Charles II and the Duchess of York (first wife of James II). She died the following year of smallpox at the age of thirty-two. Her poetry was widely read during her lifetime in manuscript, and gained widespread popularity upon publication in a pirated edition in 1664. Authorized publication took place in 1667 under Cotterell's editorship.

A Retired Friendship. To Ardelia.

Come, my Ardelia, to this bower
   Where kindly mingling souls awhile,
Let's innocently spend an hour
   And at all serious follies smile.

Here is no quarreling for crowns,
   Nor fear of changes in our fate;
No trembling at the great ones' frowns,
   Nor any slavery of state.

Here's no disguise nor treachery,
   Nor any deep concealed design;
From blood and plots this place is free
   And calm as are those looks of thine.

Here let us sit and bless our stars,
   Who did such happy quiet give,
As that removed from noise of wars:
   In one another's hearts we live.

Why should we entertain a fear?
   Love cares not how the world is turned;
If crowds of dangers should appear,
   Yet friendship can be unconcerned.

We wear about us such a charm,
   No horror can be our offence;
For mischief's self can do no harm
   To friendship and to innocence.

Let's mark how soon Apollo's beams
   Command the flocks to quit their meat,

And not entreat the neighboring springs
 To quench their thirst, but cool their heat.

In such a scorching age as this,
 Whoever would not seek a shade
Deserve their happiness to miss,
 As having their own peace betrayed.

But we (of one another's mind
 Assured) the boisterous world disdain;
With quiet souls and unconfined
 Enjoy what princes wish in vain.

Written August 23, 1651, published 1664

On 3 September 1651[1]

As when the glorious magazine of light[2]
Approaches to his canopy of night,
He with new splendor clothes his dying rays
And double brightness to his beams conveys;
As if to brave and check his ending fate,
Puts on his highest looks in's lowest state,
Dressed in such terror as to make us all
Be anti-Persians,[3] and adore his fall;
Then quits the world, depriving it of day,
While every herb and plant does droop away:
So when our gasping English royalty
Perceived her period[4] now was drawing nigh,
She summons her whole strength to give one blow,

---

1. The future Charles II led a Royalist army from Scotland into England in August 1651, which was completely destroyed at the battle of Worcester on September 3. For Loyalists such as Philips, this was a tragedy, marking the end of any hope that the monarchy could be restored by force.
2. the glorious magazine of light] i.e., the sun—a repository or warehouse of light.
3. anti-Persians] Persians were thought to be sun worshippers.
4. period] end.

To raise herself or pull down others too.
Big with revenge and hope, she now spake more
Of terror than in many months before;
And musters her attendants, or to save
Her from, or wait upon her to the grave:
Yet but enjoyed the miserable fate
Of setting majesty—to die in state.
　　　Unhappy kings, who cannot keep a throne,
Nor be so fortunate to fall alone!
Their weight sinks others: Pompey could not fly,
But half the world must bear him company;[5]
Thus captive Samson could not life conclude
Unless attended with a multitude.
Who'd trust to greatness now, whose food is air,[6]
Whose ruin sudden, and whose end despair?
Who would presume upon his glorious birth
Or quarrel for a spacious share of earth,
That sees such diadems become thus cheap,
And heroes tumble in the common heap?
　　　Oh give me virtue then, which sums up all,
And firmly stands when crowns and scepters fall.

Written shortly after September 3, 1651, published 1667

Upon the Double Murder of King Charles I, in Answer to a Libelous Copy of Rhymes by Vavasor Powell[1]

I think not on the state, nor am concerned
Which way soever the great helm is turned,
But as that son whose father's danger nigh

---

5. Pompey fled to Egypt after defeat at Pharsalus.
6. whose food is air] who live on false hopes.
UPON THE DOUBLE MURDER OF KING CHARLES I
1. Vavasor Powell was a Welsh Independent Minister with Republican leanings who had written an antimonarchical poem claiming Charles I had broken all of the Ten Commandments.

Did force his native dumbness, and untie
The fettered organs,[2] so this is a cause
That will excuse the breach of nature's laws.
Silence were now a sin—nay, passion now
Wise men themselves for merit would allow.
What noble eye could see (and careless pass)
The dying lion kicked by every ass?
Has Charles so broke God's laws, he must not have
A quiet crown, nor yet a quiet grave?
Tombs have been sanctuaries; thieves lie there
Secure from all their penalty and fear.
Great Charles his double misery was this:
Unfaithful friends, ignoble enemies.
Had any heathen been this Prince's foe,
He would have wept to see him injured so!
His title was his crime, they'd reason good
To quarrel at the Right they had withstood.
"He broke God's laws, and therefore he must die":
And what shall then become of thee and I?
Slander must follow treason; but yet stay,
Take not our reason with our King away—
Though you have seized upon all our defence,
Yet do not sequester our common sense.
"Christ will be King"; but I ne'er understood
His subjects built his kingdom up with blood
(Except their own) or that he would dispense
With his commands, though for his own defence.
Oh, to what height of horror are they come
Who dare pull down a crown, tear up a tomb?

Written between 1650 and 1654, published 1667

---

2. Croesus had an unnamed son who could not speak; the son conquered his dumbness on seeing a soldier about to strike Croesus to the ground.

On the Numerous Access of the English to Wait Upon the King in Flanders[1]

Hasten, great Prince, unto thy British Isles,
Or all thy subjects will become exiles!
To thee they flock, thy presence is their home,
As Pompey's camp—where'er it moved was Rome.
They that asserted thy just cause go hence
To testify their joy and reverence;
And those that did not, now by wonder taught,
Go to confess and expiate their fault.
So that if thou dost stay, thy gasping land
Itself will empty on the Belgic sand
Where the affrighted Dutchman does profess
He thinks it an invasion, not address;
As we unmonarched were for want of thee,
So till thou come we shall unpeopled be.
None but the close fanatic will remain,
Who by our loyalty his ends will gain,
And he the exhausted land will quickly find
As desolate a place as he designed,
For England (though grown old with woes) will see
Her long denied and sovereign remedy.
So when old Jacob could but credit give
That his prodigious Joseph still did live
(Joseph that was preserved to restore
Their lives that would have taken his before[2]),
"It is enough," said he, "to Egypt I
Will go, and see him once before I die."

Probably written March 1660, published 1667

---

1. The future Charles II arrived in Flanders (present-day Belgium) on December 26, 1659 and left it on March 30, 1660; he entered London on May 29 to be crowned king.
2. Philips refers to the story at Genesis 45.

Aphra Behn (?1640–1689)

LITTLE IS KNOWN of Behn's early years, perhaps because she suppressed information about them. She became a Royalist spy during the final years of the Interregnum, and in 1663 was sent to Surinam, a country in northern South America where there were British and Dutch plantations. Under the codename Astrea, she reported on the activities of the dangerous dissident William Scot, with whom she became personally involved. Returning to London, she married a merchant of German extraction, Johann Behn, who died shortly afterward. In 1666 she was sent to Antwerp by Secretary of State Henry Bennet, first Earl of Arlington, her mission being to extract information about the Dutch from Scot, now resident there. Back in London, she became a prolific writer of sex comedies and in ensuing years had nineteen plays staged, contributing to many others. Her most enduring play is *The Rover* (1677), set during the Interregnum. She was at the center of Restoration culture, and would come to know eminent personalities including Thomas Otway, Elizabeth Barry, and John Wilmot, Earl of Rochester (see p. 228). She claimed that Rochester assisted with her poetry, and he was the subject of an elegy she composed at his death. Her poem "On a Juniper Tree," in which a tree watches mortals having sex, is more daring than any other poem published by a woman at this period, and is probably influenced by Rochester. In the 1680s Behn turned to erotic fiction, producing *Love-Letters between a Nobleman and his Sister*, an epic of over one thousand pages, between 1684 and 1687. Her most famous work is a short story, "Oroonoko," dramatized by Thomas Southerne in 1696. She lived long enough to see the Glorious Revolution, but died shortly after, on April 16, 1689. Although she led the way for women writers of her time, the bawdiness of her writing led to its partial suppression until the last two decades of the twentieth century, when she was recognized as a significant novelist, a formidable poet, and one of the great dramatists of the English stage.

On a Juniper Tree, Cut Down to Make Busks[1]

Whilst happy I triumphant stood,
The pride and glory of the wood,
My aromatic boughs and fruit
Did with all other trees dispute,
Had right by nature to excel
In pleasing both the taste and smell,
But to the touch (I must confess)
Bore an ungrateful sullenness.
My wealth, like bashful virgins, I
Yielded with some reluctancy,
For which my value should be more,
Not giving easily my store.
My verdant branches all the year
Did an eternal beauty wear,
Did ever young and gay appear,
Nor needed any tribute pay
For bounties from the god of day;
Nor do I hold supremacy
(In all the wood) o'er every tree,
But even those too of my own race,
That grow not in this happy place.
But that in which I glory most
And do myself with reason boast,
Beneath my shade the other day
Young Philocles and Cloris lay:
Upon my root she leaned her head
And where I grew he made their bed,
Whilst I the canopy more largely spread.
Their trembling limbs did gently press
The kind supporting yielding grass:
Ne'er half so blest as now, to bear
A swain so young, a nymph so fair.
My grateful shade I kindly lent,
And every aiding bough I bent;

---

1. A busk is a piece of wood used to stiffen the front of corsets.

So low as sometimes had the bliss
To rob the shepherd of a kiss,
Whilst he in pleasures far above
The sense of that degree of love
Permitted every stealth I made,
Unjealous of his rival shade.
I saw 'em kindle to desire
Whilst with soft sighs they blew the fire,
Saw the approaches of their joy,
He growing more fierce and she less coy;
Saw how they mingled melting rays,
Exchanging love a thousand ways.
Kind was the force on every side,
Her new desire she could not hide,
Nor would the shepherd be denied.
Impatient he waits no consent
But what she gave by languishment
The blessed minute he pursued,
Whilst love her fear and shame subdued;
And now transported in his arms,
Yields to the conqueror all her charms:
His panting breast to hers now joined,
They feast on raptures unconfined—
Vast and luxuriant such as prove
The immortality of love.
For who but a divinity
Could mingle souls to that degree?
Now like the phoenix both expire
While from the ashes of their fire
Sprung up a new and soft desire.
Like charmers, thrice they did invoke
The god, and thrice new vigor took.
Nor had the mystery ended there,
But Cloris reassumed her fear,
And chid the swain for having pressed
What she (alas!) could not resist;
Whilst he (in whom love's sacred flame
Before and after was the same)

Fondly implored she would forget
A fault which he would yet repeat.
From active joys with some they haste
To a reflection on the past;
A thousand times my covert bless
That did secure their happiness;
Their gratitude to every tree
They pay, but most to happy me;
The shepherdess my bark caressed
Whilst he my root, love's pillow, kissed,
And did with sighs their fate deplore,
Since I must shelter them no more.
And if before my joys were such
In having heard and seen too much,
My grief must be as great and high
When all abandoned I shall be,
Doomed to a silent destiny—
No more the charming strife to hear
The shepherd's vows, the virgin's fear;
No more a joyful looker on
Whilst love's soft battle's lost and won.
       With grief I bowed my murmuring head
And all my crystal dew I shed,
Which did in Cloris pity move
(Cloris whose soul is made of love):
She cut me down and did translate
My being to a happier state.
No martyr for religion died
With half that unconsidering pride;
My top was on that altar laid
Where love his softest offerings paid
And was as fragrant incense burned;
My body into busks was turned
Where I still guard the sacred store
And of love's temple keep the door.

Published 1680

Song to a New Scotch Tune[1]

Young Jemmy was a lad
Of royal birth and breeding,
With every beauty clad
And every grace exceeding;
A face and shape so wondrous fine,
So charming every part,
That every lass upon the green
For Jemmy had a heart.

In Jemmy's powerful eyes
Young gods of love are playing,
And on his face there lies
A thousand smiles betraying.
But oh, he dances with a grace—
None like him e'er was seen;
No god that ever fancied was
Has so divine a mien.

To Jemmy every swain
Did lowly doff his bonnet,
And every nymph would strain
To praise him in her sonnet;
The pride of all the youths he was,
The glory of the groves,
The joy of every tender lass,
The theme of all our loves.

But oh, unlucky fate,
A curse upon ambition!
The busy fops of state
Have ruined his condition.
For glittering hopes he's left the shade,

---

1. This political poem comments on James Scott, Duke of Monmouth, illegitimate son of Charles II, whose alliance with Shaftesbury and the Whigs had led to his exile from court (see p. 210).

His peaceful hours are gone;
By flattering knaves and fools betrayed,
Poor Jemmy is undone.

Published 1681

John Wilmot, second Earl of Rochester (1647–1680)

MISANTHROPIST? CYNIC? RAKE? One of the greatest satirists and lyric poets of all time? Scholars continue to debate which, if any, Rochester might have been. Born into a Royalist family, he spent his earliest years at the Court of Henrietta Maria in exile in Paris, succeeding at the age of ten to his aristocratic titles. He abducted a court beauty, Elizabeth Malet, in May 1665, only to be apprehended and thrown in the Tower of London. A favorite of the king, Rochester was released within weeks, before being sent to fight in the Second Anglo-Dutch War in which (according to his commander, Lord Sandwich) Rochester "showed himself brave, industrious, and of useful parts." He took part in the siege of Bergen where he saw two comrades next to him cut in half by a single cannonball. In March 1666 Charles made him Gentleman of the Bedchamber, a post that entailed sleeping in the king's bedroom and waiting at table. Rochester probably found this stultifyingly dull, and ran away to fight in the Four Days' Battle against the Dutch, June 1–4, 1666, one of the bloodiest engagements in naval history. In its midst, Rochester volunteered to sail through enemy fire with a message for a neighboring boat. It was an act of madness beside which nothing, least of all civilian life, can ever have been the same, as the salient events of his biography indicate: collusion in the murder of an unfortunate quartermaster in Epsom; claims to have been "continually drunk . . . for five years together"; physical assaults on Thomas Killigrew and John Dryden; affair with the actress Elizabeth Barry; impersonation of his alter ego, Dr. Alexander Bendo; duel with John Sheffield, Earl of Mulgrave. For some scholars, such as Germaine Greer, the more lurid elements of the Rochester myth are "the accretion of speculation and opinion." Whatever the truth, his poetry remains the testimony of a sensitive man to whom any form of delusion was anathema, for Rochester was the foremost of those involved in Caroline culture, his "honorable scar"—and legacy—being a vision shaped by the meaninglessness and randomness of war. For more on Rochester's war service, see the introduction, pp. 4–6.

The Disabled Debauchee

As some brave admiral, in former war,
Deprived of force, but pressed with courage still,
Two rival fleets appearing from afar,
Crawls to the top of an adjacent hill

From whence (with thoughts full of concern) he views
The wise and daring conduct of the fight,
And each bold action to his mind renews
His present glory and his past delight;

From his fierce eyes flashes of rage he throws
(As from black clouds when lightning breaks away)—
Transported, thinks himself amid his foes,
And absent yet enjoys the bloody day:

So, when my days of impotence approach,
And I'm by pox and wine's unlucky chance
Forced from the pleasing billows of debauch,
On the dull shore of lazy temperance,

My pains at least some respite shall afford,
Whilst I behold the battles you maintain
When fleets of glasses sail about the board
From whose broadsides volleys of wit shall rain;

Nor let the sight of honourable scars
Which my too forward valour did procure,

Frighten new-listed soldiers from the wars—
Past joys have more than paid what I endure.

Should hopeful youths (worth being drunk) prove nice
And from their fair inviters meanly shrink,
'Twill please the ghost of my departed vice
If at my counsel they repent and drink.

Or should some cold-complexioned sot forbid,
With his dull morals, your bold night-alarms,
I'll fire his blood by telling what I did
When I was strong and able to bear arms.

I'll tell of whores attacked, their lords at home,
Bawds' quarters beaten up, and fortress[1] won,
Windows demolished, watches overcome,
And handsome ills by my contrivance done.

Nor shall our love fits,[2] Cloris, be forgot,
When each the well-looked link boy[3] strove to enjoy,
And the best kiss was the deciding lot
Whether the boy fucked you, or I the boy.

With tales like these, I will such thoughts inspire
As to important mischief shall incline;
I'll make him long some ancient church to fire
And fear no lewdness he's called to by wine.

Thus statesman-like, I'll saucily impose,
And safe from action valiantly advise,
Sheltered in impotence, urge you to blows,
And being good for nothing else, be wise.

Written February 1673, published c. September 1680

---

1. Scholars suggest the "fortress" may be a brothel.
2. love fits] quarrels.
3. link boy] boys who guided travelers through the streets at night, carrying lighted torches.

A Ramble in St. James's Park

Much wine had passed, with grave discourse
Of who fucks who and who does worse,
Such as you usually do hear
From those that diet at the Bear;[1]
When I, who still take care to see
Drunkenness relieved by lechery,
Went out into St. James's Park
To cool my head and fire my heart:
But though St. James has the honour on't,
'Tis consecrate to prick and cunt.
There by a most incestuous birth
Strange woods spring from the teeming earth,
For they relate how heretofore,
When ancient Pict[2] began to whore,
Deluded of his assignation
(Jilting, it seems, was then in fashion),
Poor pensive lover in this place
Would frig upon his mother's face
Whence rows of mandrakes tall did rise
Whose lewd tops fucked the very skies.
Each imitative branch does twine
In some loved fold of Aretine,[3]
And nightly now beneath their shade
Are buggeries, rapes and incests made.
Unto this all-sin-sheltering grove
Whores of the bulk[4] and the alcove,
Great ladies, chambermaids and drudges,
The ragpicker and heiress trudges;
Car men,[5] divines, great Lords, and tailors,

---

1. the Bear] a hostelry in central London.
2. Pict] Scot.
3. Rochester refers to pornographic illustrations by Giulio Romano, with sonnets by Pietro Aretino.
4. bulk] boxlike constructions outside shops which, at nighttime, could be used for assignations with prostitutes.
5. Car men] drivers of horse-drawn carts.

Prentices, poets, pimps, and jailers,
Footmen, fine fops, do here arrive,
And here promiscuously they swive.
    Along these hallowed walks it was
That I beheld Corinna pass:
Whoever had been by to see
The proud disdain she cast on me
Through charming eyes, he would have swore
She dropped from heaven that very hour,
Forsaking the divine abode
In scorn of some despairing god.
But mark what creatures women are—
How infinitely vile, when fair!
    Three knights of the elbow and the slur[6]
With wriggling tails made up to her.
The first was of your Whitehall blades,
Near kin to the mother of the maids[7]—
Graced by whose favor he was able
To bring a friend to the waiters' table
Where he had heard Sir Edward Sutton[8]
Say how the king loved Banstead mutton,[9]
Since when he'd ne'er be brought to eat
By 's good will any other meat.
In this, as well as all the rest,
He ventures to do like the best,
But wanting common sense, the ingredient
In choosing well, not least expedient,
Converts abortive imitation
To universal affectation.
Thus he not only eats and talks
But feels and smells, sits down and walks—

---

6. knights of the elbow and the slur] dishonest gamblers.
7. mother of the maids] at court, the mother of the maids took responsibility for the conduct of maids of honor; it was also the slang term for a prostitute.
8. Sir Edward Sutton was, like Rochester, a gentleman of the Privy Chamber, and would have waited on the king.
9. Banstead mutton] mutton from Banstead Downs in Surrey, a well-known delicacy up to the nineteenth century.

Nay, looks and lives and loves by rote
In an old tawdry birthday coat.
    The second was a Grays Inn wit,
A great inhabiter of the pit[10]
Where critic-like he sits and squints,
Steals pocket handkerchiefs, and hints,
From 's neighbor and the comedy,
To court and pay his landlady.
    The third, a lady's eldest son
Within few years of twenty one,
Who hopes from his propitious fate,
Against he comes to his estate,
By these two worthies to be made
A most accomplished tearing blade.
    One, in a strain 'twixt tune and nonsense
Cries, "Madam, I have loved you long since!
Permit me your fair hand to kiss,"
When at her mouth her cunt cries, "Yes!"
In short, without much more ado,
Joyful and pleased, away she flew,
And with these three confounded asses
From park to hackney coach she passes.
    So a proud bitch does lead about
Of humble curs the amorous rout
Who most obsequiously do hunt
The savory scent of salt-swoln cunt.
Some power more patient now relate
The sense of this surprising fate.
Gods, that a thing admired by me
Should fall to so much infamy!
Had she picked out, to rub her arse on,
Some stiff-pricked clown or well-hung parson,
Each job of whose spermatic sluice
Had filled her cunt with wholesome juice,
I the proceeding should have praised
In hope she'd quenched a fire I raised.

---

10. A great inhabiter of the pit] i.e. he was a theatergoer.

Such natural freedoms are but just;
There's something generous in mere lust.
But to turn damned abandoned jade
When neither head nor tail persuade;
To be a whore in understanding,
A passive pot for fools to spend in—
The devil played booty, sure, with thee
To bring a blot on infamy![11]
But why am I, of all mankind,
To so severe a fate designed?
Ungrateful! Why this treachery
To humble, fond, believing me?
Who gave you privilege above
The nice allowances of love?
Did ever I refuse to bear
The meanest part your lust could spare?
When your lewd cunt came spewing home,
Drenched with the seed of half the town,
My dram of sperm was supped up after
For the digestive surfeit water—
Full gorged at another time
With a vast meal of nasty slime
Which your devouring cunt had drawn
From porters' backs and footmen's brawn.
I was content to serve you up
My ballockful for your grace cup,[12]
Nor ever thought it an abuse
While you had pleasure for excuse—
You that could make my heart away
For noise and colour, and betray
The secrets of my tender hours
To such knight-errant paramours.
When leaning on your faithless breast,
Wrapped in security and rest,
Soft kindness all my powers did move
And reason lay dissolved in love.

---

11. The devil played booty . . . infamy!] "You conspired with the devil to dishonor infamy."
12. grace cup] the last cup of the meal, after grace has been said.

May stinking vapors choke your womb
Such as the men you dote upon!
May your depraved appetite
(That could in whiffling fools delight)
Beget such frenzies in your mind
You may go mad for the north wind,
And fixing all your hopes upon 't
To have him bluster in your cunt,
Turn up your longing arse to the air
And perish in a wild despair!
But cowards shall forget to rant,
Schoolboys to frig, old whores to paint;
The Jesuits' fraternity
Shall leave the use of buggery;
Crab-louse inspired with grace divine
From earthly cod to heaven shall climb;
Physicians shall believe in Jesus
And disobedience cease to please us—
Ere I desist with all my power
To plague this woman and undo her.
But my revenge will best be timed
When she is married that is limed.[13]
In that most lamentable state
I'll make her feel my scorn and hate,
Pelt her with scandals, truth or lies,
And her poor cur with jealousies,
Till I have torn him from her breech
While she whines like a dog-drawn bitch—
Loathed and despised, kicked out of the town
Into some dirty hole alone
To chew the cud of misery
And know she owes it all to me.
And may no woman better thrive
That dares profane the cunt I swive.

Written by March 20, 1673, published c. September 1680

---

13. limed] impregnated.

Upon Nothing

Nothing! thou elder brother even to shade,
Thou hadst a being ere the world was made
And (well fixed) art alone of ending not afraid.

Ere Time and Place were, Time and Place were not;
When primitive Nothing, Something straight begot—
Then all proceeded from the great united *what*.

Something, the general attribute of all,
Severed from thee, its sole original,
Into thy boundless self must undistinguished fall.

Yet Something did thy mighty power command
And from thy fruitful Emptiness's hand
Snatched men, beasts, birds, fire, water, air and land.

Matter, the wicked'st offspring of thy race,
By Form assisted, flew from thy embrace,
And rebel Light obscured thy reverend dusky face.

With Form and Matter, Time and Place did join;
Body (thy foe) with these did leagues combine
To spoil thy peaceful realm and ruin all thy line.

But turncoat Time assists the foe in vain,
And, bribed by thee, destroys their short-lived reign,
And to thy hungry womb drives back thy slaves again.

Though mysteries are barred from laic eyes,
And the divine alone with warrant pries
Into thy bosom, where thy truth in private lies,

Yet this of thee the wise may truly say:
"Thou from the virtuous Nothing tak'st away";
And to be part of thee, the wicked wisely pray.

Great negative, how vainly would the wise
Inquire, define, distinguish, teach, devise,
Didst thou not stand to point their blind philosophies!

Is or is not, the two great ends of fate,
And true or false, the subject of debate
That perfect or destroy the vast designs of state,

When they have racked the politician's breast
Within thy bosom most securely rest,
And when reduced to thee, are least unsafe and best.

But Nothing, why does Something still permit
That sacred monarchs should in council sit
With persons highly thought at best for nothing fit,

Whilst weighty Something modestly abstains
From princes' coffers and from statesmen's brains,
And Nothing there like stately Nothing reigns?—

Nothing, who dwellst with fools in grave disguise
For whom they reverend shapes and forms devise,
Lawn sleeves and furs and gowns, when they (like thee) look wise.

French truth, Dutch prowess, British policy,
Hibernian learning, Scotch civility,
Spaniards' dispatch, Danes' wit, are mainly seen in thee;

The great man's gratitude to his best friend,
Kings' promises, whores' vows—towards thee they bend,
Flow swiftly into thee, and in thee ever end.

Written by May 14, 1678, published 1679

Daniel Defoe (1660?–1731)

BY THE TIME he came to maturity as a novelist (at the age of fifty-nine), Defoe had experienced more than enough to qualify him for inclusion in this book. As a young man he fought in the rebellion of 1685, when James Scott, Duke of Monmouth, led an army against his father, Charles II; he fought in the deciding battle of the campaign at Sedgemoor. Having eluded capture, Defoe was pardoned for his role in the uprising two years later. His pamphlet in defense of nonconformism, *The Shortest Way with the Dissenters* (1702), marked him as a political activist and precipitated his arrest for seditious libel and subsequent imprisonment in Newgate. Sentenced to appear at the pillory three times in July 1703, he arranged for supporters to pelt him with flowers while distributing copies of his *A Hymn to the Pillory*, which condemned that form of punishment. This made him susceptible to accusations of rabble-rousing, and further arrests were threatened in subsequent years. Embroiled in the world of politics, Defoe's career as spymaster began after his first conviction, in the course of which he established an intelligence network that gave him control of newspapers in Edinburgh, with contacts in the Scottish Parliament, the Church of Scotland, and major businesses and civic organizations. His feelings concerning slavery are evident in *Robinson Crusoe* and *Captain Singleton*, but long before those novels were composed he condemned the practice in *Reformation of Manners: A Satire*.

Reformation of Manners: A Satire (extract)

Some fit out ships and double freights ensure,
And burn the ships to make the voyage secure,
Promiscuous plunders through the world commit
And with the money buy their safe retreat.
    Others seek out to Afric's torrid zone

And search the burning shores of Sierra Leone;
There in insufferable heats they fry
And run vast risks to see the gold and die;
The harmless natives basely they trepan,
And barter baubles for the souls of men;
The wretches they to Christian climes bring o'er,
To serve worse heathens than they did before.
The cruelties they suffer there are such,
Amboyna's nothing—they've outdone the Dutch.
     Cortez, Pizzarro, Guzman, Penaloe
Who drank the blood and gold of Mexico,
Who thirteen millions of souls destroyed
And left one third of God's creation void;
By birth for nature's butchery designed,
Compared to these are merciful and kind;
Death could their cruelest designs fulfill,
Blood quenched their thirst and it sufficed to kill;
But these the tender *coup de grace* deny,
And make men beg in vain for leave to die;
To more than Spanish cruelty inclined,
Torment the body and debauch the mind;
The lingering life of slavery preserve
And vilely teach them both to sin and serve.
In vain they talk to them of shades below:
They fear no hell, but where such Christians go;
Of Jesus Christ they very often hear—
Often as his blaspheming servants swear;
They hear and wonder what strange gods they be
Can bear with patience such indignity.
They look for famines, plagues, disease, and death,
Blasts from above and earthquakes from beneath,
But when they see regardless Heaven looks on,
They curse our gods, or think that we have none.
Thus thousands to religion are brought o'er
And made worse devils than they were before.

Published c. August 1702

A Hymn to the Pillory (extracts)

Hail, hieroglyphic state machine,
    Contrived to punish fancy in!
Men that are men in thee can feel no pain,
And all thy insignificants disdain.
    Contempt, that false new word for shame,
    Is without crime an empty name,
    A shadow to amuse mankind,
But never frights the wise or well-fixed mind;
    Virtue despises human scorn,
    And scandals innocence adorn.
    Exalted on thy stool of state,
What prospect do I see of sovereign fate—
    How the inscrutables of providence
    Differ from our contracted sense;
    Here by the errors of the town,
    The fools look out, the knaves look on.
Persons or crimes find here the same respect,
    And vice does virtue oft correct;
    The undistinguished fury of the street
    With mob and malice mankind greet:
    No bias can the rabble draw,
But dirt throws dirt without respect to merit or to law. . . .

    Then clap thy wooden wings for joy
    And greet the men of great employ,
The authors of the nation's discontent
And scandal of a Christian government:
Jobbers and brokers of the City stocks
With forty thousand tallies at their backs,
Who make our banks and companies obey,
    Or sink 'em all the shortest way.
    The intrinsic value of our stocks
Is stated in their calculating books;
The imaginary prizes rise and fall
    As they command who toss the ball;
    Let 'em upon thy lofty turrets stand

With bearskins[1] on the back, debentures[2] in the hand,
    And write in capitals upon the post
    That here they should remain
    Till this enigma they explain:
How stocks should fall when sales surmount the cost,
    And rise again when ships are lost.
    Great monster of the law, exalt thy head,
    Appear no more in masquerade,
In homely phrase express thy discontent
And move it in the approaching Parliament:
    Tell 'em how paper went instead of coin
With interest eight percent and discount nine,
    Of Irish transport debts unpaid,
Bills false endorsed and long accounts unmade.
And tell them all the nation hopes to see,
    They'll send the guilty down to thee
Rather than those who write their history.
Then bring those Justices upon thy bench
Who vilely break the laws they should defend
    And upon equity entrench
By punishing the crimes they will not mend.
    Set every vicious magistrate
Upon thy sumptuous chariot of the state;
    There let 'em all in triumph ride,
Their purple and their scarlet laid aside.
Let none such Bridewell[3] justices protect,
As first debauch the whores which they correct;
    Such who with oaths and drunk'ness sit
And punish far less crimes than they commit;
    These certainly deserve to stand
With trophies of authority in either hand.

Published July 29, 1703

---

1. A bearskin is a bear, or a speculator who sells stock for delivery at a future date, in the expectation that meanwhile prices will fall, and he will be able to buy in at a lower rate what he has contracted to deliver at a higher.
2. Debentures record money owed.
3. Bridewell] house of correction.

Anne Finch, Countess of Winchilsea
(1661–1720)

OFTEN CONSIDERED A nature poet, Anne Finch was engaged more directly in the political twists and turns of her time than many contemporaries. She and her husband Heneage were at the center of the Court of James II: she was maid of honor to Mary of Modena (James's wife); Heneage was Gentleman of the Bedchamber to the king. Both had a distinguished future ahead of them until the Glorious Revolution, when the unpopular Catholic monarch they served was forced into exile and replaced with the securely Protestant William and Mary, crowned 1689. Declining to pledge loyalty to them, the Finches fled to Kent, where Anne composed "The Change," about a devastated Arcadia. There was worse to come, for on April 29, 1690, her husband was arrested while attempting to join the exiled Stuart court in France, where James II was hoping to organize opposition to the new regime. (This was, perhaps, the last moment at which it could have stood a realistic chance of success.) The charges were serious as they amounted to a form of treason, for Heneage was planning to join forces that would declare war on the new king. During the summer months, Anne Finch was in anguish, as she waited for the outcome to the judicial process, and she composed "The Loss" and "A Song on Grief." The case against Heneage was dropped finally on November 28, seven months after his arrest. The Finches continued to live in retirement, becoming Earl and Countess of Winchilsea in 1712. Wordsworth praised "A Noctural Reverie" for its observation of the natural world, as a result of which it remains her best-known poem.

The Change

Poor river, now thou 'rt almost dry,
What nymph or swain will near thee lie?
Since brought, alas, to sad decay,

What flocks or herds will near thee stay?
The swans that sought thee in thy pride
Now on new streams forgetful ride,
And fish that in thy bosom lay,
Choose in more prosperous floods to play.
All leave thee now thy ebb appears,
To waste thy sad remains in tears;
Nor will thy mournful murmurs heed:
Fly, wretched stream, with all thy speed,
Among those solid rocks thy griefs bestow,
For friends, like those (alas!) thou ne'er didst know—
And thou, poor sun, that sat'st on high,
But late the splendour of the sky,
What flower, though by thy influence born,
Now clouds prevail, will towards thee turn?
Now darkness sits upon thy brow,
What Persian votary will bow?
What river will her smiles reflect,
Now that no beams thou canst direct?
By watery vapours overcast,
Who thinks upon thy glories past?
If present light nor heat we get,
Unheeded thou mayst rise and set.
Not all the past can one adorer keep—
Fall, wretched sun, to the more faithful deep.

     Nor do thou, lofty structure, boast
Since undermined by time and frost;
Since thou canst no reception give,
In untrod meadows thou mayst live.
None from his ready road will turn,
With thee thy wretched change to mourn;
Not the soft nights or cheerful days
Thou hast bestowed, can give thee praise;
No lusty tree that near thee grows
(Though it beneath thy shelter rose)
Will to thy age a staff become:
Fall, wretched building, to thy tomb!
Thou and thy painted roofs, in ruin mixed,
Fall to the earth—for that alone is fixed.

The same, poor man, the same must be
Thy fate, now Fortune frowns on thee;
Her favour everyone pursues
And, losing her, thou all must lose.
No love, sown in thy prosperous days,
Can fruit in this cold season raise;
No benefit, by thee conferred,
Can in this time of storms be heard;
All from thy troubled waters run—
Thy stooping fabric all men shun.
All do thy clouded looks decline,
As if thou ne'er didst on them shine.
     Oh wretched man! To other worlds repair,
For faith and gratitude are only there.

Written 1689/1690, published 1713

The Loss

She sighed, but soon it mixed with common air—
Too fleet a witness for her deep despair;
She wept, but tears no lasting grief can show,
For tears will fail, and ebb as well as flow;
She would her tongue to the sad subject force,
But all great passions are above discourse.
Thy heart alone, Ardelia, with it trust;
There grave it deep—alas, 'twill fall to dust!
"Urania is no more, to me no more,
All these combined can ne'er this loss deplore."

Written c. 1690, published 1903

A Song on Grief

Oh grief, why hast thou so much power?
    Why do the ruling fates decree

No state should e'er without thee be?
Why dost thou joys and hopes devour,
And clothe even Love himself in thy dark livery?

Thou and cold Fear, thy close ally,
    Do not alone on life attend,
    But following mortals to their end
Do rack the wretches whilst they die
And to eternal shades too often with them fly.

To thee, great monarch, I submit,
    Thy sables and thy cypress bring;
    I own thy Power, I own thee King;
Thy title in my heart is writ
And till that breaks, I ne'er shall freedom get.

Forced smiles thy rigor will allow,
    And whilst thy seat is in the soul
    And there all mirth thou dost control,
Thou canst admit to outward show,
The smooth appearance and dissembled brow.

Written c. 1690, published 1903

A Nocturnal Reverie

In such a night, when every louder wind
Is to its distant cavern safe confined;
And only gentle zephyr fans his wings,
And lonely Philomel, still waking, sings;
Or from some tree, famed for the owl's delight,
She, hollooing clear, directs the wanderer right;
In such a night when passing clouds give place,
Or thinly veil the heaven's mysterious face;
When in some river, overhung with green,
The waving moon and trembling leaves are seen;
When freshened grass now bears itself upright,

And makes cool banks to pleasing rest invite,
Whence springs the woodbine and the bramble rose,
And where the sleepy cowslip sheltered grows;
Whilst now a paler hue the foxglove takes,
Yet chequers still with red the dusky brakes;
When scattered glowworms, but in twilight fine,
Show trivial beauties watch their hour to shine;
When odours, which declined repelling day,
Through temperate air uninterrupted stray;
When darkened groves their softest shadows wear,
And falling waters we distinctly hear;
When through the gloom more venerable shows
Some ancient fabric, awful in repose,
While sunburned hills their swarthy looks conceal,
And swelling haycocks thicken up the vale;
When the loosed horse now, as his pasture leads,
Comes slowly grazing through the adjoining meads,
Whose stealing pace, and lengthened shade we fear,
Till torn-up forage in his teeth we hear;
When nibbling sheep at large pursue their food,
And unmolested kine rechew the cud;
When curlews cry beneath the village walls,
And to her straggling brood the partridge calls;
Their short-lived jubilee the creatures keep,
Which but endures whilst tyrant man does sleep;
When a sedate content the spirit feels,
And no fierce light disturbs, whilst it reveals;
But silent musings urge the mind to seek
Something, too high for syllables to speak;
Till the free soul to a composedness charmed,
Finding the elements of rage disarmed,
O'er all below a solemn quiet grown,
Joys in the inferior world, and thinks it like her own:
In such a night let me abroad remain
Till morning breaks, and all's confused again;
Our cares, our toils, our clamours are renewed,
Or pleasures, seldom reached, again pursued.

Published 1713

Matthew Prior (1664–1721)

No one knew the derelictions of politicians better than Prior, who encountered more of them than most of his contemporaries. During a long career he served as secretary to King William, British ambassador to the Hague and Paris, and commissioner of the Board of Trade and Plantations in London. He was also a member of the Kit-Kat Club, a gathering of intellectuals that included Joseph Addison, Richard Steele, and William Congreve. The Whiggish tendencies of the Kit-Katters went against his instincts, Prior believing the king should not be hampered by the majority opposition in Parliament. As a Tory statesman he was instrumental in the peace negotiations that led to the Treaty of Utrecht, signed in 1713, thus ending the War of the Spanish Succession. When the Whigs took power after the demise of Queen Anne he found himself vulnerable to charges of corruption and treason—not on account of anything he had done, but due to the machinations of enemies. From June 1715 he was confined at the home of the serjeant-at-arms for more than a year, unable to receive guests without permission from the Speaker of the Commons, or to receive or write letters. After release he went into retirement, devoting himself to writing, collecting, and his country estate.

True Statesmen

True statesmen only love or hate
What lessens them or makes them great.
With wondrous kindness each ascends,
Supported by his shouldering friends,
And fleering critics sometimes note
His dirt imprinted on his coat.
    Some lords like wife and husband squabble
For this fine thing, for that blue bauble,
But soon the present folly ends

And common interest makes them friends.
Whilst yet Erinnis[1] rages high
And paper darts in pamphlets fly,
He whose hot head would interpose
Is sure to have his share of blows,
But in the reconciling feast
When all the bustle proves a jest,
Where matters are adjusted fairly,
And St. John sweetly kisses Harley,[2]
The little agents of the plot,
The understrappers, are forgot.
And if the doctor, uninvited,
Afraid to fancy he was slighted,
Comes in, his labours he may spy
Fixed to the bottom of a pie
Or find how those reward his trouble
That light their pipes with dear T.D.[3]
   Be not the bully of the nation
Nor foam at mouth for moderation;
Take not thy sentiments on trust
Nor be by others' notions just.
To church and Queen and laws be hearty,
But hate a trick and scorn a party;
And if thou ever hast a voice
(Though it be only in the choice
Of vestrymen or graycoat boys[4]),
Vote right though certain to be blamed
And rather starve than be ashamed.
This method I should fancy best;
You may think otherwise. I rest.

Written between 1710 and 1714, published 1907

---

1. Erinnis] In Greek myth, the Furies; in this context, "anger."
2. Prior refers to Henry St John, first Viscount Bolingbroke, and Robert Harley, first Earl of Oxford and Mortimer, politicians who, by the time Prior composed this poem, had become rivals.
3. Prior means the pamphlets of Dr. Thomas Davenant, political economist.
4. The Grey Coat Hospital was a charitable institution that designed to educate the poor.

IV

Revolutionary Upheaval

I N CONSTITUTIONAL TERMS, the early eighteenth century was more
settled than the one preceding it, there being little appetite for changing
monarch. All the same, there were periodic Jacobite uprisings, threatened
first by James Stuart ("The Old Pretender") in 1715, then, more seriously, by
his son Charles ("The Young Pretender") in 1745–1746. Neither was success-
ful, and the Battle of Culloden (1746), still remembered in Scotland, broke
the Jacobite cause for good. There were other calls on national resources,
most obviously the Great Northern War (1700–1721) and Seven Years' War
(1756–1763)—a conflict of global proportions in which between 900,000 to
1,400,000 people were killed. Constitutional stability came under greater
pressure in subsequent years, during the reigns of George III (1760–1820),
and his son, George IV (1820–1830).

The American War of Independence was to be the harbinger of worldwide
revolution and could be said to mark the birth of the modern world, its defin-
ing feature the value it placed on the rights of the people as opposed to those
of the monarch. If we take our political rights for granted, that is due in part
to the eighteenth-century intellectuals who argued for them—Thomas Paine,
for example, active in both America and France at key moments in their
history: "the palaces of kings are built on the ruins of paradise," he told read-
ers of *Common Sense* (1776). The British have never forgiven him for putting
forward sound arguments against unelected hereditary monarchs or (in *The
Rights of Man*) defending the French Revolution.

The outcome of the American war came as a shock to George III and his lieutenants, causing government to be fearful of insurrection, an anxiety that hardened into paranoia with the outbreak of revolution in France. When unrest occurred, as in Ireland from the mid-1780s onward, the government responded with repressive measures rather than by addressing the cause, a strategy that could only make matters worse. For most of the Irish peasantry, life was unbearable under English rule, the gap between rich and poor being more pronounced than in any other country in Western Europe. With formation of the United Irishmen in 1791 it became possible for Catholics and Protestants to work together toward an independent democratic republic that would abolish payment of tithes to the Anglican Church. United Irish lodges formed across the country, and the organization was involved in the publication of four newspapers that propagated its message: the *Northern Star* (Belfast), January 1792 to May 1797; *The National Journal* (Dublin), March to May 1792; *The Press* (Dublin), September 1797 to March 1798; and *The Harp of Erin* (Cork), March 7 to 17, 1798. The United Irishmen developed connections with the revolutionary government of France (from 1793 at war with England), hoping it would invade and liberate them—and, indeed, the French and their Dutch allies would make three such attempts between 1796 and 1798, while from 1803 to 1805 Napoléon's Légion Irlandaise stood ready to land on the Irish coast. During these years Ireland was in turmoil, its "native" people resisting the tactics of the English army, which included house burnings, beatings, floggings, and torture followed by summary execution. Prison ships anchored off the coast housed vast numbers of inmates, while a blind eye was turned to atrocities committed by gangs of Orangemen and yeoman farmers.

By February 1798 the United Irishmen could boast half a million members, 280,000 of whom were armed and ready for combat. A revolutionary uprising was scheduled for May 23, 1798, but suffered from poor organization, bad luck, and disunity among leaders. Estimates of those killed vary from 30,000 to 100,000, mostly laborers who confronted British muskets with pitchforks and homemade pikes. The turning point is sometimes dated to June 5, 1798, when 1,500 rebels were slaughtered at New Ross, and over a hundred men, women and children burned to death at Scullabogue Barn, County Wexford. Guerrilla warfare continued until Robert Emmet led the United Irishmen to further insurrection in 1803, also doomed to failure (see p. 339).

The English government could not see that the most effective way of fostering unrest was to oppress its subjects, as happened on mainland Britain throughout what we now call the Romantic period (1780–1830). There are numerous examples. In 1795, poor harvests led to food riots in which large crowds shouted: "No war! No famine! No Pitt! No King!"; George III's carriage was stoned, and the windows of 10 Downing Street were attacked. The government's response was the "Two Acts," which turned critics of the constitution into criminals, and banned meetings of more than fifty people. The Luddites were already victims of a failing economy (the combined result of the Napoleonic War, harvest failures, and enclosure) when new forms of technology destroyed their livelihood. What was the government's answer? Frame breaking became a capital offense and twelve thousand troops (more than in the Peninsular Campaign) were deployed against protestors. When working people in Ely and Littleport campaigned in 1816 against high unemployment and rising grain costs, they were attacked by a militia supported by mounted dragoons. One man was killed and others injured, and in the trials that took place afterward, twenty-three men and one woman were condemned to death. At St. Peter's Field in Manchester in 1819, mounted cavalrymen charged sixty thousand people lobbying for Parliamentary reform: fourteen died and hundreds were wounded in the Peterloo Massacre.

Contrary to government suspicion, political agitation was seldom the work of revolutionaries but rather of laboring folk so deprived they had nothing to lose by peaceful protest. Wellington's victory at Waterloo only worsened their lot: direct taxation having been abolished, the national debt was discharged by levies on staples rather than luxuries, which weighed disproportionately on the poor. In a country in which laborers with full-time jobs were impoverished, many thousands lived on the verge of starvation. The obvious solution was reform of Parliament, in which only 3 percent of the population, principally the aristocracy and the landowning class, was represented. Despite the heavy-handed methods used against them, protestors were invariably nonviolent, resorting to petitions and mass meetings, but to no avail. During the nineteenth century three reform acts were passed (in 1832, 1867, and 1884), all of which succeeded in keeping political power from working people. Universal suffrage would have to wait until 1918. (In America, women received the vote in 1919; in Great Britain, they had to wait until 1928.)

Another area in which protest crystallized was the slave trade, the inhumanity of which was acknowledged by anyone who saw the manner in which slaves were manacled side by side, one above the other, like livestock. A hundred-ton ship was expected to carry a cargo of 250 slaves. Samuel Newton estimated that a third of the 60,000 who made the journey from Africa to America each year died en route. Abuses were endemic: the thumbscrew and other torture devices were used on children, while female slaves were raped by crew members. In the notorious case of the "Zong," in 1781, 132 ailing slaves were thrown overboard for the sake of an insurance claim (it would become the subject of a painting by J. M. W. Turner, *The Slave Ship*). Things were no better on plantations, where owners were a law unto themselves. John Gabriel Stedman claimed it was commonplace for owners in Surinam to cut off their slaves' noses, burn them alive, and whip them to death. On one occasion he witnessed the punishment of a slave hanged from an iron hook driven between his ribs. Stedman himself had an affair with a mulatto slave girl, Joanna.

Little wonder that slaves rebelled. They were sometimes successful, as when those in Saint-Domingue fought off the armies of England, France, and Spain, declaring independence as Haiti in 1804. Other successful rebellions include two on ships: that on the *Amistad*, off the coast of Cuba in 1839, and on the *Creole*, two years later, off the southern coast of America.

Britain was a principal culprit. During the eighteenth century, her ships transported an estimated three million from Africa to the Americas; indeed, London has been described as the hub around which the entire Atlantic trade revolved. The first step toward abolition occurred when in June 1772 Lord Mansfield removed all justification for slavery in common law. The abolitionist movement won a significant victory when in 1788 Sir William Dolben proposed a bill to the House of Commons aimed at restricting the number of slaves who could be transported from Africa to British colonies in the West Indies. The trade was abolished in 1807, and slavery ended throughout the British Empire in 1833; in America, where the South was dependent on slaves for the harvesting of cotton, the issue remained in contention until resolved at the conclusion of the Civil War in 1865.

At the start of this period, women were as subjugated as ever. Typically, they did not receive an education equivalent to that of male counterparts; they were not expected to have careers; and were dependent on men for their welfare. These attitudes prevailed in some parts of society until well into the twentieth century, yet it was during the eighteenth century, when Thomas Paine was proclaiming the rights of man, that Mary Wollstonecraft began to argue for the rights of woman: "Let woman share the rights and she will emulate the virtues of man," she wrote. Though not the first to do so (the implied agenda of the bluestocking circle that assembled round Elizabeth Montagu during the 1770s was essentially feminist), Wollstonecraft was the most coherent, articulate, and formidable to date—and by raising the issue during the French Revolution (1791), she established it as central to the debate that led to reform many decades later. Such poets as Anna Laetitia Barbauld, Charlotte Smith, Hannah More, and Ann Yearsley were no less essential to this process. Whether they wrote about slavery or the war against France, the mere fact that they engaged in political debate was an affront to a society that valued women according to their charm and physical attributes.

This period—often described as the Romantic period, referring to the cultural shift that took place after the American and French Revolutions—was one of change. Though poets occupy only a marginal place in national discourse today, they played a considerable part in changing social and political attitudes during the nineteenth century. For instance, Shelley's "The Mask of Anarchy," composed in 1819 but not published until 1832, was an inspiration to the Chartists, who reprinted it when they campaigned for Parliamentary reform in the 1840s. In subsequent years it won the admiration of such figures as Mahatma Gandhi and Bertolt Brecht. Shelley always wanted to write for a popular audience, and composed songs for working-class protestors, including a version of the British national anthem that hails as Queen the deposed figure of Liberty:

> God prosper, speed and save,
> God raise from England's grave
> > Her murdered Queen;
> Pave with swift victory
> The steps of Liberty
> Whom Britons own to be
> > Immortal Queen!

John Newton (1725–1807)

NEWTON WAS TWENTY-THREE when he was press-ganged on board HMS *Harwich* to serve in the Royal Navy during the War of the Austrian Succession; having attempted to escape, he was caught, put in irons, and flogged in front of other sailors with a cat-o'-nine tails. He was afterward transferred to a slave-trading vessel and transported its cargo for years, eventually as captain of his own ship. He became responsible, among other things, for putting sailors in irons, raping female slaves, flogging rebellious slaves, and torturing small children, including on one occasion applying thumbscrews to four boys who were afterward imprisoned in neck yokes. On March 10, 1748 he awakened in the middle of the night to find his ship breaking apart in a storm. Newton prayed for deliverance. By the following morning, the ship was in bad shape, but most of the crew survived. Though he continued as a slave trader until 1755, Newton began to read the Bible, committed himself to a form of evangelical Calvinism, and repented of his past, turning eventually to the abolitionist cause. He was a tireless campaigner against the trade, condemning it to the Privy Council in 1788. As a Church of England minister, he was a close friend of Hannah More (p. 264), William Wilberforce and William Cowper, with whom he collaborated on *Olney Hymns* (1779), "Amazing grace!" being the most famous, thanks to its adoption as an unofficial anthem by civil rights protestors in the 1960s.

Amazing Grace!

Amazing grace! (how sweet the sound)
    That saved a wretch like me;
I once was lost but now am found,
    Was blind but now I see.

'Twas grace that taught my heart to fear
    And grace my fears relieved;
How precious did that grace appear,
    The hour I first believed.

Through many dangers, toils and snares
    I have already come;
'Tis grace that brought me safe thus far
    And grace will lead me home.

The Lord has promised good to me,
    His word my hope secures;
He will my shield and portion be,
    As long as life endures.

Yes, when this flesh and heart shall fail
    And mortal life shall cease,
I shall possess within the veil
    A life of joy and peace.

The earth shall soon dissolve like snow,
    The sun forbear to shine;
But God who called me here below
    Will be forever mine.

Published 1779

Joseph Mather (1737–1804)

MATHER WAS A semiliterate Sheffield file cutter who composed and sang lyrics to well-known tunes, which he would perform at fairs and in taverns. When selling broadsides of his work, he sat on a donkey facing the animal's rump, to catch the eye of potential buyers. His lyrics would have to wait until more than half a century after his death, in 1862, to be collected in book form. Few writers better articulated the sufferings and pleasures of artisan life in England, especially during the French Revolution. Mather's best-known work is the republican version of the British national anthem, beginning "God Save Great Thomas Paine." During the 1790s it was sung at open air meetings by Sheffield Jacobins, and became a local rallying cry for anyone with radical leanings. In another lyric, Mather attacks Pitt's taxation policy, which placed an undue burden on the poor:

> In eating, drinking, working, playing,
> Sleeping, waking, swearing, praying,
> The people were forever paying.

Mather was eyewitness to a riot that took place in Norfolk Street, Sheffield, on August 4, 1795, when soldiers mustered by Colonel Cameron refused to march, part of their bounty money having been withheld, along with arrears in their pay. A large mob supported them, aware that soldiers' families suffered as much as townspeople from high food prices and misgovernment. Colonel Robert Althorpe, commander of the local volunteers, had the Riot Act read before wading into the crowd, slashing civilians with his sabre. Riflemen were summoned and began shooting, killing two men. Mather articulated his reaction in "The Norfolk Street Riots." The price of such outspoken criticism was to spend a year bound over to keep the peace—as he later recalled, "I was muzzled for a year."

God Save Great Thomas Paine

> God save great Thomas Paine,
> His *Rights of Man* to explain
>   To every soul;
> He makes the blind to see
> What dupes and slaves they be,
> And points out liberty
>   From pole to pole.
>
> Thousands cry "Church and King!"
> That well deserve to swing,
>   All must allow:
> Birmingham blush for shame,

Manchester do the same,
Infamous is your name,
    Patriot's vow.

Pull proud oppressors down,
Knock off each tyrant's crown
    And break his sword;
Down with aristocracy,
Set up democracy,
And from hypocrisy
    Save us, good Lord.

Why should despotic pride
Usurp on every side?
    Let us be free;
Grant freedom's arms success
And all her efforts bless,
Plant through the universe
    Liberty's tree.

Facts are seditious things
When they touch courts and kings,
    Armies are raised,[1]
Barracks and bastilles built,
Innocence charged with guilt,
Blood most unjustly spilt,
    Gods stand amazed.

Despots may howl and yell,
Though they're in league with hell
    They'll not reign long;
Satan may lead the van,
And do the worst he can,
Paine and his *Rights of Man*
    Shall be my song.

Probably written 1793, published 1794

---

1. This may be a reference to the outbreak of war between Britain and France in 1793.

The Norfolk Street Riots

Corruption tells me homicide
Is willful murder justified;
A striking precedent was tried
    In August ninety-five,
When armed assassins dressed in blue
Most wantonly their townsmen slew,
And magistrates and juries too
    At murder did connive.

I saw the tragic scene commence;
A madman drunk,[1] without offence
Drew out his sword in false pretence
    And wounded some more wise;
Defenceless boys he chased about,
The timid cried, the bold did shout,
Which brought the curious to shout
    To see what meant the noise.

The gazing crowd stagnated stood
To see a wretch that should know good
Insatiate thirst for human blood
    Like one sent from beneath;
This gave me well to understand
A sword put in a madman's hand,
Especially a villain grand,
    Must terminate in death.

'Twas manifest in the event
That what the bloody tyrant meant
Was murder without precedent,
    Though by injustice screened.
The *Courant* may her columns swell,[2]

---

1. A madman drunk] a reference to Colonel Robert Althorpe, who commanded the local regiment of volunteers from April 1794 to October 1799 (see headnote, p. 256 above).
2. *The Sheffield Courant*, a newspaper set up to oppose Jacobinism, published from June 10, 1793 to August 4, 1797.

Designing men may falsehoods tell,
Not all the powers of earth and hell
    Can justify the fiend.

This armed banditti, filled with spleen,
At his command, like bloodhounds keen,
In fine, to crown the horrid scene,
    A shower of bullets fired.
The consequence was deep distress,
More widows and more fatherless,
The devil blushed and did confess
    'Twas more than he required.

Corruption cried for this exploit:
"His worship shall be made a knight,
I hold his conduct just and right
    And think him all divine."
Oppression need not fear alarms
Since tyranny has got such swarms
Of gallant heroes bearing arms
    To butcher-grunting swine.[3]

The stones besmeared with blood and brains
Was the result of Robin's pains,
Surviving friends wept o'er the stains
    When dying victims bled;
As Abel's blood aloud did call
To Him whose power created all,
Eternal vengeance sure must fall
    Upon his guilty head.

Ye wanton coxcombs, fops, and fools,
Aristocratic dupes and tools,
Subject yourselves to better rules
    And cast away that badge.

---

3. butcher-grunting swine] Mather alludes to Burke's description of the working class as a "swinish multitude."

Remember on a future day
Corruption must be done away,
Then what will you presume to say
    When truth shall be your judge?

Written shortly after August 4, 1795, published 1862

Anna Laetitia Barbauld (1743–1825)

BARBAULD'S ROOTS LAY in dissenting culture, which produced such think-
ers as William Hazlitt and Samuel Taylor Coleridge. Eighteenth-century dis-
senters were pioneers of scientific and political thought; one of her father's
colleagues at the Warrington Academy was Joseph Priestley, discoverer of
phlogiston. A beautiful woman in youth, Barbauld may have been courted
by Jean-Paul Marat, among others. She wrote on behalf of liberal causes:
women's rights, the antislavery protestors, and the French Revolution. In *Civic
Sermons* (1792), she attempted to impart political literacy to the uneducated
working class, producing furious criticism from Tory reviewers who accused
her of whipping up discontent. Undeterred, her poem "On the Expected Gen-
eral Rising of the French Nation in 1792" begins with a passionate declara-
tion of Republican feeling in which the French people are enjoined to "Strike
hordes of despots to the ground!" In "The Rights of Woman," Barbauld sup-
ports Wollstonecraft's critique of Rousseau's argument that woman should
manipulate man; her view was that woman should command by moral author-
ity alone. In another prose publication, *Sins of Government, Sins of the Nation*
(1793), Barbauld attacked the unrepresentative form of government in Britain
and her country's pursuit of "a ruinous war." Tory reviewers again denounced
her adoption of "the jargon of French republicanism." Barbauld continued to
publish until her poem, *Eighteen Hundred and Eleven* (1812), a critique of the
British government, was greeted with anger at its apparent lack of patriotism.
The Tory critic John Wilson Croker satirized her, saying she was induced
"to sally forth in the magnanimous resolution of saving a sinking state by
the instrumentality of a pamphlet in prose and a pamphlet in verse." Henry
Crabb Robinson confided to his diary that "the tone and spirit of it are cer-

tainly very bad," while William Godwin called it "cowardly, time-serving, Presbyterian, besides a string of epithets which meant only that he found the work wretched." Barbauld was not to publish again, and slipped gradually into depression.

On the Expected General Rising of the French Nation in 1792

Rise, mighty nation, in thy strength,
And deal thy dreadful vengeance round;
Let thy great spirit, roused at length,
Strike hordes of despots to the ground!

Devoted land! thy mangled breast
Eager the royal vultures tear;
By friends betrayed, by foes oppressed,
And Virtue struggles with Despair.

The tocsin[1] sounds! Arise, arise!
Stern o'er each breast let country reign;
Nor virgin's plighted hand nor sighs
Must now the ardent youth detain:

Nor must the hind who tills thy soil
The ripened vintage stay to press,
Till Rapture crown the flowing bowl,
And Freedom boast of full success.

Briareus-like[2] extend thy hands,
That every hand may crush a foe;
In millions pour thy generous bands,
And end a warfare by a blow!

---

1. tocsin] alarm bell calling citizens to arms.
2. Briareus was a creature in Greek myth with fifty heads and a hundred hands.

Then wash with sad repentant tears
Each deed that clouds thy glory's page;
Each frenzied start impelled by fears,
Each transient burst of headlong rage:

Then fold in thy relenting arms
Thy wretched outcasts where they roam;
From pining want and war's alarms,
Oh, call the child of misery home!

Then build the tomb—oh, not alone,
Of him who bled in freedom's cause;
With equal eye the martyr own,
Of faith revered and ancient laws.

Then be thy tide of glory stayed;
Then be thy conquering banners furled;
Obey the laws thyself hast made,
And rise—the model of the world!

Written 1792, published November 2, 1793

The Rights of Woman[1]

Yes, injured woman, rise, assert thy right!
Woman! too long degraded, scorned, oppressed;
Oh born to rule in partial law's despite,
Resume thy native empire o'er the breast!

---

1. Although first published after Barbauld's death, this poem engages with Mary Woll-stonecraft's *Vindication of the Rights of Woman* (1792), which Barbauld read soon after its publication. Though woman may seek to use her seductive appeal to "Make treacherous man thy subject," Barbauld argues that true authority lies in moral superiority to man, and the ability to civilize and comfort. She concludes with the argument that the separate rights of the sexes are irrelevant if men and women enjoy "mutual love."

Go forth arrayed in panoply divine,
That angel pureness which admits no stain;
Go bid proud man his boasted rule resign
And kiss the golden sceptre of thy reign.

Go gird thyself with grace, collect thy store
Of bright artillery glancing from afar—
Soft melting tones thy thundering cannon's roar,
Blushes and fears thy magazine of war.

Thy rights are empire: urge no meaner claim—
Felt, not defined, and, if debated, lost;
Like sacred mysteries which, withheld from fame,
Shunning discussion, are revered the most.

Try all that wit and art suggest to bend
Of thy imperial foe the stubborn knee;
Make treacherous man thy subject, not thy friend—
Thou mayst command, but never canst be free.

Awe the licentious and restrain the rude;
Soften the sullen, clear the cloudy brow;
Be more than princes' gifts, thy favours[2] sued—
She hazards all, who will the least allow.

But hope not, courted idol of mankind,
On this proud eminence secure to stay;
Subduing and subdued, thou soon shalt find
Thy coldness soften, and thy pride give way.

Then, then, abandon each ambitious thought,
Conquest or rule thy heart shall feebly move,
In Nature's school, by her soft maxims taught
That separate rights are lost in mutual love.

Written c. 1792, published June 1825

---

2. favours] probably a reference to sexual favours.

Hannah More (1745–1833)

AFTER MORE BECAME an Evangelical Anglican, her closeness to fellow Evangelicals William Wilberforce MP and the reformed slave trader John Newton deepened her interest in abolitionism. The slave trade tainted countless details of everyday life: many children taught at the school run by More and her sisters were from slave-trading families; the sugar that people put in their tea, the tobacco smoked in their pipes, the rum consumed by sailors—all were produced by slave labor. In 1787 More assisted Thomas Clarkson in his investigation of the Bristol trade and, under his influence, became an activist. For someone resident near the slaving port of Bristol, this was dangerous, especially if they were female. When invited to friends' houses, she took an engraved cross section of a ship showing slaves manacled side by side, and displayed it to the horrified fascination of fellow guests. She canvassed MPs in person and by correspondence, hoping to persuade them to support Sir William Dolben's 1788 bill to restrict the transport of slaves between Africa and the West Indies. As part of her campaign she composed "Slavery" in a fortnight so it could be published prior to Parliament's debate on the bill. Its argument is that those who trade in human flesh are "white savages" whose conduct is inherently un-Christian. In the extract below, she describes a raid on an African village by slavers, "The burning village and the blazing town," and the forcible separation of children from their parents. By arguing the humanity of blacks, More contradicted the widespread view, held even by some abolitionists, that they were genetically conditioned to serve whites; as she says, "all mankind can feel." Though a comparatively small measure, Dolben's Bill was a first step toward abolition, and caused consternation among traders when passed into law, for it was clear the abolitionists were serious. More remained a prominent campaigner for abolition until her death in 1833, the year of West Indian emancipation.

Slavery: A Poem (extract)

Whene'er to Afric's shores I turn my eyes,
Horrors of deepest, deadliest guilt arise;
I see, by more than fancy's mirror shown,
The burning village and the blazing town,
See the dire victim torn from social life,
The shrieking babe, the agonizing wife!
She, wretch forlorn, is dragged by hostile hands,
To distant tyrants sold in distant lands!
Transmitted miseries and successive chains
The sole sad heritage her child obtains!
Even this last wretched boon their foes deny:
To weep together or together die.
By felon hands, by one relentless stroke,
See the fond links of feeling nature broke!
The fibers twisting round a parent's heart,
Torn from their grasp and bleeding as they part

     Hold, murderers, hold! Nor aggravate distress;
Respect the passions you yourselves possess!
Even you, of ruffian heart and ruthless hand,
Love your own offspring, love your native land.
Ah, leave them holy freedom's cheering smile,
The Heav'n-taught fondness for the parent soil;
Revere affections mingled with our frame,
In every nature, every clime the same;
In all, these feelings equal sway maintain;
In all, the love of home and freedom reign—
And Tempe's vale and parched Angola's sand
One equal fondness of their sons command.
The unconquered savage laughs at pain and toil,
Basking in freedom's beams which gild his native soil.

     Does thirst of empire, does desire of fame
(For these are specious crimes) our rage inflame?
No; sordid lust of gold their fate controls—
The basest appetite of basest souls!
Gold, better gained by what their ripening sky,
Their fertile fields, their arts and mines supply.
What wrongs, what injuries does Oppression plead,

To smooth the horror of the unnatural deed?
What strange offence, what aggravated sin?
They stand convicted of a darker skin!
Barbarians, hold! The opprobrious commerce spare,
Respect His sacred image which they bear.
Though dark and savage, ignorant and blind,
They claim the common privilege of kind;
Let malice strip them of each other plea,
They still are men, and men should still be free.
Insulted reason loathes the inverted trade—
Dire change! The agent is the purchase made!
Perplexed, the baffled muse involves the tale;
Nature confounded, well may language fail!
The outraged goddess, with abhorrent eyes,
Sees man the traffic, souls the merchandise!

Published February 8, 1788

Olaudah Equiano (c. 1745–1797)

"ONE DAY, WHEN all our people were gone out to their works as usual, and only I and my dear sister were left to mind the house, two men and a woman got over our walls, and in a moment seized us both; and, without giving us time to cry out, or make resistance, they stopped our mouths, tied our hands, and ran off with us into the nearest wood": so began Equiano's life as a slave. He was eight years old, the son of a Nigerian slave owner. Sold and resold until he ended up on an Atlantic trading ship, he was beaten until he responded to his new name, Gustavus Vassa. He eventually became the property of a naval officer in Virginia, serving on British ships in several battles of the Seven Years' War. Taught to read and write by sailors, he converted to Christianity and became a Methodist. Thinking he had obtained his freedom in London, he was nonetheless reenslaved in 1762, and forced to work on a ship that plied its trade between America and the West Indies. In 1766 he bought his freedom for forty pounds and entered the slave business as trader and plantation owner. After traveling the world for twenty years he eventually returned to London and became involved in radical politics, including the abolitionist cause—to which his autobiography, published in 1789, lent support. He helped found the Sons of Africa, a group of Africans who lobbied politicians and wrote to newspapers condemning slavery. He even wrote a letter to Queen Charlotte on behalf of the cause. Despite winning fame during his lifetime he was largely forgotten after his death until, in the 1960s, interest revived in his *The Interesting Narrative of the Life of Olaudah Equiano*, from which the poem below is taken.

Miscellaneous Verses[1]

Well may I say my life has been
One scene of sorrow and of pain;
From early days I griefs have known,
And as I grew my griefs have grown.

Dangers were always in my path
And fear of wrath and sometimes death;
While pale dejection in me reigned
I often wept, by grief constrained.

When taken from my native land
By an unjust and cruel band,
How did uncommon dread prevail!
My sighs no more I could conceal.

To ease my mind I often strove,
And tried my trouble to remove;
I sung and uttered sighs between,
Assayed to stifle guilt with sin.

But oh! not all that I could do
Would stop the current of my woe;
Conviction still my vileness showed—
How great my guilt, how lost to good.

---

1. The subtitle to this poem is: "Reflections on the state of my mind during my First convictions; of the necessity of believing the truth and experiencing the inestimable benefits of Christianity."

Prevented that I could not die,
Nor could to one sure refuge fly;
An orphan state I had to mourn,
Forsook by all and left forlorn.

Those who beheld my downcast mien
Could not guess at my woes unseen;
They by appearance could not know
The troubles that I waded through.

Lust, anger, blasphemy and pride
With legions of such ills beside
Troubled my thoughts, while doubts and fears
Clouded and darkened most my years.

Sighs now no more would be confined,
They breathed the trouble of my mind;
I wished for death but checked the word,
And often prayed unto the Lord.

Unhappy, more than some on earth,
I thought the place that gave me birth
Strange thoughts oppressed, while I replied,
"Why not in Ethiopia died?"

And why thus spared when nigh to hell?
God only knew, I could not tell!
A tottering fence, a bowing wall
I thought myself e'er since the fall.

Ofttimes I mused and nigh despair,
While birds melodious filled the air—
Thrice happy songsters, ever free,
How blest were they compared to me!

Thus all things added to my pain
While grief compelled me to complain;
When sable clouds began to rise,
My mind grew darker than the skies.

The English nation called to leave,
How did my breast with sorrows heave!
I longed for rest, cried "Help me, Lord—
Some mitigation, Lord, afford!"

Yet on dejected still I went,
Heart-throbbing woes within me pent;
Nor land nor sea could comfort give,
Nor aught my anxious mind relieve.

Weary with troubles yet unknown
To all but God and self alone,
Numerous months for peace I strove,
Numerous foes I had to prove.

Inured to dangers, grief and woes,
Trained up midst perils, death and foes,
I said, "Must it thus ever be?
No quiet is permitted me."

Hard hap and more than heavy lot!   *fate*
I prayed to God, "Forget me not;
What thou ordain'st help me to bear—
But oh, deliver from despair!"

Strivings and wrestling seemed in vain,
Nothing I did could ease my pain;
Then gave I up my work and will,
Confessed and owned my doom was hell!

Like some poor prisoner at the bar,
Conscious of guilt, of sin and fear,
Arraigned and self-condemned I stood,
Lost in the world and in my blood!

Yet here midst blackest clouds confined,
A beam from Christ the day-star shined;
Surely, thought I, if Jesus please,
He can at once sign my release.

I, ignorant of his righteousness,
Set up my labours in its place;
Forgot for why his blood was shed,
And prayed and fasted in his stead.

He died for sinners—I am one;
Might not his blood for me atone?
Though I am nothing else but sin
Yet surely he can make me clean!

Thus light came in and I believed;
Myself forgot, and help received!
My Savior then I know I found
For, eased from guilt, no more I groaned.

Oh happy hour, in which I ceased
To mourn, for then I found a rest;
My soul and Christ were now as one—
Thy light, oh Jesus, in me shone!

Blessed be thy name, for now I know
I and my works can nothing do;
The Lord alone can ransom man:
For this the spotless lamb was slain!

When sacrifices, works, and prayer
Proved vain, and ineffectual were,
"Lo, then I come!" the Savior cried,
And bleeding, bowed his head and died.

He died for all who ever saw
No help in them, nor by the law:
I this have seen, and gladly own
Salvation is by Christ alone.

Published March 24, 1789

James Field Stanfield (1749–1824)

BORN IN DUBLIN, Stanfield trained as a priest before serving as an ordinary seaman on slave ships. His first voyage was on board the Eagle, which left Liverpool on September 7, 1774, under the command of Captain David Wilson. Wilson was a sadist who enjoyed flogging slaves and sailors as part of a campaign of terror. If the flogger did not use sufficient violence, Wilson ensured he in turn was flogged. On arrival in Benin many sailors became ill and died; Stanfield journeyed to a slave-trading fortress at Gato and escaped the worst of the contagions. In late June 1775, he joined Captain Wilson on another ship, the *True Blue*, which took a cargo of slaves first to Jamaica, then on to Liverpool. It was, Stanfield recalled, a "floating dungeon" from which came "shrieks of woe and howlings of despair." The extract we have selected from *The Guinea Voyage* describes the horrors that greet an enslaved African when he wakes up to find the man chained to him has died, and is forced to "tug" the corpse on deck. It is clear from what Stanfield says that he witnessed many atrocities, including the rape of a small girl by the ship's captain. He left the trade in 1777, to become a touring actor, an elocution teacher, a brandy merchant and, finally, a writer. He published a damning account of his experiences in May 1788, in the form of letters to Thomas Clarkson, and the following year issued *The Guinea Voyage*, the proceeds of which he donated to the abolitionist cause. He believed he had a mission to reveal to the world the evils of "the inhuman trade" as witnessed by common sailors, many of whom either died or deserted.

The Guinea Voyage, Book 3

SLAVES IN THE HOLD (EXTRACTS)

The hateful purchase made, compressive stowed,
The floating dungeon with the unnatural load
Is crammed profane; immersed in deadly gloom

The shackled sufferers wait the expected doom
Till the bark, glutted with the purchased gore,
Hoists the full sail, and quits the wafted shore. . . .

     Soon as umbrageous night on raven wings
O'er the sad freight her dewy opiates flings,
Packed in close misery, the reeking crowd,
Sweltering in chains, pollute the hot abode.
In painful rows with studious art compressed,
Smoking they lie, and breathe the humid pest.
Moistened with gore, on the hard platform ground,
The bare-rubbed joint soon bursts the painful bound;
Sinks in the obdurate plank with racking force
And ploughs (dire task!) its agonizing course.
Nor can they turn to an exchange of pains,
Pressed in their narrow cribs and girt with chains;
The afflictive posture all relief denies.
Recruiting sleep, the squalid mansion flies,
In one long groan the feeble throng unite:
One strain of anguish wastes the lengthened night.
     With broadening disk and slow-increasing ray,
Up from old ocean climbs the orb of day;
Then the drear hatchway morning hands disclose
And point the sufferers to a change of woes.
     Soon as the gorged cell of dim disease
Opes the sick passage to a quicker breeze
From the rank maw, belched up in morbid steam,
The hot mist thickens in the sidelong beam;
When from the noisome cave, the drooping crowd
In fettered pairs break through the misty cloud.
With keen despair they eye the morning's glow
And curse the added day that swells their woe;
Wet with foul damps, behold the sad array
Disclose their misery to the unpitying day.
Look at yon wretch, a melancholy case,
Grief in his eye, despair upon his face;
His fellow—see—from orbs of bloodshot ire
On his pale tyrants darts the indignant fire.

Striving with feeble force to press the grate,
Yon struggling sufferer heaves a ponderous weight.
Stripes from the sounding lash, fierce drawn, succeed,
To give the fainting trembler hapless speed.
Alas! the sounding lash applies in vain;
For close united by the festering chain,
His dead companion up the untoward height
(Struck by the mortal ministers of night)
The living victim tugs with painful throes—
Himself, less blessed, reserved for keener woes.

Published 1789

Charlotte Smith (1749–1806)

"I WAS SOLD, a legal prostitute, in my early youth," Smith once wrote, characterizing her married life as "personal slavery." Charlotte Turner was a mere fifteen-year-old when sold by her father, an indebted gambler, to the scion of a wealthy plantation-owning family, Benjamin Smith, thus beginning a child-bearing career that would span twenty-two years, producing twelve children (eight within the first nine years of marriage). The relationship was a disaster: Smith regarded Charlotte as his property, and was abusive and violent. He turned out to be as penurious as her father. As was customary, she was imprisoned with him when he was sentenced to seven months for embezzlement of his father's trust fund. She separated from him in 1787 but the sufferings of these years would remain with her forever, as she confided to William Godwin: "I have no other consciousness of my identity than that I am the same unhappy person who was, at barely (I think) fifteen, sold to an idiot—and from the Sussex hills, condemned to be shut up in a wretched street in the city." She won literary renown in 1784 with her *Elegiac Sonnets,* which drew speculation from reviewers about her depression (the subject of her poems). Under constant pressure to raise funds to support her children, she began to write novels, of which she would publish no less than ten between 1788 and 1798. From 1791 to 1793 she resided in Brighton on the south coast of England, where she sheltered refugees from revolutionary France (principally aristocratic, middle class, and clerical). Most arrived without a penny, having spent everything they had on their passage, and many were in shock, having witnessed atrocities either in Paris or La Vendée, where a Royalist uprising had been brutally suppressed. In one of her letters, Smith records that "the emigrants who are yet here, some of whom are very agreeable men, find some consolation in the society my small book room affords them of an evening." Though a supporter of the French Revolution, Smith disapproved of what she called "the injustice and ferocity of the French republic," and (even more) of the execution of Louis XVI. These feelings inform her long poem, *The Emigrants* (1793).

The Emigrants, Book 2 (extracts)

Long wintry months are passed; the moon that now
Lights her pale crescent even at noon has made
Four times her revolution, since with step
Mournful and slow, along the wave-worn cliff,
Pensive I took my solitary way
Lost in despondence, while contemplating
Not my own wayward destiny alone
(Hard as it is, and difficult to bear!),
But in beholding the unhappy lot
Of the lorn exiles who, amid the storms
Of wild disastrous anarchy, are thrown,
Like shipwrecked sufferers, on England's coast,
To see, perhaps, no more their native land
Where Desolation riots. . . .

Shuddering, I view the pictures they have drawn
Of desolated countries where the ground,
Stripped of its unripe produce, was thick strewn
With various death—the warhorse falling there
By famine, and his rider by the sword.
The moping clouds sailed heavy-charged with rain,
And bursting o'er the mountain's misty brow

Deluged, as with an inland sea, the vales;
Where through the sullen evening's lurid gloom,
Rising like columns of volcanic fire,
The flames of burning villages illumed
The waste of water; and the wind that howled
Along its troubled surface brought the groans
Of plundered peasants and the frantic shrieks
Of mothers for their children; while the brave,
To pity still alive, listened aghast
To these dire echoes, hopeless to prevent
The evils they beheld, or check the rage
Which ever, as the people of one land
Meet in contention, fires the human heart
With savage thirst of kindred blood, and makes
Man lose his nature, rendering him more fierce
Than the gaunt monsters of the howling waste.
      Oft have I heard the melancholy tale
Which, all their native gaiety forgot,
These exiles tell—how hope impelled them on,
Reckless of tempest, hunger or the sword
Till, ordered to retreat they knew not why
From all their flattering prospects, they became
The prey of dark suspicion and regret:
Then in despondence sunk the unnerved arm
Of gallant Loyalty. At every turn
Shame and Disgrace appeared, and seemed to mock
Their scattered squadrons—which the warlike youth,
Unable to endure, often implored
As the last act of friendship, from the hand
Of some brave comrade, to receive the blow
That freed the indignant spirit from its pain.
To a wild mountain, whose bare summit hides
Its broken eminence in clouds, whose steeps
Are dark with woods, where the receding rocks
Are worn by torrents of dissolving snow,
A wretched woman, pale and breathless, flies,
And gazing round her, listens to the sound
Of hostile footsteps. No, it dies away!

Nor noise remains but of the cataract
Or surly breeze of night that mutters low
Among the thickets where she trembling seeks
A temporary shelter, clasping close
To her hard-heaving heart her sleeping child,
All she could rescue of the innocent group
That yesterday surrounded her. Escaped
Almost by miracle, fear, frantic fear,
Winged her weak feet! Yet half-repentant now
Her headlong haste, she wishes she had stayed
To die with those affrighted Fancy paints
The lawless soldier's victims. Hark, again,
The driving tempest bears the cry of Death!
And with deep sullen thunder, the dread sound
Of cannon vibrates on the tremulous earth
While, bursting in the air, the murderous bomb
Glares o'er her mansion. Where the splinters fall
Like scattered comets, its destructive path
Is marked by wreaths of flame! Then, overwhelmed
Beneath accumulated horror, sinks
The desolate mourner, yet in death itself,
True to maternal tenderness, she tries
To save the unconscious infant from the storm
In which she perishes, and to protect
This last dear object of her ruined hopes
From prowling monsters that from other hills
More inaccessible, and wilder wastes,
Lured by the scent of slaughter, follow fierce
Contending hosts, and to polluted fields
Add dire increase of horrors. But, alas,
The mother and the infant perish both!

Written c. February 1793, published July 1793

John Philpot Curran (1750–1817)

CURRAN WAS THE "fiercest imp of the pandemonium," recalled William Drennan (p. 286). As politician, Curran supported Catholic emancipation and reform of the Parliamentary system, and in those causes delivered powerful speeches. But he is more relevant to this volume as a lawyer, in which role he fought for the lives of Irish patriots, beginning in January 1794 with Archibald Hamilton Rowan, President of the United Irishmen, prosecuted for having distributed a pamphlet urging readers "to overturn the established constitution." Curran managed over the course of the next six months to secure acquittal of seven Irish patriots charged with "raising . . . insurrection"; the proprietor of the *Northern Star* (a mouthpiece of the United Irishmen); and of William Drennan. These trials took place against the backdrop of revolution. By late 1796 Ireland had become the principal theater of insurrection in Britain, and site of increasing repression by the authorities; among other tactics, the army used house searches, seizures, burnings, hangings, "half-hangings," torture, summary execution, and deportation without trial. In May 1797 Curran withdrew from Parliament with other Irish Whigs, in protest at the atrocities, declining to seek reelection. Over the next six months he defended William Orr, a farmer tried and found guilty of administering the oath of the United Irishmen to a soldier, as well as Peter Finnerty, publisher of *The Press* (successor to the *Northern Star*), accused and found guilty of libel. After the '98 uprising he became the main defender of the United Irishmen, most of whom were tried in an atmosphere of hostility. As their advocate, he was under constant surveillance by the authorities, who presumed him to be a co-conspirator (though he was not); court records reveal he conducted himself with courage and determination. He came under renewed scrutiny in 1803, because of his daughter Sarah's relationship with Robert Emmet (p. 339): his house was searched and he was interrogated by the Irish Privy Council. In later years he was the friend of Byron and Hazlitt, both of whom admired what he had done for the Irish cause. He composed poetry throughout his life, "The Deserter's Meditation" being his best-known work. It was inspired by a meeting with a soldier who faced a capital penalty for desertion. Curran is said to have asked him "whether you feel disposed to pass the little remnant of life that is left you in penitence and fasting, or whether you would prefer to drown your sorrow in a merry glass?" "The Deserter's Meditation" records his answer. "Cushla-Ma-Chree" celebrates a promised land, at peace with itself and the world, that Curran would not live to see.

The Deserter's Meditation

>   If sadly thinking,
>   With spirits sinking,
>   Could more than drinking my cares compose,
>   A cure for sorrow
>   From sighs I'd borrow,
>   And hope tomorrow would end my woes.
>
>   But as in wailing
>   There's nought availing,
>   And death unfailing will strike the blow,
>   Then for that reason,
>   And for a season,
>   Let us be merry before we go!
>
>   To joy a stranger,
>   A wayworn ranger
>   In every danger my course I've run;
>   Now hope all ending,
>   And death befriending,
>   His last aid lending, my cares are done.
>
>   No more a rover
>   Or hapless lover,
>   My griefs are over—my glass runs low;
>   Then for that reason,
>   And for a season,
>   Let us be merry before we go!

Written 1786, published 1819

Cushla-Ma-Chree[1]

Dear Erin, how sweetly thy green bosom rises,
　　An emerald set in the ring of the sea,
Each blade of thy meadows my faithful heart prizes,
　　Thou queen of the west, the world's *cushla-ma-chree.*

Thy gates open wide to the poor and the stranger,
　　There smiles hospitality, hearty and free;
Thy friendship is seen in the moment of danger,
　　And the wanderer is welcomed with *cushla-ma-chree.*

Thy sons are brave but, the battle once over,
　　In brotherly peace with their foes they agree,
And the roseate cheeks of thy daughters discover
　　The soul-speaking blush that says *cushla-ma-chree.*

Then flourish forever, my dear native Erin,
　　While sadly I wander an exile from thee,
And firm as thy mountains, no injury fearing,
　　May heaven defend its own *cushla-ma-chree.*

Composed by 1817, published 1825

Philip Freneau (1752–1832)

OF FRENCH HUGUENOT descent, Freneau was a New Yorker who, at Princeton College, would become the friend of James Madison, Hugh Henry Brackenridge, and Aaron Burr. With Brackenridge, he coauthored a poem entitled "The Rising Glory of America" in 1771. He afterward visited Jamaica, where he was appalled by the abuses of slave owners. He returned to America to fight in the Revolutionary War in 1778 and two years later attempted to return to the West Indies. En route, his ship became involved

---

1. The phrase that gives this poem its title is Irish for "pulse of my heart."

in a fight with a British warship, the *Iris*; he afterward recalled how a twelve-pound shot struck his ship's captain "in the right thigh, which it smashed to atoms, tearing part of his belly open at the same time with the splinters from the oars. He fell from the quarter-deck close by me, and for some time seemed very busily engaged in setting his legs to rights. He died about eleven the same night." Captured by the British, Freneau was transferred to a prison ship, the *Scorpion*, in New York harbor. When some of the prisoners tried to escape, the sentries "posted themselves at each hatchway, and most basely and cowardly fired fore and aft among us, pistols and muskets, for a full quarter of an hour without intermission." Badly injured, Freneau was transferred to the *Hunter*, where he was held in the dark, filthy hold of what he called "the slaughter house," a victim of repeated beatings by the ship's "doctor." Two months later, he was released in an exchange of prisoners, and returned to New Jersey to recover. Almost immediately he began to compose *The British Prison-Ship*, which describes his prisoner-of-war experiences, condemning the inhumanity with which the British treated their captives. He later became a journalist, writing on behalf of Jeffersonian causes, a profession that he maintained in subsequent decades.

The British Prison-Ship[1]

CANTO III (EXTRACT)

A scene of horror rises to the view,
Such as the boldest painter never drew:
Three hundred prisoners banished from the light
Below the decks in torment, spend the night;
Some for a bed their tattered clothing join,
And some on chests, and some on floors recline.
Shut from the blessings of the cooling air,
Pensive they lie, all anguish and despair;
Meager and sad and scorched with heat below,
They look like ghosts ere death has made them so.

---

1. This extract from Freneau's four-canto work describes his experiences as a prisoner of war in the *Hunter*, a British prison ship, during six weeks in 1780 (see headnote above).

How should they bloom where heat and hunger join,
Thus to debase the human form divine—
Where cruel thirst the parching throat invades,
Dries up the man, and fits him for the shades?
    No waters laded from the bubbling spring   *loaded*
To these dire ships the generous Britons bring;
Oft through the night in vain their captives ask
One drop of water from the stinking cask;
No drop is granted to the earnest prayer,
To Dives[2] in the regions of despair.
The loathsome cask a fatal dose contains,
Its poison bearing through the altered veins;
Hence fevers rage where health was seen before,
And the lank veins abound with blood no more.
    Oh, how they long to taste the woodland streams,
For these they pine in frantic feverish dreams;
To springs and brooks with weary steps they go
And seem to hear the gushing waters flow;
Along the purling wave they think they lie,   *flowing*
Quaff the sweet dream and all contented die—
Then start from dreams that fright the restless mind,
And still new torments in their prison find.
    Dull flow the hours till from the sky displayed,
Sweet morn dispels the horrors of the shade;
But what to them is morn's delightful ray,
Sad and distressful as the close of day;
At distance far appears the dewy green,
And leafy trees on mountaintops are seen;
But they no groves nor grassy mountains tread,
Marked for a longer journey to the dead.

Written autumn 1780, published 1781

---

2. In the Bible, Dives is a rich man who disregards the beggar at his gate and is condemned to hell.

To Sir Toby,

A sugar planter in the interior parts of Jamaica,
near the city of San Jago de la Vega, 1784

> The motions of his spirit are black as night,
> And his affections dark as Erebus. (Shakespeare)[1]

If there exists a hell, the case is clear,
Sir Toby's slaves enjoy that portion here:
Here are no blazing brimstone lakes, 'tis true,
But kindled rum too often burns as blue,
In which some fiend whom nature must detest
Steeps Toby's brand, and marks poor Cudjoe's breast.[2]
Here whips on whips excite perpetual fears
And mingled howlings vibrate on my ears;
Here nature's plagues abound, to fret and tease—
Snakes, scorpions, despots, lizards, centipedes.
No art, no care escapes the busy lash;
All have their due, and all are paid in cash;
The eternal driver keeps a steady eye
On a black herd who would his vengeance fly,
But chained, imprisoned, on a burning soil,
For the mere avarice of a tyrant, toil!
The lengthy cart-whip guards this monster's reign,
And cracks, like pistols, from the fields of cane.
          Ye powers who formed these wretched tribes, relate
What had they done to merit such a fate!
Why were they brought from Eboe's[3] sultry waste
To see that plenty which they must not taste?—
Food which they cannot buy and dare not steal;
Yams and potatoes, many a scanty meal!
One with a gibbet wakes his negro's fears,
One to the windmill nails him by the ears;
One keeps his slave in darkened dens, unfed,

---

1. From *The Merchant of Venice*, V, i, 93–94.
2. Newly imported slaves were branded on the chest in the West Indies.
3. Eboe was a name applied to any slave who had originated in Benin.

One puts the wretch in pickle ere he's dead:
This, from a tree suspends him by the thumbs,
That, from his table grudges even the crumbs!
      O'er yond rough hills a tribe of females go,
Each with her gourd, her infant and her hoe;
Scorched by a sun that has no mercy here,
Driven by a devil, whom men call overseer;
In chains, twelve wretches to their labors haste;
Twice twelve I saw, with iron collars graced!
      Are such the fruits that spring from vast domains?
Is wealth thus got, Sir Toby, worth your pains?
Who would your wealth on terms like these possess,
Where all we see is pregnant with distress?
Angola's natives scourged by ruffian hands
And toil's hard product shipped to foreign lands.
Talk not of blossoms and your endless spring;
What joy, what smile, can scenes of misery bring?
Though nature here has every blessing spread,
Poor is the laborer and how meanly fed!
Here Stygian paintings light and shade renew
Pictures of hell that Virgil's pencil drew:[4]
Here, surly Charons make their annual trip
And ghosts arrive in every Guinea ship
To find what beasts these western isles afford,
Plutonian scourges, and despotic lords;
Here, they, of stuff determined to be free,
Must climb the rude cliffs of the Liguanee;[5]
Beyond the clouds, in skulking haste repair,
And hardly safe from brother traitors there.[6]

Written c. 1784, published 1792

---

4. In his *Aeneid*, the Roman poet Virgil described the underworld.
5. Liguanee] Freneau refers to an area north of Kingston, Jamaica.
6. And hardly safe . . . there] Freneau refers to the blacks living in the blue mountains of Jamaica who captured renegade slaves and took them to the authorities.

Phillis Wheatley (c. 1753–1784)

WHEATLEY WAS BORN on the banks of the Gambia River, probably to aristocratic parents. She was kidnapped, shipped to America, and at the age of seven or eight sold to the Wheatley family, who named her after the slave ship that brought her to Boston. Kindly treated, she learned how to read and write and composed her first poem at the age of thirteen; she would also learn Latin and Greek and was composing neoclassical verse by the mid-1760s. With the encouragement of Selina Hastings, Countess of Huntingdon, she visited London to publish her *Poems on Various Subjects* (1773), where she was lionized by the intellectuals and aristocrats at the vanguard of the abolitionist movement. Her poems were well received, gaining the admiration of Voltaire, among others. Back in Boston, she was granted her freedom in October 1773 and in November 1778 married John Peters, another freed slave. She proposed a second volume of poems in 1779, but it never appeared. A vigorous supporter of the War of Independence, she addressed a poem to George Washington that ended: "A crown, a mansion, and a throne that shine, / With gold unfading, Washington, be thine!" The commander of the American army was pleased, and invited Wheatley to meet him in Cambridge, Massachusetts, which she did in March 1776. In the second of the poems included here, "To the Rt. Hon. William, Earl of Dartmouth," Wheatley presents freedom as one of the central themes of her poetry and recounts how she was first kidnapped by slave traders. She also includes a plea that slavery be abolished in her home country: "No longer shall thou dread the iron chain / Which wanton Tyranny with lawless hand / Had made . . ."

On Being Brought From Africa to America

'Twas mercy brought me from my pagan land,
Taught my benighted soul to understand
That there's a God, that there's a Savior too;

Once I redemption neither sought nor knew.
Some view our sable race with scornful eye—
"Their color is a diabolic dye!"
Remember Christians, negroes black as Cain
May be refined, and join the angelic train.

Written 1768, published September 1773

To the Rt. Hon. William, Earl of Dartmouth, His Majesty's Principal Secretary of State for North America[1]

Hail, happy day, when, smiling like the morn,
Fair Freedom rose New England to adorn!
The northern clime beneath her genial ray,
Dartmouth, congratulates thy blissful sway;
Elate with hope her race no longer mourns,
Each soul expands, each grateful bosom burns,
While in thine hand with pleasure we behold
The silken reins, and Freedom's charms unfold.
Long lost to realms beneath the northern skies
She shines supreme, while hated Faction dies:
Soon as appeared the goddess[2] long desired,
Sick at the view, she[3] languished and expired—
Thus from the splendors of the morning light
The owl in sadness seeks the caves of night.

    No more, America, in mournful strain
Of wrongs, and grievance unredressed complain,
No longer shall thou dread the iron chain
Which wanton Tyranny with lawless hand
Had made, and with it meant to enslave the land.

---

1. Wheatley addresses William Legge, second Earl of Dartmouth (1731–1801). As an Evangelical Christian, he was known to the Wesleys, George Whitefield, William Romaine, and the Countess of Huntingdon. He secured the ordination of John Newton and his installation as curate at Olney (p. 254), and became secretary of state for North America in the summer of 1772.
2. the goddess] Freedom.
3. she] Faction.

Should you, my lord, while you peruse my song,
Wonder from whence my love of Freedom sprung,
Whence flow these wishes for the common good,
By feeling hearts alone best understood,
I, young in life, by seeming cruel fate
Was snatched from Afric's fancied happy seat—
What pangs excruciating must molest,
What sorrows labour in my parent's breast?
Steeled was that soul and by no misery moved
That from a father seized his babe beloved:
Such, such my case. And can I then but pray
Others may never feel tyrannic sway?

    For favours past, great sir, our thanks are due,
And thee we ask thy favors to renew,
Since in thy power, as in thy will before,
To soothe the griefs which thou didst once deplore.
May heavenly grace the sacred sanction give
To all thy works, and thou for ever live
Not only on the wings of fleeting fame
(Though praise immortal crowns the patriot's name),
But to conduct to heaven's refulgent fane,   *shining temple*
May fiery coursers sweep the ethereal plain,
And bear thee upward to that blest abode
Where, like the prophet, thou shalt find thy God.

Written November 1772, published September 1773

William Drennan (1754–1820)

DRENNAN WAS ONE of the founders of the organization that emerged in
1791 as the Society of United Irishmen, which aimed to mobilize those of
all religious persuasions in the task of fighting for an independent republic.
As president of its Dublin branch, Drennan played a central role in formu-
lating their objectives, and wrote many of their publications. His *Address*

to the Volunteers (December 1792) exhorted the Protestant middle class who comprised the Volunteer force in Ireland to arm itself in the manner of the French National Guard—an act of open rebellion against the British government. He called also for a National Convention at a moment when Louis XVI was being tried by a similar body in France. Drennan was prosecuted for seditious libel alongside Archibald Hamilton Rowan, who printed and distributed the pamphlet, and was fortunate in having John Philpot Curran (p. 277) as his advocate, who managed to secure an acquittal. Drennan would remain a member of the United Irishmen, but was not involved in the insurrections of 1798 and 1803; in any case, he was now a marked man, and the government was watching him. His best-known ballad is "The Wake of William Orr." In 1797, Orr, a Presbyterian yeoman farmer, was found guilty on the trumped-up charge of having administered the oath of the United Irishmen to two soldiers—a capital offense. Although the jury was drunk when it found him guilty, and the only witness against him was found to have perjured himself, Orr's advocate (Curran again) was unable to get the guilty verdict overturned, and Orr became the first Presbyterian republican to be executed, on October 14, 1797. He was thirty. Indignation at Orr's fate was felt across Ireland and England: at a political banquet the Whig leader Charles James Fox proposed a toast to "the memory of the martyred Orr," while "Remember Orr" became a rallying cry during the '98 uprising. In an earlier poem, "Erin," Drennan coined the phrase, the "Emerald Isle," to describe Ireland. Both poems made their first appearance in *The Press*, house organ of the United Irishmen.

Erin

When Erin first rose from the dark-swelling flood,
God blessed the green island, he saw it was good;
The emerald of Europe, it sparkled, it shone,
In the ring of this world the most precious stone!

In her sun, in her soil, in her station thrice blessed,
With her back towards Britain, her face to the west,
Erin stands proudly insular, on her steep shore,
And strikes her high harp to the ocean's deep roar.

But when its soft tones seem to mourn and to weep,
The dark chain of silence is cast o'er the deep;
At the thought of the past, tears gush from her eyes,
And the pulse of her heart makes her white bosom rise:

"Oh, sons of green Erin, lament o'er the time
When religion was war, and our country a crime,
When men in God's image inverted his plan,
And moulded their God in the image of man.

When the interest of state wrought the general woe,
The stranger a friend, and the native a foe;
While the mother rejoiced o'er her children distressed,
And clasped the invader more close to her breast.

When with pale for the body and pale for the soul,
Church and state joined in compact to conquer the whole;
And while Shannon ran red with Milesian blood,
Eyed each other askance, and pronounced it was good.

By the groans that ascend from your forefathers' grave
For their country thus left to the brute and the slave,
Drive the demon of bigotry home to his den,
And where Britain made brutes, now let Erin make men!

Let my sons, like the leaves of their shamrock, unite,
A partition of sects from one footstalk of right;
Give each his full share of this earth and yon sky,
Nor fatten the slave where the serpent would die.

Alas, for poor Erin that some are still seen
Who would dye the grass red, in their hatred to green;
Yet, oh, when you're up, and they down, let them live,
Then yield them that mercy which they did not give.

Arm of Erin, prove strong, but be gentle as brave,
And uplifted to strike, still be ready to save;
Nor one feeling of vengeance presume to defile
The cause or the men of the Emerald Isle.

The cause it is good, and the men they are true,
And the Green shall outlive both the Orange and Blue.[1]
And the daughters of Erin her triumph shall share
With their full-swelling chest and their fair-flowing hair.

Their bosoms heave high for the worthy and brave,
But no coward shall rest on that soft-swelling wave;
Men of Erin, awake, and make haste to be blessed!
Rise, arch of the ocean; rise, queen of the west!"

Written 1795, published October 5, 1797

The Wake of William Orr

Here our brother worthy lies,
Wake not him with women's cries;
Mourn the way that mankind ought—
Sit in silent trance of thought.

Write his merits on your mind,
Morals pure and manners kind;
On his head, as on a hill,
Virtue placed her citadel.

Why cut off in palmy youth?
Truth he spoke, and acted truth:
"Countrymen, unite!," he cried,
And died for what his Savior died.

God of peace and God of love,
Let it not thy vengeance move;
Let it not thy lightnings draw—
A nation guillotined by law.

---

1. And the Green . . . Orange and Blue] Green was the color of a united Ireland; orange
and blue are those of the disunited Protestants and Catholics.

Hapless nation, rent and torn,
Early wert thou taught to mourn;
Warfare of six hundred years—
Epochs marked by blood and tears!

Hunted through thy native grounds,
A flung reward to human hounds;
Each one pulled and tore his share,
Emblem of thy deep despair.

Hapless nation, hapless land,
Heap of uncementing sand;
Crumbled by a foreign weight
Or by worse—domestic hate!

God of mercy, God of peace,
Make this mad confusion cease;
O'er the mental chaos move,
Through it speak the light of love.

Monstrous and unhappy sight!
Brothers' blood will not unite;
Holy oil and holy water
Mix and fill the world with slaughter.

Who is she with aspect wild?
The widowed mother with her child—
Child new stirring in the womb,
Husband waiting for the tomb!

Angel of this holy place,
Calm her soul and whisper peace:
Cord nor axe nor guillotine
Make the sentence, not the sin.

Here we watch our brother's sleep;
Watch with us, but do not weep;
Watch with us through dead of night,
But expect the morning light.

Conquer fortune, persevere!
Lo, it breaks, the morning clear!
The cheerful cock awakes the skies;
The day is come—arise, arise!

Written shortly after October 14, 1797, published January 13, 1798

Ann Yearsley (1756–1806)

YEARSLEY WROTE AS "Lactilla" because she was a milkmaid. She always loved books, but was an unlikely poet: having married young, she produced six children within six years—a common fate. Taken up as a working-class prodigy by Hannah More (whose table provided scraps for her pigs), she went from poverty to overnight literary stardom, her first book attracting over a thousand subscribers including seven duchesses, sixteen countesses, Sir Joshua Reynolds, Horace Walpole, and most of the bluestockings. Her poems challenge military aggression, identify with the oppressed, and advocate rebellion. She sought to influence opinion with her poetry, and her passionate, independent voice speaks clearly in her *Poem on the Inhumanity of the Slave-Trade*, published to coincide with Sir William Dolben's 1788 bill, restricting transport of slaves from Africa to the West Indies. It was dangerous for women to intervene in such issues, especially if, like Yearsley, they were citizens of a principal slave-port such as Bristol. There she was surrounded, on a daily basis, by slave-schooners, advertisements for runaways, and shops selling the paraphernalia of the trade—whips, manacles, chains, and the dreaded speculum oris, used for force-feeding slaves who tried to starve themselves to death. She spared no one, condemning traders who attended church: "Ye hypocrites, disown / The Christian name, nor shame its cause." In the extract below, Yearsley narrates the sufferings of a slave, Luco, separated from his beloved Incilanda and burned by Gorgon, a heartless Christian slave-trader. A principal source of information for this passage was probably Yearsley's friend John Newton (p. 254).

A Poem on the Inhumanity of the Slave-Trade (extract)

Gorgon, remorseless Christian, saw the slave
Stand musing mid the ranks and, stealing soft
Behind the studious Luco, struck his cheek
With a too-heavy whip that reached his eye,
Making it dark forever. Luco turned
In strongest agony, and with his hoe
Struck the rude Christian on the forehead. Pride,
With hateful malice, seized on Gorgon's soul,
By nature fierce, while Luco sought the beach
And plunged beneath the wave. But near him lay
A planter's barge, whose seamen grasped his hair,
Dragging to life a wretch who wished to die.
     Rumor now spreads the tale, while Gorgon's breath
Envenomed aids her blast. Imputed crimes
Oppose the plea of Luco, till he scorns
Even a just defence, and stands prepared.
The planters, conscious that to fear alone
They owe their cruel power, resolve to blend
New torment with the pangs of death, and hold
Their victims high in dreadful view, to fright
The wretched number left. Luco is chained
To a huge tree, his fellow slaves are ranged
To share the horrid sight; fuel is placed
In an increasing train some paces back
To kindle slowly, and approach the youth
With more than native terror. See, it burns!
He gazes on the growing flame, and calls
For "Water, water!" The small boon's denied.
E'en Christians throng each other to behold
The different alterations of his face
As the hot death approaches. (Oh shame, shame
Upon the followers of Jesus! Shame
On him that dares avow a God!) He writhes,
While down his breast glide the unpitied tears,
And in their sockets strain their scorched balls.
"Burn, burn me quick! I cannot die!" he cries,

"Bring fire more close!" The planters heed him not,
But still prolonging Luco's torture, threat
Their trembling slaves around. His lips are dry,
His senses seem to quiver ere they quit
His frame forever, rallying strong, then driven
From the tremendous conflict. Sight no more
Is Luco's, his parched tongue is ever mute;
Yet in his soul his Incilanda stays,
Till both escape together. Turn, my muse,
From this sad scene; lead Bristol's milder soul
To where the solitary spirit roves
Wrapped in the robe of innocence, to shades
Where pity breathing in the gale dissolves
The mind, when fancy paints such real woe.

    Now speak, ye Christians (who for gain enslave
A soul like Luco's, tearing her from joy
In life's short vale—and if there be a hell,
As ye believe, to *that* ye thrust her down,
A blind, involuntary victim), where
Is your true essence of religion? Where
Your proofs of righteousness, when ye conceal
The knowledge of the Deity from those
Who would adore him fervently? Your God
Ye rob of worshippers, his altars keep
Unhailed, while driving from the sacred font
The eager slave, lest *he* should hope in Jesus.

Published February 1788

William Blake (1757–1827)

"Around Saint James's glow the fires, ever to the city gate" (*America*, cancelled plate c): an image plucked not from Blake's imagination but from eyewitness experience. He may have needed little encouragement to join the Gordon rioters when they swept toward him on the evening of June 6, 1780, for at twenty-two years old he was of the same generation, and shared their disdain for the social and economic inequalities of Georgian London. He followed them to Newgate Prison, where some had been detained, and watched as they demolished it, liberating some three hundred prisoners, including five under sentence of death. Then they torched it, many clambering onto precarious parts of the structure, urinating into the flames and screaming obscenities across the rooftops. Blake was a peaceable man who unlike Wordsworth would not defend revolutionary violence (see pp. 307–8), but he cannot have been immune to the exhilaration and horror of what he saw, recalled in the painting on the cover of this book. He was almost certainly a witness to events the following night, when the district round Holborn was "like a volcano"; the King's Bench and Fleet prisons burned down; tollhouses on Blackfriars Bridge set on fire; a full-scale battle waged on the steps of the Bank of England; and scores of other fires were ignited across the capital. Small wonder that, when Blake composed "A Song of Liberty" for *The Marriage of Heaven and Hell*, he conceived of revolution in apocalyptic terms—as "the new-born fire" with "fiery limbs," bringing an end to the financial system, the British Empire, and organized religion (which Blake regarded as corrupt). The times were such that no one escaped suspicion. A few months after the riots, in September 1780, Blake was one of several artists touring the Medway taken prisoner by a group of soldiers who believed them to be French spies. (France fought on the American side in the Revolutionary War.) They were interrogated by an officer who thought a sketch showing a warship, and the defenseless state of nearby Upnor Castle, was the means by which information could be conveyed to the enemy. They were released when their membership of the Royal Academy was confirmed, but it was an indication to Blake of how easily power might be abused. That experience may have come to mind when, more than two decades later, in 1803, he found a soldier in his Sussex garden whom he ordered out. Having refused, the soldier, Private John Schofield, began arguing, at which Blake forcibly removed the man from his property. He was later charged in court, accused by Schofield with having used seditious language (it was claimed he said "Damn the King"), but was acquitted—though the stress of the trial took a severe toll on Blake's health and that of his wife. Blake espoused liberal causes, one of which was the antislavery movement. "Let the slave grinding at the mill run out into the field," he wrote. "The Little Black Boy" (from *Songs of Innocence*) critiques the social and religious assumptions that made slavery possible, from the perspective of a child victim in exile, recalling his homeland. For more on Blake and the Gordon Riots, see the introduction, pp. 7–10.

The Little Black Boy

My mother bore me in the southern wild
And I am black, but oh, my soul is white!
White as an angel is the English child,
But I am black, as if bereaved of light.

My mother taught me underneath a tree,
And sitting down before the heat of day,
She took me on her lap and kissed me,
And pointing to the east began to say,

"Look on the rising sun: there God does live
And gives his light, and gives his heat away;
And flowers and trees and beasts and men receive
Comfort in morning, joy in the noonday.

And we are put on earth a little space
That we may learn to bear the beams of love;
And these black bodies and this sunburned face
Is but a cloud, and like a shady grove.

For when our souls have learned the heat to bear
The cloud will vanish; we shall hear his voice

Saying, 'Come out from the grove, my love and care,
And round my golden tent like lambs rejoice.' "

Thus did my mother say and kissed me;
And thus I say to little English boy,
When I from black and he from white cloud free,
And round the tent of God like lambs we joy,

I'll shade him from the heat till he can bear
To lean in joy upon our Father's knee;
And then I'll stand and stroke his silver hair,
And be like him, and he will then love me.

Composed 1787–1789, published 1789

The Marriage of Heaven and Hell (extract)

A SONG OF LIBERTY[1]

1. The Eternal Female groaned! It was heard over all the Earth:
2. Albion's coast is sick, silent; the American meadows faint!
3. Shadows of Prophecy shiver along by the lakes and the rivers, and mutter across the ocean! France, rend down thy dungeon;
4. Golden Spain, burst the barriers of old Rome;
5. Cast thy keys, oh Rome, into the deep down falling, even to eternity down falling,
6. And weep!
7. In her trembling hands, she took the newborn terror howling;
8. On those infinite mountains of light now barred out by the Atlantic sea, the newborn fire stood before the starry king!
9. Flagged with gray-browed snows and thunderous visages, the jealous wings waved over the deep.

---

1. In this concluding section from Blake's prophetic work, he envisages the birth of a new revolutionary age, describing it in apocalyptic terms: among other things, he refers to the tearing down of the Bastille prison and imagines the end of the Roman Catholic Church.

10. The speary hand burned aloft, unbuckled was the shield, forth went the hand of jealousy among the flaming hair, and hurled the newborn wonder through the starry night.

11. The fire, the fire, is falling!

12. Look up! Look up! Oh citizen of London, enlarge thy countenance! Oh Jew, leave counting gold, return to thy oil and wine! Oh African! Black African! (Go, winged thought, widen his forehead.)

13. The fiery limbs, the flaming hair, shot like the sinking sun into the western sea.

14. Waked from his eternal sleep, the hoary element roaring fled away;

15. Down rushed, beating his wings in vain the jealous king; his gray-browed councilors, thunderous warriors, curled veterans, among helms and shields and chariots, horses, elephants, banners, castles, slings and rocks,

16. Falling, rushing, ruining! buried in the ruins, on Urthona's dens.[2]

17. All night beneath the ruins; then their sullen flames faded emerge round the gloomy king,

18. With thunder and fire: leading his starry hosts through the waste wilderness he promulgates his ten commands, glancing his beamy eyelids over the deep in dark dismay,

19. Where the son of fire in his eastern cloud, while the morning plumes her golden breast,

20. Spurning the clouds written with curses, stamps the stony law to dust, loosing the eternal horses from the dens of night, crying, "Empire is no more! And now the lion and wolf shall cease."

Chorus

Let the priests of the raven of dawn no longer, in deadly black, with hoarse note, curse the sons of joy; nor his accepted brethren (whom, tyrant, he calls free) lay the bound or build the roof; nor pale religious lechery call that virginity that wishes but acts not!

For everything that lives is Holy.

Probably composed 1790, published 1793

---

2. Urthona's dens] Scholars disagree as to Blake's exact meaning. Urthona is one of Blake's mythic figures (or emanations); in this context, "Urthona's dens" are the first earthly destination of Orc, as he prepares to spread revolution through the world, ending the rule of empire and the "stony law."

London

I wander through each chartered street
Near where the chartered Thames does flow,
And mark in every face I meet
Marks of weakness, marks of woe.

In every cry of every man,
In every infant's cry of fear,
In every voice, in every ban,
The mind-forged manacles I hear.

How the chimney sweeper's cry
Every black'ning church appals,
And the hapless soldier's sigh
Runs in blood down palace walls.

But most through midnight streets I hear
How the youthful harlot's curse
Blasts the newborn infant's tear
And blights with plagues the marriage-hearse.

Composed c. 1791–1792, published 1794

John Marjoribanks (1758/1759–1796)

MARJORIBANKS WAS A published poet by the time he was appointed an ensign and stationed at Stoneyhill Barracks in Kingston, Jamaica, January 1784. He felt "compassion for the sufferings of the negroes in the West Indies, of which I was for several years an indignant eyewitness." This led to composition of his most important poem, *Slavery: An Essay in Verse*, which describes how slave owners routinely cast out old and exhausted slaves to die of hunger; the flogging of a slave woman and her baby; enforced amputation of captured runaways, and other atrocities. Despite their artificiality of style, Marjoribanks's case studies are drawn from his own experience, and testify to his outrage. In a note, he argues for "the abolition of the trade to Africa for slaves; the meliorating the condition of those already in the islands; and, perhaps, in time, the gradual establishment of their freedom." Marjoribanks returned to Edinburgh in 1787, where he supported Wilberforce's abolition bill in 1792.

Slavery: An Essay in Verse (extract)

See the wretch fastened to an emmet's nest,   *anthill*
Whose stings in myriads his whole frame molest;
Or smeared with cowhage[1] all his body o'er,
His burning skin intolerably sore!
Chains, hooks, and horns of every size and shape
Mark those who've once attempted an escape;
A sister isle first used, but *this* improves,
That cursed invention called Barbados Gloves.[2]
For your own sakes, your malice and your whim
But rarely sacrifice a negro's limb—
Unless a slave of sedentary trade
(A luckless tailor well may be afraid),
Where there's no great occasion for a pair:
You may lop off the leg he has to spare.[3]
Were there a surgeon (and there may be such)
Whose heart compassion had the power to touch,
Who dared the horrid office to decline,
Your laws condemn him in a heavy fine.[4]
    If interest teaches you their limbs to spare,
Immediate murders must be still more rare,

---

1. cowhage] the stinging hairs of the pod of a tropical plant.
2. "Slips of wood are placed between every two fingers, and the whole screwed or wedged close together, so as to give most exquisite torture. I have known this infernal machine kept on house slaves for many days together" (Marjoribanks's note).
3. "The reason assigned to a gentleman of my acquaintance, by his overseer, for cutting off the leg of one of his negroes in his absence was that the fellow having run off, he thought this the most effectual method of preventing his trying it a second time; adding that, as he was a tailor, the property was not a bit less valuable" (Marjoribanks's note).
4. "The penalty, I think, is fifty pounds" (Marjoribanks's note).

Though 'tis this selfish sentiment alone
That oft deters you to destroy your own.
But should your passions hurry you away
Another person's property to slay,
The guilt's considered in a venial light—
The proof is difficult, the sentence slight.[5]
Nay, Malice, safe, may find a thousand times
When no white evidence can prove his crimes,
Since 'tis established by your partial laws
No slave bears witness in a white man's cause.[6]

Written October 1786, published 1792

Helen Maria Williams (1759–1827)

"PARIS, THE REFUGE of barbarism and the den of carnage," wrote Williams, in the wake of the Terror. She was lucky to survive it. Having emerged from dissenting circles to win fame as a poet, she visited revolutionary France in summer 1790 and would remain there for the next three decades, becoming one of the foremost English writers to witness the twists and turns of the French Revolution and the remarkable developments that followed. With her sisters and mother, she was imprisoned for six weeks during the Terror, first in the Luxembourg Palace and then at the convent Les Anglaises. She knew many who would not survive, and often believed her own life to be in the balance. Her experiences are recorded in the eight volumes of her remarkable *Letters from France* (1790–1796), in which she describes the exhilaration of the first flowerings of revolution, and the dark days of the Terror. She was able to visit her friend, Marie-Jeanne Roland, wife of the politician

---

5. "Generally payment of the price of the negro to his owner. It is then, it may be remarked, as expensive to kill another man's slave as your own. But this does not follow: in the former case, the loss is certain; in the latter, the fact must be proved (which is often impossible) before the damages can be incurred" (Marjoribanks's note).
6. "Not only slaves, but free negroes, and people of color, are excluded. They are, however, admitted as evidences against each other" (Marjoribanks's note).

Jean-Marie Roland, at the prison of Sainte-Pélagie in October 1793. "She told me she expected to die," wrote Williams (Roland was executed early the following month). Upon release, Williams saw for herself the "deep and silent gloom" that pervaded Paris, and the paranoia of those at liberty: "The citizens in general saw with stupefied terror those processions of death which daily encumbered the streets, and the feelings of sympathy and indignation were repelled by the sense of that personal danger from which no individual was secure. Even in his own habitation, and in the bosom of his family, no man dared to utter a complaint but in anxious whispers, lest a servant should overhear the forbidden expostulations of humanity, and denounce him as a counter-revolutionist." Williams became notorious in England for her relationship with John Hurford Stone, a businessman with whom she lived but never married: Richard Polwhele described her as "an intemperate advocate for Gallic licentiousness," while Horace Walpole called her a "scribbling trollop." She was also despised for her politics: to Hester Lynch Piozzi she was "a wicked little democrat." There were greater threats awaiting her in France: after the decree of 27 Germinal, Williams was forced out of Paris and compelled to report on a daily basis to local magistrates; in June 1794, she fled to Switzerland to avoid a "special proscription" against her, issued because of her sympathetic accounts of Robespierre's victims; Napoléon later put her under house arrest for days at a time. In later years she was renowned as hostess of a Paris salon in which she entertained the cream of European society including Tadeusz Kościuszko, Frédéric-César de La Harpe, Joel Barlow, Amelia Opie, Henri Grégoire, Pierre-Louis Ginguené, Thomas Erskine, and William Wordsworth.

Lines by Roucher[1]

The fate of Roucher, author of a poem called *The Months*, excited particular sympathy. He passed his time in prison in educating one of his children, and this employment seemed to charm away his cares. The

---

1. Jean-Antoine Roucher (1745–94) was born in Montpellier and moved to Paris at the age of twenty. During the revolution he was a leader of an anti-Jacobin Club. He was arrested in October 1793 and imprisoned in Sainte-Pélagie; seven months later he was transferred to Saint-Lazare. He was executed on July 25, 1794.

day he received his act of accusation, knowing well the fate that awaited him, he sent his son home, giving him his portrait which a painter who was his fellow prisoner had drawn, and which he ordered the child to give his mother. Below the picture he had written the following lines:

Ne vous étonnez pas, objets charmants et doux,
Si quelqu'air de tristesse obscurcit mon visage;
Lorsqu'un savant crayon dessinoit cet image,
On dressait l'échafaud, et je pensais à vous!

Loved objects, cease to wonder when ye trace
The melancholy air that clouds my face;
Ah, while the painter's skill this image drew,
They reared the scaffold, and I thought of you.

Written 1794, published 1795

Lines by a Young Man to His Mistress

Many young persons, after receiving their act of accusation, composed verses written with a pencil at the table where they partook their last repast with their fellow prisoners. The following, written by a young man of twenty-four years of age to his mistress, the night before his execution, are simple and affecting:

I.
L'heure avance où je vais mourir,
L'heure sonne et la mort m'appelle:
Je n'ai point de laches désirs,
Je ne fuirai point devant elle:
Je meurs plein de foi, plein d'honneur:
Mais je laisse ma douce amie
Dans le veuvage et la douleur—
Ah! je dois regretter la vie!

II.

Demain, mes yeux inanimés
Ne s'ouvriront plus sur tes charmes;
Tes beaux yeux à l'amour fermés
Demain seront noyés de larmes.
La mort glacera cette main
Qui m'unit à ma douce amie!
Je ne vivrai plus sur ton sein—
Ah! je dois regretter la vie!

IMITATION

I.

The hour that calls to death is near,
It brings to me no throb of fear;
The breast that Honour arms, can brave
The murderer's steel, the untimely grave;
But thou, to whom I gave my heart,
From thee forever must I part
And leave my mourning love to sigh?
Ah, 'tis a cruel task to die!

II.

Tomorrow my closed eyes no more
Shall gaze on beauty I adore;
Tomorrow, saddening every grace,
Unceasing tears shall bathe thy face;
Tomorrow, chilled by death's cold grasp,
This hand no longer thine shall clasp;
From thee forever I shall fly—
Ah, 'tis a cruel task to die!

Written 1794, published 1795

John Thelwall (1764–1834)

"CITIZEN" THELWALL WAS one of the best-known political activists in 1790s London. A moderate republican who supported the French revolutionary cause, he lobbied for reform in Britain. That made him a threat to the government, which placed him under surveillance from 1792 onward, well before he began to deliver talks that attracted audiences of up to 750. Among the spies who reported on his movements and activities was one James Walsh who, in 1798, would be sent to Somerset to observe the affairs of two other dangerous radicals: Wordsworth and Coleridge. Like other governments before and since, that of William Pitt attempted to intimidate dissidents into silence. Thelwall became the recipient of death threats, and his lectures were invaded by gangs of hooligans who threatened to bludgeon those who refused to leave. In May 1794 he was one of eight campaigners arrested and imprisoned in the Tower of London during the summer months. When, eventually, they were indicted, it was for high treason, which carried a capital penalty. In the Tower he composed "Short is perhaps our date of life," believing there existed a real chance he and his codefendants might be found guilty. After William Godwin published a clear-sighted attack on the government case, it became impossible for any lawyer to persuade a jury of their guilt, and they were acquitted. Still determined to put an end to Thelwall's lobbying, the government passed the Two Acts in 1795, banning political meetings of more than fifty people. He responded by lecturing on "Classical History, and particularly the Laws and Revolutions of Rome," an apparently apolitical subject. When all else failed, government agents pursued him across the country, sabotaging his speaking engagements; on at least one occasion they tried to have him kidnapped and press-ganged. By his own account, he was "proscribed and hunted—driven like a wild beast, and banished, like a contagion, from society—during those reiterated attempts by armed banditti, to kidnap and to murder me." He withdrew from politics in 1797, turning instead to speech therapy, but returned to the fray after the Napoleonic Wars as editor of *The Champion*, in which he denounced the Peterloo Massacre, supported Catholic Emancipation, and wrote sympathetically about the plight of German Jews.

The Source of Slavery

Ah, why, forgetful of her ancient fame,
Does Britain in lethargic fetters lie?
Why from the burning cheek and kindling eye
Burst no keen flashes of that sacred flame
That wont the freeborn energies proclaim
Of Albion's hardy race? Alas, we fly
The homely altars, slight the once-loved name
Of rustic liberty and deify
Luxurious pride! To her the pliant soul   *Excessive*
We bend degenerate, her vain pomps adore,
And chase the simple virtues from the shore
They wont to guard. Hence to the base control
Of Tyranny we bow, nor once complain;
But hug with servile fear the gilded chain.

Written July 17, 1794, published 1795

Stanzas on Hearing for Certainty That We Were to Be Tried for High Treason

Short is perhaps our date of life,
        But let us while we live be gay—
To those be thought and anxious care
        Who build upon the distant day.

Though in our cup tyrannic power
        Would dash the bitter dregs of fear,
We'll gaily quaff the mantling draught,
        While patriot toasts the fancy cheer.

Sings not the seaman, tempest-tossed,
      When surges wash the riven shroud,
Scorning the threatening voice of fate
      That pipes in rocking winds aloud?

Yes, he can take his cheerful glass
      And toast his mistress in the storm,
While duty and remembered joys
      By turns his honest bosom warm.

And shall not we, in storms of state,
      At base oppression's fury laugh,
And while the vital spirits flow,
      To freedom fill, and fearless quaff?

Short is perhaps our date of life,
      But let us while we live be gay—
To those be thought and anxious care
      Who build upon the distant day.

Written September 28, 1794, published 1795

The Cell

Within the dungeon's noxious gloom
The patriot still, with dauntless breast,
The cheerful aspect can assume
And smile in conscious virtue blessed!

The damp foul floor, the ragged wall
And shattered window grated high
The trembling ruffian may appall
Whose thoughts no sweet resource supply.

But he unawed by guilty fears
(To freedom and his country true)
Who o'er a race of well-spent years

Can cast the retrospective view,
Looks inward to his heart and sees
The objects that must ever please.

Written October 24, 1794, published 1795

William Wordsworth (1770–1850)

SOMETIMES PARODIED AS a harmless (and therefore irrelevant) nature poet, the real William Wordsworth was, for a time, identified by the government as a serious security threat. The Home Office was sufficiently concerned to send an agent to spy on him and his sister Dorothy in 1797, when they were resident in Somersetshire, where it was believed the French would begin their invasion of Britain. At first, James Walsh, the agent, believed them to be French emigrés. His revised opinion was that they and Coleridge comprised a "nest" of "disaffected Englishmen," and he finally concluded that the "rascals from Alfoxden" (where the Wordsworths lived) were "a set of violent democrats," potential leaders of a rebellion. This was less absurd than it sounds. Five years before, by his own admission, Wordsworth was "pretty hot in it" ("it" being the French Revolution). He was twenty when first he crossed the Channel in the summer of 1790, on a walking tour with a college friend, and would return in November 1791 for over a year, during which time he visited the National Assembly in Paris, possibly as the guest of Jacques Pierre Brissot, leader of the Girondist faction (guillotined October 1793). From February to September 1792 Wordsworth was resident in Blois, where he fell in love with Annette Vallon, who became pregnant with his daughter. While there, his militant republicanism was shaped by Bishop Henri Grégoire and the soldier Michel Beaupuy. He returned to London in late 1792, to publish his prorevolutionary couplet poem *Descriptive Sketches*. It appeared on January 29, 1793, just over a week after the execution of Louis XVI, and days before the declaration of war between France and Britain. Though composed in an eighteenth-century poetic manner, *Descriptive Sketches* is invaluable for taking us to the heart of Wordsworth's early politics. After the outbreak of war between Britain and France in early 1793 he composed a pamphlet "by a Republican" defending the revolution:

"[Liberty] is too often obliged to borrow the very arms of despotism . . . and in order to reign in peace must establish herself by violence." This apology for regicide and revolutionary excess (the Terror was then ongoing) remained in manuscript until 1876: at the time of its writing, no publisher would have risked issuing it. Wordsworth may have returned to Paris to see the Terror firsthand, possibly witnessing on October 7, 1793, the execution of Antoine-Joseph Gorsas, known to him in former times as a journalist, since a member of the National Convention. In London the following year, Wordsworth planned a magazine called *The Philanthropist* that would reflect his interest in the anarcho-socialism of his friend William Godwin, and the republicanism of John Milton (pp. 135–36) and Algernon Sidney; he may even have contributed to such a journal, issued by the radical publisher Daniel Isaac Eaton, in 1795. A decade later, the mature Wordsworth would write an autobiographical poem, *The Prelude*, the masterpiece by which his artistic achievement is now reckoned. Though completed in 1805, it was unpublished during his lifetime—a pity, as it would have enlightened such contemporaries as Percy Bysshe Shelley and his girlfriend, Mary Godwin, who, at the time Wordsworth published *The Excursion* (1814), thought him a "slave" to conservatism. They could not know that in 1792 (the year of Shelley's birth), he had been a member of the revolutionary club at Blois, Les Amis de la Constitution; an enthusiastic reader of Jacobin newspapers edited by Carra and Gorsas; the father of an illegitimate child born to a French family; defender of the September Massacres, and of regicide. He may even, as scholars suggest, have been as extreme in his views as Robespierre, warranting the attention of a government spy.

Descriptive Sketches (extract)[1]

Yet hast thou found that Freedom spreads her power
Beyond the cottage hearth, the cottage door;
All nature smiles and owns beneath her eyes

---

1. These are the concluding lines from Wordsworth's early couplet poem, *Descriptive Sketches* (1793), largely written during his stay in revolutionary France, 1791–1792, and inspired by the close attachments he formed there, which included Annette Vallon, by whom he had a daughter, Anne-Caroline, in December 1792. The extract we include here reflects Wordsworth's millenarian hopes for the newly emergent nation.

Her fields peculiar, and peculiar skies.   *distinctive*
Yes, as I roamed where Loiret's waters[2] glide
Through rustling aspens heard from side to side,
When from October clouds[3] a milder light
Fell where the blue flood rippled into white,
Methought from every cot the watchful bird   *cottage*
Crowed with ear-piercing power till then unheard;
Each clacking mill that broke the murmuring streams
Rocked the charmed thought in more delightful dreams,
Chasing those long long dreams the falling leaf
Awoke a fainter pang of moral grief;
The measured echo of the distant flail
Winded in sweeter cadence down the vale;
A more majestic tide the water rolled
And glowed the sun-gilt groves in richer gold.[4]

    Though Liberty shall soon, indignant, raise
Red on his hills his beacon's comet blaze;[5]
Bid from on high his lonely cannon sound,
And on ten thousand hearths his shout rebound;
His 'larum bell from village-tower to tower
Swing on the astounded ear its dull undying roar,
Yet, yet rejoice!—though Pride's perverted ire
Rouse Hell's own aid and wrap thy hills in fire.[6]
Lo, from the innocuous flames, a lovely birth!
With its own virtues springs another earth!
Nature, as in her prime, her virgin reign
Begins, and Love and Truth compose her train;

---

2. Wordsworth at this point has a prose explanation of the River Loire (beside which he resided during much of 1792) and its source "a league and a half south-east of Orleans."
3. October clouds] Wordsworth appears to have written the conclusion of his poem in October 1792 somewhere along the River Loiret.
4. "The duties upon many parts of the French rivers were so exorbitant that the poorer people, deprived of the benefit of water carriage, were obliged to transport their goods by land" (Wordsworth's note).
5. In the concluding part of his poem, Wordsworth imagines revolutionary action spreading far beyond France.
6. Pride's perverted ire . . . in fire] Pride is associated with the forces of counterrevolution. The fire is that of millenarian rebirth, from which will spring a new world order overseen by Nature and Justice.

With pulseless hand, and fixed unwearied gaze,
Unbreathing Justice her still beam surveys;
No more, along thy vales and viny groves,
Whole hamlets disappearing as he moves,
With cheeks o'erspread by smiles of baleful glow,
On his pale horse shall fell Consumption go.
      Oh give, great God, to Freedom's waves to ride
Sublime o'er Conquest, Avarice, and Pride,
To break: the vales where Death with Famine scours,[7]
And dark Oppression builds her thick-ribbed towers;
Where Machination her fell soul resigns,   *fierce*
Fled panting to the center of her mines;
Where Persecution decks with ghastly smiles
Her bed, his mountains mad Ambition piles;
Where Discord stalks dilating, every hour;
And (crouching fearful at the feet of Power,
Like lightnings eager for the almighty Word)
Look up for sign of havoc, Fire and Sword.[8]
Give them, beneath their breast while gladness springs,
To brood the nations o'er with Nile like wings;
And grant that every sceptred child of clay
Who cries, presumptuous, "Here their tides shall stay!"[9]
Swept in their anger from the affrighted shore,
With all his creatures sink—to rise no more!
      Tonight, my friend, within this humble cot
Be the dead load of mortal ills forgot,
Renewing, when the rosy summits glow
At morn, our various journey, sad and slow.

Written c. October 1792, published January 29, 1793

---

7. the vales where Death with Famine scours] "where Death, using Famine as his agent, scours the vales."
8. Look up . . . Fire and Sword] Wordsworth welcomes these harbingers of violence and destruction, which he compares with the role played by heavenly lightnings in God's fight against Satan. The implication is that revolution is divinely ordained.
9. presumptuous . . . stay!] Wordsworth's critique of King Canute is a condemnation of monarchical government.

September 1st, 1802[1]

We had a fellow passenger who came
From Calais with us, gaudy in array,
A negro woman like a lady gay
Yet silent as a woman fearing blame;
Dejected, meek, yea, pitiably tame
She sat, from notice turning not away,
But on our proffered kindness still did lay
A weight of languid speech, or at the same
Was silent, motionless in eyes and face.
She was a negro woman driven from France,
Rejected like all others of that race,
Not one of whom may now find footing there;
This the poor outcast did to us declare
Nor murmured at the unfeeling ordinance.

Written between August 29, and September 1, 1802,
published February 1803

The Prelude[1]

BOOK 6 (EXTRACT)[2]

. . . 'twas a time when Europe was rejoiced,
France standing on the top of golden hours,
And human nature seeming born again.
Bound, as I said, to the Alps, it was our lot

---

1. In the wake of the San Domingue campaign, Napoléon had exiled all colonial blacks from the French mainland. Wordsworth encountered this woman on his 1802 visit to France.

THE PRELUDE

1. *The Prelude*, an autobiographical poem begun in 1798 and finished as a poem in thirteen books in 1805, is Wordsworth's masterpiece. It was not published in this form until 1926.

2. This passage describes Wordsworth's first experience of revolutionary France, when he landed at Calais with his college friend Robert Jones on July 13, 1790, the eve of the first anniversary of the fall of the Bastille, which was celebrated all over France.

To land at Calais on the very eve
Of that great federal day; and there we saw
In a mean city, and among a few,
How bright a face is worn when joy of one
Is joy of tens of millions. Southward thence
We took our way direct through hamlets, towns
Gaudy with relics of that festival—
Flowers left to wither on triumphal arcs
And window-garlands. On the public roads,
And, once, three days successively, through paths
By which our toilsome journey was abridged,
Among sequestered villages we walked
And found benevolence and blessedness
Spread like a fragrance everywhere, like spring
That leaves no corner of the land untouched.
Where elms, for many and many a league in files,
With their thin umbrage, on the stately roads   *shade*
Of that great kingdom, rustled o'er our heads,
Forever near us as we paced along,
'Twas sweet at such a time, with such delights
On every side, in prime of youthful strength,
To feed a poet's tender melancholy
And fond conceit of sadness, to the noise
And gentle undulation which they made.
Unhoused, beneath the evening star we saw
Dances of liberty and, in late hours
Of darkness, dances in the open air.
Among the vine-clad hills of Burgundy,
Upon the bosom of the gentle Saone,
We glided forward with the flowing stream:
Swift Rhone, thou wert the wings on which we cut
Between thy lofty rocks! Enchanting show
Those woods and farms and orchards did present,
And single cottages and lurking towns,
Reach after reach, procession without end
Of deep and stately vales. A lonely pair
Of Englishmen we were, and sailed along
Clustered together with a merry crowd

Of those emancipated, with a host
Of travelers, chiefly delegates, returning
From the great spousals³ newly solemnized
At their chief city in the sight of heaven.
Like bees they swarmed, gaudy and gay as bees;
Some vapored in the unruliness of joy
And flourished with their swords, as if to fight
The saucy air. In this blithe company
We landed, took with them our evening meal,
Guests welcome almost as the angels were
To Abraham of old.⁴ The supper done,
With flowing cups elate and happy thoughts
We rose at signal given and formed a ring
And, hand in hand, danced round and round the board:
All hearts were open, every tongue was loud
With amity and glee; we bore a name
Honoured in France, the name of Englishmen,
And hospitably did they give us hail
As their forerunners in a glorious course,⁵
And round and round the board they danced again.
With this same throng our voyage we pursued
At early dawn; the monastery bells
Made a sweet jingling in our youthful ears,
The rapid river flowing without noise,
And every spire we saw among the rocks
Spake with a sense of peace, at intervals
Touching the heart amid the boisterous crew
With which we were environed.   *surrounded*

---

3. Wordsworth refers to the symbolic marriage between Louis XVI and the new constitution of revolutionary France.
4. In Genesis, angels visit Abraham to tell him he is to have a son.
5. The French honored the English for the Glorious Revolution of 1688, by which the Catholic James II was deposed in favor of Mary Stuart and her Dutch husband, William of Orange (p. 211).

BOOK 9 (EXTRACTS)[6]

Where silent zephyrs sported with the dust
Of the Bastille I sat in the open sun,
And from the rubbish gathered up a stone
And pocketed the relic in the guise
Of an enthusiast; yet, in honest truth,
Though not without some strong incumbencies   *obligations*
And glad (could living man be otherwise?),
I looked for something which I could not find,
Affecting more emotion than I felt.
For 'tis most certain that the utmost force
Of all these various objects, which may show
The temper of my mind as then it was,
Seemed less to recompense the traveler's pains—
Less moved me, gave me less delight—than did
A single picture merely, hunted out
Among other sights: the "Magdalene" of Le Brun[7]
A beauty exquisitely wrought, fair face
And rueful, with its ever-flowing tears. . . .

                          'Twas in truth an hour
Of universal ferment. Mildest men
Were agitated, and commotions, strife
Of passion and opinion, filled the walls
Of peaceful houses with unquiet sounds.
The soil of common life was at that time
Too hot to tread upon! Oft said I then,
And not then only, "What a mockery this
Of history, the past and that to come!
Now do I feel how I have been deceived,
Reading of nations and their works in faith—

---

6. In this extract and the next, Wordsworth recalls his time in France in 1791–1792, when he was immersed in revolutionary politics, visited the site of the Bastille prison (a symbol of the ancien régime demolished during the revolution), and came to know such eminent figures as Jean-Louis Carra and Antoine-Joseph Gorsas, journalists active in the National Assembly, who would be executed during Robespierre's reign of Terror in October 1793.
7. Charles Le Brun's painting of the penitent Mary Magdalen is now at the Louvre.

Faith given to vanity and emptiness;
Oh, laughter for the page that would reflect
To future times the face of what now is!'
The land all swarmed with passion, like a plain
Devoured by locusts—Carra, Gorsas[8]—add
A hundred other names forgotten now,
Nor to be heard of more. Yet were they powers
Like earthquakes, shocks repeated day by day,
And felt through every nook of town and field.

BOOK 10 (EXTRACTS)

       When to my native land
(After a whole year's absence) I returned,[9]
I found the air yet busy with the stir
Of a contention which had been raised up
Against the traffickers in negro blood,
An effort which, though baffled, nevertheless
Had called back old forgotten principles
Dismissed from service, had diffused some truths
And more of virtuous feeling through the heart
Of the English people. And no few of those,
So numerous (little less in verity   *truth*
Than a whole nation crying with one voice)
Who had been crossed in this their just intent
And righteous hope, thereby were well prepared
To let that journey sleep awhile, and join
Whatever other caravan appeared
To travel forward towards Liberty
With more success. For me that strife had ne'er
Fastened on my affections, nor did now

---

8. Carra, Gorsas] Jean-Louis Carra and Antoine-Joseph Gorsas were journalists; Carra edited *Annales Patriotiques*, while Gorsas edited *Courrier des Departements*. Wordsworth knew Gorsas personally, and may have returned to Paris in autumn 1793 to witness his execution.
9. Wordsworth looks back to late November/early December 1792, when he returned to England seeking the means to support his girlfriend and newborn child, both of whom were still in France.

Its unsuccessful issue much excite
My sorrow, having laid this faith to heart,
That if France prospered, good men would not long
Pay fruitless worship to humanity,
And this most rotten branch of human shame
(Object, as seemed, of superfluous pains)
Would fall together with its parent tree. . . .

Ere yet the fleet of Britain had gone forth
On this unworthy service,[10] whereunto
The unhappy counsel of a few weak men
Had doomed it, I beheld the vessels lie,
A brood of gallant creatures, on the deep.
I saw them in their rest, a sojourner
Through a whole month of calm and glassy days
In that delightful island which protects
Their place of convocation; there I heard
Each evening, walking by the still seashore,
A monitory sound which never failed—   *warning*
The sunset cannon. When the orb went down
In the tranquility of nature, came
That voice (ill requiem!), seldom heard by me
Without a spirit overcast, a deep
Imagination, thought of woes to come
And sorrow for mankind, and pain of heart.
      In France, the men who for their desperate ends
Had plucked up mercy by the roots were glad
Of this new enemy. Tyrants, strong before
In devilish pleas, were ten times stronger now,[11]
And thus beset with foes on every side

---

10. Although he wanted to return to his girlfriend and child, Wordsworth was confined to Britain by the outbreak of war, and during the summer saw the British fleet arming off Portsmouth. It was a distressing experience for him.

11. Wordsworth describes the Reign of Terror, which began in July 1793, the month Robespierre came to power. Robespierre's main justification for the slaughter that followed was the need to destroy France's enemies. At its height, in June 1794, the Terror dispensed with defense lawyers and witnesses, enabling accused parties to be condemned en masse. Over the course of forty-nine days, 1,376 people were guillotined in Paris.

The goaded land waxed mad;[12] the crimes of few
Spread into madness of the many; blasts
From hell came sanctified like airs from heaven.
The sternness of the just, the faith of those
Who doubted not that Providence had times
Of anger and of vengeance, theirs who throned
The human understanding paramount
And made of that their god, the hopes of those
Who were content to barter short-lived pangs
For a paradise of ages, the blind rage
Of insolent tempers, the light vanity
Of intermeddlers, steady purposes
Of the suspicious, slips of the indiscreet,
And all the accidents of life, were pressed
Into one service, busy with one work.
The Senate was heart-stricken, not a voice
Uplifted, none to oppose or mitigate.
Domestic carnage now filled all the year
With feast days; the old man from the chimney-nook,
The maiden from the bosom of her love,
The mother from the cradle of her babe,
The warrior from the field—all perished, all—
Friends, enemies, of all parties, ages, ranks,
Head after head, and never heads enough
For those that bade them fall. They found their joy,
They made it, ever thirsty as a child—
If light desires of innocent little ones
May with such heinous appetites be matched—
Having a toy, a windmill, though the air
Do of itself blow fresh and make the vane
Spin in his eyesight, he is not content
But with the plaything at arm's length he sets
His front against the blast and runs amain
To make it whirl the faster.

---

12. waxed mad] burst into madness.

                      In the depth
Of those enormities, even thinking minds
Forgot at seasons whence they had their being—
Forgot that such a sound was ever heard
As liberty upon earth: yet all beneath
Her innocent authority was wrought,
Nor could have been, without her blessed name.
The illustrious wife of Roland,[13] in the hour
Of her composure, felt that agony
And gave it vent in her last words. Oh friend,[14]
It was a lamentable time for man,
Whether a hope had e'er been his or not;
A woeful time for them whose hopes did still
Outlast the shock; most woeful for those few—
They had the deepest feeling of the grief—
Who still were flattered, and had trust in man.
Meanwhile, the invaders fared as they deserved:
The herculean Commonwealth had put forth her arms
And throttled with an infant godhead's might
The snakes about her cradle—that was well
And as it should be, yet no cure for those
Whose souls were sick with pain of what would be
Hereafter brought in charge against mankind.
Most melancholy at that time, oh friend,
Were my day thoughts, my dreams were miserable;
Through months, through years, long after the last beat
Of those atrocities (I speak bare truth,
As if to thee alone in private talk)
I scarcely had one night of quiet sleep,
Such ghastly visions had I of despair
And tyranny and implements of death,
And long orations which in dreams I pleaded
Before unjust tribunals, with a voice

13. Wordsworth refers to Madame Roland, a major figure among the moderate Girondins, the party with which Wordsworth was most closely associated. She was imprisoned in June 1793 and guillotined on November 9. Her last words are said to have been: "Oh liberty, what crimes are committed in thy name!"
14. As elsewhere in *The Prelude*, Wordsworth addresses Coleridge.

Labouring, a brain confounded, and a sense
Of treachery and desertion in the place
The holiest that I knew of—my own soul. . . .

      Oh friend, few happier moments have been mine
Through my whole life than that when first I heard
That this foul tribe of Moloch was o'erthrown
And their chief regent leveled with the dust.[15]
The day was one which haply may deserve   *perhaps*
A separate chronicle. Having gone abroad
From a small village where I tarried then,
To the same far-secluded privacy
I was returning. Over the smooth sands
Of Leven's ample estuary lay
My journey, and beneath a genial sun,
With distant prospect among gleams of sky
And clouds, and intermingled mountaintops,
In one inseparable glory clad—
Creatures of one ethereal substance, met
In consistory, like a diadem
Or crown of burning seraphs, as they sit
In the empyrean. Underneath this show
Lay, as I knew, the nest of pastoral vales
Among whose happy fields I had grown up
From childhood. On the fulgent spectacle   *shining*
Which neither changed, nor stirred, nor passed away,
I gazed, and with a fancy more alive
On this account—that I had chanced to find
That morning, ranging through the churchyard graves
Of Cartmel's rural town, the place in which
An honoured teacher of my youth was laid.[16]
While we were schoolboys he had died among us,
And was borne hither, as I knew, to rest

---

15. Wordsworth recalls the late summer of 1794, which he spent at Rampside, a small village on the west coast of England close to the mouth of the River Leven, where he first heard of Robespierre's death.
16. The Reverend William Taylor, headmaster of Hawkshead Grammar School, had died in June 1786 at the age of thirty-two. His gravestone is still to be seen in Cartmel Priory.

With his own family. A plain stone inscribed
With name, date, office, pointed out the spot,
To which a slip of verses was subjoined
(By his desire as afterward I learned)—
A fragment from the *Elegy* of Gray.
A week, or little less, before his death
He had said to me, "My head will soon lie low,"
And when I saw the turf that covered him
After the lapse of full eight years, those words,
With sound of voice and countenance of the man,
Came back upon me, so that some few tears
Fell from me in my own despite. And now,
Thus traveling smoothly o'er the level sands,
I thought with pleasure of the verses graven
Upon his tombstone, saying to myself,
"He loved the poets, and if now alive
Would have loved me, as one not destitute
Of promise, nor belying the kind hope
Which he had formed, when I at his command
Began to spin, at first, my toilsome song."
         Without me and within, as I advanced,
All that I saw, or felt, or communed with,
Was gentleness and peace. Upon a small
And rocky island near, a fragment stood
(Itself like a sea-rock) of what had been
A Romish chapel[17] where in ancient times
Masses were said at the hour which suited those
Who crossed the sands with ebb of morning tide.
Not far from this still ruin all the plain
Was spotted with a variegated crowd
Of coaches, wains and travelers, horse and foot,
Wading, beneath the conduct of their guide,
In loose procession through the shallow stream
Of inland water;[18] the great sea meanwhile

17. Chapel Island is a limestone outcrop in the Levens estuary; its chapel was built in the fourteenth century by Cistercian monks from the nearby Conishead Priory.
18. Wordsworth describes the two-mile guided crossing at low tide of Levens Sands, taking travelers from Cartmel to Ulverston.

Was at safe distance, far retired. I paused,
Unwilling to proceed, the scene appeared
So gay and cheerful, when a traveler
Chancing to pass, I carelessly inquired
If any news were stirring; he replied
In the familiar language of the day
That *Robespierre was dead.* Nor was a doubt,
On further question, left within my mind
But that the tidings were substantial truth:
That he and his supporters all were fallen.[19]

     Great was my glee of spirit, great my joy
In vengeance, and eternal justice, thus
Made manifest. "Come now, ye golden times,"
Said I, forth-breathing on those open sands
A hymn of triumph, "as the morning comes
Out of the bosom of the night, come ye.
Thus far our trust is verified; behold,
They who with clumsy desperation brought
Rivers of blood, and preached that nothing else
Could cleanse the Augean stable, by the might
Of their own helper have been swept away!
Their madness is declared and visible,
Elsewhere will safety now be sought, and earth
March firmly towards righteousness and peace. . . ."

     Bliss was it in that dawn to be alive,
But to be young was very heaven![20]—oh, times
In which the meager, stale, forbidding ways
Of custom, law and statute took at once
The attraction of a country in romance;
When reason seemed the most to assert her rights
When most intent on making of herself
A prime enchanter to assist the work
Which then was going forward in her name.
Not favored spots alone, but the whole earth

---

19. Robespierre and twenty-one associates were guillotined on July 28, 1794. His death was reported by *The Times* on August 16.
20. Wordsworth digresses to remember his early belief that the French Revolution would create a brave new world.

The beauty wore of promise, that which sets,
To take an image which was felt, no doubt,
Among the bowers of paradise itself,
The budding rose above the rose full blown.
What temper at the prospect did not wake
To happiness unthought of? The inert
Were roused and lively natures rapt away:
They who had fed their childhood upon dreams,
The playfellows of fancy who had made
All powers of swiftness, subtlety, and strength
Their ministers, used to stir in lordly wise
Among the grandest objects of the sense,
And deal with whatsoever they found there
As if they had within some lurking right
To wield it; they too who, of gentle mood,
Had watched all gentle motions and to these
Had fitted their own thoughts, schemers more mild,
And in the region of their peaceful selves,
Did now find helpers to their hearts' desire,
And stuff at hand, plastic as they could wish,
Were called upon to exercise their skill
Not in Utopia, subterraneous fields,
Or some secreted island Heaven knows where,
But in the very world which is the world
Of all of us, the place on which, in the end,
We find our happiness, or not at all.

Written 1804–1805, published 1926

James Orr (1770–1816)

WHAT WAS IT like to participate in the uprising of the United Irishmen in 1798? The most powerful testimony in verse is the work of James Orr, a native of Ballycarry, County Antrim. Taught by his parents to read and write, Orr followed his father into handloom weaving. He seems to have begun his writing career as contributor to the *Northern Star*, a Belfast newspaper that supported the United Irishmen. His radical politics were shaped by millenarian convictions (as were those of Blake, Wordsworth, and Coleridge). On June 7, 1798, he led over one hundred men to the mustering ground at Donegore Hill, to participate in the battle of Antrim. There were numerous desertions along the way, but Orr led his remaining men into battle all the same. It soon became clear the battle was over: the yeomanry was slaughtering wounded rebels and English soldiers were rounding up prisoners and preparing to execute them. Surrounded by retreating insurgents, Orr watched as his men abandoned the fight. He was now in acute personal danger, for as a rebel commander he had a bounty of fifty pounds on his head. That was a sizeable reward to the impoverished country folk who knew of his role. Orr fled to America, though the Amnesty Act of July 1799 allowed him to return to Ballycarry where he resumed his livelihood as weaver and tenant farmer, continuing to publish poetry, including his remarkable poem about the '98 uprising, "Donegore Hill." To a modern reader its language may at first seem opaque, but it is worth the effort. Orr writes in the vernacular of Ulster-Scots, which makes his evocation all the more powerful, for not only is this his native tongue, it is that of the country folk he describes, and the rhythms and sounds are those of their own speech—as wives hand loaves of home-made bread ("bonnocks") to husbands they may never see again, girlfriends make green cockades for their boyfriends, while men manufacture pikes, pitchforks, and primitive firearms. The cowards among them hide, like hens, in the crevices of cow barns ('byre neuks'). A phrase like "Moilie wad dunch the yeomen" comes straight from Orr's comrades. A "moilie" is a hornless cow—a symbol of the impoverished peasants who supported the republican cause; "dunch" is a verb meaning "to butt." What the men who march so bravely to the battlefield are saying is that, though provided only with improvised pikes, they could take on the better-equipped yeomanry. It takes us to the heart of the culture, as well as to the men's conflicted psyches, for their words belie the fear that will, within moments, compel them to slink away. "Come back, ye dastards!" Perhaps Orr spoke those words on the battlefield as he watched them disappear; he would certainly have been witness to the "leuks o' wheens wha stayed behind"—men brave enough to fight, but who understood that, in much-reduced numbers, they had little chance of survival, far less of victory. Such closely observed detail makes "Donegore Hill" the most evocative account we have of this remarkable episode in Irish history.

Donegore Hill

> Ephie's base bairntime, trail-pike brood,
> Were armed as weel as tribes that stood;
> Yet on the battle ilka cauf
> Turned his backside, an' scampered aff.
>
> —PSALM 78, VERSE 9[1]

> The dew-draps wat the fiels o' braird[2]
> That soon the warhorse thortured;   *obstructed*
> An falds were oped by monie a herd[3]
> Wha lang ere night lay tortured;
> Whan chiels wha grudged to be sae taxed   *farmers*
> An tythed by rack-rent blauth'ry[4]
> Turned out en masse, as soon as axed—
> An unco throuither squath'ry[5]
>   Were we, that day.

---

1. In the authorized version, this verse of the Bible reads: "The children of Ephraim, being armed, and carrying bows, turned back in the day of battle."
2. braird] the first shoots of corn in a field are watered by dewdrops.
3. Folds where animals were penned were opened by many herdsmen.
4. Poor Irish peasants were overtaxed by the Anglican Church, from whom their land was rented.
5. An unco throuither squath'ry] a thoroughly disheveled group.

While close-leagued crappies[6] raised the hoards
O' pikes, pike-shafts, forks, firelocks,
Some melted lead, some sawed deal-boards,
Some hade, like hens in byre-neuks;[7]
Wives baket bonnocks[8] for their men
Wi' tears instead o' water;
An' lasses made cockades o' green
For chaps wha used to flatter
                    Their pride ilk day.

A brave man firmly leain' hame
I ay was proud to think on;
The wife-obeyin' son o' shame
Wi' kindlin e'e I blink on:
"Peace, peace be wi' ye! Ah, return
Ere lang and lea the daft anes"[9]—
"Please guid," quo he, "before the morn
In spite o' a' our chieftains
                    An' guards, this day."

But when the pokes o' provender   *bags of food*
Were slung on ilka shou'der,
Hags, wha to henpeck didna spare,
Loot out the yells the louder.
Had they, whan blood about their heart
Cauld fear made cake an' crudle,
Ta'en twa rash gills[10] frae Herdman's quart,
'Twad roused the calm, slow puddle
                    I' their veins that day.

---

6. crappies] the croppies of 1798 were so called because they had their hair cropped short.
7. Some hade, like hens in byre-neuks] some hid, like hens in cow sheds.
8. bonnocks] unleavened loaves of bread.
9. the daft anes] from the wife's point of view, the daft ones are those who continue into battle.
10. twa rash gills] two gills make a pint. The container held a quart (or two pints) of liquid—which in this case must have been whiskey, or some other beverage that would have roused rebel blood. Herdman was a local innkeeper.

Now leaders, laith to lea the rigs
Whase leash they feared was broken,
An' privates, cursin' purse-proud prigs,
Wha brought 'em balls to sloken;[11]
Repentant Painites[12] at their pray'rs
An' dastards crousely craikin',   *complaining loudly*
Move on, heroic, to the wars
They meant na to partake in
              By night or day.

Some fastin' yet, now strave to eat
The piece, that butter yellowed;
An' some, in flocks, drank out cream crocks,
That wives but little valued:
Some lettin' on their burn to mak',
The rear-guard, goadin', hastened;
Some hunk'rin' at a lee dyke back,
Boost houghel on, ere fastened   *have to walk awkwardly*
           Their breeks that day.   *breeches*

The truly brave, as journeyin' on
They pass by weans an' mithers,   *children and mothers*
Think on red fiel's,[13] whare soon may groan
The husbands an' the fathers:
They think how soon thae bonie things
May lose the youths they're true to;
An' see the rabble, strife ay brings,
Ravage their mansions, new to
            Sic scenes, that day.

When to the tap o' Donegore   *top*
Braid-islan' corps cam' postin',
The red-wud, warpin, wild uproar   *angry*

---

11. The privates curse penny-pinching comrades who provide them with only a glass of malt whiskey ("ball") to slake their thirst ("sloken").
12. The Painites are enthusiastic readers of the works of Thomas Paine, advocate of republicanism.
13. red fiel's] fields red with the blood of the dead and dying.

Was like a bee scap castin';
For ***** ***** took ragweed farms
(Fears e'e has ay the jaundice[14])
For Nugent's redcoats,[15] bright in arms,
An' rush! the pale-faced randies   *reckless fellows*
         Took leg, that day.

The camp's brak up. Owre braes an' bogs
The patriots seek teeir sections;
Arms, ammunition, bread-bags, brogues,[16]
Lye skailed in a' directions;   *scattered*
Ane half, alas, wad feared to face
Auld fogies, faps, or women;
Though strong, untried, they swore in pride,
"Moilie wad dunch the yeomen,"[17]
         Some wissed-for day.

Come back, ye dastards! Can ye ought
Expect at your returnin',
But wives an' weans stripped, cattle hought,
An' cots an' claughin's burnin'?   *cottages, hamlets*
Na, haste ye hame; ye ken ye'll 'scape,
'Cause martial worth ye're clear o';
The nine-tailed cat or choakin' rape
Is maistly for some hero
         On sic a day.

Saunt Paul (auld Knacksie![18]) counsels weel—
Pope somewhere does the samen,
That, "first o' a, folk sud themsel's
Impartially examine";

---

14. Fears e'e has ay the jaundice] a jaundiced eye is tainted by its owner's expectations.
15. Nugent's redcoats] Major General George Nugent (1757–1849) commanded the northern district of Ireland during the uprising.
16. brogues] a kind of crude shoe worn by Irish peasants.
17. Moilie wad dunch the yeomen] A moilie was a hornless cow, the symbol of republicanism, which would butt ("dunch") the yeomen cavalry.
18. auld Knacksie!] familiar name for St. Paul.

Gif that's na done, whate'er ilk loun   *each low, idle fellow*
May swear to, never swith'rin,   *hesitating*
In ev'ry pinch, he'll basely flinch—
"Guidbye to ye, my brethren,"
          He'll cry that day.

The leuks o' wheens wha stayed behin'   *The faces of several of those*
Were marked by monie a passion;
By dread to staun, by shame to rin,   *stay, run*
By scorn an' consternation;
Wi' spite they curse, wi' grief they pray,
Now move, now pause a bit ay;
"'Tis mad to gang, 'tis death to stay!"—   *to go*
An unco dolefu' ditty   *very sad refrain*
          On sic a day.

What joy at hame our entrance gave!   *home*
"Guid God! Is't you? Fair fa' ye!
'Twas wise, though fools may ca't no' brave,
To rin or e'er they saw ye."[19]
"Aye wife, that's true without dispute,
But lest saunts fail in Zion,
I'll hae to swear Orr[20] forced me out:
Better he swing than I, on
          Some hangin' day."

My story's done, an' to be free,
Owre sair, I doubt, they smarted,   *over-worked*
Wha wad hae belled the cat awee,[21]
Had they no' been deserted:
Thae warks pat skill, though in my min'

---

19. 'Twas wise . . . saw ye] Although fools may not call it brave, it was wise to run before the enemy saw you.
20. In the 1804 text, Orr does not spell out the name, rendering three asterisks instead. I follow Carol Baranuik's suggestion that Orr means he knew there were some who would have betrayed him in order to save themselves.
21. "Wha daur bell the cat?" is a question supposedly asked by one mouse of another, when one of them has the idea of securing a bell to the cat's neck, to warn of its approach.

That ne'er was in't before, mon,
In tryin' times, maist folk, you'll fin',
Will act like Donegore men
              On onie day.

Written after June 7, 1798, published 1804

Samuel Taylor Coleridge (1772–1834)

COLERIDGE ENLISTED IN the King's Light Dragoons as Silas Tomkyn Comberbache in December 1793, and remained a "horse soldier" until April 8 the following year. Peculiar behavior for a utopian revolutionary opposed to the war with France, who would later propose a commune in America where he and like-minded individuals would practice free love under the banner of Pantisocracy—but then, Coleridge was no ordinary activist. In August 1794, he regarded Robespierre as "the benefactor of mankind" whose death was "the greatest misfortune Europe could have sustained," and went on to deliver public lectures sufficiently radical to incite physical violence: "Mobs and mayors, blockheads and brickbats, placards and press-gangs have leagued in horrible conspiracy against me," he complained. "Two or three uncouth and unbrained automata have threatened my life, and in the last lecture the genus infimum ["the lowest kind"] were scarcely restrained from attacking the house in which the 'damned Jacobin was jawing away.'" E. P. Thompson notes that Coleridge's ideology followed the same trajectory as others who were imprisoned, and only retirement to Nether Stowey saved him from the same fate. Even there, however, Coleridge remained a "downright zealous leveler" (as Thelwall described him) sufficiently notorious to invite the attentions of a government spy, James Walsh, whose initial report was that Coleridge, William and Dorothy Wordsworth were "French people"; a later report suggested they were "a mischievous gang of disaffected Englishmen," and his final verdict was that the "rascals from Alfoxden" (where the Wordsworths lived) were "a set of violent democrats." This helps explain why Coleridge and the Wordsworths emigrated in 1798, preferring to live, at least for a time, in Germany. Our selections from Coleridge's verse date from the period when he continued to think as a Leveler, while writing at the peak of his powers. "Kubla Khan" has been read as apolitical, though the "ancestral voices prophesying war" suggest some insight into recent history; after all, it is the inherent propensity for conflict, something we now understand as part of our genetic inheritance, that turns revolution (however well motivated) into bloodshed. "Fire, Famine, and Slaughter: A War Eclogue," from the original text of 1798, deplores the British-aided Royalist revolt in La Vendée, as well as the burning of huts and cottages in Ulster in March 1797. Many years later, an older Coleridge anxious to atone for his youthful politics apologized for the poem in an essay that declared admiration for Pitt "both as a good man and a great statesman," adding: "there was never a moment in my existence in which I should have been more ready, had Mr. Pitt's person been in hazard, to interpose my own body, and defend his life at the risk of my own." Coleridge and Southey coauthored "The Devil's Thoughts" in August 1799, Southey contributing four stanzas to the version that appeared in *The Morning Post* on September 6, 1799 (our source for the text below). It takes its inspiration from Job 1:7: "And the Lord said unto Satan, Whence comest thou? Then Satan answered the Lord, and said, From going to and fro in the earth, and from walking up and down in it." The poem describes a locked-down, reactionary England through the eyes of the Devil, who sees the country as ripe for apocalypse. Such was its popularity, the editor of *The Morning Post* had to print several hundred extra copies of the paper, which remained "in demand for days and weeks afterwards." It is the model for Shelley's "The Devil's Walk" (1812) and Byron's "The Devil's Drive" (1813).

Kubla Khan

In Xanadu did Kubla Khan
A stately pleasure dome decree,
Where Alph, the sacred river, ran
Through caverns measureless to man
  Down to a sunless sea.
So twice five miles of fertile ground
With walls and towers were girdled round;
And here were gardens bright with sinuous rills
Where blossomed many an incense-bearing tree;

And here were forests ancient as the hills,
And folding sunny spots of greenery.

But oh, that deep romantic chasm which slanted
Down the green hill athwart a cedarn cover!
A savage place, as holy and enchanted
As e'er beneath a waning moon was haunted
By woman wailing for her demon lover!
And from this chasm, with ceaseless turmoil seething,
As if this earth in fast thick pants were breathing,
A mighty fountain momently was forced
Amid whose swift half-intermitted burst
Huge fragments vaulted like rebounding hail,
Or chaffy grain beneath the thresher's flail!
And mid these dancing rocks at once and ever,
It flung up momently the sacred river.

Five miles meandering with a mazy motion
Through wood and dale the sacred river ran,
Then reached the caverns measureless to man
And sank in tumult to a lifeless ocean:
And mid this tumult Kubla heard from far
Ancestral voices prophesying war!

  The shadow of the dome of pleasure
  Floated midway on the waves,
  Where was heard the mingled measure
  From the fountain and the caves;
It was a miracle of rare device,
A sunny pleasure dome with caves of ice!

  A damsel with a dulcimer
  In a vision once I saw:
  It was an Abyssinian maid
  And on her dulcimer she played,
  Singing of Mount Abora.
  Could I revive within me
  Her symphony and song,

To such a deep delight 'twould win me
That with music loud and long,
I would build that dome in air,
That sunny dome, those caves of ice!
And all who heard should see them there,
And all should cry, "Beware, beware!
His flashing eyes, his floating hair!
Weave a circle round him thrice,
And close your eyes with holy dread—
For he on honey dew hath fed
And drank the milk of paradise."

Written c. November 1797, published May 25, 1816

Fire, Famine, and Slaughter: A War Eclogue

(SCENE: A DEPOPULATED TRACT IN LA VENDÉE.[1] FAMINE IS DISCOVERED
STRETCHED ON THE GROUND; TO HER ENTER SLAUGHTER AND FIRE.)

FAMINE
Sisters, sisters! Who sent you here?

SLAUGHTER
I will name him in your ear.

FIRE
      No! no! no!
Spirits hear what spirits tell:
'Twill make an holiday in hell.
      No! no! no!
Myself, I named him once below
And all the souls that damned be

---

1. Royalist sympathizers led a rebellion against the new French Republic from 1793 to
1799, when they were suppressed. It was an exceptionally bloody war, in which many
hundreds of thousands were killed.

Leaped up at once in anarchy,
Clapped their hands and danced for glee;
They no longer heeded *me*
But laughed to hear hell's burning rafters
Unwillingly re-echo laughters!
        No! no! no!
Spirits hear what spirits tell:
'Twill make an holiday in hell!

FAMINE

Then sound it not, yet let me know—
Darkly hint it, soft and low.

SLAUGHTER

Four letters form his name.[2]
And who sent you?

FAMINE

        The same, the same!

SLAUGHTER

He came by stealth and unlocked my den,
And I have spilled the blood since then
Of thrice ten hundred thousand men.

FIRE AND FAMINE

Who bade you do 't?

SLAUGHTER

        The same, the same!
Four letters form his name.
He let me loose and cried "Halloo!"—
To him alone the praise is due.

---

2. Four letters form his name] This is usually taken to refer to the prime minister, William Pitt, though (as John Barrell has argued) it could refer also to George III (K,I,N,G). Coleridge detested Pitt, and in his antiwar lecture of 1795 said that he had "an actual presence in the sacraments of Hell."

FAMINE

Thanks, sisters, thanks! The men have bled,
Their wives and children faint for bread.
I stood in a swampy field of battle;
With bones and skulls I made a rattle
To frighten the wolf and the carrion crow
And the homeless dog—but they would not go.
So off I flew: for how could I bear
To see them gorge their dainty fare?
I heard a groan and a peevish squall,
And through the chink of a cottage wall—
Can you guess what I saw there?

SLAUGHTER AND FIRE

Whisper it, sister, in our ear!

FAMINE

A baby beat its dying mother:
I had starved the one, and was starving the other!

SLAUGHTER AND FIRE

Who bade you do 't?

FAMINE

The same, the same!
Four letters form his name.
He let me loose and cried, "Halloo!"—
To him alone the praise is due.

FIRE

Sisters, I from Ireland came![3]
Huts and cornfields all on flame,
I triumphed o'er the setting sun,
And all the while the work was done.
As on I strode with monstrous strides,

---

3. Fears that Ireland would prove the source of invasion from France prompted the British government to impose martial law in March 1797, in the form of house burnings, torture, and execution.

I flung back my head and held my sides;
It was so rare a piece of fun
To see the sweltered cattle run
With uncouth gallop, all the night,
Scared by the red and noisy light!
By the light of his own blazing cot
Was many a naked rebel shot;
The house stream met the fire and hissed,
While crash! the roof fell in, I wish
On some of those old bedrid nurses
That deal in discontent and curses!

SLAUGHTER AND FIRE
Who bade you do 't?

FIRE
      The same, the same!
Four letters form his name.
He let me loose and cried "Halloo!"—
How shall I give him honour due?

ALL
He let us loose and cried "Halloo!"
How shall I give him honour due?

FAMINE
Wisdom comes with lack of food;
I'll gnaw, I'll gnaw the multitude
Till the cup of rage o'erbrim:
They shall seize him of his brood.

SLAUGHTER
They shall tear him limb from limb!

FIRE
Oh, thankless beldames, and untrue,
And is this all that you can do
For him that did so much for you?
(to SLAUGHTER)

For *you* he turned the dust to mud
With his fellow creatures' blood!
(to FAMINE)
And hunger scorched as many more
To make *your* cup of joy run o'er!
(*to both*)
Full ninety moons he, by my troth,
Hath richly catered for you both;
And in an hour you would repay
An eight years' debt, away, away!
I alone am faithful, I
Cling to him everlastingly.

LABERIUS[4]

Written probably December 1797, published January 8, 1798

The Devil's Thoughts
Co-authored With Robert Southey[1]

From his brimstone bed at break of day,
        A-walking the Devil is gone,
To look at his little snug farm of the earth,
        And see how his stock went on.

Over the hill and over the dale,
        And he went over the plain,
And backward and forward he swished his long tail
        As a gentleman swishes his cane.

He saw a lawyer killing a viper
        On the dunghill beside his stable;

---

4. The pen name chosen by Coleridge probably refers to Decimus Laberius (105–43 BC), a Roman satirist.
THE DEVIL'S THOUGHTS
1. The first three stanzas are by Southey, as is the one mentioning Coldbath Fields prison; see footnote 4, next page.

"Oh, oh!," quoth he, for it put him in mind
    Of the story of Cain and Abel.

An apothecary on a white horse
    Rode by on his vocation,
And the Devil thought of his old friend—
    Death, in the Revelation.[2]

He went into a rich bookseller's shop,
    Quoth he, "We are both of one college,
For I sat myself like a cormorant once
    Upon the tree of knowledge."[3]

He saw a turnkey in a trice
    Handcuff a troublesome blade;
"Nimbly," quoth he, "the fingers move,
    If a man is but used to his trade."

He saw the same turnkey unfettering a man
    With but little expedition,
And he laughed, for he thought of the long debates
    On the slave-trade abolition.

As he went through Coldbath Fields[4] he looked
    At a solitary cell—
And the Devil was pleased, for it gave him a hint
    For improving the prisons of hell.

He passed a cottage with a double coach-house,
    A cottage of gentility;

---

2. At this point Coleridge notes Revelation 6:8: "And I looked, and behold a pale horse, and his name that sat on him was Death."

3. "This anecdote is related by that most interesting of the Devil's biographers, Mr. John Milton, in his *Paradise Lost*, and we have here the Devil's own testimony to the truth and accuracy of it" (Coleridge's note).

4 Coldbath Fields] This stanza is by Southey. Coldbath Fields was a prison in the Farringdon Road, noted for its austerity. Southey may allude to the cell occupied by Colonel Despard, a mutineer, which was seven feet square, completely dark, and freezing cold.

And he grinned at the sight, for his favorite vice
    Is pride, that apes humility.

He saw a pig right rapidly
    Adown the river float;
The pig swam well, but every stroke
    Was cutting his own throat.

Old Nicholas grinned, and swished his tail
    For joy and admiration,
And he thought of his daughter, Victory,
    And her darling babe, Taxation.[5]

He met an old acquaintance
    Just by the Methodist meeting;
She held a consecrated flag,
    And the Devil nods a greeting.[6]

She tipped him the wink, then frowned and cried,
    "Avaunt, my name's Religion!"
And turned to Mr. Wilberforce
    And leered like a love-sick pigeon.

General ———'s[7] burning face
    He saw with consternation,
And back to hell his way did take—
For the Devil thought, by a slight mistake,
    It was general conflagration.

Written August–September 1799, published September 6, 1799

---

5. her darling babe, Taxation] In 1798 the national debt reached 407 million pounds sterling. The prime minister, William Pitt, was compelled to introduce income tax in late 1798, which affected those who earned more than sixty pounds a year.

6. a consecrated flag . . . a greeting] Coleridge criticized Methodists for their conservatism and practice of consecrating regimental banners: to him, it seemed ungodly to practice religious rites upon instruments of war.

7. General ———'s] suggested candidates include Isaac Gascoigne and Banastre Tarleton, both involved in the brutal suppression of the Irish uprising, both opposed to the abolition of slavery.

Robert Emmet (1778–1803)

ROBERT EMMET WAS an active member of the Society of United Irishmen well before the uprising of May 23, 1798, though he saw none of the fighting and evaded imprisonment, unlike his brother Thomas Addis Emmet. All the same, he was aware of the summary manner with which the British army executed rebels, most of whom were hanged or shot. He also knew the refuse dump at Arbour Hill, the "Croppies' Hole," between the main entrance to the Royal Barracks and the north bank of the Liffey, where the mutilated bodies of United Irishmen were left exposed to the elements with pikes tied to their bodies. After the '98 uprising, Emmet helped reorganize the society, and was secretary of a secret delegation to France, where he met Talleyrand and Napoléon (then first consul), with whom he discussed the possibility of a French invasion, though without reaching agreement. By the time he returned to Ireland in autumn 1802, he was contemplating further rebellion. "We war not against property," Emmet declared, "We war against English dominion." His plan, scheduled for July 23, 1803, was to take control of principal government buildings in Dublin, but it was ill timed, ill prepared, and virtually everything went wrong that could go wrong. The coup failed and he went on the run. He was hunted down, imprisoned, and tried on September 19, 1803. He made no attempt to defend himself from the capital charge of high treason, and called no witnesses, wishing to implicate no one else. Aware his life was approaching its end, he rose and made a speech that would inspire future generations. It culminated with an attack on the British government, "which reigns amid the cries of orphans and of the widows it has made." His concluding words were to be his most famous:

> I have not been allowed to vindicate my character. I have but one request to ask at my departure from this world: it is the charity of its silence. Let no man write my epitaph; for as no man who knows my motives dares now vindicate them, let not prejudice or ignorance asperse them. Let them rest in obscurity and peace: my memory be left in oblivion and my

tomb remain uninscribed, until other times and other men can do justice to my character. When my country takes her place among the nations of the earth, then, and not till then, let my epitaph be written. I have done.

Emmet was condemned to be hanged and beheaded the following day, September 20, 1803. He was twenty-five years old. His speech in court, maltreatment in Kilmainham Gaol, courage on the scaffold, and affair with Sarah Curran (daughter of John Philpot Curran, see p. 277), are the stuff of Republican legend, and continue to inspire biographers and historians. His memory was kept alive by the writings of his friend and fellow student Thomas Moore, particularly such lyrics as "Oh, breathe not his name," inspired by Emmet's courtroom speech.

Arbour Hill

No rising column marks this spot
    Where many a victim lies;
But oh, the blood which here has streamed
    To heaven for justice cries!

It claims it on the oppressor's head
    Who joys in human woe,
Who drinks the tears by misery shed
    And mocks them as they flow.

It claims it on the callous judge
    Whose hands in blood are dyed,
Who arms injustice with the sword,
    The balance thrown aside;

It claims it for this ruined isle,
    Her wretched children's grave,
Where withered Freedom droops her head
    And man exists a slave.

Oh, sacred Justice! free this land
    From tyranny abhorred;
Resume thy balance and thy seat,
    Resume—but sheathe thy sword.

No retribution should we seek,
    Too long has Horror reigned;
By Mercy marked, may Freedom rise,
    By Cruelty unstained.

Nor shall a tyrant's ashes mix
    With those our martyred dead;
This is the place where Erin's sons
    In Erin's cause have bled.

And those who here are laid at rest—
    Oh, hallowed be each name!
Their memories are forever blessed,
    Consigned to endless fame.

Unconsecrated is this ground,
    Unblessed by holy hands;
No bell here tolls its solemn sound,
    No monument here stands.

But here the patriot's tears are shed,
    The poor man's blessing given;
These consecrate the virtuous dead,
    These waft their fame to heaven.

Written May 1799, published 1846

The Exile

Ah, where is now my peaceful cot?
    Ah, where my happy home?

No peaceful cot, alas, is mine—
    An exile now I roam.

Far from the country I am driven,
    A wanderer sent from thee,
But still my constant prayer to heaven
    Shall be to make thee free.

Written c. 1802, published 1847

Francis Scott Key (1779–1843)

HAD HE COMPOSED the great blank verse epic on the history of world, it would make no difference; Key will always be known for the four-verse poem by which he is represented here, probably the best-known in this volume. Key was a lawyer who worked in Georgetown near Washington, DC. He visited Baltimore with a volunteer artillery company, charged with the mission of negotiating for the release of prisoners held by the British during the 1812 war. "Detained" by his hosts on the truce ship, Key was compelled to watch the British rocket attack on the star-shaped Fort McHenry during the battle of Baltimore; it lasted twenty-five hours, in the course of which twenty British ships were sunk by American cannon. For all their efforts, the British soon realized they could not take Baltimore and retreated into the Chesapeake. At the end of the bombardment, the American flag at the fort emerged unscathed; as Key saw it fluttering in the wind on the early morning of September 14, 1814, he began to compose "Defence of Fort McHenry," which, under a catchier title—"The Star-Spangled Banner"—would become America's national anthem.

The Star-Spangled Banner

Oh say, can you see, by the dawn's early light,
    What so proudly we hailed, at the twilight's last gleaming,

Whose broad stripes and bright stars, through the perilous fight
    O'er the ramparts we watched, were so gallantly streaming?
And the rockets' red glare, the bombs bursting in air,
Gave proof through the night that our flag was still there—
        Oh say, does that star-spangled banner yet wave
        O'er the land of the free and the home of the brave?

On that shore dimly seen through the mists of the deep,
    Where the foe's haughty host in dread silence reposes,
What is that which the breeze o'er the towering steep,
    As it fitfully blows, now conceals, now discloses?
Now it catches the gleam of the morning's first beam,
In full glory reflected now shines in the stream—
        'Tis the star-spangled banner; oh, long may it wave
        O'er the land of the free and the home of the brave!

And where are the foes who so vauntingly swore
    That the havoc of war and the battle's confusion,
A home and a country should leave us no more?
    Their blood has washed out their foul footsteps' pollution;
No refuge could save the hireling and slave
From the terror of flight or the gloom of the grave;
        And the star-spangled banner in triumph doth wave
        O'er the land of the free and the home of the brave!

Oh, thus be it ever, when freemen shall stand
    Between their loved homes and the war's desolation;
Blessed with victory and peace, may the heaven-rescued land
    Praise the Power that hath made and preserved us a nation!
Then conquer we must, when our cause it is just,
And this be our motto, "In God is our trust"—
        And the star-spangled banner in triumph shall wave
        O'er the land of the free and the home of the brave!

Written September 14, 1814, published September 20, 1814

Leigh Hunt (1784–1859)

HUNT IS FAMOUS for having occupied a prison cell lined with rose-trellised wallpaper, in which he was allowed to place busts of his favorite poets; all the same, the experience of confinement was a chastening one. His crime was to have declared in his newspaper, *The Examiner*, that the Prince Regent (not known for laughing at himself), "this Adonis in loveliness, was a corpulent gentleman of fifty! . . . a libertine over head and ears in debt and disgrace, a despiser of domestic ties, the companion of gamblers and demireps, a man who has just closed half a century without one single claim on the gratitude of his country or the respect of posterity!" Able to bear only so much reality, the regent ensured Hunt's prosecution for libel, resulting in a two-year prison sentence. Hunt was severely traumatized by the experience, and on the day of his release (February 2, 1815) found himself disabled by a psychological ailment akin to agoraphobia, described in his autobiography: "two years' confinement, and illness in combination, had acted so injuriously upon a sensitive temperament, that for many months I could not leave home without a morbid wish to return, and a fear of being seized with some fit or other in the streets, perhaps with sudden death." Unable to make the journey to Hampstead, he fled to the house of a friend yards from the prison gates in Horsemonger Lane—and there remained until he could bear to venture out: "I had not the courage to continue looking at the shoals of people passing to and fro." Eventually, he returned to his cottage in Hampstead, and in sonnets written over ensuing weeks spoke as frankly as he could of his gradual readjustment. As the friend of Keats, Shelley, and Byron, Hunt was a friend also to their liberal ideologies. It is no coincidence that he was the editor to whom Shelley sent "The Mask of Anarchy" in 1819 (see pp. 357–70), hoping for swift publication. But the experience of imprisonment had marked Hunt forever, and he knew a further jail term would be the inevitable result of its printing. Instead he stuck it in his bottom drawer until the political climate made it less likely to agitate government attorneys.

To Hampstead

Sweet upland, to whose walks with fond repair
    Out of thy western slope I took my rise
    Day after day, and on these feverish eyes
Met the moist fingers of the bathing air;
If health, unearned of thee, I may not share,
    Keep it, I pray thee, where my memory lies,
    In thy green lanes, brown dells, and breezy skies
Till I return, and find thee doubly fair.
Wait then my coming, on that lightsome land,
    Health, and the joy that out of nature springs,
      And Freedom's air-blown locks—but stay with me,
Friendship, frank entering with the cordial hand,
    And Honour, and the Muse with growing wings,
      And Love Domestic, smiling equably.

SURREY JAIL, 27 AUGUST 1813

Written August 27, 1813, published August 29, 1813

To Hampstead

The baffled spell that bound me is undone,
    And I have breathed once more beneath thy sky,
Lovely browed Hampstead; and my looks have run
    O'er and about thee; and had scarce drew nigh
When I beheld, in momentary sun,
    One of thy hills gleam bright and bosomy,
Just like that orb of orbs, a human one,
    Let forth by chance upon a lover's eye.
Forgive me, then, that not till now I spoke;
    For all the comforts missed in close distress
      With airy nod came up from every part
O'er smiling speech; and so I gazed and took
    A long, deep draught of silent freshfulness
      Ample, and gushing round my fevered heart.

Written May 3, 1815, published May 7, 1815

To Hampstead

As one who after long and far-spent years
    Comes on his mistress in an hour of sleep,
    And half-surprised that he can silence keep
Stands smiling o'er her through a flash of tears,
To see how sweet and self-same she appears;
    Till at his touch, with little moving creep
    Of joy, she wakes from out her calmness deep,
And then his heart finds voice, and dances round her ears—
So I, first coming on my haunts again,
    In pause and stillness of the early prime,[1]
    Stood thinking of the past and present time
With earnest eyesight, scarcely crossed with pain;
    Till the fresh moving leaves, and startling birds,
    Loosened my long-suspended breath in words.

Written May 7, 1815, published May 14, 1815

Eliza Lee Follen (1787–1860)

IN ADDITION TO being an intellectual, capable of translating some of the most challenging works of the French philosopher François Fénelon, Follen believed in the ability of women to reform the political structure of the world, something she demonstrated in word and deed. This was nowhere more clear than in her hatred of the slave trade, against which she campaigned with her German husband; her essay, "Women's Work," leaves no doubt of her sentiments: "The abolition of slavery is indeed women's work. As imitators of him who came to seek and to save that which was lost, we are called to it. Let neither fathers, nor brothers, nor husbands, nor false or weak friends keep us back from it." These were brave words, for abolitionists were "most hated, most reviled" at this period. She and her husband were outcasts, such

---

1. early prime] the time just after sunrise.

that when he died in a steamship disaster in 1840 it took four months to find a chapel that would agree to host his memorial service. Often religious in content, her poetry has much in common with that of the British Romantics in its preoccupation with the natural world and the numinous forces that flow through it—though it is worth remembering Follen was also one of the great children's writers of the day, responsible for a much-loved version of "The Three Little Kittens."

For the Fourth of July

My country, that nobly could dare
    The hand of oppression to brave—
Oh how the foul stain canst thou bear
    Of being the land of the slave?

His groans and the clank of his chains
    Shall rise with the shouts of the free,
And turn into discord the strains
    They raise, God of mercy, to thee.

The proud knee at his altar we bend,
    On God as our Father we call:
We call him our Father and Friend
    And forget he's the Father of all.

His children he does not forget;
    His mercy, his power can save;
And, sure as God liveth, he yet
    Will liberty give to the slave.

Oh, talk not of freedom and peace
    With the blood of the slave on our sod—
Till the groans of the negro shall cease,
    Hope not for a blessing from God.

He asks, "Am I not a man?"
    He pleads, "Am I not a brother?"
Then dare not, and hope not you can
    The cry of humanity smother.

'Twill be heard from the south to the north
    In our halls and in poverty's shed;
It will go like a hurricane forth
    And wake up the living and dead.

The dead whom the white man has slain,
    They cry from the ground and the waves;
They once cried for mercy in vain,
    They plead for their brothers, the slaves.

Oh, let them, my country, be heard!
    Be the land of the free and the brave!
And send forth the glorious word—
    This is not the land of the slave!

Published 1839

Children in Slavery

When children play the livelong day
    Like birds and butterflies,
As free and gay, sport life away,
    And know not care nor sighs,
Then earth and air seem fresh and fair,
    All peace below, above,
Life's flowers are there, and everywhere
    Is innocence and love.

When children pray with fear all day,
    A blight must be at hand;
Then joys decay and birds of prey

Are hovering o'er the land;
When young hearts weep as they go to sleep
Then all the world seems sad;
The flesh must creep and woes are deep
When children are not glad.

Published 1839

The Slave Boy's Wish

I wish I was that little bird
Up in the bright blue sky,
That sings and flies just where he will
And no one asks him why.

I wish I was that little brook
That runs so swift along
Through pretty flowers and shining stones,
Singing a merry song.

I wish I was that butterfly
Without a thought or care,
Spreading my pretty, brilliant wings
Like a flower in the air.

I wish I was that wild, wild deer
I saw the other day,
Who swifter than an arrow flew,
Through the forest far away.

I wish I was that little cloud
By the gentle south wind driven,
Floating along so free and bright
Far, far up into heaven.

I'd rather be a cunning fox
    And hide me in a cave,
I'd rather be a savage wolf
    Than what I am—a slave.

My mother calls me her good boy,
    My father calls me brave;
What wicked action have I done
    That I should be a slave?

I saw my little sister sold,
    So will they do to me;
My heavenly Father, let me die
    For then I shall be free.

Published 1845

Samuel Bamford (1788–1872)

PROMINENT AMONG WORKING-CLASS radicals, Bamford was identified in a Home Office report of January 1817 as secretary of his local branch of the Hampden Club (which argued for universal suffrage and annual Parliaments) and soon after arrested on a charge of high treason, to be interrogated by members of the Privy Council, including Lord Sidmouth (the Home Secretary) and Viscount Castlereagh (Foreign Secretary). This was a serious charge that carried a capital penalty, but he was acquitted for lack of evidence. Undeterred in the fight for a more equitable political system, he helped organize a mass demonstration at St. Peter's Field in Manchester on August 16, 1819, when he led workers from his home town of Middleton to join a crowd of sixty thousand agitating for Parliamentary reform, who were to listen to a speech by Henry "Orator" Hunt. That day he witnessed what took place when mounted hussars charged into crowds of unarmed men, women, and children. "The cavalry were in confusion," he later recalled, "and their sabers were plied to hew a way through naked held-up hands and defenseless heads; and then chopped limbs and wound-gaping skulls were seen; and groans and cries were mingled with the din of that horrid confusion. . . . For a moment the crowd held back as in a pause; then was a rush, heavy and resistless as a headlong sea, and a sound like low thunder, with screams, prayers, and imprecations from the crowd-moiled and saber-doomed who could not escape." It was the bloodiest political event of the nineteenth century on British soil; as E. P. Thompson wrote, "It really was a massacre. . . . [t]here is no term for this but class war." Of those who reported the aftermath, Bamford is the most eloquent:

> The hustings remained, with a few broken and hewed flag-staves erect, and a torn and gashed banner or two drooping; whilst over the whole field were strewed caps, bonnets, hats, shawls and shoes, and other parts of male and female dress—trampled, torn, and bloody. The yeomanry had dismounted. Some were easing their horses' girths, others adjusting their accoutrements, and some were wiping their sabers. Several mounds of human beings still remained where they had fallen, crushed down and smothered. Some of these were still groaning,—others with staring eyes were gaping for breath, and others would never breathe more. All was silent save those low sounds, and the occasional snorting and pawing of steeds. Persons might sometimes be noticed peeping from attics and over the tall ridgings of houses, but they quickly withdrew as if fearful of being observed, or unable to sustain the full gaze of a scene so hideous and abhorrent.

Fourteen people died and 654 were seriously injured. Although Bamford's conduct had been nonviolent, he was put on trial for high treason, along with Hunt, and found guilty of unlawful assembly and of attempting to change the law of the country by force, for which he received a year in Lincoln jail. His "Lancashire Hymn" had appeared in the *Manchester Observer* in two parts, on July 17 and August 7, 1819, as encouragement to those preparing to march on St. Peter's Field. We publish that early text here, including a verse deleted from subsequent versions, which refers to the martyrdom of two seventeenth-century Republicans, John Hampden and Algernon Sidney ("By the dear blood which Hampden bled," p. 354). "The Song of the Slaughter" was published by Orator Hunt in a pamphlet written from prison, which urged readers to sing Bamford's poem on the anniversary of Peterloo: "It will be very proper to be chaunted over the graves of those who were murdered on that never-to-be-forgotten day." That was exactly what happened: on the third anniversary of the massacre in Ashton-under-Lyne (a town in Lancashire), a number of people displayed a flag inscribed "Murder, 16th August," as they sang Bamford's poem. Of the various early versions of "The Song of the Slaughter," we include here the most polished, which appeared in the *Manchester Observer* on August 5, 1820.

The Lancashire Hymn

PART ONE

Great God, who did of old inspire
    The patriot's ardent heart,
And filled him with a warm desire
    To die or do his part,
Oh, let our shouts be heard by thee,
Genius great of liberty!

Here, 'fore creation's million worlds,
    Our wrongs we do proclaim,
And when thy banner thou unfurls,
    We will redress the same;
Triumph ever waits on thee,
God of love and liberty.

When fell oppression o'er the land
    Hung like a darksome day,
And crushed beneath a tyrant's hand
    The groaning people lay,[1]
The patriot band impelled by thee
Nobly strove for liberty.[2]

And shall *we* tamely now forego
    The rights for which they bled?

---

1. And crushed . . . lay] in a note, Bamford indicates that the tyrant is Charles I.
2. The patriot band . . . liberty] by the "band," Bamford means "Hampden and his compatriots." John Hampden (1595–1643) was prominent among the parliamentarians who took England to war against Charles I.

And crouch beneath a minion's blow[3]
    And basely bow the head?
Ah no, it cannot, cannot be—
Death for us, or liberty!

PART TWO

Behold, yon midnight, dark divan,[4]
    The plunderers of our right;
Fell sorcerers, mustering every ban,
    Our happiness to blight.
Why lingers yet the nation's ire?
Why bursteth not the bolt of fire?

The dungeon door hath opened wide
    Its victims to immure,
And blood hath yonder scaffold dyed,[5]
    Betrayed by hellish lure;[6]
Oh Justice, why so long delay
To judge the judges of that day?

Have we not heard the infant's cry
    And marked its mother's tear,
That look which told us mournfully
    That woe and want were there?
And shall they ever weep again?
And shall their pleadings be in vain?

---

3. a minion's blow] Bamford has in mind Henry Addington, first viscount Sidmouth, Home Secretary since 1812, and George Canning, president of the Board of Control within the cabinet.

4. divan] Bamford refers to the Privy Council, which had detained and interrogated him for his involvement in the Hampden Club, which sought parliamentary reform (see headnote, p. 350 above).

5. Bamford refers to the Pentrich uprising of June 1817, when a large group of working men protested by marching to Nottingham. They were routed by dragoons, and their leaders (Jeremiah Brandreth, William Turner, and Isaac Ludlam) hanged and beheaded.

6. Bamford refers to W. J. Oliver, a government agent who informed on the marchers and acted as an agent provocateur.

By the dear blood which Hampden bled
　　In freedom's noble strife,
By gallant Sidney's gory head,[7]
　　By all that's dear to life,
They shall not supplicate in vain,
No longer will we wear the chain.

Souls of our mighty sires, behold
　　This band of brothers join;
Oh never, never be it told
　　That we disgrace your line.
If England wills the glorious deed,
We'll have another Runnymede.[8]

Written July 1819, published July 17, and August 7, 1819

The Song of the Slaughter

　　Written to commemorate the anniversary
　　of the fatal 16th of August

PART ONE

Parent of the wide creation,
　　We would counsel ask of thee:
Look upon a mighty nation,
　　Rousing from its slavery.

If to men our wrongs are stated,
　　We are but the faster bound;

---

7. gallant Sidney's gory head] Bamford refers to Algernon Sidney (1623–1683), republican, who, with Hampden, became involved in discussions concerning a rebellion led by the Duke of Monmouth against Charles II. The plot was discovered, Sidney was found guilty of treason, and beheaded on December 7, 1683.
8. The Magna Carta, which itemized the liberties he was willing to give to the population of England, was signed by King John at Runnymede in 1215.

All our actions reprobated—
    No redress for us is found.

Thou hast made us to inherit
    Strength of body, daring mind;
Shall we rise and in Thy spirit
    Tear away the chains that bind?

Chains, but forged to degrade us—
    Oh, the base indignity!
In the name of God who made us,
    We will perish or be free!

PART TWO

Can we e'er forget our brothers,
    Cold and gory as they lay?
Can we e'er forgive the others
    For their cruel treachery?

Ah, behold their sabers gleaming,
    Never, never known to spare!
See the flood of slaughter streaming!
    Hear the cries that rend the air!

Youth and valour nought availed;
    Nought availed beauty's prayer;
E'en the lisping infant failed
    To arrest the ruin there.

Give the ruffians time to glory,
    Theirs is but a waning day;
We have yet another story
    For the page of history!

LINCOLN CASTLE, 13 JULY 1820

Published August 5, 1820

Percy Bysshe Shelley (1792–1822)

NO POET HATED tyranny more, and none devoted more energy to its denunciation. After expulsion from Oxford (for having published an atheist pamphlet), Shelley became a political activist, attempting to foment revolution in Ireland. But the Dublin poor were so beaten down, he believed, there was no rousing them. "I had no conception of the depth of human misery until now," he wrote, "The poor of Dublin are assuredly the meanest and most miserable of all. In their narrow streets thousands seem huddled together—one mass of animated filth!" (March 8, 1812). On return to England in April, Shelley was under suspicion as a dangerous radical, his activities under surveillance by agents of the Home Secretary, Lord Sidmouth. Having settled in north Devon, Shelley instructed his Irish servant, Daniel Hill, to distribute copies of his radical publications—which led to Hill's imprisonment for six months. Shelley came face to face with Sidmouth's colleague, John Scott, Lord Eldon, the Lord Chancellor, in 1817, when attempting to take custody of his children by his first wife. Eldon was the public face of government—one that had just suspended habeas corpus, made meetings of more than fifty people illegal, and ordered the arrest of authors of seditious material. Eldon refused Shelley guardianship and the poet never saw his children again. These brushes with Lord Liverpool's government help explain his response to the Peterloo Massacre in August 1819. When he heard that mounted cavalrymen had charged into a crowd of unarmed demonstrators in Manchester, leaving 654 injured and 14 dead, he was incensed: "the torrent of indignation has not yet done boiling in my veins," he wrote, "I wait anxiously to hear how the country will express its sense of this bloody murderous oppression of its destroyers. Something must be done" (September 6, 1819). Shelley expected working people to take revenge: "The tyrants here, as in the French Revolution, have shed first blood" (September 9, 1819). His response was "The Mask of Anarchy," which urges a form of nonviolent resistance (and mentions both Eldon and Sidmouth, along with other members of Lord Liverpool's government). It was completed within days, and on September 23 he sent it to Leigh Hunt in London for publication in his newspaper, *The Examiner*. But Hunt had already spent two years in prison for expressing his political opinions, and the law had become more restrictive since then. He chose the politic course of not publishing, retaining Shelley's manuscript until 1832, by which time its author was dead. However, "The Mask of Anarchy" was reprinted many times subsequently, and gave encouragement to the Chartists, who would agitate for reforms advocated by Shelley decades before.

The Mask of Anarchy

Written on the Occasion of the Massacre
at Manchester[1]

As I lay asleep in Italy
There came a voice from over the sea,
And with great power it forth led me
To walk in the visions of poesy.

I met Murder on the way—
He had a mask like Castlereagh[2]—
Very smooth he looked, yet grim;
Seven bloodhounds followed him.

All were fat, and well they might
Be in admirable plight,   *condition*
For one by one, and two by two,
He tossed them human hearts to chew,
Which from his wide cloak he drew.

---

1. On August 16, 1819 at St. Peter's Field on the outskirts of Manchester, a peaceful political demonstration was dispersed by mounted Hussars with a violence that left 14 dead and 654 seriously injured. Shelley, who was resident in Livorno, Italy, was outraged, and responded with this plea for nonviolent protest.
2. Castlereagh] Robert Stewart, Viscount Castlereagh (1769–1822), was Foreign Secretary in 1819. Years before, as Chief Secretary to Ireland, he was responsible for the arrest of the United Irishmen in September 1796. Shelley may have held him responsible for the summary execution of United Irishmen after the 1798 uprising.

Next came Fraud, and he had on,
Like Eldon,[3] an ermined gown;
His big tears, for he wept well,
Turned to millstones as they fell.

And the little children, who
Round his feet played to and fro,
Thinking every tear a gem,
Had their brains knocked out by them.

Clothed with the Bible, as with light,
And the shadows of the night,
Like Sidmouth,[4] next Hypocrisy
On a crocodile rode by.

And many more Destructions played
In this ghastly masquerade,
All disguised, even to the eyes,
Like bishops, lawyers, peers, or spies.

Last came Anarchy:[5] he rode
On a white horse, splashed with blood;
He was pale even to the lips,
Like Death in the Apocalypse.[6]

And he wore a kingly crown,
And in his grasp a scepter shone;
On his brow this mark I saw—
"I AM GOD, AND KING, AND LAW."

---

3. John Scott, Baron Eldon, was Lord Chancellor. On March 27, 1817, he was responsible for denying Shelley custody of his children, Ianthe and Charles, whom he did not see again.

4. Henry Addington (1757–1844), created Viscount Sidmouth in 1805, was Home Secretary in 1819. He applauded the Peterloo Massacre in the House of Commons.

5. Anarchy] an idol of both the people and their oppressive rulers, Anarchy is something against which Shelley warns his readers. Shelley knows that the people want revenge, but argues that, were they to take it, the government would respond with greater ruthlessness than ever.

6. Death in the Apocalypse] Revelation 6:8: "And I looked, and behold a pale horse, and his name that sat on him was Death, and Hell followed him."

With a pace stately and fast,
Over English land he passed,
Trampling to a mire of blood
The adoring multitude.

And a mighty troop around,
With their trampling shook the ground,
Waving each a bloody sword,
For the service of their lord.

And with glorious triumph, they
Rode through England proud and gay,
Drunk as with intoxication
Of the wine of desolation.

O'er fields and towns, from sea to sea,
Passed the pageant swift and free,
Tearing up, and trampling down,
Till they came to London town.

And each dweller, panic-stricken,
Felt his heart with terror sicken
Hearing the tempestuous cry
Of the triumph of Anarchy.

For with pomp to meet him came
Clothed in arms like blood and flame,
The hired murderers, who did sing
"Thou art God, and Law, and King.

We have waited, weak and lone,
For thy coming, Mighty One!
Our purses are empty, our swords are cold,
Give us glory, and blood, and gold."

Lawyers and priests, a motley crowd,
To the earth their pale brows bowed;
Like a bad prayer, not overloud,
Whispering, "Thou art Law and God."

Then all cried with one accord,
"Thou art King, and God, and Lord;
Anarchy, to thee we bow,
By thy name made holy now!"

And Anarchy, the skeleton,
Bowed and grinned to everyone,
As well as if his education
Had cost ten millions to the nation.

For he knew the palaces
Of our kings were rightly his—
His the scepter, crown, and globe[7]
And the gold-enwoven robe.

So he sent his slaves before
To seize upon the Bank and Tower,[8]
And was proceeding with intent
To meet his pensioned Parliament,[9]

When one fled past, a maniac maid,
And her name was Hope, she said;
But she looked more like Despair,
And she cried out in the air:

"My father Time is weak and gray
With waiting for a better day;
See how idiot-like he stands,
Fumbling with his palsied hands!

He has had child after child
And the dust of death is piled

---

7. globe] orb, symbol of kingship.
8. Bank and Tower] The Bank of England, in Threadneedle Street in the City of London, since 1734, and the Tower of London, situated on Tower Hill since around 1066. They were strongholds of power.
9. pensioned Parliament] Anarchy pays those in Parliament to oppress the people by whatever means necessary.

Over everyone but me—
Misery, oh misery!"

Then she lay down in the street,
Right before the horses' feet,
Expecting, with a patient eye,
Murder, Fraud and Anarchy.

When between her and her foes
A mist, a light, an image rose,
Small at first, and weak and frail
Like the vapour of a vale;

Till as clouds grow on the blast,
Like tower-crowned giants striding fast,
And glare with lightnings as they fly,
And speak in thunder to the sky,

It grew—a shape arrayed in mail
Brighter than the viper's scale,
And upborne on wings whose grain   *color*
Was as the light of sunny rain.

On its helm, seen far away,   *helmet*
A planet, like the morning's, lay;
And those plumes its light rained through   *feathers*
Like a shower of crimson dew.

With step as soft as wind it passed
O'er the heads of men—so fast
That they knew the presence there,
And looked—and all was empty air.

As flowers beneath May's footstep waken,
As stars from night's loose hair are shaken,
As waves arise when loud winds call,
Thoughts sprung where'er that step did fall.

And the prostrate multitude
Looked—and ankle deep in blood,
Hope, that maiden most serene,
Was walking with a quiet mien.

And Anarchy, the ghastly birth,
Lay dead earth upon the earth;
The horse of Death, tameless as wind,
Fled, and with his hoofs did grind
To dust the murderers thronged behind.

A rushing light of clouds and splendor,
A sense awakening and yet tender,
Was heard and felt—and at its close
These words of joy and fear arose

(As if their own indignant earth
Which gave the sons of England birth
Had felt their blood upon her brow,
And shuddering with a mother's throe

Had turned every drop of blood
By which her face had been bedewed
To an accent unwithstood—
As if her heart had cried aloud):

"Men of England, heirs of Glory,
Heroes of unwritten story,
Nurslings of one mighty mother,
Hopes of her and one another,

Rise like lions after slumber
In unvanquishable number,
Shake your chains to earth like dew
Which in sleep had fallen on you—
Ye are many; they are few.

What is freedom? Ye can tell
That which slavery is, too well—

For its very name has grown
To an echo of your own.

'Tis to work and have such pay
As just keeps life from day to day
In your limbs, as in a cell
For the tyrants' use to dwell.

So that ye for them are made
Loom, and plough, and sword, and spade,
With or without your own will bent
To their defence and nourishment.

'Tis to see your children weak
With their mothers pine and peak,[10]
When the winter winds are bleak—
They are dying whilst I speak.

'Tis to hunger for such diet
As the rich man in his riot   *extravagance*
Casts to the fat dogs that lie
Surfeiting beneath his eye.

'Tis to let the ghost of gold[11]
Take from toil a thousandfold—
More than ere its substance could
In the tyrannies of old.

Paper coin—that forgery
Of the title deeds, which ye
Hold to something of the worth
Of the inheritance of earth.

'Tis to be a slave in soul
And to hold no strong control

---

10. pine and peak] grow thin and emaciated.
11. the ghost of gold] paper money, which Shelley regarded as a trick to inflate currency and depress the cost of labor.

Over your own wills, but be
All that others make of ye.

And at length when ye complain
With a murmur weak and vain,
'Tis to see the tyrant's crew
Ride over your wives and you—
Blood is on the grass like dew.

Then it is to feel revenge
Fiercely thirsting to exchange
Blood for blood and wrong for wrong—
Do not thus when ye are strong.

Birds find rest in narrow nest
When weary of their winged quest;
Beasts find fare in woody lair
When storm and snow are in the air.

Asses, swine, have litter spread
And with fitting food are fed;
All things have a home but one—
Thou, oh Englishman, hast none!

This is slavery—savage men
Or wild beasts within a den
Would endure not as ye do;
But such ills they never knew.

What art thou, freedom? Oh, could slaves
Answer from their living graves
This demand, tyrants would flee
Like a dream's dim imagery.

Thou art not, as impostors say,
A shadow soon to pass away,
A superstition and a name
Echoing from the cave of fame.   *rumor, gossip*

For the labourer thou art bread,
And a comely table spread
From his daily labour come
To a neat and happy home.

Thou art clothes, and fire, and food
For the trampled multitude;
No—in countries that are free
Such starvation cannot be
As in England now we see.

To the rich thou art a check:
When his foot is on the neck
Of his victim, thou dost make
That he treads upon a snake.

Thou art justice: ne'er for gold
May thy righteous laws be sold
As laws are in England—thou
Shieldst alike the high and low.

Thou art wisdom: freemen never
Dream that God will damn forever
All who think those things untrue
Of which priests make such ado.

Thou art peace: never by thee
Would blood and treasure wasted be,
As tyrants wasted them, when all
Leagued to quench thy flame in Gaul.[12]

What if English toil and blood
Was poured forth, even as a flood?
It availed, oh liberty,
To dim, but not extinguish thee!

---

12. Gaul] revolutionary France. In 1793, England formed an alliance with Prussia and Austria against France.

Thou art love—the rich have kissed
Thy feet, and like him following Christ,
Give their substance to the free
And through the rough world follow thee;

Or turn their wealth to arms, and make
War for thy beloved sake
On wealth, and war, and fraud—whence they
Drew the power which is their prey.

Science, poetry and thought   *knowledge*
Are thy lamps; they make the lot
Of the dwellers in a cot   *cottage*
So serene, they curse it not.

Spirit, patience, gentleness,
All that can adorn and bless
Art thou—let deeds, not words, express
Thine exceeding loveliness.

Let a great assembly be
Of the fearless and the free
On some spot of English ground
Where the plains stretch wide around.

Let the blue sky overhead
The green earth on which ye tread,
All that must eternal be
Witness the solemnity.

From the corners uttermost
Of the bounds of English coast;
From every hut, village and town
Where those who live and suffer moan
For others' misery or their own;

From the workhouse and the prison
Where pale as corpses newly risen,

Women, children, young and old,
Groan for pain and weep for cold;

From the haunts of daily life
Where is waged the daily strife
With common wants and common cares
Which sows the human heart with tares;   *weeds, anxieties*

Lastly from the palaces
Where the murmur of distress
Echoes, like the distant sound
Of a wind alive around,

Those prison halls of wealth and fashion,
Where some few feel such compassion
For those who groan, and toil, and wail
As must make their brethren pale—

Ye who suffer woes untold,
Or to feel, or to behold
Your lost country bought and sold
With a price of blood and gold—

Let a vast assembly be,
And with great solemnity
Declare with measured words that ye
Are, as God has made ye, free.

Be your strong and simple words
Keen to wound as sharpened swords,
And wide as targes let them be   *shields*
With their shade to cover ye.

Let the tyrants pour around
With a quick and startling sound,
Like the loosening of a sea,
Troops of armed emblazonry.

Let the charged artillery drive
Till the dead air seems alive
With the clash of clanging wheels,
And the tramp of horses' heels.

Let the fixed bayonet
Gleam with sharp desire to wet
Its bright point in English blood,
Looking keen as one for food.

Let the horsemen's scimitars
Wheel and flash, like sphereless stars
Thirsting to eclipse their burning
In a sea of death and mourning.

Stand ye calm and resolute
Like a forest close and mute,
With folded arms and looks which are
Weapons of an unvanquished war;

And let Panic, who outspeeds
The career of armed steeds
Pass, a disregarded shade
Through your phalanx undismayed.

Let the laws of your own land,
Good or ill, between ye stand
Hand to hand, and foot to foot,
Arbiters of the dispute;

The old laws of England—they
Whose reverend heads with age are gray,
Children of a wiser day;
And whose solemn voice must be
Thine own echo—liberty!

On those who first should violate
Such sacred heralds in their state,

Rest the blood that must ensue,
And it will not rest on you.

And if then the tyrants dare,
Let them ride among you there,
Slash, and stab, and maim, and hew—
What they like, that let them do.

With folded arms and steady eyes,
And little fear, and less surprise,
Look upon them as they slay,
Till their rage has died away.

Then they will return with shame
To the place from which they came,
And the blood thus shed will speak
In hot blushes on their cheek.

Every woman in the land
Will point at them as they stand—
They will hardly dare to greet
Their acquaintance in the street.

And the bold, true warriors
Who have hugged danger in wars
Will turn to those who would be free,
Ashamed of such base company.

And that slaughter to the nation
Shall steam up like inspiration,
Eloquent, oracular—
A volcano heard afar.

And these words shall then become
Like oppression's thundered doom
Ringing through each heart and brain,
Heard again—again—again—

Rise like lions after slumber
In unvanquishable number;
Shake your chains to earth like dew
Which in sleep had fallen on you—
Ye are many, they are few."

Written between September 5 and 23, 1819, published October 1832

Ode to the West Wind[1]

I

Oh wild west wind, thou breath of autumn's being;
Thou, from whose unseen presence the leaves dead
Are driven, like ghosts from an enchanter fleeing,

Yellow, and black, and pale, and hectic red,
Pestilence-stricken multitudes; oh thou
Who chariotest to their dark wintry bed

The winged seeds, where they lie cold and low,
Each like a corpse within its grave, until
Thine azure sister of the spring shall blow

Her clarion o'er the dreaming earth, and fill
(Driving sweet buds like flocks to feed in air)
With living hues and odors plain and hill—

Wild spirit, which art moving everywhere,
Destroyer and preserver, hear, oh hear!

---

1. Though on the surface a nature poem, Shelley's great ode expounds a myth of world-wide apocalypse followed by regeneration. It envisions the oppression of the "pestilence-stricken multitudes," their disease and death, which will be followed by regeneration and rebirth, a process Shelley regards as a form of revolution of which he is the prophet.

II

Thou on whose stream, mid the steep sky's commotion,
Loose clouds like earth's decaying leaves are shed,
Shook from the tangled boughs of heaven and ocean,

Angels of rain and lightning; there are spread
On the blue surface of thine airy surge,
Like the bright hair uplifted from the head

Of some fierce maenad,[2] even from the dim verge
Of the horizon to the zenith's height,
The locks of the approaching storm. Thou dirge

Of the dying year, to which this closing night
Will be the dome of a vast sepulchre,
Vaulted with all thy congregated might

Of vapours, from whose solid atmosphere
Black rain, and fire, and hail will burst—oh hear!

III

Thou who didst waken from his summer dreams
The blue Mediterranean where he lay,
Lulled by the coil of his crystalline streams,

Beside a pumice isle in Baiae's bay,
And saw in sleep old palaces and towers
Quivering within the wave's intenser day,

All overgrown with azure moss and flowers
So sweet, the sense faints picturing them! Thou
For whose path the Atlantic's level powers

Cleave themselves into chasms, while far below
The sea blooms and the oozy woods which wear
The sapless foliage of the ocean, know

---

2. maenad] bacchante, follower of Bacchus, god of wine.

Thy voice, and suddenly grow gray with fear,
And tremble and despoil themselves—oh hear!

IV

If I were a dead leaf thou mightest bear;
If I were a swift cloud to fly with thee;
A wave to pant beneath thy power and share

The impulse of thy strength, only less free
Than thou, oh uncontrollable! If even
I were as in my boyhood, and could be

The comrade of thy wanderings over heaven,
As then, when to outstrip thy skyey speed
Scarce seemed a vision; I would ne'er have striven

As thus with thee in prayer in my sore need.
Oh lift me as a wave, a leaf, a cloud!
I fall upon the thorns of life! I bleed!

A heavy weight of hours has chained and bowed
One too like thee—tameless, and swift, and proud.

V

Make me thy lyre, even as the forest is:
What if my leaves are falling like its own?
The tumult of thy mighty harmonies

Will take from both a deep autumnal tone,
Sweet though in sadness. Be thou, spirit fierce,
My spirit! Be thou me, impetuous one!

Drive my dead thoughts over the universe
Like withered leaves to quicken a new birth!
And, by the incantation of this verse,

Scatter, as from an unextinguished hearth,
Ashes and sparks, my words among mankind!
Be through my lips to unawakened earth

The trumpet of a prophecy! Oh wind,
If winter comes, can spring be far behind?

Written c. October 25, 1819, published August 14, 1820

England in 1819

An old, mad, blind, despised, and dying king;[1]
Princes, the dregs of their dull race, who flow
Through public scorn—mud from a muddy spring;
Rulers who neither see, nor feel, nor know,
But leech-like to their fainting country cling,
Till they drop, blind in blood, without a blow;
A people starved and stabbed on the untilled field;
An army, which liberticide[2] and prey
Makes as a two-edged sword to all who wield;
Golden and sanguine laws which tempt and slay;
Religion Christless, Godless—a book sealed;
A senate, time's worst statute, unrepealed—
Are graves from which a glorious phantom may
Burst, to illumine our tempestuous day.

Written by December 23, 1819, published 1839

Song to the Men of England

Men of England, wherefore plough
For the lords who lay ye low?
Wherefore weave with toil and care
The rich robes your tyrants wear?

---

1. George III, on the throne since 1760, was old and ill, and had been insane for years. He died on January 29, 1820.
2. liberticide] the killing of liberty.

Wherefore feed and clothe and save
From the cradle to the grave
Those ungrateful drones who would
Drain your sweat—nay, drink your blood?

Wherefore, Bees of England, forge
Many a weapon, chain and scourge,
That these stingless drones may spoil
The forced produce of your toil?

Have ye leisure, comfort, calm,
Shelter, food, love's gentle balm?
Or what is it ye buy so dear
With your pain and with your fear?

The seed ye sow, another reaps;
The wealth ye find, another keeps;
The robes ye weave, another wears;
The arms ye forge, another bears.

Sow seed, but let no tyrant reap;
Find wealth, let no impostor heap;
Weave robes, let not the idle wear;
Forge arms in your defence to bear.

Shrink to your cellars, holes, and cells;
In halls ye deck another dwells.
Why shake the chains ye wrought? Ye see
The steel ye tempered glance on ye.

With plough and spade and hoe and loom,
Trace your grave, and build your tomb,
And weave your winding-sheet till fair
England be your sepulcher.

Probably written between December 1819
and January 1820, published 1839

John Clare (1793–1864)

BETWEEN 1700 AND 1845 the English countryside changed beyond recognition by the enclosure of over 7,175,000 acres of land that had once been freely accessible to all. In parts of the country the effects were damaging—including, in Warwickshire, two decades of high unemployment, increased infant mortality, and mass emigration. Clare's county of Northamptonshire suffered, too: between 1750 and 1815, two-thirds of its agricultural holdings were turned from open fields and commons to enclosed farmland. When local opposition was ignored (as was usual), residents engaged in sporadic guerrilla action— destroying live hedges; throwing down posts and rails; and pulling down fences, gates, and stiles, as happened on the bridle path between Northampton and neighboring villages in 1786. Frequently, such resistance was met by force: in Wilbarston in summer 1799, local villagers hoping to prevent enclosure of their common were confronted by two troops of yeoman cavalry. Clare's home town of Helpston was unenclosed at the time of his birth, and in boyhood he "wandered the heath in raptures among the rabbit burrows and golden blossomed furze," as he later recalled. But the Enclosure Act of 1809 changed all that, taking from him, and everyone else, countryside formerly owned in common. With that gesture, the landowning class of Northamptonshire declared war on those who, like Clare and his family, were dependent on common land for fuel and grazing rights; those who lived off the gleanings of stray ears of corn after harvest, who fed on nuts and berries growing wild, and gathered wool from the fields. Easy access to common land had defined their existence, and that of their forebears, for centuries. Now, in one fell swoop, they were made dependent on wage labor or charity, in the worst cases being rendered destitute. It was an act of oppression to match anything on the national stage. Not only was Clare a witness to the economic consequences of enclosure, he felt deeply the psychologically alienating effects of losing touch with the landscape in which he had grown up, and in which he had once lived. It is the single most important reason why he writes as an elegist: when he wrote, "I dreaded walking where there was no path," he did so as representative of a newly minted underclass, stripped of birthright and heritage.

The Village Minstrel (extract)

There once was days (the woodman knows it well)
When shades e'en echoed with the singing thrush;
There once was hours, the ploughman's tale can tell,
When morning's beauty wore its earliest blush;
How woodlarks caroled from each stumpy bush—
Lubin[1] himself has marked 'em soar and sing!
The thorns are gone, the woodlark's song is hushed;
Spring more resembles winter now than spring;
The shades are banished all, the birds betook to wing.

There once was lanes in nature's freedom dropped;
There once was paths that every valley wound:
Enclosure came and every path was stopped—
Each tyrant fixed his sign where pads was found.   *paths*
To hint a trespass now, who crossed the ground?
Justice is made to speak as they command;
The high road now must be each stinted bound.
Enclosure, thou'rt a curse upon the land,
And tasteless was the wretch who thy existence planned![2]

Oh, England, boasted land of liberty,
With strangers still thou mayst thy title own;
But thy poor slaves the alteration see—
With many a loss to them the truth is known.
Like emigrating bird thy freedoms flown,
While mongrel clowns, low as their rooting plough,   *peasants*
Disdain thy laws to put in force their own;

---

1. Lubin] The name given by Clare to the protagonist of this poem.
2. In the manuscript, Clare's patron Lord Radstock wrote, against this stanza, "This is radical Slang."

And every village owns its tyrants now,
And parish slaves must live as parish kings allow.

Composed between October 20, 1819 and
January 21, 1820, published September 1821

The Moors[1]

Far spread the moory ground, a level scene
Bespread with rush and one eternal green,
That never felt the rage of blundering plough
Though centuries' wreathed spring's blossoms on its brow,
Still meeting plains that stretched them far away
In unchecked shadows of green, brown, and gray;
Unbounded freedom ruled the wandering scene,
Nor fence of ownership crept in between
To hide the prospect of the following eye—
Its only bondage was the circling sky:
One mighty flat undwarfed by bush and tree
Spread its faint shadow of immensity
And lost itself, which seemed to eke its bounds   *extend*
In the blue mist the horizon's edge surrounds.
     Now this sweet vision of my boyish hours,
Free as spring clouds and wild as summer flowers,
Is faded all—a hope that blossomed free,
And hath been once, no more shall ever be:
Enclosure came and trampled on the grave
Of labour's rights and left the poor a slave,
And memory's pride, ere Want to Wealth did bow,
Is both the shadow and the substance now.
The sheep and cows were free to range as then
Where change might prompt, nor felt the bonds of men;
Cows went and came with evening, morn and night

---

1. Clare's manuscript spells the title as "The Mores." Some editors retitle this poem "Enclosure."

To the wild pasture as their common right;
And sheep, unfolded[2] with the rising sun,
Heard the swains shout and felt their freedom won,
Tracked the red fallow field and heath and plain
Then met the brook, and drank and roamed again—
The brook that dribbled on, as clear as glass,
Beneath the roots, then hid among the grass;
While the glad shepherd traced their tracks along,
Free as the lark and happy as her song.

      But now all's fled, and flats of many a dye
That seemed to lengthen with the following eye—
Moors, losing from the sight, far, smooth, and blea[3]
Where swooped the plover in its pleasure free,
Are vanished now, with commons wild and gay,
As poet's visions of life's early day;
Mulberry bushes where the boy would run
To fill his hands with fruit are grubbed and done,
And hedgerow briars—flower lovers overjoyed
Came and got flowerpots—these are all destroyed;
And sky-bound moors in mangled garbs are left
Like mighty giants of their limbs bereft.
Fence now meets fence in owners' little bounds
Of field and meadow, large as garden grounds—
In little parcels little minds to please,
With men and flocks imprisoned ill at ease;
Each little path that led its pleasant way
As sweet as morning leading night astray,
Where little flowers bloomed round a varied host
That travel felt delighted to be lost,   *traveler*
Nor grudged the steps that he had taken as vain
When right roads traced his journey's end again—
Nay, on a broken tree he'd sit awhile
To see the moors and fields and meadows smile;
Sometimes with cowslips smothered—then all white
With daisies—then the summer's splendid sight

---

2. unfolded] allowed to wander from the sheepfold.
3. blea] bleak, exposed.

Of cornfields crimson o'er the "headache"[4] bloomed,
Like splendid armies for the battle plumed:
He gazed upon them with wild fancy's eye
As fallen landscapes from an evening sky.
      These paths are stopped—the rude philistine's thrall
Is laid upon them and destroyed them all;
Each little tyrant with his little sign
Shows where man claims earth glows no more divine;
On paths to freedom and to childhood dear
A board sticks up to notice "no road here,"
And on the tree with ivy overhung
The hated sign by vulgar taste is hung,
As though the very birds should learn to know
When they go there they must no further go.
Thus with the poor, scared Freedom bade good-bye,
And much they feel it in the smothered sigh;
And birds and trees and flowers without a name,
All sighed when lawless laws' enclosure came
And dreams of plunder in such rebel schemes
Have found too truly that they were but dreams.

Written c. 1822, published 1996

I dreaded walking where there was no path

I dreaded walking where there was no path,
And pressed with cautious tread the meadow swath,
And always turned to look with wary eye,
And always feared the owner coming by;
Yet everything about where I had gone
Appeared so beautiful I ventured on,
And when I gained the road where all are free
I fancied every stranger frowned at me,
And every kinder look appeared to say,

---

4. headache] poppy.

"You've been on trespass in your walk today."
I've often thought the day appeared so fine—
How beautiful if such a place were mine;
But having nought I never feel alone,
And cannot use another's as my own.

Perhaps written 1835, published 1995

John Keats (1795–1821)

"THE PRESENT DISTRESSES of this nation are a fortunate thing," wrote Keats on hearing of the Peterloo Massacre, "though so horrid in their experience" (September 18, 1819). He meant that the sufferings of ordinary people were so intense that the time had come for revolution, however bloody. The government's prosecution of Richard Carlile for publishing his own eyewitness account of Peterloo was, Keats wrote, "of great moment in my mind"—enough for him to add, "I hope sincerely to put a mite of help to the liberal side of the question before I die" (September 22, 1819). One by-product of his premature death (at the age of twenty-five, in Rome) is that he would not do so, but there can be no doubting his strength of feeling. He was sufficiently opposed to the government to suspect his mail was monitored ("they open my letters"), such was the paranoia of the moment. And when Henry "Orator" Hunt, the principal speaker in St. Peter's Field, returned to London on September 13, Keats joined the crowd of thirty thousand who welcomed him: "The whole distance from the Angel Islington to the Crown and Anchor was lined with multitudes" (September 18, 1819). Until recently, critics tended to regard Keats as immune to the upheaval of the times, but recent research shows he was as ideologically engaged as those with whom he consorted (Leigh Hunt and Shelley, among others); moreover, his views aligned him with liberal, if not radical, figures of his time. It was not for nothing that, the day after Peterloo, Keats compared himself with Samuel Bamford (see p. 350): "My name with the literary fashionables is vulgar: I am a weaver boy to them" (September 17, 1819). His opinions were fostered by *The Examiner*, a newspaper edited by Leigh Hunt (jailed for having ridiculed the Prince Regent), whose release from prison Keats celebrated in a sonnet (p. 382). The author of "Ode to a Nightingale" was Republican, as the first poem in this selection indicates, which declares his sympathies with English Republicans of the seventeenth century. If that were not evidence enough, one need only glance at the opening of *Endymion*, Book 3, where Keats attacks panjandrums who wore "empurpled vests / And crowns," a sentiment that prompted one critic to accuse him of "lisping sedition" (a crime that entailed a prison sentence). We also include "Lines on the Mermaid Tavern" and "Robin Hood," which denounce the capitalist economy in which "honey / Can't be got without hard money!" while praising a more equitable past in which "men knew nor rent nor leases." In a letter written shortly after he wrote "Robin Hood," Keats spoke of his longing for a world in which "every human might become great, and humanity (instead of being a wide heath of furze and briars with here and there a remote oak or pine) would become a grand democracy of forest trees" (February 19, 1818). To have made such a declaration in 1818 was to ally oneself with those lobbying for fairer Parliamentary representation and a broadening of the franchise—in short, with those slaughtered at Peterloo. Keats regarded himself as radical, and was unafraid of declaring as much in his published work.

Written on 29 May, the Anniversary of Charles's Restoration, on Hearing the Bells Ringing[1]

Infatuate Britons, will you still proclaim
His memory, your direst, foulest shame?
    Nor patriots revere?
Ah, when I hear each traitorous lying bell,
'Tis gallant Sidney's, Russell's, Vane's[2] sad knell
    That pains my wounded ear.

Written May 29, 1814 or 1815, published 1925

---

1. In his copy of Milton's poems, Keats wished that Milton's Republican views "should have had power to pull that feeble animal Charles II from his bloody throne."

2. Sidney's, Russell's, Vane's] Keats refers to Algernon Sidney (1623–1683), Lord William Russell (1639–1683) and Sir Henry Vane the younger (1613–1662). Their Republican beliefs led to execution.

Written on the Day That Mr. Leigh Hunt Left Prison[1]

What though, for showing truth to flattered state,
    Kind Hunt was shut in prison, yet has he,
    In his immortal spirit, been as free
As the sky-searching lark, and as elate.
Minion of grandeur, think you he did wait?
    Think you he nought but prison walls did see
    Till, so unwilling, thou unturn'dst the key?
Ah no, far happier, nobler was his fate!
In Spenser's halls he strayed, and bowers fair,
    Culling enchanted flowers; and he flew
With daring Milton through the fields of air:
    To regions of his own his genius true
Took happy flights. Who shall his fame impair
    When thou art dead, and all thy wretched crew?

Written February 2, 1815, published March 3, 1817

Lines on the Mermaid Tavern[1]

Souls of poets dead and gone,
What Elysium have ye known,
Happy field or mossy cavern,
Choicer than the Mermaid Tavern?
Have ye tippled drink more fine
Than mine host's Canary wine?
Or are fruits of paradise

---

1. Keats gave a copy of this poem to his friend, Charles Cowden Clarke, on the day in question—Thursday, February 2, 1815. Leigh Hunt's actual departure from the Surrey prison was traumatic; see p. 344 above.

LINES ON THE MERMAID TAVERN
1. Keats composed this poem, and the one that follows, in what he described as "the spirit of outlawry," drawing on the popular idea of Robin Hood as a quasi-Republican figure whose time was past, but whose fame "Can never, never die." Contrary to what some scholars suggest, Keats could not have visited the Mermaid, as it was destroyed in the Great Fire of 1666.

Sweeter than those dainty pies
Of venison? Oh generous food,
Dressed as though bold Robin Hood
Would, with his Maid Marian,
Sup and bowse from horn and can.   *drink*
I have heard that on a day
Mine host's signboard flew away
Nobody knew whither, till
An astrologer's old quill
To a sheepskin gave the story,
Said he saw you in your glory,
Underneath a new old sign
Sipping beverage divine,
And pledging with contented smack
The Mermaid in the Zodiac.
　　　Souls of poets dead and gone,
What Elysium have ye known,
Happy field or mossy cavern,
Choicer than the Mermaid Tavern?

Written c. February 3, 1818, published July 1820

Robin Hood

To a friend

No! those days are gone away
And their hours are old and gray,
And their minutes buried all
Under the downtrodden pall
Of the leaves of many years;
Many times have winter's shears,
Frozen north and chilling east,
Sounded tempests to the feast
Of the forest's whispering fleeces,
Since men knew nor rent nor leases.

No, the bugle sounds no more
And the twanging bow no more;
Silent is the ivory[1] shrill
Past the heath and up the hill;
There is no mid-forest laugh,
Where lone Echo gives the half
To some wight, amazed to hear
Jesting, deep in forest drear.

On the fairest time of June
You may go, with sun or moon,
Or the seven stars to light you,
Or the polar ray to right you;
But you never may behold
Little John, or Robin bold;
Never one, of all the clan,
Thrumming on an empty can
Some old hunting ditty, while
He doth his green way beguile
To fair hostess Merriment,
Down beside the pasture Trent;
For he left the merry tale
Messenger for spicy ale.

Gone, the merry morris din;
Gone, the song of Gamelyn;[2]
Gone, the tough-belted outlaw
Idling in the "grenè shawe";[3]   *green wood*
All are gone away and past!
And if Robin should be cast
Sudden from his turfed grave,
And if Marian should have
Once again her forest days,
She would weep and he would craze: *go mad*
He would swear, for all his oaks,
Fallen beneath the dockyard strokes,

---

1. ivory] probably a reference to the hunting horn.
2. *The Tale of Gamelyn* is a poem written in Middle English about an outlaw in the forest.
3. grenè shawe] from Chaucer, "The Friar's Tale," 1386.

Have rotted on the briny seas;
She would weep that her wild bees
Sang not to her; strange that honey
Can't be got without hard money!
    So it is: yet let us sing
Honour to the old bowstring!
Honour to the bugle horn!
Honour to the woods unshorn!
Honour to the Lincoln green!
Honour to the archer keen!
Honour to tight little John
And the horse he rode upon!
Honour to bold Robin Hood
Sleeping in the underwood!
Honour to Maid Marian
And to all the Sherwood clan!
Though their days have hurried by,
Let us two a burden try.   *sing a chorus*

Written c. February 3, 1818, published July 1820

V

Civil War and Civil Liberties

🙰🙲

T HE NINETEENTH CENTURY was a period of international upheaval. Britain, whose empire was at its height, fought more wars across the world during the sixty-four years of Queen Victoria's reign than during the preceding two hundred years. Across Europe and parts of South America, revolution was rife. The constitutional monarchy of France finally stuttered to a long-overdue end; Italy was united as a single country; and in Germany there were uprisings against the autocratic confederation of states by which it was ruled. No longer was it possible for monarchs to claim absolute power unchallenged, thanks to an increasingly skeptical middle class.

The plight of working people was as bad as ever, made worse by the global recession of 1840–1842 and agricultural failures that led to high food prices in the 1840s and 1850s. In Britain, poor working conditions, low wages, and inadequate representation within a flawed political system led to the formation of unions and the Chartist movement that, between 1838 and 1848, lobbied for reform. Their demands were reasonable: universal male suffrage, a secret ballot, the abolition of property qualifications for Members of Parliament, a system of payment for MPs, equal electoral districts, and yearly elections. The newspaper, which had come into its own as a tool of mass communication during the revolutionary period, was instrumental in mobilizing (for instance) a general strike in 1842. Despite a government clampdown, Chartist activity continued, culminating in a general convention in 1848 that inspired meetings across the country, provoking the arrest (among others) of

Ernest Jones (p. 433). Millions of working people signed a petition presented to Parliament in April, only for it to be ridiculed by politicians. Alarmed by the possibility of revolution, the British government put down the movement calmly and confidently, detaining its leaders in conditions designed to undermine health and sanity.

In America, where slavery remained legal, there were vigorous debates over abolition. The "land of the free" was well behind the rest of the world; by 1850, slavery had been abolished across the British Empire, Prussia, Haiti, lower Canada, Spain, Portugal, France, the Netherlands, Greece, Chile, Bolivia, Mexico, Tunisia, Sweden, and Denmark. Although the importation of slaves was abolished in 1808, there were still four million slaves working in the South in 1860, and it was legal to trade them. The Northern and Southern states were increasingly divided on this question, a principal source of income for the South being cotton, production of which was reliant on slave labor. In 1860, the election of Abraham Lincoln as president was bound to inflame opinion, as it brought home to the Southern states they were losing the fight. The Civil War began in April 1861 and would continue for four arduous, bloody years. After the Union victory, slavery was finally abolished with adoption of the Thirteenth Amendment to the Constitution in 1865; the Fourteenth and Fifteenth Amendments guaranteed civil rights for African Americans, including (for men) the right to vote.

Yet postwar Reconstruction was to prove a failure. Despite the efforts of radical Republicans, attitudes in the South proved hard to shift. Paramilitary organizations such as the White League terrorized blacks, deterring them from exercising newly granted voting rights. Even when Congress imposed military rule on the South in 1867, the Ku Klux Klan, a vigilante organization, attacked blacks as well as white sympathizers. The imposition of Jim Crow laws between 1876 and 1965 institutionalized segregation and imposed on blacks a quality of life lower than that enjoyed by white counterparts, so that in 1903 Charles Chesnutt could write: "the rights of negroes are at a lower ebb than at any time during the thirty-five years of their freedom, and the race prejudice more intense and uncompromising." It represented the betrayal of everything for which the war had been fought, and would be the cause of enduring bitterness to those who, like Ambrose Bierce, fought on the Union side, only to watch the opportunity for a more equal society squandered by politicians.

That land full surely hastens to its end
Where public sycophants in homage bend
The populace to flatter, and repeat
The doubled echoes of its loud conceit.
Lowly their attitude but high their aim:
They creep to eminence through paths of shame
Till, fixed securely in the seats of pow'r,
The dupes they flattered they at last devour.

(AMBROSE BIERCE, "POLITICS")

Eliza Hamilton Dunlop (1796–1880)

ON JUNE 10, 1838, a gang of European stockmen tied up and hacked to death some thirty unarmed Aborigines in northern New South Wales, Australia, including a number of women and children; some days later they returned to burn the bodies. At that time such incidents were not uncommon, as whites believed indigenous Australians not to be human; they were, according to a typical correspondent in the *Sydney Herald*, "the most degenarate, despicable, and brutal race of beings in existence . . . a scoff and a jest upon humanity" (September 19, 1838). Murderers of Aborigines usually went unpunished, but on this occasion seven of the stockmen were caught, tried, and sentenced to death. Five days before their execution, Eliza Hamilton Dunlop, an Ulsterwoman who had arrived in Australia with her husband and four children only in February, published "The Aboriginal Mother" in *The Australian* (December 13, 1838). The speaker of her poem was a survivor of the massacre, whose husband had been killed. Dunlop's objective was to plead the humanity of Indigenous Australians. Such enlightened attitudes won enemies, and when "The Aboriginal Mother" enjoyed renewed popularity in 1841, the composer Isaac Nathan having set it to music and his daughter Jessy Rosetta having sung it before a Sydney audience, they ridiculed the poem and its subject—a mother "with a ghastly, toad-like looking brat, gnawing a raw opossum" (*Sydney Herald*, October 29, 1841). This drew from Dunlop the most forceful of her defenses for attributing "the sweetest emotions of the heart" to Aboriginals. Her hope was to awaken "the sympathies of the English nation for a people whom it is averred are rendered desperate and revengeful by continued acts of outrage. . . . the clear wellsprings of love and kindred ties bestow their healing influences, even now, for the children of the desert" (*Sydney Herald*, November 29, 1841). In 1840, Dunlop followed her husband to Wollombi in the Hunter Valley, where he assumed the post of Police Magistrate and Protector of Aborigines. There she made friends with the Darkinung tribespeople with whom she worked, recording their songs for publication in Australian newspapers and journals.

She was unafraid of comparing their melodies with those of Handel (see *South Australian Register*, February 25, 1843).

> Our home is the gibber-gunyah,   *caves*
> Where hill joins hill on high;
> Where the turruma and berrambo   *war arms*
> Like sleeping serpents lie;
> And the rushing of wings, as the wangas pass,   *pigeons*
> Sweeps the wallaby's print from the glistening grass.
>   (*Band of Hope Journal*, June 5, 1858)

Dunlop was among the few to appreciate native culture and promote it among white settlers—an activity nearly as perilous as to oppose the slave trade in America. She would continue to compose verse, and translate from Irish and Aboriginal sources, for several years. And she collaborated with Nathan on other works including an Australian national anthem, "Hail, star of the south!" which, when attacked by the *Sydney Morning Herald*, she defended against the paper's "flippant remarks, or vulgarly familiar style of criticism" (August 30, 1842). Dunlop and her husband lived at Mulla Villa in Wollombi, today a guesthouse; she was eighty-four at the time of her death in Sydney, and was buried alongside her husband at Wollombi. Our text of "The Aboriginal Mother" comes from its first printing in *The Australian*; it contains a number of native words which we have glossed with information provided by Elizabeth Webby and John O'Leary.

The Aboriginal Mother (from Myall's Creek)

Oh, hush thee, hush my baby,
    I may not tend thee yet,
Our forest home is distant far
    And midnight's star is set.
Now, hush thee, or the pale-faced men
    Will hear thy piercing wail,
And what would then thy mother's tears
    Or feeble strength avail?

Oh could'st thy little bosom
    That mother's torture feel,
Or could'st thou know thy father lies,
    Struck down by English steel,
Thy tender form would wither
    Like the *kniven* on the sand
And the spirit of my perished tribe
    Would vanish from our land.

For thy young life, my precious,
    I fly the field of blood,
Else had I, for my chieftain's sake,
    Defied them where they stood;
But basely bound my woman's arm,
    No weapon might it wield;
I could but cling round him I loved
    To make my heart a shield.

I saw my firstborn treasure
    Lie headless at my feet,
The goro[1] on this hapless breast
    In his life-stream is wet!
And thou—I snatched thee from their sword,
    It harmless passed by thee,
But clave the binding cords—and gave,
    Haply, the power to flee.

To flee, my babe—but whither,
    Without my friend, my guide?
The blood that was our strength is shed,
    He is not by my side!
Thy sire!—oh never, never
    Shall Toon Bakra[2] hear our cry:
My bold and stately mountain-bird,
    I thought not he could die.

---

1. goro] possibly a reed ornament.
2. Toon Bakra] the father's name, literally translated, means "hawk's tail."

Now who will teach thee, dearest,
    To poise the shield and spear,
To wield the koopin³ or to throw
    The *boommering*, void of fear;
To breast the river in its might,
    The mountain tracks to tread?
The echoes of my homeless heart
    Reply, "The dead, the dead!"

And ever must their murmur
    Like an ocean torrent flow;
The parted voice comes never back,
    To cheer our lonely woe:
Even in the region of our tribe,
    Beside our summer streams,
'Tis but a hollow symphony—
    In the shadowland of dreams.

Oh hush thee, dear—for weary
    And faint I bear thee on—
His name is on thy gentle lips;
    My child, my child, *he's gone*!
Gone o'er the golden fields that lie
    Beyond the rolling cloud,
To bring thy people's murder cry
    Before the Christian's God.

Yes, o'er the stars that guide us
    He brings my slaughtered boy,
To show their God how treacherously
    The stranger men destroy;
To tell how hands in friendship pledged
    Piled high the fatal pyre;
To tell, to tell of the gloomy ridge
    And the stockmen's human fire.

Published December 13, 1838

---

3. koopin] some sort of weapon or club.

Lydia Maria Child (1802–1880)

"HER LIFE WAS a battle," wrote John Greenleaf Whittier, "a constant row-ing hard against the stream of popular prejudice and hatred. And through it all—pecuniary privation, loss of friends and position, the painfulness of being suddenly thrust from 'the still air of delightful studies' into the bit-terest and sternest controversy of the age—she bore herself with patience, fortitude and unshaken reliance upon the justice and ultimate triumph of the cause she had espoused." Child came from a middle-class Massachusetts family in which she was home educated. A successful writer and journalist, she was responsible for (among other things) the first historical novel by an American, *Hobomok* (1824), which described a white woman's marriage to a Native American—at the time regarded as savages. The extent of her moral courage was revealed when she published her *Appeal in Favor of that Class of Americans Called Africans* (1833), which attacked slavery for being unchristian, condemned racist attitudes in the North, and demanded immediate aboli-tion. The result was outrage. Friends and relatives ostracized her; doors were slammed in her face; those who continued to speak to her were themselves ostracized. The *Appeal* was banned in the South, while readers across the country boycotted her books, cancelling subscriptions to the *Juvenile Mis-cellany*, which she edited. It folded within the year. Her library, the Boston Athenaeum, revoked her library privileges. She had known what to expect: "I am fully aware of the unpopularity of the task I have undertaken; but though I expect ridicule and censure, I do not fear them." After John Brown's foiled attempt to lead a slave revolt in October 1859, seizing an arsenal at Harpers Ferry, she wrote to his captors asking whether she might be allowed "to dress his wounds, and speak soothingly to him"—a request they denied. All the same, she published her correspondence with him in a pamphlet that sold three hundred thousand copies. During the Civil War she assisted escaped slaves, gave them supplies and taught them how to read. Her antislavery poems are among the best of their kind; they include "The Hero's Heart," inspired by the apocryphal story that, on his way to the gallows, John Brown stooped to kiss a little black girl.

The World That I Am Passing Through

Few, in the days of early youth,
Trusted like me in love and truth;
I've learned sad lessons from the years,
But slowly, and with many tears—
For God made me to kindly view
The world that I was passing through.

How little did I once believe
That friendly tones could e'er deceive,
That kindness and forbearance long
Might meet ingratitude and wrong!
I could not but kindly view
The world that I was passing through.

And though I've learned some souls are base
I would not, therefore, hate the race;
I still would bless my fellow men
And trust them, though deceived again.
God help me still to kindly view
The world that I am passing through.

Through weary conflicts I have passed
And struggled into rest at last,
Such rest as comes when the rack has broke
A joint or nerve at every stroke;
But the wish survives to kindly view
The world that I am passing through.

From all that fate has brought to me
I strive to learn humility,
And trust in Him who rules above,
Whose universal law is love.
Thus only can I kindly view
The world that I am passing through.

When I approach the setting sun
And feel my journey nearly done,

May earth be veiled in genial light
And her last smile to me seem bright!
Help me till then to kindly view
The world that I am passing through.

And all who tempt a trusting heart
From faith and hope to drift apart,
May they themselves be spared the pain
Of losing power to trust again.
God help us all to kindly view
The world that we are passing through.

Published 1857

The Hero's Heart[1]

A winter sunshine, still and bright,
The blue hills bathed with golden light,
And earth was smiling to the sky
When calmly he went forth to die.

Infernal passions festered there,
Where peaceful nature looked so fair;
And fiercely, in the morning sun,
Flashed glittering bayonet and gun.

The old man met no friendly eye
When last he looked on earth and sky;
But one small child, with timid air,
Was gazing on his hoary hair.

---

1. The poem's manuscript contains a note: "At eleven o'clock, on the morning of his execution, he left the jail his face wearing an expression of serene cheerfulness. As he stepped out of the door, he noticed a negro woman with her little child. He stooped and kissed the child tenderly."

As that dark brow to his upturned,
The tender heart within him yearned
And, fondly stooping o'er her face,
He kissed her for her injured race.

The little one, she knew not why
That kind old man went forth to die;
Nor why, mid all that pomp and stir,
He stooped to give a kiss to her.

But Jesus smiled that sight to see,
And said, "He did it unto me."
The golden harps then sweetly rung,
And this the song the angels sung:

"Who loves the poor doth love the Lord;
Earth cannot dim thy bright reward:
We hover o'er yon gallows high,
And wait to bear thee to the sky."

Written by January 26, 1860, published February 3, 1860

Thomas Cooper (1805–1892)

BORN IN LEICESTER, the illegitimate son of a dyer, Thomas Cooper trained as a shoemaker but in his free time taught himself Latin, Greek, and French. A supporter of the Chartist leader Feargus O'Connor, he branched out as a journalist for ultraradical papers, and was a keen activist: thanks to his efforts, Leicester became a Chartist stronghold. Hardly surprising, then, that the government targeted him for special treatment. They had their opportunity during the General Strike of 1842, the year in which more Britons were imprisoned and transported for political crimes than in any other that century. On August 15, Cooper delivered a speech at Crown Bank in Hanley, north Staffordshire, to a gathering of mineworkers, urging them to "cease [all labor] until the People's Charter becomes the law of the land." Whether he sparked off the two-day orgy of rioting, looting, and vandalism that followed is still debated, but the consequences were far-reaching: pits were flooded; Hanley police station was taken over and prisoners set free; local government offices burned to the ground, as well as houses belonging to a magistrate, a poor-rate collector, a pottery manufacturer, and two ministers who worked as Poor Law Guardians. Led by women, the crowd marched north, joining with groups from Manchester and Stockport. At Burslem, to the north of Stoke-on-Trent, they were charged by dragoons and fired on by troops, killing one man and seriously wounding several others. There followed a "Tory reign of terror" in which the Potteries were placed under martial law: in the first two weeks of October, 23 women and 256 men were put on trial, 116 of whom were jailed, 56 men being transported. Cooper was tried for seditious conspiracy, precipitating a two-year prison term that plunged him into a period of intense religious doubt, political despair, and physical illness. These events are recounted at the beginning of *The Purgatory of Suicides: A Prison-Rhyme in Ten Books* (1845), written in Stafford Prison. Cooper began writing his poem without pen and paper, committing it to memory. It would have been a remarkable achievement under any circumstances, but given that it was written in conditions of extreme privation, it is nothing short of astonishing—an epic poem in Spenserian stanzas that considers different forms of government, poverty, and economic exploitation. In Canto Ten it culminates with a vision of a future in which the working class educates itself and becomes politically empowered. Cooper's masterpiece won the admiration of Benjamin Disraeli, who tried to find it a publisher, as well as that of Thomas Carlyle, who described it as a "dark Titanic rhapsody" and its author "a tiger marked with smallpox."

The Purgatory of Suicides

BOOK I (EXTRACT)

I

"Slaves, toil no more![1] Why delve and moil and pine   *drudge*
To glut the tyrant forgers of your chain?

---

1. Cooper begins his poem by versifying the speech he delivered on August 15, 1842, which would lead directly to his imprisonment.

Slaves, toil no more! Up from the midnight mine,
Summon your swarthy thousands to the plain;
Beneath the bright sun marshaled, swell the strain
Of liberty and, while the lordlings view
Your banded hosts, with stricken heart and brain,
Shout as one man: 'Toil we no more renew
Until the many cease their slavery to the few!'

2

'We'll crouch and toil and weave no more—to weep!'
Exclaim your brothers from the weary loom;
Yea, now, they swear with one resolve—dread, deep,
'We'll toil no more to win a pauper's doom!'
And while the millions swear, fell famine's gloom
Spreads from their haggard faces like a cloud
Big with the fear and darkness of the tomb:
How, 'neath its terrors, are the tyrants bowed!
Slaves, toil no more—to starve! Go forth and tame the proud!

3

And why not tame them all? Of more than clay
Do your high lords proclaim themselves? Of blood
Illustrious boast they? Or that reason's ray
Beams from the brows of Rollo's robber-brood[2]
More brightly than from yours? Let them make good
Their vaunt of nobleness, or now confess
The majesty of ALL! Raise *ye* the feud—
Not, like their sires, to murder and possess,
But for unbounded power to gladden and to bless.

4

What say ye? That the priests proclaim content?
So taught their master who the hungry fed
As well as taught; who wept with men, and bent

---

2. Rollo's robber-brood] that is, the descendants of Rollo (c. 860–c. 932) Scandinavian robber baron who founded the duchy of Normandy. After raiding Scotland, England, Flanders, and France on pirating expeditions, he took lands along the Seine River as his base.

In gentleness and love, o'er bier and bed
Where wretchedness was found, until it fled?
Rebuked he not the false ones till his zeal
Drew down their hellish rage upon his head?
And who that yearns for world-spread human weal
Doth not, erelong, the weight of priestly vengeance feel?

5

Away! The howl of wolves in sheep's disguise
Why suffer ye to fill your ears? Their pride
Why suffer ye to stalk before your eyes?
Behold in pomp the purple prelate ride,
And on the beggar by his chariot's side
Frown sullenly, although in rags and shame
His brother cries for food! Up, swell the tide
Of retribution, till ye end the game
Long practiced by proud priests in old religion's name.[3]

6

Slaves, toil no more! Despite their boast, even kings
Must cease to sit in pride without your toil,
Spite of their potency (the surpliced things
Who through all time have thirsted to embroil
Man with his neighbor, and pollute the soil
Of holiest mother Earth with brothers' gore):
Join but to fold your hands, and ye will foil
To utter helplessness—yea, to the core
Strike their pale craft with paler death! Slaves, toil no more!"

7

For that these words of truth I boldly spake
To labour's children in their agony
Of want and insult; and, like men awake
After drugged slumbers, they did wildly flee

---

3. Cooper was consistent with radical thought from the French Revolution, in regarding
the established church as complicit with the government. There were, after all, bishops in
the House of Lords, who had legislative authority.

To do they knew not what until, with glee,
The cellar of a Christian priest they found
And with its poison fired their misery
To mad revenge, swift hurling to the ground
And flames bed, cassock, wine cups of the tippler gowned;

8

For that I boldly spake these words of truth
And the starved multitude, to fury wrought
By sense of injury, and void of ruth,
Rushed forth to deeds of recklessness, but nought
Achieved of freedom since nor plan nor thought
Their might directed—for this treason foul
'Gainst evil tyrants I was hither brought
A captive, mid the vain derisive howl
Of some who thought the iron now should pierce my soul.

9

Let them howl on! Their note, perchance, may change
(The earthquake oft is presaged by dull rest—
Kings may tomorrow feel its heavings strange!).
For my lorn dove, who droopeth in her nest,
I mourn in tenderness; but, to this breast
Again to clasp my meek one I confide
With fervid trustfulness! And for the rest,
Since Truth shall one day triumph, let betide
What may, within these bars in patience I can 'bide.

10

I had a vision on my prison bed
Which took its tinct from the mind's waking throes: *color*
Of patriot blood on field and scaffold shed;
Of martyrs' ashes; of the demon foes
Ubiquitous, relentless, that oppose
And track through life the footsteps of the brave
Who champion Truth; of evil that arose
Within the universe of good, and gave
To sovereign man the soul to live his brother's slave;

11

Of knowledge which, from sire to son bequeathed,
Hath ever on the few with bounty smiled,
But on the many wastingly hath breathed   *destructively*
A pestilence, from the scourged crowd that piled
Of yore the pyramids, to the dwarfed child
Whose fragile bloom steam and starvation blast;
Of specious arts whereby the bees beguiled,
Yield to the sable drones their sweet repast,
And creep themselves the path to heaven by pious fast;

12

Of infamy for him who gives himself
A sacrifice to stem the tyrant's rage;
And, for the tyrant's pander (peerage, pelf,   *property, loot*
And honours blazed with lies on history's page);
Of giant Wrong who, fed from age to age
With man's best blood and woman's purest tears,
Seems with our poor humanity to wage
Exterminating war; of hopes and fears
That mock the human worm from youth to grayest years. . . .

BOOK 10 (EXTRACT)[4]

15

Oh, not by changeling, tyrant, tool, or knave,
Thy march, blessed Liberty, can now be stayed;
The wand of Gutenberg, behold it wave!—
The spell is burst! The dark enchantments fade
Of wrinkled Ignorance! ('Twas she betrayed
Thy firstborn children, and so oft threw down
The mounds of freedom.) Lo, the book its aid
Hath brought! The feudal serf, though still a clown,   *peasant*
Doth read and, where his sires gave homage, pays a frown!

---

4. In Book 10, Cooper demonstrates how self-education enables the working class to liberate itself.

16

The sinewy artisan, the weaver lean,
The shrunken stockinger, the miner swarth,   *stocking weaver*
Read, think and feel; and in their eyes the sheen
Of burning thought betokens thy young birth
Within their souls, blithe Liberty! That earth
Would thus be kindled from the humble spark
Ye caught from him of Mainz,[5] and scattered forth
Faust, Koster, Caxton![6]—not "the clerk"
Himself could prophesy in your own mid-age dark!

17

And yet, oh Liberty, these humble toilers
The true foundation for thy reign begun.
Aye, and while thronecraft decks man's murderous spoilers,
While feverous Power mocks the weary sun
With steed-throned effigies of Wellington
And columned piles to Nelson, labour's child
Turns from their haughty forms to muse upon
The page by their blood-chronicle defiled;
Then, bending o'er his toil, weighs well the record wild.

18

Aye, they are thinking at the frame and loom,
At bench and forge and in the bowelled mine,
And when the scanty hour of rest is come
Again they read—to think and to divine
How it hath come to pass that Toil must pine
While Sloth doth revel; how the game of blood
Hath served their tyrants; how the scheme malign
Of priests hath crushed them, and resolve doth bud
To band and to bring back the primal Brotherhood.

---

5. him of Mainz] Johannes Gensfleisch zur Laden zum Gutenberg (c. 1398–1468) born in Mainz, inventor of the printing press.
6. Johann Fust (1400–1466), Laurens Coster (1370–1440), and William Caxton (c. 1415–1492), all associated with early developments in printing.

19

What though awhile the braggart-tongued poltroon,
False demagogue or hireling base impede
The union they affect to aid? Right soon
Deep thought to such "conspiracy" shall lead
As will result in a successful deed
Not forceful but fraternal: for the past
Hath warned the million that they must succeed
By will and not by war. Yet to hold fast
Men's rage when they are starving, 'tis a struggle vast!—

20

A struggle that were vain unless the book
Had kindled light within the toiler's soul
And taught him though 'tis difficult to brook
Contempt with hunger, yet he must control
Revenge or it will leave him more a thrall;   *slave*
"The pike, the brand, the blaze," his lesson saith,
"Would leave Old England as they have left Gaul—
Bondaged to sceptered Cunning." Thus their wrath
The million quell, but look for Right with firmest faith.

21

Oh, might I see that triumph ere I die—
The poor, oppressed, contemned, and hungered throng
Hold festival for Labour's victory
O'er Mammon, Pride, and Sloth; for Right o'er Wrong;
Oh, might I hear them swell the choral song:
"The toiler's rights are won! Our fatherland
Is fully free!"—with joy to rest among
The solemn dead, at Nature's high command,
I'd haste, not ask to stay the speed of one life-sand!

22

Nor selfish is the wish, however vain;
From boyhood, Greece and our old Commonweal⁷

---

7. Commonweal] Cooper refers to the Protectorate of Oliver Cromwell.

I worshipped, but 'twas gnawing hunger's pain
I saw your lank and fainting forms reveal
(Poor trampled stockingers!) that made me feel
'Twas time to be in earnest, nor regard
Man's freedom merely as a theme for zeal
In hours of emulous converse, or for bard
Weaving rapt fancies in pursuit of fame's reward.

23

I threw me in the gap, defying scorn,
Threats, hatred, poisonous tongues, to front your foes;
And this hath come of it—that I have worn
The fetters for your sake. Yet now the close
Of this captivity is near, no throes
Of anger, sorrow, or regret are mine
For aught that I have suffered; but your woes
(Poor victims who by grinding tricksters pine)
Breed thoughts that with my hopes their tortures intertwine.

Written between 1842 and 1844, published January 1845

Elizabeth Barrett Browning (1806–1861)

HER STATUS AS physical invalid makes Browning (or EBB) an unlikely poet of witness. She earns her place here as an activist: aligned consistently with the cause of freedom, whether it was the antislavery campaign or the Italian Risorgimento, EBB had the courage to face down her opponents. The repressive influence of her family was the making of her: when in 1845 she was invited to write in support of the Anti-Corn Law League, her brothers ridiculed the idea and her father forbade it. (The Corn Law placed a tariff on imported corn that made bread too expensive for working-class people.) Henry Chorley, editor of *The Athenaeum*, warned that to publish such a poem would be her "ruin." She bowed to these prohibitions and remained silent—a decision she later described as "a remorse to me for life." Never again would she submit to such cautions. By this time she was already the victim of a spinal disorder and chronic lung ailment making her dependent on opiates, so it took courage for her secretly to marry Robert Browning and elope with him to the Continent. Despite her letters, her father declined ever again to communicate with her, while her brothers scorned her husband as a social upstart. Having agreed to write a poem for the Anti-Slavery Bazaar in Boston, she worked on it during her honeymoon: "The Runaway Slave at Pilgrim's Point" was completed in Italy. It tells the story of a slave girl whose lover, another slave, is killed, and who is raped by a white man. Having given birth to that man's child, she strangles it with her shawl. Once captured, she is whipped and dies, her religious faith intact. It is (in her words) a "ferocious" work that both condemns enslavement and analyzes the female experience of oppression by men. The other two poems in this selection come from a later period when she had been resident in Italy for over fifteen years. "A Curse for a Nation" returns to the antislavery cause, and was written, again, at the behest of the Anti-Slavery Bazaar. EBB's curse on Americans is that the injustices of which they are guilty prevent them from denouncing the ill deeds of others. Both antislavery poems are published here in the form in which they first appeared, from *The Liberty Bell*, an annual edited by Lydia Maria Child (p. 394). EBB was already the recipient of hate mail from Americans when "A Curse for a Nation" appeared in England and was interpreted as an attack on her homeland: she did nothing to correct the misapprehension. *The Saturday Review* criticized her "delirium of imbecile one-sidedness" and "hysterical antipathy to England," while *The Athenaeum* deplored the poem as "a malediction against England—infallible, arrogant." "Heavens and earth!" was her response, "What a crime!" As that suggests, she was unmoved. Writing to her friend Isa Blagden, she commented: "The fact is, between you and me, Isa, certain of those quoted stanzas do 'fit' England 'as if they were made for her,' which they were *not* though." EBB's attachment to the Italian Risorgimento cannot be overstated; "the word Venice makes my heart beat," she once said. She loved the Italian people, "their heroic constancy and union," and worshipped freedom fighter Giuseppe Garibaldi. On the first anniversary of her marriage (September 12, 1847), she watched from the windows of Casa Guidi as Florentines celebrated their new civic guard, granted by Grand Duke Leopold II of Tuscany. She witnessed further celebration when, in March 1848, the duke gave Tuscans legislative powers, a parliament, and religious freedom to Protestants and Jews. "I have been living and dying for Italy lately," she wrote. In "Italy and the World" she hails, in apocalyptic terms, unification of her adoptive country. Within weeks of its completion she was exultant at King Victor Emanuel's triumphant entry to Florence on April 16, 1860. She died on June 29, 1861, having lived to see the new kingdom of Italy declared a few months before, though the Risorgimento would not finally be achieved until 1871.

The Runaway Slave at Pilgrim's Point

I stand on the mark beside the shore
    Of the first white pilgrim's bended knee,
Where exile changed to ancestor
    And God was thanked for liberty.
I have run through the night (my skin is as dark),
I bend my knee down on this mark,
    I look on the sky and the sea.

Oh, pilgrim souls, I speak to you,
    I see you come out proud and slow
From the land of the spirits, pale as dew,
    And round me and round me ye go.
Oh, pilgrims, I have gasped and run
All night long from the whips of one
    Who, in your names, works sin and woe.

And thus I thought that I would come
    And kneel here where ye knelt before,
And feel your souls around me hum
    In undertone to the ocean's roar;
And lift my black face, my black hand
Here in your names, to curse this land
    Ye blessed in Freedom's, heretofore.

I am black—I am black,
    And yet God made me, they say;
But if he did so, smiling, back
    He must have cast his work away

Under the feet of his white creatures
With a look of scorn, that the dusky features
    Might be trodden again to clay.

And yet he has made dark things
    To be glad and merry as light;
There's a little dark bird sits and sings,
    There's a dark stream ripples out of sight,
And the dark frogs chant in the safe morass,
And the sweetest stars are made to pass
    O'er the face of the darkest night.

But we who are dark, we are dark!
    Oh God, we have no stars!
About our souls, in care and cark,   *anxiety*
    Our blackness shuts like prison bars!
And crouch our souls so far behind
That never a comfort can they find
    By reaching through their prison bars.

Howbeit God's sunshine and his frost,   *Be that as it may*
    They make us hot, they make us cold
As if we were not black and lost;
    And the beasts and birds in wood and wold
Do fear and take us for very men:
Could the whipoorwill or the cat of the glen
    Look into my eyes and be bold?

I am black, I am black,
    And once I laughed in girlish glee,
For one of my color stood in the track
    Where the drivers drove, and looked at me,
And tender and full was the look he gave!
A slave looked so at another slave;
    I look at the sky and the sea.

And from that hour our spirits grew
    As free as if unsold, unbought;

We were strong enough, since we were two,
  To conquer the world—we thought.
The drivers drove us day by day;
We did not mind, we went one way
  And no better a liberty sought.

In the open ground between the canes
  He said "I love you" as he passed;
Where the shingle roof rang sharp with the rains,
  I heard how he vowed it fast.
While others trembled, he sat in the hut
And carved me a bowl of the coconut
  Through the roar of the hurricanes.

I sang his name instead of a song,
  Over and over I sang his name;
Backward and forward I sang it along
  With my sweetest notes, it was still the same!
But I sang it low, that the slave girls near
Might never guess, from what they could hear,
  That all the song was a name.

I look on the sky and the sea!
  We were two to love, and two to pray—
Yes, two, oh God, who cried on thee,
  Though nothing didst thou say.
Coldly thou satst behind the sun
And now I cry, who am but one;
  Thou wilt not speak today.

We were black, we were black,
  We had no claim to love and bliss;
What marvel ours was cast to wrack?
  They wrung my cold hands out of his,
They dragged him—why, I crawled to touch
His blood's mark in the dust—not much,
  Ye pilgrim souls, though plain as this!

Wrong followed by a greater wrong!
　　　Grief seemed too good for such as I;
So the white men brought the shame erelong
　　　To stifle the sob in my throat thereby.
They would not leave me for my dull
Wet eyes; it was too merciful
　　　To let me weep pure tears and die.

I am black, I am black!
　　　I wore a child upon my breast—
An amulet that hung too slack
　　　And, in my unrest, could not rest;
Thus we went moaning, child and mother,
One to another, one to another,
　　　Until all ended for the best.

For hark! I will tell you low, low—
　　　I am black, you see,
And the babe that lay on my bosom so
　　　Was far too white—too white for me;
As white as the ladies who scorned to pray
Beside me at church but yesterday,
　　　Though my tears had washed a place for my knee.

And my own child—I could not bear
　　　To look in his face, it was so white;
So I covered him up with a kerchief rare,
　　　I covered his face in, close and tight!
And he moaned and struggled as well as might be,
For the white child wanted his liberty—
　　　Ha, ha! He wanted his master's right.

He moaned and beat with his head and feet,
　　　His little feet that never grew!
He struck them out as it was meet,
　　　Against my heart to break it through.
I might have sung like a mother mild
But I dared not sing to the white-faced child
　　　The only song I knew.

And yet I pulled the kerchief close:
    He could not see the sun, I swear,
More then, alive, than now he does
    From between the roots of the mangles—where?
I know where. Close! A child and mother
Do wrong to look at one another
    When one is black and one is fair.

Even in that single glance I had
    Of my child's face (I tell you all),
I saw a look that made me mad—
    The master's look that used to fall
On my soul like his lash, or worse—
Therefore, to save it from my curse,
    I twisted it round in my shawl.

And he moaned and trembled from foot to head,
    He shivered from head to foot,
Till after a time he lay instead
    Too suddenly still and mute;
And I felt, beside, a creeping cold,
I dared to lift up just a fold,
    As in lifting a leaf of the mango fruit.

But *my* fruit! Ha, ha! There had been
    (I laugh to think on't at this hour!)
Your fine white angels (who have seen
    God's secret nearest to His power),
And gathered my fruit to make them wine,
And sucked the soul of that child of mine
    As the hummingbird sucks the soul of the flower.

Ha, ha! For the trick of the angels white!
    They freed the white child's spirit so;
I said not a word but day and night
    I carried the body to and fro
And it lay on my heart like a stone—as chill;
The sun may shine out as much as he will—
    I am cold, though it happened a month ago.

From the white man's house and the black man's hut
    I carried the little body on;
The forest's arms did round us shut
    And silence through the trees did run!
They asked no questions as I went,
They stood too high for astonishment,
    They could see God rise on his throne.

My little body, kerchiefed fast,
    I bore it on through the forest—on—
And when I felt it was tired at last,
    I scooped a hole beneath the moon.
Through the forest tops the angels far
With a white fine finger in every star
    Did point and mock at what was done.

Yet when it all was done aright,
    Earth twixt me and my baby strewed,
All changed to black earth, nothing white,
    A dark child in the dark—ensued
Some comfort, and my heart grew young;
I sat down smiling there, and sung
    The song I told you of, for good.

And thus we two were reconciled,
    The white child and black mother thus;
For as I sang it—soft and wild—
    The same song, more melodious,
Rose from the grave whereon I sat!
It was the dead child singing that,
    To join the souls of both of us.

I look on the sea and the sky
    Where the pilgrims' ships first anchored lay;
The great sun rideth gloriously,
    But the pilgrims' ghosts have slid away
Through the first faint streaks of the morn!
My face is black, but it glares with a scorn
    Which they dare not meet by day.

Ah, in their stead their hunter sons!
    Ah, ah! They are on me! They form in a ring!
Keep off! I brave you all at once!
    I throw off your eyes like a noisome thing!
You have killed the black eagle at nest, I think:
Did you never stand still in your triumph and shrink
    From the stroke of her wounded wing?

Man, drop that stone you dared to lift!
    I wish you who stand there, seven abreast,
Each for his own wife's grace and gift,
    A little corpse as safely at rest,
Hid in the mangles! Yes, but *she*
May keep live babies on her knee
    And sing the song she liketh best.

I am not mad, I am black!
    I see you staring in my face;
I know you staring, shrinking back!
    Ye are born of the Washington race!
And this land is the free America,
And this mark on my wrist (I prove what I say)—
    Ropes tied me up here to the flogging-place.

You think I shrieked there? Not a sound!
    I hung as a gourd hangs in the sun:
I only cursed them all around
    As softly as I might have done
My own child after. From these sands
Up to the mountains, lift your hands,
    Oh slaves, and end what I begun!

Whips, curses; these must answer those!
    For in this union, you have set
Two kinds of men in adverse rows,
    Each loathing each! And all forget
The seven wounds in Christ's body fair;
While he sees gaping everywhere
    Our countless wounds that pay no debt.

Our wounds are different; your white men
  Are, after all, not gods indeed,
Nor able to make Christ's again
  Do good with bleeding. *We* who bleed
(Stand off!), we help not in our loss,
We are too heavy for our cross,
  And fall and crush you and your seed.

I fall, I swoon! I look at the sky!
  The clouds are breaking on my brain;
I am floated along, as if I should die
  Of liberty's exquisite pain;
In the name of the white child waiting for me
In the deep black death where our kisses agree,
White men, I leave you all curse-free
  In my broken heart's disdain!

       Written autumn 1846, published December 1847

A Curse for a Nation[1]

PROLOGUE

I heard an angel speak last night,
  And he said "Write!
Write a nation's curse for me
And send it over the western sea."

I faltered, taking up the word:
  "Not so, my lord!
If curses must be, choose another
To send thy curse against my brother;

---

1. When "A Curse for a Nation" was published in London in 1860, it caused outrage as it was interpreted not as a condemnation of American slavery but as an attack on England's refusal to assist the Italians in their fight for independence. It led to accusations of "hysterical antipathy to England" and EBB's blacklisting by British publishers; see p. 13.

For I am bound by gratitude,
    In love and blood,
To brothers of mine across the sea,
Who have stretched out kindly hands to me."

"Therefore," the voice said, "shalt thou write
    My curse tonight.
From the summits of love a curse is driven,
As lightning from the tops of heaven."

"Not so," I answered. "Evermore
    My heart is sore
For my own land's sins; for the little feet
Of children bleeding along the street;

For parked-up honours that gainsay
    The right of way;
For almsgiving through a door that is
Not open enough for two friends to kiss;

For an oligarchic parliament
    And classes rent.
What curse to another land assign,
When heavy-souled for the sins of mine?"

"Therefore," the voice said, "shalt thou write
    My curse tonight.
Because thou hast strength to see and hate
An ill thing done within thy gate."

"Not so," I answered once again;
    "To curse, choose men.
For I, a woman, have only known
How the heart melts and the tears run down."

"Therefore," the voice said, "shalt thou write
    My curse tonight.
There are women who weep and curse, I say,
And no one marvels, night and day.

And thou shalt take their part tonight:
> Weep and write!
A curse from the depths of womanhood
Is very salt, and bitter, and good."

So thus I wrote and mourned indeed,
> What all may read.
And thus, as was enjoined on me,
I send it over the western sea.

THE CURSE

I

Because ye have broken your own chain
> With the strain
Of brave men climbing a nation's height,
Yet thence bear down with chain and thong
>> On the souls of others—for this wrong
>> This is the curse. Write.

Because yourselves are standing straight
> In the state
Of Freedom's foremost acolyte,
Yet keep calm footing all the time
>> On writhing bondslaves—for this crime
>> This is the curse. Write.

Because ye prosper in God's name,
> With a claim
To honour in the whole world's sight,
Yet do the fiend's work perfectly
>> On babes and women—for this lie
>> This is the curse. Write.

II

Ye shall watch while kings conspire
Round the people's smoldering fire,
> And, warm for your part,
Shall never dare—oh shame!—

To utter the thought into flame
    Which burns at your heart.
        This is the curse. Write.

Ye shall watch while nations strive
With the bloodhounds, die or survive,
    Drop faint from their jaws,
Or throttle them backward to death;
And only under your breath
    Shall ye bless the cause.
        This is the curse. Write.

Ye shall watch while strong men draw
The nets of feudal law
    To strangle the weak;
Ye shall count the sin for a sin,
But your soul shall be sadder within
    Than the word which ye speak.
        This is the curse. Write.

Ye shall watch while rich men dine
And poor men hunger and pine
    For one crust in seven;
But shall quail from the signs which present
God's judgment as imminent
    To make it all even.
        This is the curse. Write.

When good men are praying erect
That Christ may avenge his elect
    And deliver the earth,
The prayer in your ears, said low,
Shall sound like the tramp of a foe
    That's driving you forth.
        This is the curse. Write.

When wise men give you their praise,
They shall pause in the heat of the phrase

And sicken afar;
When ye boast your own charters kept true,
Ye shall blush; for the thing which ye do
    Derides what ye are.
        This is the curse. Write.

When fools cast taunts on your gate,
Your scorn ye shall somewhat abate
    As ye look o'er the wall;
For your conscience, tradition, and name
Strike back with a deadlier blame
    Than the worst of them all.
        This is the curse. Write.

Go, while ill deeds shall be done,
Plant on your flag in the sun
    Beside the ill-doers!
And shrink from clenching the curse
Of the witnessing universe
    With a curse of yours.
        This is the curse. Write.

FLORENCE, ITALY, 1854

Published December 1855

Italy and the World[1]

Florence, Bologna, Parma, Modena:
    When you named them a year ago,
So many graves reserved by God, in a

---

1. At the time this poem was composed, EBB was dismayed by the fact that the Italians had recently lost an ally in Napoléon III, who made peace with the Austrians in the summer of 1859 after the battle of Solferino. Just when it seemed the French and the Austrians would carve up Italy between themselves while Britain stood idly by and watched, EBB composed a poem that hailed in prophetic and apocalyptic terms her adoptive country's reunification. It was an act of faith justified by the creation of the kingdom of Italy in March 1861.

Day of Judgment, you seemed to know,
To open and let out the resurrection.

And meantime (you made your reflection
    If you were English), was nought to be done
But sorting sables, in predilection
    For all those martyrs dead and gone
Till the new earth and heaven made ready.

And if your politics were not heady,
    Violent, "Good," you added, "good
In all things! Mourn on sure and steady.
    Churchyard thistles are wholesome food
For our European wandering asses.

The date of the resurrection passes
    Human foreknowledge: men unborn
Will gain by it (even in the lower classes),
    But none of these. It is not the morn
Because the cock of France is crowing.

Cocks crow at midnight, seldom knowing
    Starlight from dawnlight! 'Tis a mad
Poor creature." Here you paused and, growing
    Scornful, suddenly (let us add)
The trumpet sounded, the graves were open.

Life and life and life—agrope in
    The dusk of death, warm hands stretched out
For swords, proved more life still to hope in,
    Beyond and behind. Arise with a shout,
Nation of Italy, slain and buried!

Hill to hill and turret to turret
    Flashing the tricolor, newly created
Beautiful Italy, calm, unhurried—
    Rise heroic and renovated,
Rise to the final restitution.

Rise; prefigure the grand solution
    Of earth's municipal, insular schisms—
Statesmen draping self-love's conclusion
    In cheap vernacular patriotisms,
Unable to give up Judea for Jesus.

Bring us the higher example; release us
    Into the larger coming time,
And into Christ's broad garment piece us
    Rags of virtue as poor as crime,
National selfishness, civic vaunting.

No more Jew nor Greek then, taunting
    Nor taunted; no more England nor France!
But one confederate brotherhood planting
    One flag only, to mark the advance,
Onward and upward, of all humanity.

For fully developed Christianity.
    Is civilization perfected
"Measure the frontier," shall it be said,
    "Count the ships," in national vanity?
Count the nation's heartbeats sooner.

For though behind by a cannon or schooner,
    That nation still is predominant
Whose pulse beats quickest in zeal to oppugn or
    Succor another, in wrong or want,
Passing the frontier in love and abhorrence.

Modena, Parma, Bologna, Florence,
    Open us out the wider way!
Dwarf in that chapel of old Saint Lawrence,
    Your Michelangelo's giant day,
With the grandeur of this day breaking o'er us!

Ye who, restrained as an ancient chorus,
    Mute while the coryphaeus[2] spake,
Hush your separate voices before us,
    Sink your separate lives for the sake
Of one sole Italy's living forever!

Givers of coat and cloak too, never
    Grudging that purple of yours at the best,
By your heroic will and endeavor
    Each sublimely dispossessed,
That all may inherit what each surrenders!

Earth shall bless you, oh noble emenders
    On egotist nations! Ye shall lead
The plough of the world, and sow new splendors
    Into the furrow of things for seed,
Ever the richer for what ye have given.

Lead us and teach us, till earth and heaven
    Grow larger around us and higher above.
Our sacrament-bread has a bitter leaven;
    We bait our traps with the name of love
Till hate itself has a kinder meaning.

Oh, this world: this cheating and screening
    Of cheats! This conscience for candlewicks,
Not beacon fires! This overweening
    Of underhand diplomatical tricks,
Dared for the country while scorned for the counter!

Oh, this envy of those who mount here,
    And oh, this malice to make them trip!
Rather quenching the fire there, drying the fount here,
    To frozen body and thirsty lip,
Than leave to a neighbour their ministration.

---

2. coryphaeus] leader of a chorus.

I cry aloud in my poet-passion,
    Viewing my England o'er Alp and sea.
I loved her more in her ancient fashion:
    She carries her rifles too thick for me
Who spares them so in the cause of a brother.

Suspicion, panic? End this pother.
    The sword, kept sheathless at peacetime, rusts.
None fears for himself while he feels for another:
    The brave man either fights or trusts
And wears no mail in his private chamber.

Beautiful Italy! Golden amber
    Warm with the kisses of lover and traitor!
Thou who hast drawn us on to remember,
    Draw us to hope now: let us be greater
By this new future than that old story.

Till truer glory replaces all glory,
    As the torch grows blind at the dawn of day;
And the nations, rising up, their sorry
    And foolish sins shall put away,
As children their toys when the teacher enters.

Till Love's one center devour these centers
    Of many self-loves; and the patriot's trick
To better his land by egotist ventures,
    Defamed from a virtue, shall make men sick,
As the scalp at the belt of some red hero.

For certain virtues have dropped to zero,
    Left by the sun on the mountain's dewy side;
Churchman's charities, tender as Nero,
    Indian suttee,[3] heathen suicide,
Service to rights divine, proved hollow:

---

3. suttee] a Hindu widow who throws herself on the funeral pyre with the burning corpse of her husband.

And heptarchy patriotisms[4] must follow.
    National voices, distinct yet dependent,
Ensphering each other, as swallow does swallow,
    With circles still widening and ever ascendant,
In multiform life to united progression,

These shall remain. And when, in the session
    Of nations, the separate language is heard,
Each shall aspire, in sublime indiscretion,
    To help with a thought or exalt with a word
Less her own than her rival's honour.

Each Christian nation shall take upon her
    The law of the Christian man in vast:
The crown of the getter shall fall to the donor,
    And last shall be first while first shall be last,
And to love best shall still be, to reign unsurpassed.

Written by February 1860, published March 1860

Frederick Douglass (1818–1895)

"IT CANNOT BE that I will live and die a slave. I will take to the water. This very bay shall yet bear me into freedom." Born into slavery in Maryland, Douglass escaped by fleeing to New York City, before settling in New Bedford, Massachusetts. He spent years campaigning for abolition, beginning each appearance by announcing to his audience he was still a slave. It was a dangerous ploy, because it invited the unwelcome attention of "slave catchers." Members of the public accosted him in the streets, he was chased by mobs, beaten. On one occasion his hand was broken, and healed badly; it

---

4. heptarchy patriotisms] the seven kingdoms established by the Angles and Saxons in Britain. Browning means that "patriotic" attachments to the former city-states and kingdoms by which Italy was comprised after the Congress of Vienna in 1815 will be superceded by a united interdependence.

was deformed for the rest of his life. His courage was acknowledged by such contemporaries as Thomas Clarkson, the British abolitionist; John Brown, the American abolitionist; Daniel O'Connell, the Irish politician; and President Lincoln, among others. His autobiographical *Narrative of the Life of Frederick Douglass* (1845) remains his best-known book; it appeared when he was twenty-seven years old, still a fugitive slave. The *Narrative* was more than autobiography; it was written to promulgate William Lloyd Garrison's agenda for abolition of the slave trade by recalling the cruelties Douglass had witnessed: the whippings, beatings, and murders of slaves by their owners; the clergyman who prided himself on whipping his slaves "in advance of deserving it"; and the church elders who violently broke up the Sabbath school for slaves that Douglass organized. From its pages we have selected "A Parody," described by Douglass as a "portrait of the religion of the south (which is, by communion and fellowship, the religion of the north) which I soberly affirm is 'true to the life,' and without caricature or the slightest exaggeration." Its author, he claimed, was "a northern Methodist preacher, who, while residing at the South, had an opportunity to see slaveholding morals, manners, and piety, with his own eyes." No such preacher has ever been identified, and there is little doubt Douglass was its author; the poem is unstinting in its condemnation of Southern hypocrisy, and the misguided belief that heavenly grace is bestowed in proportion to a slave owner's inhumanity toward his charges.

A Parody

Come, saints and sinners, hear me tell
How pious priests whip Jack and Nell,
And women buy and children sell,
And preach all sinners down to hell,
    And sing of heavenly union.

They'll bleat and baa, dona[1] like goats,
Gorge down black sheep, and strain at motes,[2]

---

1. dona] presumably a misprint; uncorrected by scholars.
2. strain at motes] find fault with their slaves, failing to see their own shortcomings; see Matthew 7:3.

Array their backs in fine black coats,
Then seize their negroes by their throats
    And choke for heavenly union.

They'll church you if you sip a dram,
And damn you if you steal a lamb,
Yet rob old Tony, Doll, and Sam
Of human rights and bread and ham—
    Kidnapper's heavenly union.

They'll loudly talk of Christ's reward
And bind his image with a cord,
And scold and swing the lash abhorred,
And sell their brother in the Lord
    To handcuffed heavenly union.

They'll read and sing a sacred song,
And make a prayer both loud and long,
And teach the right and do the wrong,
Hailing the brother, sister throng
    With words of heavenly union.

We wonder how such saints can sing
Or praise the Lord upon the wing,
Who roar and scold, and whip and sting,
And to their slaves and mammon cling
    In guilty conscience union.

They'll raise tobacco, corn, and rye,
And drive and thieve, and cheat and lie,
And lay up treasures in the sky
By making switch and cowskin fly,
    In hope of heavenly union.

They'll crack old Tony on the skull,
And preach and roar like Bashan bull,[3]

---

3. Bashan bull] a person with a powerful body and loud voice is often compared with the cattle of Bashan; see also Psalm 22:12.

Or braying ass, of mischief full,
Then seize old Jacob by the wool,
    And pull for heavenly union.

A roaring, ranting, sleek man-thief
Who lived on mutton, veal, and beef,
Yet never would afford relief
To needy, sable sons of grief
    Was big with heavenly union.

"Love not the world," the preacher said,
And winked his eye, and shook his head;
He seized on Tom, and Dick, and Ned,
Cut short their meat and clothes and bread,
    Yet still loved heavenly union.

Another preacher whining spoke
Of One whose heart for sinners broke:
He tied old Nanny to an oak
And drew the blood at every stroke,
    And prayed for heavenly union.

Two others oped their iron jaws,
And waved their children-stealing paws;
There sat their children in gewgaws;
By stinting negroes' backs and maws,
    They kept up heavenly union.

All good from Jack another takes,
And entertains their flirts and rakes,
Who dress as sleek as glossy snakes,
And cram their mouths with sweetened cakes;
    And this goes down for union.

Written by April 28, 1845, published May 1845

Arthur Hugh Clough (1819–1861)

CLOUGH WAS BY temperament an ivory-tower intellectual—an unlikely poet of witness. He was a Fellow of Oriel College, Oxford, and during the 1840s became involved in radical politics, urging that food be conserved to help the Irish poor. In 1848 he toured the Continent, witnessing the French Revolution firsthand. He then traveled south to Italy; this was an exciting moment to do so. In February 1849 Rome declared itself an independent republic under the effective dictatorship of Giuseppe Mazzini, and in March Garibaldi's irregulars arrived to defend it against the onslaught of a French expeditionary force led by Oudinot, charged with restoring papal supremacy. Clough arrived on April 16 and settled at the Hotel d'Angleterre, long since deserted by its English residents. He quickly acquainted himself with nearby amenities including Monaldini's reading room in Piazza di Spagna, where he could read copies of *The Times*. He met Mazzini on April 22, whom he thought "in excellent spirits, and generally confident and at ease." Oudinot's regiment arrived at Civita Vecchia the following day, and began exchanging fire with the Roman Republicans. On April 30 Clough wrote to his sister: "I went up to the Pincian Hill and saw the smoke and heard the occasional big cannon, and the sharp succession of skirmishers' volleys—bang, bang, bang—away beyond St. Peter's." That day, he witnessed Garibaldi's victory over the French. The conflict soon intensified with the arrival of pro-Papal Neapolitan forces. In letters home, Clough joked that the art galleries had been shut down; it was his way of staving off anxiety, for he was at that moment in danger. The Romans were suspicious of strangers wandering around with maps, thinking all foreigners potential spies. They were volatile enough that news of the Neapolitan advance led them to attack and kill four or five priests, thought to be agents of the pope, who had condemned the revolutionaries as "a forest of wild animals." Clough was present throughout the Siege of Rome: in a letter on June 3 he described the sound of battle: "This is being written while guns are going off, there—, there—, there! For the French are attacking us again. May the Lord scatter and confound them!" The seventeen-hour assault determined the outcome of the siege, though the Romans held out bravely until the end of the month. In letters home, Clough praised their courage and peaceability: "The soldiers, so far as I see, are extremely well behaved, far more seemly than our regulars; they are about of course in the streets and cafés, but make no disorder." On June 22, when the French bombarded the city, he witnessed the fallout: "I do not think much harm was done, and the people took it coolly enough. I found a crowd assembled about 9 p.m. in the northeast corner of the Piazza Colonna, watching these pretty fireworks, 'ecco un altro!' One first saw the 'lightning' over the Post-office; then came the missive itself, describing its tranquil parabola; then the distant report of the mortar; and finally the near explosion, which occasionally took place in the air." Cannon balls and grenades fell in Piazza di Spagna on June 29, forcing Clough to take shelter in the basement of the building in Via della Croce, where he was now living. The following day, Garibaldi left the city, taking his soldiers north; the French entered Rome on July 3: "It is a sight to make one gnash one's very wisdom teeth to go about the fallen Jerusalem and behold the abomination of desolation standing where it ought not; not that the French misbehave, so far as I see." Clough would mediate these experiences through the character of Claude, in his verse novel, *Amours de Voyage*, parts of which were composed in Rome.

Amours de Voyage

CANTO 2 (EXTRACTS)

V. CLAUDE TO EUSTACE
Yes, we are fighting at last, it appears. This morning as usual
(Murray, as usual, in hand), I enter the Cafe Nuovo;
Seating myself with a sense as it were of a change in the weather,
Not understanding, however, but thinking mostly of Murray—
And (for today is their day) of the Campidoglio Marbles.[1]
"Caffe latte!" I call to the waiter, and *Non c'e latte*—
This is the answer he makes me, and this is the sign of a battle.
So I sit: and truly they seem to think anyone else more
Worthy than me of attention. I wait for my milkless nero,[2]
Free to observe undistracted all sorts and sizes of persons,

---

1. Claude is carrying Murray's guidebook to Rome, which describes the marble statues of Castor and Pollux in the Piazza del Campidoglio.
2. nero] black coffee.

Blending civilian and soldier in strangest costume, coming in, and
Gulping in hottest haste, still standing, their coffee—withdrawing
Eagerly, jangling a sword on the steps, or jogging a musket
Slung to the shoulder behind. They are fewer, moreover, than usual,
Much, and silenter far; and so I begin to imagine
Something is really afloat. Ere I leave, the Cafe is empty,
Empty too the streets, in all its length the Corso
Empty, and empty I see to my right and left the Condotti.[3]

    Twelve o'clock, on the Pincian Hill,[4] with lots of English,
Germans, Americans, French (the Frenchmen, too, are protected),
So we stand in the sun, but afraid of a probable shower;
So we stand and stare, and see, to the left of St. Peter's,
Smoke from the cannon, white—but that is at intervals only—
Black, from a burning house, we suppose, by the Cavalleggieri;[5]
And we believe we discern some lines of men descending
Down through the vineyard slopes, and catch a bayonet gleaming.
Every ten minutes, however (in this there is no misconception),
Comes a great white puff from behind Michelangelo's dome, and
After a space the report of a real big gun—not the Frenchman's?—
That must be doing some work. And so we watch and conjecture.

    Shortly, an Englishman comes, who says he has been to St. Peter's,
Seen the Piazza and troops, but that is all he can tell us;
So we watch and sit—and indeed, it begins to be tiresome.
All this smoke is outside; when it has come to the inside,
It will be time, perhaps, to descend and retreat to our houses.

    Half-past one, or two. The report of small arms frequent,
Sharp and savage, indeed; that cannot all be for nothing:
So we watch and wonder; but guessing is tiresome, very.
Weary of wondering, watching, and guessing, and gossiping idly,
Down I go, and pass through the quiet streets with the knots of
National Guards patrolling, and flags hanging out at the windows—
English, American, Danish—and, after offering to help an
Irish family moving *en masse* to the Maison Serny,[6]

---

3. The Corso and Via dei Condotti are fashionable streets in central Rome, close to the area round Piazza di Spagna.
4. The Pincian Hill is in the northeast quadrant of Rome.
5. Clough refers to the Porta Cavalleggieri, now demolished, to the immediate south of the Vatican in Rome.
6. Maison Serny] hotel in Piazza di Spagna, popular with British tourists.

After endeavoring idly to minister balm to the trembling
Quinquagenarian fears of two lone British spinsters,[7]
Go to make sure of my dinner before the enemy enter.
But by this there are signs of stragglers returning; and voices
Talk, though you don't believe it, of guns and prisoners taken;
And on the walls you read the first bulletin of the morning.
This is all that I saw, and all that I know of the battle.

VI. CLAUDE TO EUSTACE

Victory! Victory! Yes, ah, yes, thou republican Zion,
Truly the kings of the earth are gathered and gone by together;
Doubtless they marveled to witness such things, were astonished, and
    so forth.
Victory! Victory! Victory! Ah, but it is, believe me,
Easier, easier far, to intone the chant of the martyr
Than to indite any paean of any victory. Death may
Sometimes be noble; but life, at the best, will appear an illusion.
While the great pain is upon us, it is great; when it is over,
Why, it is over. The smoke of the sacrifice rises to heaven,
Of a sweet savour, no doubt, to Somebody; but on the altar,
Lo, there is nothing remaining but ashes and dirt and ill odor.
    So it stands, you perceive; the labial muscles that swelled with
Vehement evolution of yesterday Marseillaises,
Articulations sublime of defiance and scorning, today col-
Lapse and languidly mumble, while men and women and papers
Scream and re-scream to each other the chorus of Victory. Well, but
I am thankful they fought, and glad that the Frenchmen were beaten.

VII. CLAUDE TO EUSTACE[8]

So, I have seen a man killed! An experience that, among others!
Yes, I suppose I have; although I can hardly be certain,
And in a court of justice could never declare I had seen it.
But a man was killed, I am told, in a place where I saw
Something; a man was killed, I am told, and I saw something.
I was returning home from St. Peter's; Murray, as usual,

---

7. The spinsters, and their fears, are aged between 50 and 59 ("Quinquagenarian").
8. This letter refers to the Roman Terror, the anticlerical outbreak of violence during the
first few days of May 1849.

Under my arm, I remember; had crossed the St. Angelo bridge; and
Moving towards the Condotti, had got to the first barricade, when
Gradually, thinking still of St. Peter's, I became conscious
Of a sensation of movement opposing me—tendency this way
(Such as one fancies may be in a stream when the wave of the tide is
Coming and not yet come—a sort of noise and retention);
So I turned and, before I turned, caught sight of stragglers
Heading a crowd, it is plain, that is coming behind that corner.
Looking up, I see windows filled with heads; the Piazza,
Into which you remember the Ponte St. Angelo enters,
Since I passed, has thickened with curious groups; and now the
Crowd is coming, has turned, has crossed that last barricade, is
Here at my side. In the middle they drag at something. What is it?—
Ha! Bare swords in the air, held up! There seem to be voices
Pleading and hands putting back; official, perhaps; but the swords are
Many, and bare in the air. In the air? They descend; they are smiting,
Hewing, chopping—at what? In the air, once more upstretched! And—
Is it blood that's on them? Yes, certainly blood! Of whom, then?
Over whom is the cry of this furor of exultation?
While they are skipping and screaming, and dancing their caps on the
        points of
Swords and bayonets, I to the outskirts back, and ask a
Mercantile-seeming bystander, "What is it?"—and he, looking always
That way, makes me answer, "A priest who was trying to fly to
The Neapolitan army," and thus explains the proceeding.
"You didn't see the dead man?" "No." I began to be doubtful;
I was in black myself, and didn't know what mightn't happen,
But a National Guard close by me, outside of the hubbub,
Broke his sword with slashing a broad hat covered with dust, and
Passing away from the place with Murray under my arm, and
Stooping, I saw through the legs of the people the legs of a body.
You are the first, do you know, to whom I have mentioned the matter.
Whom should I tell it to else? These girls? The heavens forbid it!
Quidnuncs at Monaldini's?[9] Idlers upon the Pincian?
If I rightly remember, it happened on that afternoon when
Word of the nearer approach of a new Neapolitan army
First was spread. I began to bethink me of Paris Septembers,

9. Monaldini's reading room in Piazza di Spagna stocked English-language newspapers.

Thought I could fancy the look of that old 'ninety-two.[10] On that evening
Three or four or (it may be) five of these people were slaughtered;
Some declared they had, one of them, fired on a sentinel; others
Say they were only escaping; a priest, it is currently stated,
Stabbed a National Guard on the very Piazza Colonna:
History, Rumor of Rumors, I leave to thee to determine!
    But I am thankful to say the government seems to have strength to
Put it down; it has vanished, at least; the place is most peaceful.
Through the Trastevere walking last night, at nine of the clock, I
Found no sort of disorder; I crossed by the island bridges,
So by the narrow streets to the Ponte Rotto, and onward
Thence by the Temple of Vesta, away to the great Coliseum,
Which at the full of the moon is an object worthy a visit.

IX. CLAUDE TO EUSTACE

It is most curious to see what a power a few calm words (in
Merely a brief proclamation) appear to possess on the people.
Order is perfect, and peace; the city is utterly tranquil;
And one cannot conceive that this easy and *nonchalant* crowd, that
Flows like a quiet stream through street and marketplace, entering
Shady recesses and bays of church, *osteria*, and *caffè*,
Could in a moment be changed to a flood as of molten lava,
Boil into deadly wrath and wild homicidal delusion.
    Ah, 'tis an excellent race, and even in old degradation,
Under a rule that enforces to flattery, lying, and cheating,
E'en under pope and priest, a nice and natural people.
Oh, could they but be allowed this chance of redemption!—but clearly
That is not likely to be. Meantime, notwithstanding all journals,
Honour for once to the tongue and the pen of the eloquent writer!
Honour to speech, and all honour to thee, thou noble Mazzini![11]

Written by June 1849; published February to May 1858

---

10. Clough refers to the September Massacres during the French Revolution in summer 1792; the massacres began as an outbreak of violence against the Catholic Church.
11. Giuseppe Mazzini (1805–1872), Italian activist and politician. He entered Rome with Garibaldi's irregulars and was appointed "triumvir" of the new republic on March 29, during Clough's stay in the city. Mazzini was compelled to leave Rome in July—after these lines were written.

Ernest Jones (1819–1869)

BORN INTO THE gentrified middle class, Jones would always prefer a Tory to a Whig, yet his principles were Chartist. Trained as a lawyer, he remained indifferent to politics until declared bankrupt in 1844. Then, at the age of twenty-seven, he became committed to the politics of the oppressed, and was drawn ineluctably toward Chartism. His *Chartist Songs* (1846) were recited across the land, and thanks to his friendship with Feargus O'Connor and George Julian Harney he advanced to the forefront of the movement, befriending Marx and Engels in London. In 1848 he was among a small delegation that visited Paris to congratulate the new provisional government, but in June was arrested in Manchester and charged with sedition and unlawful behavior. There followed an imprisonment of two years, which severely damaged his health. His poems on solitary confinement, memorized as a means of maintaining sanity, testify to the brutality with which the government punished its opponents. By the time he was released, Chartism was no longer a national force, and he devoted his energies to socialism, writing in the *Northern Star*: "as Whig and Tory unite, when there is danger, to crush their common foe—the people—so the people are beginning to unite against their common enemy: THE RICH! Aye! THE RICH!" (September 14, 1850). He stood for election three times between 1852 and 1857, without success, and was compelled by financial hardship to return to the law courts where he defended the Manchester Fenians, among others.

Our Destiny

Labour! Labour! Labour! Toil! Toil! Toil!
    With the wearing of the bone and the drowning of the mind,
Sink like shriveled parchment, in the flesh-devouring soil
        And die when ye have shouted it till centuries shall hear!
        Pass away unheeded like the waving of the wind!

Build the marble palace! Sound the hollow fame!
    Be the trodden pathway for a conqueror's career;
Exhale your million breathings to elevate one name,
    And die when ye have shouted it till centuries shall hear!

"By right divine we rule ye. God made ye but for us!"
    Thus cry the lords of nations to the slaves whom they subdue.
Unclasp God's book of nature: its writings read not thus!
    Hear, tramplers of the millions! Hear, benders to the few!

God gave us hearts of ardour, God gave us noble forms,
    And God has poured around us his paradise of light!
Has he bade us sow the sunshine, and only reap the storms?
    Created us in glory, to pass away in night?

"No!" say the sunny heavens, that smile on all alike;
    The waves that upbear navys, yet hold them in their thrall;
"No!" shouts the dreadful thunder, that teaches to strike
    The proud, for one usurping, what the Godhead meant for all.

"No! No!" we cry, united by our suffering's mighty length;
    "Ye—Ye have ruled for ages, now we will rule as well!"
"No! No!" we cry, triumphant in our right's resistless strength,
    "We—we will share your heaven, or ye shall share our hell!"

                    Written June 15, 1846, published July 11, 1846

Prison Fancies

> Composed when confined to a solitary cell, on bread and water,
> without books or writing materials, May 1849.

Troublesome fancies beset me
    Sometimes as I sit in my cell,
That comrades and friends may forget me,
    And foes may remember too well.

That plans which I thought well digested
    May prove to be bubbles of air,
And hopes when they come to be tested
    May turn to the seed of despair.

But though I may doubt all beside me
    And anchor and cable my part,
Whatever—whatever betide me,
    Forbid me to doubt my own heart!

For sickness may wreck a brave spirit,
    And time wear the brain to a shade;
And dastardly age disinherit
    Creations that manhood has made.

But, God, let me ne'er cease to cherish
    The truths I so fondly have held!
Far sooner, at once let me perish,
    Ere firmness and courage are quelled.

Though my head in the dust may be lying,
    And bad men exult o'er my fall,
I shall smile at them—smile at them, dying,
    The Right is the Right, after all!

Written May 1849, published 1851

The Silent Cell

> Composed, during illness, on the sixth day of my incarceration
> in a solitary cell, on bread and water, and without books, August
> 1849.

They told me 'twas a fearful thing
    To pine in prison lone:

The brain became a shriveled scroll,
    The heart a living stone.

Nor solitude, nor silent cell
    The teeming mind can tame;
No tribute needs the granite well,
    No food the planet-flame.

Denied the fruit of others' thought,
    To write my own denied,
Sweet sisters, Hope and Memory, brought
    Bright volumes to my side.

And oft we trace, with airy pen,
    Full many a word of worth;
For time will pass, and freedom then
    Shall flash them on the earth.

They told me that my veins would flag,
    My ardor would decay;
And heavily their fetters drag
    My blood's young strength away.

Like conquerors bounding to the goal,
    Where cold white marble gleams,
Magnificent red rivers, roll!
    Roll, all you thousand streams!

Oft to Passion's stormy gale
    When sleep I seek in vain,
Fleets of fancy up them sail
    And anchor in my brain.

But never a wish for base retreat
    Or thought of a recreant part,
While yet a single pulse shall beat
    Proud marches in my heart.

They'll find me still unchanged and strong
   When breaks their puny thrall;
  With hate for not one living soul
   And pity for them all.

Written August 1849, published December 7, 1850

Walt Whitman (1819–1892)

"OH GOD!" WROTE Whitman after Gettysburg, "that whole damned War business is about nine hundred and ninety nine parts diarrhea to one part glory." He had reason to know. Though ready to fight on the Union side, Whitman was unacceptable as a recruit, being forty-two years old. He left home in Brooklyn and headed to Washington, DC, in early 1863, to find his brother George, wounded at the Battle of Fredericksburg. He remained long after he found his brother (who was not seriously hurt) because he felt it his duty to visit wounded soldiers—"a profound conviction of necessity, affinity, coming into closest relations—relations O so close and dear." Six days a week, afternoon and evening, he performed the office of "wound dresser," comforting the dying and diseased, including veterans of the First Battle of Fredericksburg (December 1862) and Gettysburg (July 1863). They were sheltered in makeshift hospitals all over the city—in the Patent Office (now the National Portrait Gallery), the Capitol, Georgetown College, and the south lawn of the White House. Whitman visited all these places, bearing witness to human suffering where the injured were not always kindly or compassionately treated—reading to them and writing letters (including love letters) at their dictation. He held and kissed them, too, exposing himself to pneumonia, typhoid, malaria, and diarrhea. "O how one gets to love them," he reflected, "so suffering, so good, so manly and affectionate." Whitman also visited numerous Union encampments in Virginia, some close to enemy lines, where he helped soldiers suffering from dysentery: "how often and how many I have seen come into Washington from this dreadful complaint," he told his mother. As he worked, Whitman carried a notebook in which he composed poems that described the suffering of war, collected as *Drum-Taps* (1865); the poems we include here are taken from that volume, which was incorporated into *Leaves of Grass* (1867) and, with the 1871 edition of that huge work, positioned centrally within it.

Drum-Taps (extracts)

COME UP FROM THE FIELDS, FATHER

Come up from the fields, father, here's a letter from our Pete;
And come to the front door, mother, here's a letter from thy dear son.

Lo, 'tis autumn;
Lo, where the trees, deeper green, yellower and redder,
Cool and sweeten Ohio's villages, with leaves fluttering in the moderate
    wind;
Where apples ripe in the orchards hang, and grapes on the trellised vines;
(Smell you the smell of the grapes on the vines?
Smell you the buckwheat, where the bees were lately buzzing?)

Above all, lo, the sky so calm, so transparent after the rain, and with
    wondrous clouds;
Below too, all calm, all vital and beautiful, and the farm prospers well.

Down in the fields all prospers well,
But now from the fields come, father, come at the daughter's call;
And come to the entry, mother, to the front door come right away.

Fast as she can she hurries—something ominous—her steps trembling;
She does not tarry to smooth her hair nor adjust her cap.

Open the envelope quickly;
Oh, this is not our son's writing, yet his name is signed;
Oh, a strange hand writes for our dear son, oh stricken mother's soul!
All swims before her eyes, flashes with black, she catches the main
    words only;
Sentences broken—*gunshot wound in the breast, cavalry skirmish, taken to
    hospital,*
At present low, but will soon be better.

Ah, now the single figure to me,
Amid all teeming and wealthy Ohio, with all its cities and farms,
Sickly white in the face, and dull in the head, very faint,
By the jamb of a door leans.

Grieve not so, dear mother (the just-grown daughter speaks through her
 sobs;
The little sisters huddle around, speechless and dismayed);
See, dearest mother, the letter says Pete will soon be better.

Alas, poor boy, he will never be better (nor maybe needs to be better,
 that brave and simple soul):
While they stand at home at the door, he is dead already,
The only son is dead.

But the mother needs to be better,
She with thin form presently dressed in black;
By day her meals untouched, then at night fitfully sleeping, often
 waking,
In the midnight waking, weeping, longing with one deep longing,
Oh, that she might withdraw unnoticed, silent from life, escape and
 withdraw,
To follow, to seek, to be with her dear dead son.

Published May 1865

VIGIL STRANGE I KEPT ON THE FIELD ONE NIGHT[1]

Vigil strange I kept on the field one night;
When you, my son and my comrade, dropped at my side that day,
One look I but gave which your dear eyes returned with a look I shall
 never forget;

---

1. This poem appears to dramatize the true story of William Giggie, killed in the Second Battle of Manassas on August 29, 1862, while serving under Union General John Pope, and buried in the war zone by his comrade, Arthur, who relayed the tale to Whitman. Whitman scribbled the details into his notebook: "William Giggee, Sept. 18th '62. I heard of poor Bill's death—he was shot on Pope's retreat—Arthur took him in his arms, and he died in about an hour and a half—Arthur buried him himself he dug his grave."

One touch of your hand to mine, oh boy, reached up as you lay on the
    ground;
Then onward I sped in the battle, the even-contested battle,
Till late in the night relieved, to the place at last again I made my way,
Found you in death so cold, dear comrade—found your body, son of
    responding kisses (never again on earth responding),
Bared your face in the starlight, curious the scene, cool blew the
    moderate night-wind;
Long there and then in vigil I stood, dimly around me the battlefield
    spreading;
Vigil wondrous and vigil sweet, there in the fragrant silent night;
But not a tear fell, not even a long-drawn sigh; long, long I gazed,
Then on the earth partially reclining, sat by your side, leaning my chin
    in my hands,
Passing sweet hours, immortal and mystic hours with you, dearest com-
    rade—not a tear, not a word;
Vigil of silence, love and death; vigil for you, my son and my soldier,
As onward silently stars aloft, eastward new ones upward stole,
Vigil final for you, brave boy (I could not save you, swift was your death,
I faithfully loved you and cared for you living, I think we shall surely
    meet again);
Till at latest lingering of the night, indeed just as the dawn appeared,
My comrade I wrapped in his blanket, enveloped well his form,
Folded the blanket well, tucking it carefully over head and carefully
    under feet,
And there and then, and bathed by the rising sun, my son in his grave,
    in his rude-dug grave I deposited,
Ending my vigil strange with that, vigil of night and battlefield dim;
Vigil for boy of responding kisses (never again on earth responding);
Vigil for comrade swiftly slain, vigil I never forget, how as day
    brightened,
I rose from the chill ground and folded my soldier well in his blanket,
And buried him where he fell.

Written September and October 1863, published May 1865

AS TOILSOME I WANDERED VIRGINIA'S WOODS

As toilsome I wandered Virginia's woods,
To the music of rustling leaves kicked by my feet (for 'twas autumn),
I marked at the foot of a tree the grave of a soldier;
Mortally wounded he and buried on the retreat (easily all could I
    understand),
The halt of a midday hour, when up! no time to lose—yet this sign left,
On a tablet scrawled and nailed on the tree by the grave,
Bold, cautious, true, and my loving comrade.

Long, long I muse, then on my way go wandering,
Many a changeful season to follow, and many a scene of life;
Yet at times through changeful season and scene, abrupt, alone, or in
    the crowded street
Comes before me the unknown soldier's grave, comes the inscription
    rude in Virginia's woods,
Bold, cautious, true, and my loving comrade.

Published May 1865

THE WOUND-DRESSER

1

An old man bending I come among new faces,
Years looking backward resuming, in answer to children,
Come tell us, old man, as from young men and maidens that love me;
(Aroused and angry, I'd thought to beat the alarum and urge relentless
    war,
But soon my fingers failed me, my face drooped and I resigned myself,
To sit by the wounded and soothe them, or silently watch the dead;)
Years hence of these scenes, of these furious passions, these chances
Of unsurpassed heroes (Was one side so brave? The other was equally
    brave)—
Now be witness again, paint the mightiest armies of earth;
Of those armies so rapid, so wondrous, what saw you to tell us?
What stays with you latest and deepest? of curious panics,
Of hard-fought engagements, or sieges tremendous, what deepest remains?

2

Oh, maidens and young men I love, and that love me,
What you ask of my days, those the strangest and sudden your talking
    recalls;
Soldier alert I arrive, after a long march, covered with sweat and dust,
In the nick of time I come, plunge in the fight, loudly shout in the
    rush of successful charge;
Enter the captured works—yet lo, like a swift-running river they fade,
Pass and are gone, they fade; I dwell not on soldiers' perils or soldiers'
    joys
(Both I remember well—many the hardships, few the joys, yet I was
    content).

But in silence, in dreams' projections,
While the world of gain and appearance and mirth goes on,
So soon what is over forgotten, and waves wash the imprints off the
    sand,
With hinged knees returning I enter the doors (while for you up there,
Whoever you are, follow me without noise and be of strong heart).

Bearing the bandages, water and sponge,
Straight and swift to my wounded I go
Where they lie on the ground after the battle brought in,
Where their priceless blood reddens the grass, the ground
Or to the rows of the hospital tent, or under the roofed hospital;
To the long rows of cots, up and down, each side I return;
To each and all, one after another, I draw near, not one do I miss;
An attendant follows, holding a tray; he carries a refuse pail
Soon to be filled with clotted rags and blood, emptied, and filled again.

I onward go, I stop
With hinged knees and steady hand to dress wounds;
I am firm with each, the pangs are sharp yet unavoidable;
One turns to me his appealing eyes—poor boy, I never knew you!
Yet I think I could not refuse this moment to die for you, if that would
    save you.

3

On, on I go! (open, doors of time! open, hospital doors!)

The crushed head I dress (poor crazed hand, tear not the bandage
away);

The neck of the cavalryman with the bullet through and through I
examine;

Hard the breathing rattles, quite glazed already the eye, yet life
struggles hard.

(Come, sweet death! Be persuaded, oh beautiful death!

In mercy come quickly.)

From the stump of the arm, the amputated hand,

I undo the clotted lint, remove the slough, wash off the matter and
blood;

Back on his pillow the soldier bends with curved neck and side-falling
head;

His eyes are closed, his face is pale, he dares not look on the bloody
stump

And has not yet looked on it.

I dress a wound in the side, deep, deep;

But a day or two more, for see, the frame all wasted and sinking,

And the yellow-blue countenance see.

I dress the perforated shoulder, the foot with the bullet-wound,

Cleanse the one with a gnawing and putrid gangrene, so sickening, so
offensive,

While the attendant stands behind aside me holding the tray and pail.

I am faithful, I do not give out;

The fractured thigh, the knee, the wound in the abdomen,

These and more I dress with impassive hand (yet deep in my breast a
fire, a burning flame).

4

Thus in silence, in dreams' projections,

Returning, resuming, I thread my way through the hospitals;

The hurt and wounded I pacify with soothing hand,

I sit by the restless all the dark night, some are so young;
Some suffer so much, I recall the experience sweet and sad;
Many a soldier's loving arms about this neck have crossed and rested,
Many a soldier's kiss dwells on these bearded lips.

Published May 1865

Herman Melville (1819–1891)

MELVILLE SAW ENOUGH human suffering as a sailor, including 163 flog-gings, a man permanently crippled by a fall from the mizzen topsail yard, and five deaths, to make him hostile to war of any kind—so that when in May 1846 America declared war on Mexico, he lamented that now "we will be able to talk of our killed and wounded like some of the old eastern conquerors reckoning them up by thousands." All the same, he regarded slavery as "a grave evil," and as a Union man accepted the necessity for the Civil War. He knew the cost would be great, and was horrified by the First Battle of Bull Run (known as the First Manassas) on July 21, 1861, the largest and bloodiest encounter in the Civil War up to that point, with a death toll of 460 Union soldiers and 387 Confederates. Aged forty-two, with bad eyesight and back trouble, Melville was not expected to enlist, but did so nonetheless, attend-ing drills for nearly two years. In April 1864 he obtained a pass to visit the Union army in Vienna, Virginia, where his cousin, Henry Gansevoort, was stationed, and accompanied the New York cavalrymen on a two-day trip into the Wilderness where John Singleton Mosby and his Partisan Rangers (43rd Battalion Virginia Cavalry) were operating, during which they captured a handful of guerrilla fighters who were planning to destroy a bridge crucial to the Union army's supply. This provided Melville with material for his only Civil War poem based on firsthand experience, *The Scout Toward Aldie*, one of seventy-odd elegies, narratives, and reflections published as *Battle-Pieces and Aspects of the War* (1866), which was dedicated to the three hundred thousand who "fell devotedly under the flag of their fathers."

The Scout Toward Aldie[1]

The cavalry camp lies on the slope
    Of what was late a vernal hill,
But now like a pavement bare—
An outpost in the perilous wilds
    Which ever are lone and still;
        But Mosby's men are there—
        Of Mosby best beware.[2]

Great trees the troopers felled, and leaned
    In antlered walls about their tents;
Strict watch they kept—'twas "Hark!" and "Mark!"
Unarmed none cared to stir abroad
    For berries beyond their forest-fence:
        As glides in seas the shark,
        Rides Mosby through green dark.

All spake of him, but few had seen
    Except the maimed ones or the low;
Yet rumor made him everything—
A farmer—woodman—refugee—
    The man who crossed the field but now;
        A spell about his life did cling—
        Who to the ground shall Mosby bring?

The morning-bugles lonely play,
    Lonely the evening-bugle calls—
Unanswered voices in the wild;
The settled hush of birds in nest
    Becharms, and all the wood enthralls:
        Memory's self is so beguiled
        That Mosby seems a satyr's child.

---

1. This is the only one of Melville's *Battle-Pieces* based on firsthand experience of the war; see headnote, p. 444 above.
2. The refrain of the poem refers to John Singleton Mosby (1833–1916) who, since January 1863, had been commander of the 43rd Virginia Battalion Cavalry, Partisan Rangers, based in Northern Virginia. They carried out guerrilla raids on Union targets—blowing up bridges, robbing trains, stealing livestock, food, and ammunition.

They lived as in the Eerie Land;
   The fireflies showed with fairy gleam;
And yet from pine-tops one might ken
The Capitol dome—hazy—sublime—
   A vision breaking on a dream:
      So strange it was that Mosby's men
      Should dare to prowl where the dome was seen.[3]

A scout toward Aldie broke the spell.[4]
   The leader[5] lies before his tent
Gazing at heaven's all-cheering lamp
Through blandness of a morning rare;
   His thoughts on bitter sweets are bent:
      His sunny bride is in the camp—
      But Mosby—graves are beds of damp!

The trumpet calls; he goes within;
   But none the prayer and sob may know:
Her hero he, but bridegroom too.
Ah, love in a tent is a queenly thing,
   And fame, be sure, refines the vow;
      But fame fond wives have lived to rue,
      And Mosby's men fell deeds can do.

Tan-tara! tan-tara! tan-tara!
   Mounted and armed he sits a king;
For pride she smiles if now she peep—
Elate he rides at the head of his men;
   He is young, and command is a boyish thing:

---

3. The dome of the Capitol in Washington, DC, was rebuilt and completed in December 1863, months before this poem was written. It rises 96 feet.
4. Aldie is a village in Loudoun County, Virginia.
5. The leader] Melville bases this character on Colonel Charles Russell Lowell, Jr. (1835–1864), of the 2nd Massachusetts Cavalry, whose job was to keep supply lines open and protect Washington, DC, against Mosby's Raiders. Shortly after meeting Melville he became involved in the Valley Campaigns, and would die in October 1864, mortally wounded at the Battle of Cedar Creek. In October 1863 he married Josephine Shaw (1843–1905), who Melville did not meet, although he knew of her presence in camp shortly before his arrival.

They file out into the forest deep—
Do Mosby and his rangers sleep?

The sun is gold, and the world is green,
   Opal the vapors of morning roll;
The champing horses lightly prance—
Full of caprice, and the riders too
    Curving in many a caracol.[6]
      But marshaled soon, by fours advance—
      Mosby had checked that airy dance.

By the hospital tent the cripples stand—
   Bandage, and crutch, and cane, and sling,
And palely eye the brave array;
The froth of the cup is gone for them
    ("Caw, caw!" the crows through the blueness wing):
      Yet these were late as bold, as gay;
      But Mosby—a clip, and grass is hay.

How strong they feel on their horses free,
   Tingles the tendoned thigh with life;
Their cavalry jackets make boys of all—
With golden breasts like the oriole;
    The chat, the jest, and laugh are rife.
      But word is passed from the front—a call
      For order; the wood is Mosby's hall.

To which behest one rider sly
   (Spurred, but unarmed) gave little heed—
Of dexterous fun not slow or spare,
He teased his neighbors of touchy mood,
    Into plungings he pricked his steed:
      A black-eyed man on a coal-black mare,
      Alive as Mosby in mountain air.

---

6. caracol] a turning maneuver.

His limbs were long, and large, and round;
   He whispered, winked, did all but shout:
A healthy man for the sick to view;
The taste in his mouth was sweet at morn;
    Little of care he cared about.
      And yet of pains and pangs he knew—
      In others, maimed by Mosby's crew.

The hospital steward—even he
   (Sacred in person as a priest),
And on his coat-sleeve broidered nice
Wore the caduceus, black and green.
    No wonder he sat so light on his beast;
      This cheery man in suit of price
      Not even Mosby dared to slice.

They pass the picket by the pine
   And hollow log—a lonesome place;
His horse a-droop, and pistol clean;
'Tis cocked—kept leveled toward the wood;
    Strained vigilance ages his childish face.
      Since midnight has that stripling been
      Peering for Mosby through the green.

Splashing they cross the freshet flood,   *stream*
   And up the muddy bank they strain;
A horse at a spectral white ash shies—
One of the span of the ambulance,
    Black as a hearse. They give the rein:
      Silent speed on a scout were wise,
      Could cunning baffle Mosby's spies.

Rumor had come that a band was lodged
   In green retreats of hills that peer
By Aldie (famed for the swordless charge[7]).

---

7. Melville refers to Colonel Louis di Cesnola, of the 4th New York Cavalry; prior to the
Battle of Aldie in June 1863 he was arrested and stripped of his saber by his command-

Much store they'd heaped of captured arms
   And, peradventure, pilfered cheer;
      For Mosby's lads oft hearts enlarge
      In revelry by some gorge's marge.

"Don't let your sabers rattle and ring;
   To his oat-bag let each man give heed—
There now, that fellow's bag's untied,
Sowing the road with the precious grain.
   Your carbines swing at hand—you need!
      Look to yourselves, and your nags beside,
      Men who after Mosby ride."

Picked lads and keen went sharp before—
   A guard, though scarce against surprise;
And rearmost rode an answering troop,
But flankers none to right or left.
   No bugle peals, no pennon flies:
      Silent they sweep, and fain would swoop
      On Mosby with an Indian whoop.

On, right on through the forest land,
   Nor man, nor maid, nor child was seen,
Not even a dog. The air was still;
The blackened hut they turned to see,
   And spied charred benches on the green;
      A squirrel sprang from the rotting mill
      Whence Mosby sallied late, brave blood to spill.

By worn-out fields they cantered on—
   Drear fields amid the woodlands wide;
By crossroads of some olden time
In which grew groves; by gate stones down,
   Grassed ruins of secluded pride:

---

ing officer for protesting promotion of a less-experienced officer to the post of brigadier general. Melville understood that di Cesnola, undeterred, "insisted upon charging at the head of his men, which he did, and the onset proved victorious."

A strange lone land, long past the prime,
    Fit land for Mosby or for crime.

The brook in the dell they pass. One peers
    Between the leaves: "Aye, there's the place—
There, on the oozy ledge—'twas there
We found the body (Blake's, you know);
    Such whirlings, gurglings round the face—
        Shot drinking! Well, in war all's fair,
        So Mosby says. The bough—take care!"

Hard by, a chapel. Flowerpot mould
    Danked and decayed the shaded roof;
The porch was punk;[8] the clapboards spanned
With ruffled lichens gray or green;
    Red coral-moss was not aloof;
        And mid dry leaves green dead-man's-hand[9]
        Groped toward that chapel in Mosby-land.

The road they leave and take the wood,
    And mark the trace of ridges there—
A wood where once had slept the farm—
A wood where once tobacco grew
    Drowsily in the hazy air,
        And wrought in all kind things a calm—
        Such influence, Mosby, bids disarm.

To ease even yet the place did woo—
    To ease which pines unstirring share,
For ease the weary horses sighed:
Halting, and slackening girths, they feed,
    Their pipes they light, they loiter there;
        Then up, and urging still the guide,
        On, and after Mosby ride.

---

8. punk] of poor quality.
9. dead-man's-hand] *Scleroderma geaster*, also known as Devils Snuffbox, a large round poisonous mushroom.

This guide in frowzy coat of brown,
   And beard of ancient growth and mould,
Bestrode a bony steed and strong,
As suited well with bulk he bore—
   A wheezy man with depth of hold
     Who jouncing went. A staff he swung—
     A wight whom Mosby's wasp had stung.

Burned out and homeless—hunted long!
   That wheeze he caught in autumn wood
Crouching (a fat man) for his life,
And spied his lean son 'mong the crew
   That probed the covert. Ah! black blood
     Was his 'gainst even child and wife—
     Fast friends to Mosby. Such the strife.

A lad, unhorsed by sliding girths,
   Strains hard to readjust his seat
Ere the main body show the gap
'Twixt them and the rearguard; scrub-oaks near
   He sidelong eyes, while hands move fleet;
     Then mounts and spurs. One drops his cap—
     "Let Mosby find!" nor heeds mishap.

A gable time-stained peeps through trees:
   "You mind the fight in the haunted house?
That's it; we clenched them in the room—
An ambuscade of ghosts, we thought,
   But proved sly rebels on a bouse!   *drinking bout*
     Luke lies in the yard." The chimneys loom:
     Some muse on Mosby, some on doom.

Less nimbly now through brakes they wind,
   And ford wild creeks where men have drowned;
They skirt the pool, avoid the fen,
And so till night, when down they lie,
   Their steeds still saddled, in wooded ground:
     Rein in hand they slumber then,
     Dreaming of Mosby's cedarn den.

But Colonel and Major[10] friendly sat
    Where boughs deformed low made a seat.
The young man talked (all sworded and spurred)
Of the partisan's blade he longed to win,
    And frays in which he meant to beat.
        The grizzled Major smoked, and heard:
        "But what's that—Mosby?" "No, a bird."

A contrast here like sire and son,
    Hope and Experience sage did meet;
The youth was brave, the senior too;
But through the Seven Days[11] one had served,
    And gasped with the rearguard in retreat:
        So he smoked and smoked, and the wreath he blew—
        "Any *sure* news of Mosby's crew?"

He smoked and smoked, eyeing the while
    A huge tree hydra-like in growth,
Moon-tinged, with crooked boughs rent or lopped,
Itself a haggard forest. "Come!"
    The Colonel cried, "to talk you're loath;
        D'ye hear? I say he must be stopped,
        This Mosby—caged, and hair close cropped."[12]

"Of course; but what's that dangling there?"
    "Where?" "From the tree, that gallows-bough."
"A bit of frayed bark, is it not?"
"Aye, or a rope; did *we* hang last?
    Don't like my neckerchief anyhow."
        He loosened it: "Oh aye, we'll stop
        This Mosby—but that vile jerk and drop!"[13]

---

10. Melville based this character on Major William H. Forbes of the 2nd Massachusetts Cavalry, who commanded the scouting party on which Melville was taken, and showed him parts of the Wilderness near to Aldie.
11. the Seven Days] a series of six major battles fought over a week, June 25–July 1, 1862, the culmination of the Peninsula Campaign.
12. Hair was usually cropped prior to execution.
13. In a note, Melville pointed out that six of Mosby's Partisans were hanged by Union

By peep of light they feed and ride,
　　Gaining a grove's green edge at morn,
And mark the Aldie hills[14] uprear
And five gigantic horsemen carved
　　Clear-cut against the sky withdrawn;
　　　　Are more behind? An open snare?
　　　　Or Mosby's men but watchmen there?

The ravaged land was miles behind,
　　And Loudoun spread her landscape rare;
Orchards in pleasant lowlands stood,
Cows were feeding, a cock loud crew,
　　But not a friend at need was there;
　　　　The valley-folk were only good
　　　　To Mosby and his wandering brood.

What best to do? What mean yon men?
　　Colonel and guide their minds compare;
Be sure some looked their leader through;
Dismounted, on his sword he leaned
　　As one who feigns an easy air;
　　　　And yet perplexed he was they knew,
　　　　Perplexed by Mosby's mountain crew.

The Major hemmed as he would speak,
　　But checked himself, and left the ring
Of cavalrymen about their chief—
Young courtiers mute who paid their court
　　By looking with confidence on their king;
　　　　They knew him brave, foresaw no grief—
　　　　But Mosby—the time to think is brief.

The surgeon (sashed in sacred green)
　　Was glad 'twas not for *him* to say

---

cavalrymen in summer 1864; in retaliation they hanged Union soldiers when they came across them.
14. Aldie hills] Bull Run Mountains.

What next should be; if a trooper bleeds,
Why he will do his best, as wont,
   And his partner in black will aid and pray;
      But judgment bides with him who leads,
      And Mosby many a problem breeds.

This surgeon was the kindliest man
   That ever a callous trade professed;
He felt for him, that leader young,
And offered medicine from his flask:
   The Colonel took it with marvelous zest.
      For such fine medicine good and strong,
      Oft Mosby and his foresters long.

A charm of proof. "Ho, Major, come;
   Pounce on yon men! Take half your troop,
Through the thickets wind—pray speedy be—
And gain their rear. And, Captain Morn,
   Picket these roads, all travelers stop;
      The rest to the edge of this crest with me,
      That Mosby and his scouts may see."

Commanded and done. Ere the sun stood steep,
   Back came the Blues, with a troop of Grays,
Ten riding double—luckless ten!—
Five horses gone, and looped hats lost,
   And love-locks dancing in a maze—
      Certes, but sophomores from the glen
      Of Mosby—not his veteran men.

"Colonel," said the Major, touching his cap,
   "We've had our ride, and here they are."
"Well done! How many found you there?"
"As many as I bring you here."
   "And no one hurt?" "There'll be no scar;
      One fool was battered." "Find their lair?"
      "Why, Mosby's brood camp everywhere."

He sighed, and slid down from his horse,
    And limping went to a spring-head nigh.
"Why bless me, Major—not hurt, I hope?"
"Battered my knee against a bar
    When the rush was made; all right by-and-by.
        Halloa! they gave you too much rope—
        Go back to Mosby, eh? Elope?"

Just by the low-hanging skirt of wood
    The guard, remiss, had given a chance
For a sudden sally into the cover,
But foiled the intent, nor fired a shot,
    Though the issue was a deadly trance;
        For, hurled 'gainst an oak that humped low over,
        Mosby's man fell, pale as a lover.

They pulled some grass his head to ease
    (Lined with blue shreds a ground-nest stirred).
The surgeon came—"Here's a to-do!"
"Ah!" cried the Major, darting a glance,
    "This fellow's the one that fired and spurred
        Downhill, but met reserves below;
        My boys, not Mosby's—so we go!"

The surgeon (bluff, red, goodly man)
    Kneeled by the hurt one; like a bee
He toiled. The pale young chaplain too
(Who went to the wars for cure of souls,
    And his own student ailments), he
        Bent over likewise; spite the two,
        Mosby's poor man more pallid grew.

Meanwhile the mounted captives near
    Jested; and yet they anxious showed;
Virginians; some of family pride,
And young, and full of fire, and fine
    In open feature and cheek that glowed;
        And here thralled vagabonds now they ride—   *captured*
        But list! one speaks for Mosby's side.

"Why, three to one—your horses strong—
    Revolvers, rifles, and a surprise—
Surrender we account no shame!
We live, are gay, and life is hope;
      We'll fight again when fight is wise.
         There are plenty more from where we came;
         But go find Mosby, start the game!"

Yet one there was who looked but glum;
    In middle age, a father he,
And this his first experience too:
"They shot at my heart when my hands were up—
      This fighting's crazy work, I see!"
         But noon is high; what next to do?
         The woods are mute, and Mosby is the foe.

"Save what we've got," the Major said;
    "Bad plan to make a scout too long;
The tide may turn, and drag them back,
And more beside. These rides I've been,
      And every time a mine was sprung.
         To rescue, mind, they won't be slack:
         Look out for Mosby's rifle crack."

"We'll welcome it! give crack for crack!
    Peril, old lad, is what I seek."
"Oh then, there's plenty to be had—
By all means on, and have our fill!"
      With that, grotesque, he writhed his neck,
         Showing a scar by buckshot made;
         "Kind Mosby's Christmas gift," he said.

"But, Colonel, my prisoners—let a guard
    Make sure of them, and lead to camp.
That done, we're free for a darkroom fight
If so you say." The other laughed;
      "Trust me, Major, nor throw a damp.
         But first to try a little sleight—
         Sure news of Mosby would suit me quite."

Herewith he turned—"Reb, have a dram?"
    Holding the surgeon's flask with a smile
To a young scapegrace from the glen.
"Oh yes!" he eagerly replied,
    "And thank you, Colonel, but—any guile?
      For if you think we'll blab—why, then
      You don't know Mosby or his men."

The leader's genial air relaxed.
    "Best give it up," a whisperer said.
"By heaven, I'll range their rebel den!"
"They'll treat you well," the captive cried;
    "They're all like us—handsome—well bred;
      In wood or town, with sword or pen,
      Polite is Mosby, bland his men."

"Where were you, lads, last night? Come, tell!"
    "We? At a wedding in the vale—
The bridegroom our comrade; by his side
Belisent, my cousin, oh so proud
    Of her young love with old wounds pale—
      A Virginian girl! God bless her pride—
      Of a crippled Mosby man the bride!"

"Four walls shall mend that saucy mood,
    And moping prisons tame him down,"
Said Captain Cloud. "God help that day,"
Cried Captain Morn, "and he so young.
    But hark, he sings—a madcap one!"
      "Oh, we multiply merrily in the May,
      The birds and Mosby's men, they say!"

While echoes ran, a wagon old,
    Under stout guard of Corporal Chew,
Came up; a lame horse, dingy white,
With clouted harness; ropes in hand,
    Cringed the humped driver, black in hue;
      By him (for Mosby's band a sight)
      A sister rebel sat, her veil held tight.

"I picked them up," the Corporal said,
    "Crunching their way over stick and root,
Through yonder wood. The man here, Cuff,
Says they are going to Leesburg town."
    The Colonel's eye took in the group;
        The veiled one's hand he spied—enough!
        Not Mosby's. Spite the gown's poor stuff,

Off went his hat: "Lady, fear not;
    We soldiers do what we deplore—
I must detain you till we march."
The stranger nodded. Nettled now,
    He grew politer than before:
        "'Tis Mosby's fault, this halt and search."
        The lady stiffened in her starch.

"My duty, madam, bids me now
    Ask what may seem a little rude.
Pardon—that veil, withdraw it, please
(Corporal, make every man fall back!);
    Pray, now, I do but what I should;
        Bethink you, 'tis in masks like these
        That Mosby haunts the villages."

Slowly the stranger drew her veil,
    And looked the soldier in the eye—
A glance of mingled foul and fair;
Sad patience in a proud disdain,
    And more than quietude. A sigh
        She heaved, as if all unaware,
        And far seemed Mosby from her care.

She came from Yewton Place, her home,
    So ravaged by the war's wild play—
Campings, and foragings, and fires—
That now she sought an aunt's abode.
    Her kinsmen? In Lee's army, they.
        The black? A servant, late her sire's.
        And Mosby? Vainly he inquires.

He gazed, and sad she met his eye:
   "In the wood yonder were you lost?"
No; at the forks they left the road
Because of hoof-prints (thick they were—
     Thick as the words in notes thrice crossed),
       And fearful, made that episode.
       In fear of Mosby? None she showed.

Her poor attire again he scanned:
   "Lady, once more; I grieve to jar
On all sweet usage, but must plead
To have what peeps there from your dress;
     That letter—'tis justly prize of war."
       She started—gave it—she must need.
       "'Tis not from Mosby? May I read?"

And straight such matter he perused
   That with the guide he went apart.
The hospital steward's turn began:
"Must squeeze this darkey; every tap
     Of knowledge we are bound to start."
       "Garry," she said, "tell all you can
       Of Colonel Mosby, that brave man."

"Dun know much, sare; and missis here
     Know less dan me. But dis I know—"
"Well, what?" "I dun know what I know."
"A knowing answer!" The humpback coughed,
     Rubbing his yellowish wool like tow.
       "Come—Mosby—tell!" "Oh dun look so!
       My gal nursed missis—let we go."

"Go where?" demanded Captain Cloud;
     "Back into bondage? Man, you're free!"
"Well, *let* we free!" The Captain's brow
Lowered; the Colonel came—had heard:
     "Pooh! pooh! his simple heart I see—
       A faithful servant. Lady—" (a bow)
       "Mosby's abroad; with us you'll go.

Guard, look to your prisoners; back to camp!
    The man in the grass, can he mount and away?
Why, how he groans!" "Bad inward bruise;
Might lug him along in the ambulance."
    "Coals to Newcastle! let him stay.
        Boots and saddles! Our pains we lose,
        Nor care I if Mosby hear the news!"

But word was sent to a house at hand,
    And a flask was left by the hurt one's side.
They seized in that same house a man,
Neutral by day, by night a foe—
    So charged his neighbor late, the guide.
        A grudge? Hate will do what it can;
        Along he went for a Mosby-man.

No secrets now; the bugle calls;
    The open road they take, nor shun
The hill; retrace the weary way.
But one there was who whispered low,
    "This is a feint; we'll back anon;
        Young hairbrains don't retreat, they say;
        A brush with Mosby is the play!"

They rode till eve. Then on a farm
    That lay along a hillside green,
Bivouacked. Fires were made, and then
Coffee was boiled; a cow was coaxed
    And killed, and savory roasts were seen;
        And under the lee of a cattle-pen
        The guard supped freely with Mosby's men.

The ball was bandied to and fro;
    Hits were given and hits were met:
"Chickamauga, Feds—take off your hat!"
"But the Fight in the Clouds repaid you, Rebs!"
    "Forgotten about Manassas yet?"
        Chatting and chaffing, and tit for tat,
        Mosby's clan with the troopers sat.

"Here comes the moon!" a captive cried;
   "A song, what say? Archie, my lad!"
Hailing the still one of the clan,
A boyish face with girlish hair,
   "Give us that thing poor Pansy made
     Last year." He brightened, and began;
     And this was the song of Mosby's man:

Spring is come; she shows her pass—
   Wild violets cool!
South of woods a small close grass—
   A vernal wool!
Leaves are a-bud on the sassafras—
   They'll soon be full:
Blessings on the friendly screen—
I'm for the South! says the leafage green.

Robins, fly, and take your fill
   Of out-of-doors;
Garden, orchard, meadow, hill,
   Barns and bowers;
Take your fill, and have your will—
   Virginia's yours!
But bluebirds,[15] *keep away, and fear*
The ambuscade in bushes here.

"A green song that," a sergeant said;
   "But where's poor Pansy? Gone, I fear."
"Aye, mustered out at Ashby's Gap."[16]
"I see; now for a live man's song;
   Ditty for ditty—prepare to cheer.
     My bluebirds, you can fling a cap!
     You barehead Mosby boys, why, clap!"

Nine Bluecoats went a-nutting
   Slyly in Tennessee;

---

15. bluebirds] Northern soldiers.
16. Ashby's Gap] Pansy was killed at the Battle of Ashby's Gap, July 19, 1864.

Not for chestnuts—better than that—
  Hush, you bumble bee!
    Nutting, nutting—
    All through the year there's nutting!

A tree they spied so yellow,
  Rustling in motion queer;
In they fired, and down they dropped—
  Butternuts,[17] *my dear!*
    Nutting, nutting—
    Who'll 'list to go a-nutting?

Ah, why should good fellows foemen be?
  And who would dream that foes they were,
Larking and singing so friendly then—
A family likeness in every face?
  But Captain Cloud made sour demur:
    "Guard, keep your prisoners *in* the pen,
    And let none talk with Mosby's men."

That captain was a valorous one
  (No irony, but honest truth),
Yet down from his brain cold drops distilled,
Making stalactites in his heart—
  A conscientious soul, forsooth;
    And with a formal hate was filled
    Of Mosby's band; and some he'd killed.

Meantime the lady rueful sat,
  Watching the flicker of a fire
Where the Colonel played the outdoor host
In brave old hall of ancient Night.
  But ever the dame grew shyer and shyer,
    Seeming with private grief engrossed—
    Grief far from Mosby, housed or lost.

---

17. Butternuts] soldiers from the South.

The ruddy embers showed her pale.
    The soldier did his best devoir:
"Some coffee? No? A cracker? One?"
Cared for her servant—sought to cheer:
      "I know, I know, a cruel war!
        But wait, even Mosby'll eat his bun;
        The Old Hearth—back to it anon!"

But cordial words no balm could bring;
    She sighed, and kept her inward chafe,
And seemed to hate the voice of glee,
Joyless and tearless. Soon he called
      An escort: "See this lady safe
        In yonder house. Madam, you're free.
        And now for Mosby. Guide—with me!"

("A night-ride, eh?") "Tighten your girths!
    But, buglers, not a note from you.
Fling more rails on the fires—a blaze!"
("Sergeant, a feint—I told you so—
    Toward Aldie again. Bivouac, adieu!")
      After the cheery flames they gaze,
      Then back for Mosby through the maze.

The moon looked through the trees, and tipped
    The scabbards with her elfin beam;
The leader backward cast his glance,
Proud of the cavalcade that came—
    A hundred horses, bay and cream:
      "Major, look how the lads advance—
      Mosby we'll have in the ambulance!"

"No doubt, no doubt; was that a hare?
    First catch, then cook; and cook him brown."
"Trust me to catch," the other cried;
"The lady's letter!—a dance, man, dance
    This night is given in Leesburg town!"
      "He'll be there too!" wheezed out the guide;
      "That Mosby loves a dance and ride!"

"The lady, ah, the lady's letter—
   A *lady*, then, is in the case,"
Muttered the Major. "Aye, her aunt
Writes her to come by Friday eve
   (Tonight), for people of the place,
     At Mosby's last fight jubilant,
      A party give, though table-cheer be scant."

The Major hemmed. "Then this night ride
   We owe to her? One lighted house
In a town else dark. The moths, begar,
Are not quite yet all dead!" "How? how?"
   "A mute, meek, mournful little mouse!
     Mosby has wiles which subtle are;
     But woman's wiles in wiles of war!"

"Tut, Major, by what craft or guile—"
   "Can't tell! but he'll be found in wait.
Softly we enter, say, the town—
Good! pickets post, and all so sure—
   When, crack! the rifles from every gate,
     The graybacks fire, dash up and down,
     Each alley unto Mosby known!"

"Now, Major, now, you take dark views
   Of a moonlight night." "Well, well, we'll see";
And smoked as if each whiff were gain.
The other mused, then sudden asked,
   "What would you do in grand decree?"
     "I'd beat, if I could, Lee's armies, then
     Send constables after Mosby's men."

"Aye, aye! You're odd." The moon sailed up;
   On through the shadowy land they went.
"Names must be made and printed be!"
Hummed the blithe Colonel. "Doc, your flask!
   Major, I drink to your good content.
     My pipe is out; enough for me!
     One's buttons shine; does Mosby see?

"But what comes here?" A man from the front
    Reported a tree athwart the road.
"Go round it, then; no time to bide;
All right, go on! Were one to stay
    For each distrust of a nervous mood,
        Long miles we'd make in this our ride
        Through Mosby-land. On, with the Guide!"

Then sportful to the surgeon turned:
    "Green sashes hardly serve by night!"
"Nor bullets nor bottles," the Major sighed,
"Against these moccasin-snakes—such foes
    As seldom come to solid fight:
        They kill and vanish; through grass they glide;
        Devil take Mosby!" His horse here shied.

"Hold, look! The tree, like a dragged balloon;
    A globe of leaves—some trickery here;
My nag is right—best now be shy."
A movement was made, a hubbub and snarl;
    Little was plain—they blindly steer.
        The Pleiads, as from ambush sly,
        Peep out: Mosby's men in the sky!

As restive they turn, how sore they feel,
    And cross, and sleepy, and full of spleen,
And curse the war. "Fools, North and South!"
Said one right out. "Oh for a bed!
    Oh now to drop in this woodland green!"
        He drops as the syllables leave his mouth;
        Mosby speaks from the undergrowth—

Speaks in a volley! Out jets the flame!
    Men fall from their saddles like plums from trees;
Horses take fright, reins tangle and bind;
"Steady—dismount—form—and into the wood!"
    They go but find what scarce can please:
        Their steeds have been tied in the field behind,
        And Mosby's men are off like the wind.

Sound the recall! Vain to pursue;
   The enemy scatters in wilds he knows,
To reunite in his own good time;
And, to follow, they need divide—
     To come lone and lost on crouching foes:
       Maple and hemlock, beech and lime
       Are Mosby's confederates, share the crime.

"Major," burst in a bugler small,
   "The fellow we left in Loudon grass,
Sir Slyboots with the inward bruise,
His voice I heard—the very same—
     Some watchword in the ambush pass;
       Aye, sir, we had him in his shoes,
       We caught him—Mosby!—but to lose."

"Go, go! These saddle dreamers! Well,
   And here's another. Cool, sir, cool!"
"Major, I saw them mount and sweep,
And one was humped, or I mistake,
     And in the scurry dropped his wool."
       "A wig? Go fetch it; the lads need sleep;
       They'll next see Mosby in a sheep!"

"Come, come, fall back; reform your ranks!
   All's jackstraws here! Where's Captain Morn?
We've parted like boats in a raging tide!
But stay—the Colonel—did he charge?
     And comes he there? 'Tis streak of dawn;
       Mosby is off, the woods are wide—
       Hist! there's a groan—this crazy ride!"

As they searched for the fallen, the dawn grew chill;
   They lay in the dew: "Ah, hurt much, Mink?
And—yes—the Colonel!" Dead! but so calm
That death seemed nothing, even death,
     The thing we deem everything heart can think;
       Amid wilding roses that shed their balm,
       Careless of Mosby he lay—in a charm!

The Major took him by the hand,
   Into the friendly clasp it bled
(A ball through heart and hand he rued):
"Good-bye!" and gazed with humid glance;
    Then in a hollow reverie said,
      "The weakest thing is lustihood;   *vigor*
      But Mosby—" and he checked his mood.

"Where the advance? Cut off, by heaven!
   Come, surgeon, how with your wounded there?"
"The ambulance will carry all."
"Well, get them in; we go to camp.
    Seven prisoners gone? for the rest have care."
      Then to himself, "This grief is gall;
      That Mosby! I'll cast a silver ball!"

"Ho!" turning—"Captain Cloud, you mind
   The place where the escort went—so shady?
Go search every closet low and high,
And barn, and bin, and hidden bower—
    Every covert; find that lady!
      And yet I may misjudge her—aye,
      Women (like Mosby) mystify.

"We'll see. Aye, Captain, go with speed!
   Surround and search; each living thing
Secure; that done, await us where
We last turned off. Stay! Fire the cage
    If the birds be flown." By the crossroad spring
      The bands rejoined; no words; the glare
      Told all. Had Mosby plotted there?

The weary troop that wended now—
   Hardly it seemed the same that pricked
Forth to the forest from the camp:
Foot-sore horses, jaded men;
    Every backbone felt as nicked,
      Each eye dim as a sickroom lamp,
      All faces stamped with Mosby's stamp.

In order due the Major rode,
   Chaplain and surgeon on either hand;
A riderless horse a negro led;
In a wagon the blanketed sleeper went;
     Then the ambulance with the bleeding band;
       And, an emptied oat bag on each head,
       Went Mosby's men, and marked the dead.

What gloomed them, what so cast them down
   And changed the cheer that late they took,
As double guarded now they rode
Between the files of moody men?
     Some sudden consciousness they brook,
       Or dread the sequel. That night's blood
       Disturbed even Mosby's brotherhood.

The flagging horses stumbled at roots,
   Floundered in mires, or clinked the stones;
No rider spake except aside;
But the wounded cramped in the ambulance,
     It was horror to hear their groans—
       Jerked along in the woodland ride,
       While Mosby's clan their reverie hide.

The hospital steward (even he),
   Who on the sleeper kept his glance,
Was changed; late bright-black beard and eye
Looked now hearse-black; his heavy heart,
     Like his fagged mare, no more could dance;
       His grape was now a raisin dry:
       'Tis Mosby's homily: *man must die.*

The amber sunset flushed the camp
   As on the hill their eyes they fed;
The pickets dumb looks at the wagon dart;
A handkerchief waves from the bannered tent—
     As white, alas! the face of the dead:
       Who shall the withering news impart?
       The bullet of Mosby goes through heart to heart!

They buried him where the lone ones lie
   (Lone sentries shot on midnight post)—
A greenwood graveyard hid from ken,
Where sweetfern flings an odor nigh,
     Yet held in fear for the gleaming ghost!
       Though the bride should see threescore and ten,
       She will dream of Mosby and his men.

Now halt the verse, and turn aside—
   The cypress falls athwart the way;
No joy remains for bard to sing;
And heaviest dole of all is this,
     That other hearts shall be as gay
       As hers that now no more shall spring:
       To Mosby-land the dirges cling.

Written c. summer 1864; published August 17, 1866

Emily Dickinson (1830–1886)

"So many brave—have died, this year—it dont seem lonely—as it did—before Battle begun," Dickinson told her Uncle Joel in the spring of 1862. At the end of the year, she would write: "Sorrow seems more general than it did, and not the estate of a few persons, since the war began; and if the anguishes of others helped one with one's own, now would be many medicines. I noticed that Robert Browning had made another poem, and was astonished—till I remembered that I, myself, in my smaller way, sang off charnel steps." Singing off charnel steps: no bad way of describing her career, for Dickinson wrote more than half her surviving poetry during the American Civil War, and in February and March 1864 published three poems in a newspaper called *Drum Beat*, established to buy medical supplies for the Union army, edited by an Amherst graduate known to the Dickinson family. She was friendly with combatants: Francis H. Dickinson, the first Amherst casualty of the war, killed in action at Ball's Bluff, Virginia, October 21, 1861; Colonel Thomas Wentworth Higginson, who commanded the 1st South Carolina Regiment in the Civil War (which comprised African American soldiers); and Frazar Stearns, son of the president of Amherst College. A few months before Stearns was killed in battle at New Berne, North Carolina, March 14, 1862 (a Union victory), she hoped "that ruddy face won't be brought home frozen." "Blazing in Gold" was one of those published in *Drum Beat*; the other five poems selected here refer to the war or were inspired by it. For more on Dickinson, see the introduction, p. 7.

Blazing in Gold and quenching in Purple[1]

Blazing in Gold and quenching in Purple
Leaping like Leopards to the Sky
Then at the feet of the old Horizon
Laying her Spotted Face to die
Stooping as low as the Otter's Window
Touching the Roof and tinting the Barn
Kissing her Bonnet to the Meadow
And the Juggler of Day is gone

Written early 1862, published February 29, 1864

It dont sound so terrible—quite—as it did—[1]

It dont sound so terrible—quite—as it did—
I run it over—"Dead," Brain—"Dead."
Put it in Latin—left of my school—
Seems it don't shriek so—under rule.

---

1. This is one of the poems Dickinson published in *Drum Bea*t, proceeds from which were used to fund medical supplies for the Union army. Scholars believe that, unlike some of her lifetime publications, the *Drum Beat* poems appeared with Dickinson's approval.

IT DONT SOUND SO TERRIBLE—QUITE—AS IT DID—
1. This poem may have been inspired by the death in action of Frazar Stearns, March 14, 1862.

Turn it, a little—full in the face
A Trouble looks bitterest—
Shift it—just—
Say "When Tomorrow comes this way—
I shall have waded down one Day."

I suppose it will interrupt me some
Till I get accustomed—but then the Tomb
Like other new Things—shows largest—then—
And smaller, by Habit—

It's shrewder then
Put the Thought in advance—a Year—
How like "a fit"—then—
Murder—wear!

Written autumn 1862, published 1945

The name—of it—is "Autumn"[1]

The name—of it—is "Autumn"—
The hue—of it—is Blood—
An artery—upon the Hill—
A Vein—along the Road—

Great Globules—in the Alleys—
And Oh, the Shower of Stain—
When Winds—upset the Basin—
And spill the Scarlet Rain—

It sprinkles Bonnets—far below—
It gathers ruddy Pools—

---

1. This poem may be inspired in part by news of the Battle of Antietam on September 17, 1862, which still ranks as the bloodiest in American history, with casualties of over 23,000 out of 100,000 combatants.

Then—eddies like a Rose—away—
Upon Vermillion Wheels—

Written late 1862, published September 8, 1862

It feels a shame to be Alive—

It feels a shame to be Alive—
When Men so brave—are dead—
One envies the Distinguished Dust—
Permitted—such a Head—

The Stone—that tells defending Whom
This Spartan put away
What little of Him we—possessed
In Pawn for Liberty—

The price is great—Sublimely paid—
Do we deserve—a Thing—
That lives—like Dollars—must be piled
Before we may obtain?

Are we that wait—sufficient worth—
That such Enormous Pearl
As life—dissolved be—for Us—
In Battle's—horrid Bowl?

It may be—a Renown to live—
I think the Men who die—
Those unsustained—Saviors—
Present Divinity—

Written c. spring 1863, published 1929

They dropped like Flakes—[1]

They dropped like Flakes—
They dropped like stars—
Like Petals from a Rose—
When suddenly across the June
A Wind with fingers—goes—

They perished in the seamless Grass—
No eye could find the place—
But God can summon every face
On his Repealless—List.

Written c. spring 1863, published 1891

When I was small, a Woman died—[1]

When I was small, a Woman died—
Today—her Only Boy
Went up from the Potomac—
His face all Victory

To look at her—How slowly
The Seasons must have turned
Till Bullets clipt an Angle
And He passed quickly round—

If pride shall be in Paradise—
Ourself cannot decide—
Of their imperial conduct—
No person testified—

1. In manuscript, this poem is entitled "The Battle-Field."
WHEN I WAS SMALL, A WOMAN DIED—
1. This poem may have been prompted by the death of Francis H. Dickinson, killed at the Battle of Ball's Bluff, Virginia, October 21, 1861.

But, proud in Apparition—
That Woman and her Boy
Pass back and forth, before my Brain
As even in the sky—

I'm confident, that Bravoes—
Perpetual break abroad
For Braveries, remote as this
In Yonder Maryland—

Written c. spring 1863, published 1890

Ambrose Bierce (1842–?1914)

No POET SAW as much active service on the front line of the American Civil War as Ambrose Bierce. He was eighteen when he enlisted in the Union army's 9th Indiana Regiment at the start of the conflict, and was not discharged until April 1865, when it ended. During that time he participated in some of its most bitter, bloody encounters, including those at Chickamauga, Lookout Mountain, and Missionary Ridge. He rescued a badly injured comrade at great physical risk at the Battle of Rich Mountain in July 1861, winning favorable newspaper comment, and the following year fought at the Battle of Shiloh, the bloodiest encounter of the Civil War up to that point. Even after incurring a serious head wound at the Battle of Kennesaw Mountain in June 1864 he returned to active service in September. The failure of the Reconstruction Era (1865–1877) and enactment of Jim Crow laws in the South, by which blacks were subjugated, left Bierce bitterly disappointed, leading him to regard the Civil War as a wasted effort. In that frame of mind he composed the war stories and poems on which his reputation now rests. In 1913 he accompanied Pancho Villa's army as it waged war against the Mexican government, and in the chaos of the revolution disappeared, never to be heard of again.

At a National Encampment

You're grayer than one would have thought you:
      The climate you have over there
In the East has apparently brought you
      Disorders affecting the hair
      Which (pardon me) seems a bit spare.

You'll not take offence at my giving
      Expression to notions like these.
You might have been stronger if living
      Out here in our sanative breeze.
      It's unhealthy here for disease.

No, I'm not so plump as a pullet,
      But that's the old wound, you see.
Remember my paunching a bullet?—
      And how that it didn't agree
      With—? Well, honest hardtack for me.   *hard bread*

Just pass me the wine—I've a helly
      And horrible kind of drouth!
When a fellow has that in his belly
      Which didn't go in at his mouth,
      He's hotter than all down south!

Great Scott! What a nasty day *that* was—
      When every galoot in our crack
Division who didn't lie flat was
      Dissuaded from further attack
      By the bullet's felicitous whack.

'Twas there that our major slept under
      Some cannon of ours on the crest,
Till they woke him by stilling their thunder,
      And he cursed them for breaking his rest,
      And died in the midst of his jest.

That night, it was late in November,
        The dead seemed uncommonly chill
To the touch; and a chap I remember
        Who took it exceedingly ill
        When I dragged myself over his bill.

Well, comrades, I'm off now—good morning.
        Your talk is as pleasant as pie,
But, pardon me, one word of warning:
        Speak little and seldom, say I.
        That's my way. God bless you. Good-bye.

Published July 31, 1886

The Hesitating Veteran

When I was young and full of faith
    And other fads that youngsters cherish,
A cry rose as of one that saith
    With unction, "Help me or I perish!"
'Twas heard in all the land, and men
    The sound were each to each repeating.
It made my heart beat faster then
    Than any heart can now be beating.

For the world is old and the world is gray,
    Grown prudent and, I guess, more witty.
She's cut her wisdom teeth, they say,
    And doesn't now go in for pity.
Besides, the melancholy cry
    Was that of one ('tis now conceded)
Whose plight no one beneath the sky
    Felt half so poignantly as he did.

Moreover, he was black. And yet
    That sentimental generation
With an austere compassion set

Its face and faith to the occasion.
Then there were hate and strife to spare
　　And various hard knocks a-plenty;
And I ('twas more than my true share,
　　I must confess) took five-and-twenty.

That all is over now; the reign
　　Of love and trade stills all dissensions,
And the clear heavens arch again
　　Above a land of peace and pensions.
The black chap—at the last we gave
　　Him everything that he had cried for,
Though many white chaps in the grave
　　'Twould puzzle to say what they died for.

I hope he's better off; I trust
　　That his society and his master's
Are worth the price we paid, and must
　　Continue paying, in disasters;
But sometimes doubts press thronging round
　　('Tis mostly when my hurts are aching)
If war for Union was a sound
　　And profitable undertaking.

'Tis said they mean to take away
　　The negro's vote for he's unlettered.
'Tis true he sits in darkness day
　　And night, as formerly, when fettered;
But pray observe: howe'er he vote
　　To whatsoever party turning,
He'll be with gentlemen of note
　　And wealth and consequence and learning.

With Hales and Morgans on each side,
　　How could a fool through lack of knowledge
Vote wrong? If learning is no guide
　　Why ought one to have been in college?
Oh son of day, oh son of night,
　　What are your preferences made of?

I know not which of you is right,
    Nor which to be the more afraid of.

The world is old and the world is bad,
    And creaks and grinds upon its axis;
And man's an ape and the gods are mad!
    There's nothing sure, not even our taxes.[1]
No mortal man can truth restore
    Or say where she is to be sought for.
I know what uniform I wore;
    Oh, that I knew which side I fought for!

Published 1903

A Year's Casualties

Slain as they lay by the secret, slow,
Pitiless hand of an unseen foe,
Two score thousand old soldiers have crossed
The river to join the loved and lost[1]
In the space of a year their spirits fled,
Silent and white, to the camp of the dead.

One after one, they fall asleep
And the pension agents awake to weep,
And orphaned statesmen are loud in their wail
As the souls flit by on the evening gale.
Oh, Father of Battles, pray give us release
From the horrors of peace, the horrors of peace!

Published 1903

---

1. not even our taxes] Bierce contradicts Benjamin Franklin: "The only thing certain in life is death and taxes."

A YEAR'S CASUALTIES

1. This alludes to the dying words of Confederate General "Stonewall" Jackson, having been mortally wounded by his own men at the Battle of Chancellorsville: "Let us cross the river and rest under the shade of the trees."

The Passing Show

I

I know not if it was a dream. I viewed
A city where the restless multitude,
    Between the eastern and the western deep
Had reared gigantic fabrics, strong and rude.

Colossal palaces crowned every height;
Towers from valleys climbed into the light;
    O'er dwellings at their feet, great golden domes
Hung in the blue, barbarically bright.

But now, new glimmering to east, the day
Touched the black masses with a grace of gray,
    Dim spires of temples to the nation's God
Studding high spaces of the wide survey.

Well did the roofs their solemn secret keep
Of life and death stayed by the truce of sleep,
    Yet whispered of an hour when sleepers wake,
The fool to hope afresh, the wise to weep.

The gardens greened upon the builded hills
Above the tethered thunders of the mills
    With sleeping wheels unstirred to service yet
By the tamed torrents and the quickened rills.

A hewn acclivity, reprieved a space,
Looked on the builder's blocks about his base
    And bared his wounded breast in sign to say
"Strike! 'tis my destiny to lodge your race.

'Twas but a breath ago the mammoth browsed
Upon my slopes, and in my caves I housed
    Your shaggy fathers in their nakedness,
While on their foemen's offal they caroused."

Ships from afar afforested the bay.
Within their huge and chambered bodies lay
    The wealth of continents; and merrily sailed
The hardy argosies to far Cathay.

Beside the city of the living spread
(Strange fellowship!) the city of the dead;
    And much I wondered what its humble folk,
To see how bravely they were housed, had said.

Noting how firm their habitations stood,
Broad-based and free of perishable wood,
    How deep in granite and how high in brass
The names were wrought of eminent and good,

I said: "When gold or power is their aim,
The smile of beauty or the wage of shame,
    Men dwell in cities; to this place they fare
When they would conquer an abiding fame."

From the red east the sun—a solemn rite—
Crowned with a flame the cross upon a height
    Above the dead; and then, with all his strength,
Struck the great city all aroar with light!

II

I know not if it was a dream. I came
Unto a land where something seemed the same
    That I had known as 'twere but yesterday,
But what it was I could not rightly name.

It was a strange and melancholy land,
Silent and desolate. On either hand
    Lay waters of a sea that seemed as dead,
And dead above it seemed the hills to stand.

Grayed all with age, those lonely hills—ah me!
How worn and weary they appeared to be.

Between their feet, long dusty fissures clove
The plain in aimless windings to the sea.

One hill there was which, parted from the rest,
Stood where the eastern water curved a-west.
    Silent and passionless it stood. I thought
I saw a scar upon its giant breast.

The sun with sullen and portentous gleam
Hung like a menace on the sea's extreme;
    Nor the dead waters, nor the far, bleak bars
Of cloud were conscious of his failing beam.

It was a dismal and a dreadful sight,
That desert in its cold, uncanny light;
    No soul but I alone to mark the fear
And imminence of everlasting night!

All presages and prophecies of doom
Glimmered and babbled in the ghastly gloom,
    And in the midst of that accursèd scene
A wolf sat howling on a broken tomb.

Published 1903

John Boyle O'Reilly (1844–1890)

AS A BOY growing up in County Meath, O'Reilly must have heard tales of Robert Emmet's 1803 uprising, for his mother was closely related to John Allen (d. 1855), who took part in it. He became a printer's apprentice at the age of eleven, moving to Preston in England to complete his training with *The Guardian* four years later. In 1863 O'Reilly joined the Irish Republican Brotherhood or Fenian movement, the most radical of the groups committed to violent overthrow of British rule in Ireland. He was instructed to join the

10th Hussars (Prince of Wales Regiment), stationed at Dundalk, where he converted eighty out of the hundred Irishmen in the unit to the nationalist cause. His plan was to organize a mutiny but before that could happen the British Police raided the offices of the *Irish People*, a Fenian newspaper, and found a list of IRB members including O'Reilly. His plot exposed, he was court-martialed and condemned to death on July 9, 1866, a sentence commuted to twenty years' penal servitude on account of his youth. After thirteen months at various prisons he was transported to Western Australia on the last of the convict ships; in prison at Fremantle he began an affair with the Warden's daughter before escaping and, after weeks on the run, boarded an American-bound whaler, the *Gazelle*. He arrived in Philadelphia on November 23, 1869, and settled in Boston, where he became a journalist, editor and part owner of the *Pilot*. But he was no stay-at-home: he continued to speak and lobby on behalf of Irish causes, and was involved in a daring mission to rescue six Irish political prisoners from the Fremantle prison from which he had escaped, landing them in New York in August 1876. During the 1880s, when people of color were more persecuted than ever, he agitated on their behalf, envisaging a time when "the races shall vote and work and study and pray side by side." Appalled by segregation and lynchings, he declared at a protest meeting at Faneuil Hall, "If ever the colored question comes up again as long as I live, I will be counted in with the black men." O'Reilly died from an overdose of chloral, which he took as a cure for insomnia, on August 10, 1890. He remains underrated as a poet, capable of articulating within a short, tightly constructed lyric everything he had learned about injustice and cruelty.

There is blood on the earth

There is blood on the face of the earth—
    It reeks through the years, and is red:
Where Truth was slaughtered at birth
    And the veins of Liberty bled.

Lo! vain is the hand that tries
    To cover the crimson stain:
It spreads like a plague, and cries
    Like a soul in writhing pain.

It wasteth the planet's flesh;
    It calleth on breasts of stone:
God holdeth His wrath in a leash
    Till the hearts of men atone.

Blind like the creatures of time;
    Cursed like all the race,
They answer, "The blood and crime
    Belong to a sect and place!"

What are these things to Heaven—
    Races or places of men?
The world through one Christ was forgiven,
    Nor question of races then.

The wrong of today shall be rued
    In a thousand coming years;
The debt must be paid in blood,
    The interest in tears.

Shall none stand up for right
    Whom the evil passes by?
But God has the globe in sight,
    And hearkens the weak ones' cry.

Wherever a principle dies—
    Nay, principles never die!
But wherever a ruler lies,
    And a people share the lie;

Where right is crushed by force,
    And manhood is stricken dead,
There dwelleth the ancient curse,
    And the blood on the earth is red!

Published 1882

The Cry of the Dreamer

I am tired of planning and toiling
    In the crowded hives of men;
Heart-weary of building and spoiling,
    And spoiling and building again.
And I long for the dear old river
    Where I dreamed my youth away;
For a dreamer lives forever,
    And a toiler dies in a day.

I am sick of the showy seeming
    Of a life that is half a lie;
Of the faces lined with scheming
    In the throng that hurries by.
From the sleepless thoughts' endeavor,
    I would go where the children play;
For a dreamer lives forever,
    And a thinker dies in a day.

I can feel no pride, but pity
    For the burdens the rich endure;
There is nothing sweet in the city
    But the patient lives of the poor.
Oh, the little hands too skillful,
    And the child-mind choked with weeds;
The daughter's heart grown wilful
    And the father's heart that bleeds!

No, no! from the street's rude bustle,
    From trophies of mart and stage,
I would fly to the woods' low rustle
    And the meadows' kindly page.
Let me dream as of old by the river,
    And be loved for the dream alway;
For a dreamer lives forever,
    And a toiler dies in a day.

Published May 8, 1886

Oscar Wilde (1854–1900)

"ALL TRIALS ARE trials for one's life," Wilde once remarked: his life was effectively destroyed by the prosecution that ended his career as a dramatist in 1895. Found guilty of "gross indecency," he was given the maximum sentence of two years' hard labor, which entailed imprisonment at Pentonville, Wandsworth, and Reading. At Pentonville he spent six hours a day on the treadmill, turned a "crank" that ground corn or pumped water, or picked oakum, which involved separating fibers of a tarry rope. Not allowed to speak or look at each other, prisoners were locked in their cells alone, for up to sixteen hours a day. The diet of thin cocoa, stale bread, and gruel gave him chronic diarrhea. When his wife visited, she hardly recognized him. He was a "wreck," thanks to a combination of fatigue, malnutrition, and illness. All in all, his prison experience was physically and psychologically destructive, and the ultimate cause of his premature death in 1900. (A fall in the prison chapel at Wandsworth brought on the middle-ear disease that would kill him five years later.) At Reading, he was installed in the third cell on the third floor of block C—prisoner C.3.3. One day he saw the hangman preparing to execute a fellow prisoner, Charles Thomas Wooldridge (1866–1897), former trooper of the Royal Horse Guards, who had murdered his twenty-three-year-old wife in a fit of jealous rage, slitting her throat three times over with a razor. Wilde knew Wooldridge and never forgot him. "The man's face will haunt me till I die," he said, for he regarded the punishment as an injustice. This was the inspiration for *The Ballad of Reading Gaol*, composed during the six months following his release, and published in February 1898. It proposes that all men kill (or betray) the thing they love, only to be punished by others guilty of the same crime. It was his greatest poem, and last major work.

The Ballad of Reading Gaol

IN MEMORIAM

C.T.W.

SOMETIME TROOPER OF THE ROYAL HORSE GUARDS

OBIIT H.M. PRISON, READING, BERKSHIRE

JULY 7, 1896

I

He did not wear his scarlet coat
    For blood and wine are red,
And blood and wine were on his hands
    When they found him with the dead—
The poor dead woman whom he loved
    And murdered in her bed.

He walked among the Trial Men[1]
    In a suit of shabby gray;
A cricket cap was on his head
    And his step seemed light and gay;
But I never saw a man who looked
    So wistfully at the day.

I never saw a man who looked
    With such a wistful eye
Upon that little tent of blue
    Which prisoners call the sky
And at every drifting cloud that went
    With sails of silver by.

I walked with other souls in pain
    Within another ring,
And was wondering if the man had done
    A great or little thing,
When a voice behind me whispered low,
    "That fellow's got to swing."

---

1. Trial Men] prisoners given leave to appeal after sentencing.

Dear Christ! the very prison walls
    Suddenly seemed to reel,
And the sky above my head became
    Like a cask of scorching steel,
And though I was a soul in pain,
    My pain I could not feel.

I only knew what hunted thought
    Quickened his step, and why
He looked upon the garish day
    With such a wistful eye:
The man had killed the thing he loved
    And so he had to die.

        *

Yet each man kills the thing he loves
    By each let this be heard;
Some do it with a bitter look,
    Some with a flattering word;
The coward does it with a kiss,
    The brave man with a sword!

Some kill their love when they are young
    And some when they are old;
Some strangle with the hands of lust,
    Some with the hands of gold;
The kindest use a knife because
    The dead so soon grow cold.

Some love too little, some too long,
    Some sell and others buy;
Some do the deed with many tears
    And some without a sigh:
For each man kills the thing he loves,
    Yet each man does not die.

He does not die a death of shame
    On a day of dark disgrace

Nor have a noose about his neck,
  Nor a cloth upon his face,
Nor drop feet-foremost through the floor
  Into an empty space.

  *

He does not sit with silent men
  Who watch him night and day;
Who watch him when he tries to weep
  And when he tries to pray;
Who watch him lest himself should rob
  The prison of its prey.

He does not wake at dawn to see
  Dread figures throng his room—
The shivering chaplain robed in white,
  The sheriff stern with gloom,
And the governor all in shiny black
  With the yellow face of doom.

He does not rise in piteous haste
  To put on convict clothes,
While some coarse-mouthed doctor gloats and notes
  Each new and nerve-twitched pose,
Fingering a watch whose little ticks
  Are like horrible hammer-blows.

He does not know that sickening thirst
  That sands one's throat before
The hangman with his gardener's gloves
  Slips through the padded door
And binds one with three leathern thongs
  That the throat may thirst no more.

He does not bend his head to hear
  The Burial Office read,
Nor while the terror of his soul
  Tells him he is not dead,

Cross his own coffin as he moves
    Into the hideous shed.

He does not stare upon the air
    Through a little roof of glass;
He does not pray with lips of clay
    For his agony to pass,
Nor feel upon his shuddering cheek
    The kiss of Caiaphas.[2]

II

Six weeks the guardsman walked the yard
    In the suit of shabby gray;
His cricket cap was on his head
    And his step seemed light and gay,
But I never saw a man who looked
    So wistfully at the day.

I never saw a man who looked
    With such a wistful eye
Upon that little tent of blue
    Which prisoners call the sky
And at every wandering cloud that trailed
    Its raveled fleeces by.

He did not wring his hands as do
    Those witless men who dare
To try to rear the changeling Hope
    In the cave of black Despair;
He only looked upon the sun
    And drank the morning air.

He did not wring his hands nor weep,
    Nor did he peak or pine,
But he drank the air as though it held

---

2. Caiaphas, high priest of the Jews, presided at Jesus's trial, and agreed to pay Judas thirty pieces of silver when he kissed Christ.

Some healthful anodyne;
With open mouth he drank the sun
    As though it had been wine!

And I and all the souls in pain
    Who tramped the other ring
Forgot if we ourselves had done
    A great or little thing,
And watched with gaze of dull amaze
    The man who had to swing.

And strange it was to see him pass
    With a step so light and gay,
And strange it was to see him look
    So wistfully at the day,
And strange it was to think that he
    Had such a debt to pay.

                *

For oak and elm have pleasant leaves
    That in the springtime shoot,
But grim to see is the gallows-tree
    With its adder-bitten root,
And green or dry, a man must die
    Before it bears its fruit!

The loftiest place is that seat of grace
    For which all worldlings try,
But who would stand in hempen band
    Upon a scaffold high
And through a murderer's collar take
    His last look at the sky?

It is sweet to dance to violins
    When love and life are fair;
To dance to flutes, to dance to lutes
    Is delicate and rare;
But it is not sweet with nimble feet
    To dance upon the air!

So with curious eyes and sick surmise
    We watched him day by day,
And wondered if each one of us
    Would end the self-same way,
For none can tell to what red hell
    His sightless soul may stray.

At last the dead man walked no more
    Among the Trial Men,
And I knew that he was standing up
    In the black dock's dreadful pen,
And that never would I see his face
    In God's sweet world again.

Like two doomed ships that pass in storm
    We had crossed each other's way;
But we made no sign, we said no word,
    We had no word to say;
For we did not meet in the holy night
    But in the shameful day.

A prison wall was round us both,
    Two outcast men we were:
The world had thrust us from its heart
    And God from out His care;
And the iron gin that waits for sin   *trap*
    Had caught us in its snare.

III

In Debtors' Yard the stones are hard
    And the dripping wall is high
So it was there he took the air
    Beneath the leaden sky,
And by each side a warder walked
    For fear the man might die.

Or else he sat with those who watched
    His anguish night and day,
Who watched him when he rose to weep

And when he crouched to pray,
Who watched him lest himself should rob
    Their scaffold of its prey.

The governor was strong upon
    The Regulations Act;[3]
The doctor said that death was but
    A scientific fact;
And twice a day the chaplain called
    And left a little tract.

And twice a day he smoked his pipe
    And drank his quart of beer;
His soul was resolute and held
    No hiding place for fear;
He often said that he was glad
    The hangman's hands were near.

But why he said so strange a thing
    No warder dared to ask;
For he to whom a watcher's doom
    Is given as his task
Must set a lock upon his lips
    And make his face a mask.

Or else he might be moved and try
    To comfort or console;
And what should human pity do,
    Pent up in Murderer's Hold?
What work of grace in such a place
    Could help a brother's soul?

            *

With slouch and swing around the ring
    We trod the Fool's Parade!
We did not care, we knew we were

---

3. The Regulations Act] These determined how condemned prisoners were to be treated.

The Devil's Own Brigade;
And shaven head and feet of lead
   Make a merry masquerade.

We tore the tarry rope to shreds
   With blunt and bleeding nails;
We rubbed the doors and scrubbed the floors,
   And cleaned the shining rails;
And rank by rank, we soaped the plank
   And clattered with the pails.

We sewed the sacks, we broke the stones,
   We turned the dusty drill;
We banged the tins and bawled the hymns
   And sweated on the mill;
But in the heart of every man
   Terror was lying still—

So still it lay that every day
   Crawled like a weed-clogged wave:
And we forgot the bitter lot
   That waits for fool and knave,
Till once, as we tramped in from work
   We passed an open grave.

With yawning mouth the yellow hole
   Gaped for a living thing;
The very mud cried out for blood
   To the thirsty asphalt ring;
And we knew that ere one dawn grew fair
   Some prisoner had to swing.

Right in we went, with soul intent
   On death and dread and doom:
The hangman with his little bag
   Went shuffling through the gloom;
And I trembled as I groped my way
   Into my numbered tomb.

*

That night the empty corridors
   Were full of forms of fear,
And up and down the iron town
   Stole feet we could not hear,
And through the bars that hide the stars
   White faces seemed to peer.

He lay as one who lies and dreams
   In a pleasant meadowland;
The watchers watched him as he slept,
   And could not understand
How one could sleep so sweet a sleep
   With a hangman close at hand.

But there is no sleep when men must weep
   Who never yet have wept:
So we (the fool, the fraud, the knave)
   That endless vigil kept,
And through each brain on hands of pain
   Another's terror crept.

Alas, it is a fearful thing
   To feel another's guilt!
For right within, the sword of sin
   Pierced to its poisoned hilt,
And as molten lead were the tears we shed
   For the blood we had not spilt.

The warders with their shoes of felt
   Crept by each padlocked door,
And peeped and saw, with eyes of awe,
   Gray figures on the floor,
And wondered why men knelt to pray
   Who never prayed before.

All through the night we knelt and prayed,
    Mad mourners of a corse!   *corpse*
The troubled plumes of midnight were
    The plumes upon a hearse;
And bitter wine upon a sponge
    Was the savour of remorse.

      *

The gray cock crew, the red cock crew,
    But never came the day:
And crooked shapes of Terror crouched
    In the corners where we lay:
And each evil sprite that walks by night
    Before us seemed to play.

They glided past, they glided fast
    Like travelers through a mist;
They mocked the moon in a rigadoon   *lively dance*
    Of delicate turn and twist,
And with formal pace and loathsome grace
    The phantoms kept their tryst.

With mop and mow, we saw them go,
    Slim shadows hand in hand;
About, about, in ghostly rout
    They trod a saraband;   *slow Spanish dance*
And the damned grotesques made arabesques
    Like the wind upon the sand!

With the pirouettes of marionettes
    They tripped on pointed tread;
But with flutes of fear they filled the ear
    As their grisly masque they led,
And loud they sang, and long they sang,
    For they sang to wake the dead.

"Oho!" they cried, "The world is wide,
    But fettered limbs go lame!

And once or twice to throw the dice
    Is a gentlemanly game,
But he does not win who plays with Sin
    In the secret House of Shame."

No things of air these antics were
    That frolicked with such glee:
To men whose lives were held in gyves   *leg irons*
    And whose feet might not go free—
Ah, wounds of Christ, they were living things
    Most terrible to see!

Around, around, they waltzed and wound,
    Some wheeled in smirking pairs;
With the mincing step of a demirep[4]
    Some sidled up the stairs;
And with subtle sneer and fawning leer
    Each helped us at our prayers.

The morning wind began to moan
    But still the night went on;
Through its giant loom the web of gloom
    Crept till each thread was spun;
And as we prayed, we grew afraid
    Of the justice of the sun.

The moaning wind went wandering round
    The weeping prison wall,
Till like a wheel of turning steel
    We felt the minutes crawl:
Oh moaning wind, what had we done
    To have such a seneschal?   *steward*

At last I saw the shadowed bars
    Like a lattice wrought in lead
Move right across the whitewashed wall

---

4. demirep] woman of dubious repute.

That faced my three-plank bed,
And I knew that somewhere in the world
 God's dreadful dawn was red.

At six o'clock we cleaned our cells,
 At seven all was still,
But the sough[5] and swing of a mighty wing
 The prison seemed to fill,
For the Lord of Death with icy breath
 Had entered in to kill.

He did not pass in purple pomp,
 Nor ride a moon-white steed;
Three yards of cord and a sliding board
 Are all the gallows' need:
So with rope of shame the herald came
 To do the secret deed.

We were as men who through a fen
 Of filthy darkness grope:
We did not dare to breathe a prayer
 Or to give our anguish scope:
Something was dead in each of us,
 And what was dead was hope.

For man's grim justice goes its way
 And will not swerve aside;
It slays the weak, it slays the strong,
 It has a deadly stride;
With iron heel it slays the strong,
 The monstrous parricide![6]

We waited for the stroke of eight,
 Each tongue was thick with thirst,
For the stroke of eight is the stroke of Fate

---

5. sough] rushing sound.
6. parricide] a force that kills a fellow human being.

That makes a man accursed,
    And Fate will use a running noose
        For the best man and the worst.

We had no other thing to do
    Save to wait for the sign to come,
So like things of stone in a valley lone,
    Quiet we sat and dumb;
But each man's heart beat thick and quick
    Like a madman on a drum!

With sudden shock the prison clock
    Smote on the shivering air,
And from all the gaol rose up a wail
    Of impotent despair
Like the sound that frightened marshes hear
    From some leper in his lair.

And as one sees most dreadful things
    In the crystal of a dream,
We saw the greasy hempen rope
    Hooked to the blackened beam,
And heard the prayer the hangman's snare
    Strangled into a scream.

And all the woe that moved him so
    That he gave that bitter cry,
And the wild regrets, and the bloody sweats
    None knew so well as I:
For he who lives more lives than one
    More deaths than one must die.

IV
There is no chapel on the day
    On which they hang a man;
The chaplain's heart is far too sick,
    Or his face is far too wan,

Or there is that written in his eyes
    Which none should look upon.

So they kept us close till nigh on noon
    And then they rang the bell,
And the warders with their jingling keys
    Opened each listening cell,
And down the iron stair we tramped,
    Each from his separate hell.

Out into God's sweet air we went
    But not in wonted way,
For this man's face was white with fear
    And that man's face was gray,
And I never saw sad men who looked
    So wistfully at the day.

I never saw sad men who looked
    With such a wistful eye
Upon that little tent of blue
    We prisoners called the sky,
And at every careless cloud that passed
    In happy freedom by.

But there were those amongst us all
    Who walked with downcast head,
And knew that, had each got his due,
    They should have died instead:
He had but killed a thing that lived,
    Whilst they had killed the dead.

For he who sins a second time
    Wakes a dead soul to pain,
And draws it from its spotted shroud
    And makes it bleed again,
And makes it bleed great gouts of blood
    And makes it bleed in vain!

*

Like ape or clown, in monstrous garb
　　With crooked arrows starred,
Silently we went round and round
　　The slippery asphalt yard;
Silently we went round and round
　　And no man spoke a word.

Silently we went round and round,
　　And through each hollow mind
The memory of dreadful things
　　Rushed like a dreadful wind,
And Horror stalked before each man,
　　And Terror crept behind.

*

The warders strutted up and down
　　And watched their herd of brutes,
Their uniforms were spick and span
　　And they wore their Sunday suits,
But we knew the work they had been at
　　By the quicklime on their boots.

For where a grave had opened wide,
　　There was no grave at all:
Only a stretch of mud and sand
　　By the hideous prison wall,
And a little heap of burning lime,
　　That the man should have his pall.[7]

For he has a pall, this wretched man,
　　Such as few men can claim:
Deep down below a prison yard,
　　Naked for greater shame,

---

7. pall] a pall is usually a fine cloth spread over a coffin; for this man, the only pall he will
get is the quicklime that has been used to dissolve his corpse.

He lies, with fetters on each foot,
 Wrapt in a sheet of flame!

And all the while the burning lime
 Eats flesh and bone away,
It eats the brittle bone by night
 And the soft flesh by day,
It eats the flesh and bone by turns,
 But it eats the heart alway.

   *

For three long years they will not sow
 Or root or seedling there;
For three long years the unblessed spot
 Will sterile be and bare,
And look upon the wondering sky
 With unreproachful stare.

They think a murderer's heart would taint
 Each simple seed they sow.
It is not true! God's kindly earth
 Is kindlier than men know,
And the red rose would but blow more red,
 The white rose whiter blow.

Out of his mouth a red, red rose!
 Out of his heart a white!
For who can say by what strange way
 Christ brings His will to light,
Since the barren staff the pilgrim bore
 Bloomed in the great Pope's sight?[8]

But neither milk-white rose nor red
 May bloom in prison air;

---

8. the barren staff . . . great Pope's sight] Wilde refers to the legend of Tannhäuser, a knight who sought absolution for his sins from Pope Urban IV, who told him that forgiveness was as impossible as for his papal staff to sprout blossoms; three days later that was exactly what happened.

The shard, the pebble and the flint
    Are what they give us there:
For flowers have been known to heal
    A common man's despair.

So never will wine-red rose or white
    Petal by petal fall
On that stretch of mud and sand that lies
    By the hideous prison wall,
To tell the men who tramp the yard
    That God's Son died for all.

*

Yet though the hideous prison wall
    Still hems him round and round,
And a spirit may not walk by night
    That is with fetters bound,
And a spirit may but weep that lies
    In such unholy ground,

He is at peace, this wretched man,
    At peace—or will be soon;
There is no thing to make him mad,
    Nor does Terror walk at noon,
For the lampless earth in which he lies
    Has neither sun nor moon.

They hanged him as a beast is hanged;
    They did not even toll
A requiem that might have brought
    Rest to his startled soul,
But hurriedly they took him out
    And hid him in a hole.

The warders stripped him of his clothes
    And gave him to the flies;
They mocked the swollen purple throat
    And the stark and staring eyes,

And with laughter loud they heaped the shroud
   In which the convict lies.

The chaplain would not kneel to pray
   By his dishonored grave,
Nor mark it with that blessed cross
   That Christ for sinners gave,
Because the man was one of those
   Whom Christ came down to save.

Yet all is well, he has but passed
   To life's appointed bourne,   *destination*
And alien tears will fill for him
   Pity's long-broken urn,
For his mourners will be outcast men,
   And outcasts always mourn.

v

I know not whether laws be right
   Or whether laws be wrong;
All that we know who lie in gaol
   Is that the wall is strong;
And that each day is like a year,
   A year whose days are long.

But this I know, that every law
   That men have made for man,
Since first man took his brother's life
   And the sad world began,
But straws the wheat and saves the chaff
   With a most evil fan.

This too I know (and wise it were
   If each could know the same):
That every prison that men build
   Is built with bricks of shame,
And bound with bars lest Christ should see
   How men their brothers maim.

With bars they blur the gracious moon
    And blind the goodly sun,
And they do well to hide their hell,
    For in it things are done
That Son of God nor son of man
    Ever should look upon!

     *

The vilest deeds like poison weeds
    Bloom well in prison air;
It is only what is good in man
    That wastes and withers there:
Pale Anguish keeps the heavy gate,
    And the warder is Despair.

For they starve the little frightened child
    Till it weeps both night and day,
And they scourge the weak and flog the fool,
    And gibe the old and gray,   *mock*
And some grow mad, and all grow bad,
    And none a word may say.

Each narrow cell in which we dwell
    Is a foul and dark latrine,
And the fetid breath of living death
    Chokes up each grated screen,
And all but lust is turned to dust
    In humanity's machine.

The brackish water that we drink
    Creeps with a loathsome slime,
And the bitter bread they weigh in scales
    Is full of chalk and lime,
And Sleep will not lie down, but walks
    Wild-eyed, and cries to Time.

     *

But though lean Hunger and green Thirst
    Like asp with adder fight,

We have little care of prison fare,
    For what chills and kills outright
Is that every stone one lifts by day
    Becomes one's heart by night.

With midnight always in one's heart,
    And twilight in one's cell,
We turn the crank or tear the rope,
    Each in his separate hell,
And the silence is more awful far
    Than the sound of a brazen bell.

And never a human voice comes near
    To speak a gentle word,
And the eye that watches through the door
    Is pitiless and hard,
And by all forgot, we rot and rot,
    With soul and body marred.

And thus we rust life's iron chain
    Degraded and alone;
And some men curse, and some men weep,
    And some men make no moan;
But God's eternal laws are kind
    And break the heart of stone.

    *

And every human heart that breaks
    In prison cell or yard
Is as that broken box that gave
    Its treasure to the Lord,
And filled the unclean leper's house
    With the scent of costliest nard.[9]

---

9. Wilde refers to an event in the life of Jesus, described in the Gospels: "And being in Bethany in the house of Simon the leper, as he sat at meat, there came a woman having an alabaster box of ointment of spikenard very precious; and she brake the box, and poured it on his head" (Mark 14:3).

Ah, happy they whose hearts can break
    And peace of pardon win!
How else may man make straight his plan
    And cleanse his soul from sin?
How else but through a broken heart
    May Lord Christ enter in?

      *

And he of the swollen purple throat
    And the stark and staring eyes
Waits for the holy hands that took
    The thief to Paradise;
And a broken and a contrite heart
    The Lord will not despise.

The man in red who reads the law[10]
    Gave him three weeks of life,
Three little weeks in which to heal
    His soul of his soul's strife,
And cleanse from every blot of blood
    The hand that held the knife.

And with tears of blood he cleansed the hand,
    The hand that held the steel,
For only blood can wipe out blood,
    And only tears can heal;
And the crimson stain that was of Cain
    Became Christ's snow-white seal.

VI

In Reading Gaol by Reading town
    There is a pit of shame,
And in it lies a wretched man
    Eaten by teeth of flame:
In a burning winding sheet he lies,
    And his grave has got no name.

---

10. The man in red who reads the law] High court judges in England wore scarlet robes with fur collars.

And there, till Christ call forth the dead,
    In silence let him lie;
No need to waste the foolish tear
    Or heave the windy sigh;
The man had killed the thing he loved
    And so he had to die.

And all men kill the thing they love,
    By all let this be heard,
Some do it with a bitter look,
    Some with a flattering word,
The coward does it with a kiss,
    The brave man with a sword!

Written July 1897; published February 9, 1898

VI

The Age of World War

THE ARRIVAL OF the twentieth century was accompanied by hope. Technological advances fueled the utopian belief that the pains and sufferings of life could be ameliorated and even transcended: two world wars and the threat of nuclear annihilation put paid to that. More than fifteen million died during the course of the First World War; sixty-six million in the second—a figure that includes those killed in the Shoah (Holocaust) and the bombings of Hiroshima and Nagasaki.

The Spanish Civil War (1936–1939) was caused by an alliance of right-wing generals who refused to serve under the Second Spanish Republic of President Manuel Azaña; it was, in effect, the beginning of the war against fascism, which continues into the present. Their coup was only partially successful, precipitating a drawn-out conflict in which the generals were backed by Nazi Germany, Mussolini's Italy, and Portugal. The republic was assisted by citizens of other European countries who came to its aid, including Sylvia Townsend Warner and John Cornford—but hindered by the refusal of the British and French governments to intervene. It was not helped, either, by hostilities between the Spanish Communist Party (PCE) and the *Partido Obrero de Unificación Marxista* (POUM), which opposed Stalin and was accused of Trotskyite tendencies.

Modern readers may experience bafflement at the powerfully motivating force Communism provided for so many intelligent people. With hindsight, we recognize certain things not evident to them: that Communism was to fail, and (worse still) become the name in which countless atrocities would be committed. All the same, the Communist Party did particularly well in France, Finland, and Italy during the early part of the twentieth century, and for many elsewhere in both Europe and America it offered a political formula for the just society, at least for a time. The fast-growing Soviet economy, with its Five-Year Plans and full employment, made Russia seem like a model for the rest of the world, especially at a time of worldwide economic depression. Fascism became a greater threat after Hitler came to power in the elections of March 1933 and began his systematic takeover of state governments in Germany. Indeed, the establishment of Oranienburg concentration camp in Berlin in 1933, where the Nazis imprisoned Communists and social democrats, was emblematic of everything to which Cornford and Warner were opposed. There was no irony in Cornford's hopeful declaration, at the conclusion of "Full Moon at Tierz": "Raise the red flag triumphantly / For Communism and for liberty" (p. 588). Even during the period 1936 to 1938, when Stalin was conducting show trials and mass purges, new recruits flocked to the Communist Party in Europe and America, believing it the only ideological answer to fascism.

The Second World War replayed the Spanish conflict on a global scale; in its course, Nazi Germany expanded its use of concentration camps, turning itself into a genocidal state. Of the 9 million Jews resident in Europe before the war, two-thirds were exterminated in the Holocaust (including over a million children), while the persecution of other "undesirables" (blacks, homosexuals, Gypsies, and political opponents) brought the death toll to between 11 and seventeen million. Germany pursued its policy in what are now thirty-five separate countries; had it been victorious, it would have been extended to Great Britain, Ireland, Switzerland, Portugal, and Spain.

The war came to an end in the Far East only when, other measures having failed, the allies detonated nuclear bombs over the Japanese cities of Hiroshima and Nagasaki. The acute effects killed 90,000 to 166,000 people in Hiroshima and 60,000 to 80,000 in Nagasaki, nearly all civilians. Victory was a mixed blessing, for it brought the realization that mankind had, for the first time in history, the ability to destroy himself—a threat that continues to overshadow life in the twenty-first century.

Mutually assured destruction was an inevitable by-product of a situation in which nuclear weapons were placed in the hands of opposing "superpowers." Since the end of the cold war, that threat has increased as countries besides America and Russia have entered the arms race. The potential danger can be observed in strains between India and Pakistan, both of which have had nuclear weapons since 1998, which it is feared they might use in the event of conflict over the disputed territory of Kashmir. In the meantime, declared nuclear states (the United Kingdom, the United States, France, Russia, and China) decline to abolish their weapons under the provisions of the nuclear Non-Proliferation Treaty, which dates back to 1968, thus providing other countries with incentive for developing their own nuclear arsenals. At the time of writing, this problem is generating tension in the Middle East.

Despite the Holocaust, civilized nations appear unable to prevent genocide, which has continued throughout the postwar period. In Cambodia, Pol Pot exterminated 2 million people between 1975 and 1979; there were 800,000 deaths in Rwanda in 1994; and 200,000 in Bosnia-Herzegovina during the three years leading up to 1995. At the time of writing, the Sudanese government pursues an openly genocidal policy in Darfur and South Sudan, and as long ago as 2009 its president was indicted by the International Criminal Court for mass killing, rape, and pillage of civilians. He has yet to be brought to trial. Whether or not they are victims of genocide, civilians continue to be slaughtered on an industrial scale, often as a result of indiscriminate aerial bombing. In recent years the Sri Lankan government has targeted its own citizens (mainly women and children).

Asymmetrical warfare continued to proliferate in the Korean War, the Vietnam War, the Soviet War in Afghanistan, the wars in Iran and Afghanistan of the present century, as well as the 2006 Lebanon War and 2011 Libyan War. Terrorism seized global attention at the beginning of the new century with the attack on the World Trade Center in New York City on September 11, 2001.

Most poets in this period testify to warfare and what it exacted from them, either as combatants or observers. Even William Stafford, a conscientious objector, was scarred by wartime experience: for him, it meant becoming an object of hatred, to the point of facing down lynch mobs (see p. 589). It is remarkable how many witnesses to war had psychological problems, suffered from alcoholism, or led lives that were in some way troubled. That seems to have been the price of survival—of coping with "something that will never yield to the restoratives of time."

> For months and years in a forgotten war
> I rode the battle-gray Diesel-stinking ships
> Among the brilliantly advertised Pacific Islands,

Coasting the sinister New Guinea Coasts,
All during the killing and hating of a forgotten war.
Now when I drive behind a Diesel-stinking bus
On the way to the university to teach
Stevens and Pound and Mallarmé,
I am homesick for war.

(KARL SHAPIRO, "HUMAN NATURE")

W. B. Yeats (1865–1939)

On Easter Monday, March 24, 1916, seven hundred revolutionaries led by Patrick Pearse (p. 530) and James Connolly of the Irish Republican Brotherhood took possession of several Dublin landmarks, most notably the General Post Office on O'Connell Street, from where they proclaimed an Irish Republic. Martial law was declared, and for the rest of the working week the city center became a battleground. By Saturday, several landmarks in the city were in ruins, including the Hibernian Academy and the Hotel Metropole; at four o'clock that afternoon, the revolutionaries surrendered. The English army then embarked on a spree of summary executions, including that of the pacifist Francis Sheehy-Skeffington; the thirty-five hundred people they held without trial were lucky to be spared. In the meantime, fifteen rebel leaders, including Pearse and Connolly, were tried by a kangaroo court convened by the army, shot, and buried in Kilmainham Gaol. Yeats's reaction was one of horror. "I had no idea that any public event could so deeply move me—and I am very despondent about the future," he wrote on May 11, by which time he was meditating a poem. His reaction was complex: at times he disapproved of the rising, regarding its leaders as "innocent and patriotic theorists"; at others he admired their bravery and felt responsibility for what they had done, wondering "if I could have done anything to turn those young men in some other direction." (Nearly all the protagonists were known to him.) In June he returned to Dublin to see the ruins for himself, and to witness the authorities' tight grip on the city; he had to apply to the police for a pass to travel to Greystones, a mere fifteen miles away. He finished his poem about the rising in September. At first he wanted to call it "1916," but eventually published it as "Easter 1916" in a limited edition of twenty-five copies, in October. Anxious that widespread circulation might lead to controversy, Yeats withheld it from further printings until October 23, 1920, when it appeared in *The New Statesman*. The impact of these events is clear from two other poems of the period. "The Rose Tree" was the closest he came in print to sympathizing with the revolutionaries; it attempts to reimagine the convictions held by Pearse and Connolly. "On a Political Prisoner" is more ambiguous; Yeats described it as a denunciation of the Republican socialist Countess Constance Markievicz, another participant in the rising. At the time he composed it (January 1919), she was in prison for alleged involvement in a "German plot." Though released in March she was imprisoned again in June for sedition and sentenced to four months' hard labor. Condemned to a further term of two years, she was released under the general amnesty that followed signing of the Anglo-Irish Treaty.

Easter 1916

I have met them at close of day
Coming with vivid faces
From counter or desk among gray
Eighteenth-century houses.
I have passed with a nod of the head
Or polite meaningless words,
Or have lingered awhile and said
Polite meaningless words,
And thought before I had done
Of a mocking tale or a gibe
To please a companion
Around the fire at the club,
Being certain that they and I
But lived where motley is worn:
All changed, changed utterly:
A terrible beauty is born.

That woman's days[1] were spent
In ignorant goodwill,
Her nights in argument
Until her voice grew shrill.
What voice more sweet than hers

---

1. Yeats refers to Countess Constance Markievicz, who took part in the uprising and was imprisoned for life; she was released under the general amnesty of 1917.

When, young and beautiful,
She rode to harriers?
This man[2] had kept a school
And rode our wingèd horse;
This other[3] his helper and friend
Was coming into his force;
He might have won fame in the end,
So sensitive his nature seemed,
So daring and sweet his thought.
This other man[4] I had dreamed
A drunken, vainglorious lout.
He had done most bitter wrong
To some who are near my heart,
Yet I number him in the song;
He, too, has resigned his part
In the casual comedy;
He, too, has been changed in his turn,
Transformed utterly:
A terrible beauty is born.

Hearts with one purpose alone
Through summer and winter seem
Enchanted to a stone
To trouble the living stream.
The horse that comes from the road,
The rider, the birds that range
From cloud to tumbling cloud,
Minute by minute they change;
A shadow of cloud on the stream
Changes minute by minute;

---

2. Patrick Pearse had founded St. Enda's School for Boys; he was commandant general and president of the provisional government declared at the Post Office in Easter Week 1916. Executed May 3, 1916. See p. 530.

3. Thomas MacDonagh was a poet, dramatist, and critic. He was one of seven signatories of the proclamation of the provisional government read by Pearse outside the General Post Office at noon on Easter Monday. Executed May 3, 1916.

4. Major John MacBride was the husband of Maud Gonne, Yeats's lover. He served as second in command to Thomas MacDonagh during the rising. Executed May 5, 1916.

A horse-hoof slides on the brim,
And a horse plashes within it;
The long-legged moorhens dive,
And hens to moorcocks call;
Minute by minute they live:
The stone's in the midst of all.

Too long a sacrifice
Can make a stone of the heart.
O when may it suffice?
That is Heaven's part, our part
To murmur name upon name,
As a mother names her child
When sleep at last has come
On limbs that had run wild.
What is it but nightfall?
No, no, not night but death;
Was it needless death after all?
For England may keep faith
For all that is done and said.
We know their dream; enough
To know they dreamed and are dead;
And what if excess of love
Bewildered them till they died?
I write it out in a verse—
MacDonagh and MacBride
And Connolly[5] and Pearse
Now and in time to be,
Wherever green is worn,
Are changed, changed utterly:
A terrible beauty is born.

Completed between May 11 and September 25, 1916,
privately published October 1916

---

5. James Connolly was a trade union organizer, who served as military commander of
Republican forces in Dublin during the rising. Executed May 12, 1916.

The Rose Tree

"O words are lightly spoken,"
Said Pearse to Connolly,
"Maybe a breath of politic words
Has withered our rose tree;
Or maybe but a wind that blows
Across the bitter sea."

"It needs to be but watered,"
James Connolly replied,
"To make the green come out again
And spread on every side,
And shake the blossom from the bud
To be the garden's pride."

"But where can we draw water,"
Said Pearse to Connolly,
"When all the wells are parched away?
O plain as plain can be
There's nothing but our own red blood
Can make a right rose tree."

Completed April 7, 1917, published November 1920

On a Political Prisoner[1]

She that but little patience knew,
From childhood on, had now so much
A gray gull lost its fear and flew
Down to her cell and there alit,

---

1. Countess Constance Markievicz, a Republican socialist whose zealotry was far removed from Yeats's own politics, was involved in the 1916 uprising. Though sentenced to death for her part in the rising, her sentence was commuted to life imprisonment, and she was released during the general amnesty of June 1917. She was arrested, with other Sinn Féin members, on account of their alleged involvement in a "German plot," in May 1918.

And there endured her fingers' touch
And from her fingers ate its bit.

Did she in touching that lone wing
Recall the years before her mind
Became a bitter, an abstract thing,
Her thought some popular enmity:
Blind and leader of the blind
Drinking the foul ditch where they lie?

When long ago I saw her ride
Under Ben Bulben[2] to the meet,
The beauty of her countryside
With all youth's lonely wildness stirred,
She seemed to have grown clean and sweet
Like any rock-bred, sea-borne bird:

Sea borne, or balanced on the air
When first it sprang out of the nest
Upon some lofty rock to stare
Upon the cloudy canopy,
While under its storm-beaten breast
Cried out the hollows of the sea.

Written between January 10 and 29, 1919, published November 1920

---

2. Ben Bulben] Gulban's Peak is a mountain to the north of Sligo.

Rudyard Kipling (1865–1936)

KIPLING CAME UNDER fire for the first time in his life at the Battle of Karee Siding in Bloemfontein in March 1900. Forced to remain on his stomach for several hours "in great bodily and mental stress," he would never forget how it felt to be "under aimed fire—being, as it were, required as a head." Nor would he ever forget a pom-pom shell hitting a rock face making a "yowl like a cat," or "a small piece of hanging woodland filled and fumed with our shrapnel much as a man's moustache fills with cigarette smoke." Having known such danger, he understood from the outset the possible fate of his son John who, having at first been rejected for service in World War One, was accepted in the Irish Guards after Kipling lobbied its colonel, Lord Roberts. "The Hun is at the gates!" Kipling wrote in a poem published shortly after, which emphasized the importance of duty, service, and sacrifice. His son was reported missing in action at the Battle of Loos in September 1915, a month after his eighteenth birthday. "My Boy Jack" evokes the grief of a parent who has received no confirmation as to his son's fate but fears the worst. (John Kipling's remains were not identified until 1992.) Kipling's unappeasable hatred of the Germans can be attributed in part to grief at John's death—for which he would eventually admit his own culpability: "If any question why we died, / Tell them, because our fathers lied."

My Boy Jack

"Have you news of my boy Jack?"
  Not this tide.
"When d'you think that he'll come back?"
  Not with this wind blowing, and this tide.

"Has any one else had word of him?"
  Not this tide.
For what is sunk will hardly swim,
  Not with this wind blowing, and this tide.

"Oh, dear, what comfort can I find?"
  None this tide,
  Nor any tide,
Except he didn't shame his kind—
  Not even with that wind blowing and that tide.

Then hold your head up all the more,
  This tide,
  And every tide;
Because he was the son you bore,
  And gave to that wind blowing and that tide!

    Written late September/early October 1916, published October 19, 1916

The Children

These were our children who died for our lands: they were dear in our
  sight.
We have only the memory left of their home-treasured sayings and
  laughter.
The price of our loss shall be paid to our hands, not another's
  hereafter.
Neither the Alien nor Priest shall decide on it. That is our right.
  But who shall return us the children?

At the hour the Barbarian chose to disclose his pretences,
And raged against Man, they engaged, on the breasts that they bared
  for us,
The first felon-stroke of the sword he had long time prepared for us—
Their bodies were all our defence while we wrought our defences.

They bought us anew with their blood, forbearing to blame us,
Those hours which we had not made good when the Judgment
    o'ercame us.
They believed us and perished for it. Our statecraft, our learning
Delivered them bound to the Pit and alive to the burning
Whither they mirthfully hastened as jostling for honour—
Not since her birth has our Earth seen such worth loosed upon her!

Nor was their agony brief, or once only imposed on them.
The wounded, the war-spent, the sick received no exemption:
Being cured they returned and endured and achieved our redemption,
Hopeless themselves of relief, till Death, marveling, closed on them.

That flesh we had nursed from the first in all cleanness was given
To corruption unveiled and assailed by the malice of Heaven—
By the heart-shaking jests of Decay where it lolled on the wires—
To be blanched or gay-painted by fumes—to be cindered by fires—
To be senselessly tossed and retossed in stale mutilation
From crater to crater. For this we shall take expiation.
    But who shall return us our children?

                                Published 1917

Stephen Crane (1871–1900)

IT IS AN irony that, at the time Crane wrote what is now regarded as one of the great war novels in the canon, *The Red Badge of Courage* (1895), he had not set foot on the battlefield. Anxious to put that right, he set out for Cuba in January 1897, intending to report on the atrocities that would lead to the Spanish-American War; however, his ship sank and he nearly drowned. His first experience of conflict would instead be the Battle of Velestino in May 1897, part of the Greco-Turkish War. The "crash" of noise as shells fell around him was, he wrote, "the most beautiful sound of my experience, barring no symphony." After laying over in England, where he met George Bernard Shaw and befriended Joseph Conrad, Crane sailed to Cuba to report on the developing Spanish-American conflict, assisting marines when they seized Guantánamo Bay: he was cited for "material aid during the action." Compelled to leave after contracting malaria, he returned to England, suffering from tuberculosis, the disease that would kill him in Germany. The poems included here, rather than his great novel, reflect his firsthand experience of war.

Unwind my riddle

Unwind my riddle.
Cruel as hawks the hours fly,
Wounded men seldom come home to die,
The hard waves see an arm flung high,
Scorn hits strong because of a lie,
Yet there exists a mystic tie.
Unwind my riddle.

Written probably in early 1899, published 1900

There exists the eternal fact of conflict

There exists the eternal fact of conflict
And—next—a mere sense of locality.
Afterward, we derive sustenance from the winds.
Afterward we become patriots.
The godly vice of patriotism makes us slaves,
And—let us surrender to this falsity
Let us be patriots

Then welcome us the practical men
Thrumming on a thousand drums
The practical men, God help us.
    They cry aloud to be led to war

Ah—
They have been poltroons on a thousand fields
And the sacked sad city of New York is their record
Furious to face the Spaniard, these people,
     and crawling worms before their task
They name serfs and send charity in bulk to better men
They play at being free, these people of New York
Who are too well dressed to protest against infamy.

Written late 1898 or early 1899, published 1957

A gray and boiling street

A gray and boiling street
Alive with rickety noise.
Suddenly, a hearse,
Trailed by black carriages
Takes a deliberate way
Through this chasm of commerce;
And children look eagerly
To find the misery behind the shades.
Hired men, impatient, drive with a longing
To reach quickly the graveside, the end of solemnity.

Yes, let us have it over.
Drive, man, drive.
Flog your sleek-hided beasts,
Gallop—gallop—gallop.
Let us finish it quickly.

Written early 1899, published 1957

Paul Laurence Dunbar (1872–1906)

ONE OF THE most popular poets of his era and the first professional black literary man in America, Dunbar wrote, he said, "to prove to the many that we are more human than African." He was born in Dayton, Ohio, the son of two former Kentucky slaves, his father having escaped to join the Union Army in the Civil War, his mother emancipated at the war's end. Dunbar wanted to study law at Harvard but was compelled by poverty to remain in Dayton, where he found work as an elevator operator. It was here, on the job, that Dunbar began writing poetry; when he was twenty-one, he met Frederick Douglass, who introduced him to other black writers and gave him much-needed encouragement: "I've been knowing you for some time and you're one of my boys," he said. In ensuing years Dunbar's poetry was praised and loved by readers of all races, Booker T. Washington hailing him as "The Poet Laureate of the Negro race." "The Haunted Oak," one of his finest ballads, was inspired by a story Dunbar heard from an elderly former slave who lived on the campus of Howard University in Washington, DC. He related the tale of his nephew in Alabama, hanged on an oak tree by a mob of whites. Soon after, the leaves on the limb from which the boy was hanged went yellow, the branch withered, and eventually died: the oak was haunted. (Lynchings were common at this time; in the last decade of the nineteenth century, an estimated 1,665 blacks were slaughtered in this way by whites.) "Sympathy" was written while Dunbar worked at the Library of Congress, the bars in the bookstacks suggesting to him those in a bird's cage.

We Wear the Mask

We wear the mask that grins and lies,
It hides our cheeks and shades our eyes—
This debt we pay to human guile;

With torn and bleeding hearts we smile,
And mouth with myriad subtleties.

Why should the world be overwise
In counting all our tears and sighs?
Nay, let them only see us while
    We wear the mask.

We smile but, oh great Christ, our cries
To thee from tortured souls arise.
We sing but, oh, the clay is vile
Beneath our feet, and long the mile;
But let the world dream otherwise,
    We wear the mask!

Published 1895

Sympathy

I know what the caged bird feels, alas!
    When the sun is bright on the upland slopes;
When the wind stirs soft through the springing grass,
And the river flows like a stream of glass;
    When the first bird sings and the first bud opes,
And the faint perfume from its chalice steals—
I know what the caged bird feels!

I know why the caged bird beats his wing
    Till its blood is red on the cruel bars;
For he must fly back to his perch and cling
When he fain would be on the bough a-swing;
    And a pain still throbs in the old, old scars
And they pulse again with a keener sting—
I know why he beats his wing!

I know why the caged bird sings, ah me,
    When his wing is bruised and his bosom sore,
When he beats his bars and he would be free;
It is not a carol of joy or glee,
    But a prayer that he sends from his heart's deep core,
But a plea, that upward to Heaven he flings—
I know why the caged bird sings!

Written between 1897 and 1899, published 1899

The Haunted Oak

Pray why are you so bare, so bare,
    Oh, bough of the old oak tree;
And why, when I go through the shade you throw,
    Runs a shudder over me?

My leaves were green as the best, I trow,
    And sap ran free in my veins,
But I saw in the moonlight dim and weird
    A guiltless victim's pains.

I bent me down to hear his sigh,
    I shook with his gurgling moan,
And I trembled sore when they rode away
    And left him here alone.

They'd charged him with the old, old crime
    And set him fast in jail—
Oh, why does the dog howl all night long,
    And why does the night wind wail?

He prayed his prayer and he swore his oath,
    And he raised his hand to the sky;
But the beat of hoofs smote on his ear,
    And the steady tread drew nigh.

Who is it rides by night, by night,
   Over the moonlit road?
And what is the spur that keeps the pace,
   What is the galling goad?

And now they beat at the prison door,
   "Ho, keeper, do not stay!
We are friends of him whom you hold within,
   And we fain would take him away

From those who ride fast on our heels
   With mind to do him wrong;
They have no care for his innocence,
   And the rope they bear is long."

They have fooled the jailer with lying words,
   They have fooled the man with lies;
The bolts unbar, the locks are drawn,
   And the great door open flies.

Now they have taken him from the jail
   And hard and fast they ride,
And the leader laughs low down in his throat,
   As they halt my trunk beside.

Oh, the judge, he wore a mask of black,
   And the doctor one of white,
And the minister, with his oldest son,
   Was curiously bedight.   *dressed*

Oh, foolish man, why weep you now?
   'Tis but a little space,
And the time will come when these shall dread
   The memory of your face.

I feel the rope against my bark
   And the weight of him in my grain,
I feel in the throe of his final woe

The touch of my own last pain.

And never more shall leaves come forth
   On a bough that bears the ban;
I am burned with dread, I am dried and dead
   From the curse of a guiltless man.

And ever the judge rides by, rides by,
   And goes to hunt the deer,
And ever another rides his soul
   In the guise of a mortal fear.

And ever the man he rides me hard,
   And never a night stays he;
For I feel his curse as a haunted bough,
   On the trunk of a haunted tree.

Written and published 1900

John McCrae (1872–1918)

"SEVENTEEN DAYS OF HADES!" was how McCrae described the terrible experience of ministering to wounded soldiers during the Second Battle of Ypres. He trained as a doctor in his native Canada and had become professor of medicine at McGill University by the time he served in the artillery during the Second Boer War in South Africa (1899–1901). He signed up as a surgeon when Canada entered World War One, and at Ypres (April to May 1915) was in charge of a small field hospital. He was deeply affected by the death of a friend and former student, Alex Helmer, killed by shellfire on May 2; in the absence of a chaplain, McCrae performed Helmer's funeral ceremony. The following day, sitting on the rear step of an ambulance, McCrae composed "In Flanders Fields," a heartfelt lament he imagined to be spoken by dead soldiers. It was a brave, audacious poem by which its author was so bemused he crumpled it up and threw it away. But it was picked up by one of his colleagues and sent to *Punch*, which published it in December. It is now one of the most famous poems about the war that inspired it, the first to propose the poppy as a flower of remembrance. McCrae would not survive the war; wounded in May 1918, he died in hospital of pneumonia and meningitis.

In Flanders Fields

In Flanders fields the poppies blow
Between the crosses, row on row,
    That mark our place; and in the sky
    The larks, still bravely singing, fly
Scarce heard amid the guns below.

We are the Dead. Short days ago
We lived, felt dawn, saw sunset glow,
    Loved and were loved, and now we lie,
        In Flanders fields.

Take up our quarrel with the foe:
To you from failing hands we throw
    The torch; be yours to hold it high.
    If ye break faith with us who die
We shall not sleep, though poppies grow
        In Flanders fields.

Written May 3, 1915, published December 8, 1915

The Anxious Dead

Oh guns, fall silent till the dead men hear
Above their heads the legions pressing on!
(These fought their fight in time of bitter fear,
And died not knowing how the day had gone.)

Oh flashing muzzles, pause, and let them see
The coming dawn that streaks the sky afar;
Then let your mighty chorus witness be
To them, and Caesar, that we still make war.

Tell them, oh guns, that we have heard their call,
That we have sworn, and will not turn aside,
That we will onward till we win or fall,
That we will keep the faith for which they died.

Bid them be patient, and some day, anon,
They shall feel earth enwrapped in silence deep;
Shall greet, in wonderment, the quiet dawn,
And in content may turn them to their sleep.

Published 1917

Patrick Pearse (1879–1916)

JUST BEFORE EXECUTION, Pearse declared there was "no nobler death than to die a soldier in the cause of Irish freedom." He made an unlikely combatant, for he was really an intellectual. Trained as a lawyer, he was called to the Irish Bar and was an active member of the Gaelic League, which promoted Irish language and culture. He also founded two bilingual schools, for boys and girls, which ministered to the needs of the individual child. As a writer he was proficient in English and Gaelic, the author of poetry, plays, and fiction; he was a skilled orator in both tongues, and a renowned scholar. His acquaintances included W. B. Yeats (p. 513) and Rabindranath Tagore, with whom he corresponded. Politically, he was an ardent supporter of home rule, by which the Irish would be allowed self-government by the English Parliament, and in March 1913 he addressed a rally in Dublin, telling listeners he would lead a revolution were Parliament to refuse it. His word would be tested: though there was support for home rule in England, the legislation was delayed, first by opposition in the House of Lords, then by outbreak of the First World War. Colleagues in the Irish Republican Brotherhood persuaded him change could come only with insurrection, and on Easter Monday 1916 Pearse was designated commandant general and president of the new Irish republic, leading seven hundred armed revolutionaries to occupy strategic Dublin buildings. It was a suicide mission: forewarned, the English army confronted them with a division of troops backed by 18-pounder cannon and a battleship. After five days of fighting, Pearse and his comrades surrendered at 4 p.m. the following Saturday, handing themselves to a military commander who swiftly turned them into martyrs. One by one, they were court-martialed, executed by firing squad, and buried in the grounds of Kilmainham Gaol. Pearse was among the first to be shot on May 3. He was thirty-seven. "We seem to have lost," he remarked at his trial, "but we have not lost; we have kept faith with the past and handed on a tradition to the future." A terrible beauty had been born. Pearse remains the most famous of the 1916 rebels, exponent of the belief that self-sacrifice is the ultimate price to be paid for one's country; it is the argument of "Renunciation," his most famous poem, composed hours before his death.

Renunciation

Naked I saw thee,
O beauty of beauty,
And I blinded my eyes
For fear I should fail.

I heard thy music,
O melody of melody,
And I closed my ears
For fear I should falter.

I tasted thy mouth,
O sweetness of sweetness,
And I hardened my heart
For fear of my slaying.

I blinded my eyes,
And I closed my ears,
And I hardened my heart
And I smothered my desire.

I turned my back
On the vision I had shaped,
And to this road before me
I turned my face.

I have turned my face
To this road before me,
To the deed that I see,
And the death I shall die.

Written early May 1916, published July 8, 1916

The Wayfarer

The beauty of the world hath made me sad,
This beauty that will pass;
Sometimes my heart hath shaken with great joy
To see a leaping squirrel in a tree,
Or a red ladybird upon a stalk,
Or little rabbits in a field at evening,
Lit by a slanting sun,
Or some green hill where shadows drifted by
Some quiet hill where mountainy man hath sown
And soon would reap; near to the gate of Heaven;
Or children with bare feet upon the sands
Of some ebbed sea, or playing on the streets
Of little towns in Connacht,
Things young and happy.
And then my heart hath told me:
These will pass,
Will pass and change, will die and be no more,

Things bright and green, things young and happy;
And I have gone upon my way
Sorrowful.

Written May 2, 1916, published July 7, 1917

D. H. Lawrence (1885–1930)

"FOR ME THE War is utterly wrong, stupid, monstrous and contemptible," Lawrence told Lady Cynthia Asquith in November 1916, "and nothing, neither life nor death, can make it right." He would have found it difficult to kill Germans in part because he married one—Frieda Emma Maria Johanna, née von Richthofen (1879–1956), cousin to the German flying ace—on July 13, 1914; World War I began at the end of the month. It was a difficult time to be German in England—even the royal family changed their name (from Saxe-Coburg-Gotha to Windsor)—and the Lawrences were harassed both by civilians and the authorities, who kept them under constant surveillance. Their living quarters were searched by the police. When they attempted to leave for America, the Foreign Office refused to give Lawrence a passport; when they tried to settle in Cornwall, they were served with a military exclusion order prohibiting them from living near the coast; Lawrence was twice given a medical inspection to see whether he was fit to serve in the military, on both occasions leaving him humiliated and degraded. These experiences had a terrible effect on him. "The war is just hell for me," he wrote, "I can't get away from it for a minute: live in a sort of coma, like one of those nightmares when you can't move." By confronting him with authoritarian tendencies within his own culture, and the jingoism so beloved of the mob, the war generated in him a hatred of his own country. That was why, in January 1915, he could declare: "The War finished me: it was the spear through the side of all sorrows and hopes." The experience of living through these years had a profound influence on his novels: the militaristic Skrebensky in *The Rainbow* (1915) embodies attitudes that created conflict; in *Women in Love* (1920) Lawrence wanted "the bitterness of the war [to be] taken for granted in the characters"; in *Kangaroo* (1923), Somers describes the years 1916 to 1919 as those in which "the damage was done. The years when the world lost its real manhood"; and in *Lady Chatterley's Lover* (1928), that view is literally embodied in Clifford Chatterley, paralyzed from the waist down. During the war, Lawrence recorded his anxieties in a series of poems published in *Bay* (1919).

Rondeau of a Conscientious Objector

The hours have tumbled their leaden, monotonous sands
And piled them up in a dull gray heap in the west.
I carry my patience sullenly through the waste lands;
Tomorrow will pour them all back, the dull hours I detest.

I force my cart through the sodden filth that is pressed
Into ooze, and the somber dirt spouts up at my hands
As I make my way in twilight now to rest.
The hours have tumbled their leaden, monotonous sands.

A twisted thorn tree still in the evening stands
Defending the memory of leaves and the happy round nest.
But mud has flooded the homes of these weary lands
And piled them up in a dull gray heap in the west.

All day has the clank of iron on iron distressed
The nerve-bare place. Now a little silence expands
And a gasp of relief. But the soul is still compressed:
I carry my patience sullenly through the wastelands.

The hours have ceased to fall, and a star commands
Shadows to cover our stricken manhood, and blest
Sleep to make us forget: but he understands:
Tomorrow will pour them all back, the dull hours I detest.

Written c. spring 1918, published July 1919

Bombardment

The town has opened to the sun.
Like a flat red lily with a million petals
She unfolds, she comes undone.

A sharp sky brushes upon
The myriad glittering chimney-tips
As she gently exhales to the sun.

Hurrying creatures run
Down the labyrinth of the sinister flower.
What is it they shun?

A dark bird falls from the sun.
It curves in a rush to the heart of the vast
Flower: the day has begun.

Written c. spring 1918, published November 20, 1919

Ruination

The sun is bleeding its fires upon the mist
That huddles in gray heaps coiling and holding back.
Like cliffs abutting in shadow a dead gray sea
Some street-ends thrust forward their stack.

On the misty wastelands, away from the flushing gray
Of the morning, the elms are loftily dimmed, and tall
As if moving in air towards us, tall angels
Of darkness advancing steadily over us all.

Published November 20, 1919

Edith Sitwell (1887–1964)

"I HAVE LIVED through the shattering of two civilizations, have seen two Pandora's boxes opened," Sitwell wrote, "One contained horror, the other emptiness." Those words could be written only by someone who, after both world wars, survived into the nuclear age. Her brothers Osbert and Sacheverell served in the Grenadier Guards during the First World War, and to the end of her days she vividly recalled "the terrible good-byes to sons, brothers, husbands" (her brothers were unusual in surviving). "The Dancers" is her most haunting poem of that period, condemning those who "dance and batten" at a time of bloodshed. Her finest poetry was inspired by World War Two, when she experienced what she later described as "the minor restrictions and major terrors of this time." At her country house, Renishaw, she hosted evacuees fleeing the air raids. She visited Blitz-torn London in December 1944 and gave a poetry reading; hearing a buzz bomb suddenly cut out (a sign it was about to descend), she stopped reciting for a moment, before the nearby explosion allowed her to continue. "Fortunately I always wear long skirts, so no one saw my knocking knees," she joked. Sitwell composed "Still Falls the Rain" during the Blitz of 1940; though not to convert to Catholicism until 1955, she comments on the war in overtly religious terms.

The Dancers

during a great battle, 1916

The floors are slippery with blood:
The world gyrates too. God is good
That while His wind blows out the light
For those who hourly die for us—
We still can dance, each night.

The music has grown numb with death—
But we will suck their dying breath,
The whispered name they breathed to chance,
To swell our music, make it loud
That we may dance,—may dance.

We are the dull blind carrion fly
That dance and batten. Though God die
Mad from the horror of the light—
The light is mad, too, flecked with blood,—
We dance, we dance, each night.

Written 1916, published 1918

Still Falls the Rain

THE RAIDS, 1940. NIGHT AND DAWN.

Still falls the Rain—
Dark as the world of man, black as our loss—
Blind as the nineteen hundred and forty nails
Upon the Cross.

Still falls the Rain
With a sound like the pulse of the heart that is changed to the ham-
    mer beat
In the Potter's Field, and the sound of the impious feet

On the Tomb:
                Still falls the Rain
In the Field of Blood where the small hopes breed and the human
    brain
Nurtures its greed, that worm with the brow of Cain.

Still falls the Rain
At the feet of the Starved Man hung upon the Cross.

Christ that each day, each night, nails there, have mercy on us—
On Dives and on Lazarus:
Under the Rain the sore and the gold are as one.

Still falls the Rain—
Still falls the Blood from the Starved Man's wounded Side:
He bears in His Heart all wounds—those of the light that died,
The last faint spark
In the self-murdered heart, the wounds of the sad uncomprehending
     dark,
The wounds of the baited bear—
The blind and weeping bear whom the keepers beat
On his helpless flesh . . . the tears of the hunted hare.

Still falls the Rain—
Then—O Ile leape up to my God: who pulles me doune—
See, see where Christ's blood streames in the firmament:[1]
It flows from the Brow we nailed upon the tree
Deep to the dying, to the thirsting heart
That holds the fires of the world—dark smirched with pain
As Caesar's laurel crown.

Then sounds the voice of One who like the heart of man
Was once a child who among beasts has lain—
"Still do I love, still shed my innocent light, my Blood, for thee."

Written c. September 1940, published 1942

---

1. Sitwell quotes Faustus's words in Marlowe's tragedy, as Faustus realizes he is damned.

Claude McKay (1889–1948)

FESTUS CLAUDIUS MCKAY (better known as Claude) grew up the youngest of eleven children in Sunny Ville, Jamaica, where his brother, Uriah Theophilus McKay, and a neighboring Englishman, Walter Jekyll, introduced him to the canon of English poetry. At the age of nineteen he moved to Kingston to become a constable and for the first time in his life experienced the violence of Jamaica's racial prejudice (the island was still a British crown colony). After publishing two books of poetry, McKay visited America in 1912, where he was appalled by racism in Alabama and New York City: "It was the first time I had ever come face to face with such manifest, implacable hate of my race, and my feelings were indescribable. . . . I had heard of prejudice in America but never dreamed of it being so intensely bitter." In London in 1919 he met George Bernard Shaw and Sylvia Pankhurst; they urged him to read Karl Marx and as a result he became a "black Bolshevik," representing the American Workers Party at the Fourth Congress of the Communist International in Moscow in November 1922. He loved Soviet Russia and its people: "Whenever I appeared in the street I was greeted by all of the people with enthusiasm . . . a spontaneous upsurging of folk feeling." He befriended principal Russian politicians of the day, including Zinoviev and Bukharin. Trotsky consulted McKay on the negro question, resulting in his 1923 "Letter to Comrade McKay." By now McKay was prominent in the Harlem Renaissance, publishing novels, poems, and short stories. "If We Must Die" remains his most famous poem, inspired by race riots in Harlem during the notorious "Red Summer" of 1919, when unrest broke out in twenty-five cities across America. It was written while McKay worked as a waiter in a railroad car: it "exploded out of me," as he later recalled.

To the White Fiends

Think you I am not fiend and savage too?
Think you I could not arm me with a gun
And shoot down ten of you for every one
Of my black brothers murdered, burned by you?
Be not deceived, for every deed you do
I could match—outmatch: am I not Afric's son,
Black of that black land where black deeds are done?
But the Almighty from the darkness drew
My soul and said: Even thou shalt be a light
Awhile to burn on the benighted earth,
Thy dusky face I set among the white
For thee to prove thyself of highest worth;
Before the world is swallowed up in night,
To show thy little lamp: go forth, go forth!

Published September 1918

If We Must Die

If we must die, let it not be like hogs
Hunted and penned in an inglorious spot,
While round us bark the mad and hungry dogs,
Making their mock at our accursèd lot.
If we must die, oh let us nobly die
So that our precious blood may not be shed
In vain; then even the monsters we defy
Shall be constrained to honor us though dead!
Oh kinsmen! we must meet the common foe!
Though far outnumbered let us show us brave,
And for their thousand blows deal one deathblow!
What though before us lies the open grave?
Like men we'll face the murderous, cowardly pack—
Pressed to the wall, dying, but fighting back!

Published July 1919

The Tropics in New York

Bananas ripe and green, and ginger-root,
Cocoa in pods and alligator pears,
And tangerines and mangoes and grapefruit
Fit for the highest prize at parish fairs,

Set in the window, bringing memories
Of fruit trees laden by low-singing rills,
And dewy dawns, and mystical blue skies
In benediction over nun-like hills.

My eyes grew dim, and I could no more gaze;
A wave of longing through my body swept,
And, hungry for the old, familiar ways,
I turned aside and bowed my head and wept.

Published May 1920

Subway Wind

Far down, down through the city's great, gaunt gut
The gray train rushing bears the weary wind;
In the packed cars the fans the crowd's breath cut,
Leaving the sick and heavy air behind.
And pale-cheeked children seek the upper door
To give their summer jackets to the breeze;
Their laugh is swallowed in the deafening roar
Of captive wind that moans for fields and seas;
Seas cooling warm where native schooners drift
Through sleepy waters, while gulls wheel and sweep,
Waiting for windy waves the keels to lift
Lightly among the islands of the deep;
Islands of lofty palm trees blooming white
That lend their perfume to the tropic sea,

Where fields lie idle in the dew-drenched night,
And the Trades float above them fresh and free.

Published August 1921

Ivor Gurney (1890–1937)

HAD IT NOT been for the war, Gurney would have been a musician: in earlier years he was a chorister at Gloucester Cathedral, a pupil of the cathedral organist, and in 1911 won a composition scholarship at the Royal College of Music. He was at first rejected by the army because of poor eyesight, but accepted as a private in 1915. During this period he mailed poetry home, his first collection appearing in October 1917 under the title *Severn and Somme*; "To His Love" commemorates the loss of a friend on the front line. His first posting was at Sarras in the Ypres Salient; it had been a battlefield for the preceding two years, and was a wasteland of mud, death, and darkness. The woods that had once graced the gentle contours of the land were no more, and human bones could be seen sticking out of the mire. Gurney concealed the more gruesome details when he described "masses of unburied dead strewn over the battlefields; no sign of organized trenches, but merely shell holes joined up to one another." For a sensitive artist like Gurney, the experience of warfare quickly became an ordeal; as he confessed, "it sometimes comes that death would be preferable to such a life." He spent the end of 1916 on the front line at Ypres, where "the shelling was so incessant that we were compelled to live more like rats than men." He was fortunate to sustain a bullet wound in his arm on Good Friday 1917, which caused his removal from the disastrous Nivelle Offensive. Six weeks later he was back at the front for the Third Battle of Ypres (Passchendaele). He inhaled mustard gas in September and by the end of the month was hospitalized in England. Gurney's behavior thereafter became erratic, culminating in a suicide attempt in June 1918. He attempted to resume his music studies but was unable to concentrate; diagnosed a paranoid schizophrenic, he was committed against his will to an asylum and in 1922 entered a mental hospital where he remained until his death. Gurney published only two small volumes of poetry during his lifetime; not until his

Collected Poems appeared in 1982 was the scale and quality of his achievement fully appreciated.

To His Love[1]

He's gone, and all our plans
Are useless indeed.
We'll walk no more on Cotswold
Where the sheep feed
Quietly and take no heed.

His body that was so quick
Is not as you
Knew it, on Severn River
Under the blue
Driving our small boat through.

You would not know him now . . .
But still he died
Nobly, so cover him over
With violets of pride
Purple from Severn side.

Cover him, cover him soon!
And with thick-set
Masses of memoried flowers
Hide that red wet
Thing I must somehow forget.

Written c. August/September 1916, published November 1917

---

1. This is a monologue addressed by a soldier to the fiancée of a dead soldier, inspired by the reported death of Gurney's friend Willy Harvey in August 1916. Though Gurney did not know it at the time, Harvey was not dead but had been captured, and would survive the war.

The Silent One

Who died on the wires, and hung there, one of two—
Who for his hours of life had chattered through
Infinite lovely chatter of Bucks accent:
Yet faced unbroken wires; stepped over, and went
A noble fool, faithful to his stripes—and ended.
But I, weak, hungry, and willing only for the chance
Of line—to fight in the line, lay down under unbroken
Wires, and saw the flashes and kept unshaken,
Till the politest voice—a finicking accent, said:
"Do you think you might crawl through, there: there's a hole?" In the
    afraid
Darkness, shot at: I smiled, as politely replied—
"I'm afraid not, Sir." There was no hole, no way to be seen,
Nothing but chance of death, after tearing of clothes.
Kept flat, and watched the darkness, hearing bullets whizzing—
And thought of music—and swore deep heart's deep oaths
(Polite to God) and retreated and came on again,
Again retreated—and a second time faced the screen.

Written between 1919 and 1925, published 1954

First Time In

After the dread tales and red yarns of the Line
Anything might have come to us; but the divine
Afterglow brought us up to a Welsh colony
Hiding in sandbag ditches, whispering consolatory
Soft foreign things. Then we were taken in
To low huts candle lit, shaded close by slitten
Oilsheets, and there the boys gave us kind welcome,
So that we looked out as from the edge of home,
Sang us Welsh things, and changed all former notions
To human hopeful things. And the next day's guns
Nor any line-pangs ever quite could blot out

That strangely beautiful entry to war's rout;
Candles they gave us, precious and shared over-rations—
Ulysses found little more in his wanderings without doubt.
"David of the White Rock," the "Slumber Song" so soft, and that
Beautiful tune to which roguish words by Welsh pit boys
Are sung—but never more beautiful than there under the guns' noise.

Written between 1920 and 1922, rejected for
publication in 1924, published 2000

On Somme

Suddenly into the still air burst thudding
And thudding, and cold fear possessed me all,
On the gray slopes there, where winter in sullen brooding
Hung between height and depth of the ugly fall
Of Heaven to earth; and the thudding was illness' own.
But still a hope I kept that were we there going over,
I in the line, I should not fail, but take recover
From others' courage, and not as coward be known.
No flame we saw, the noise and the dread alone
Was battle to us; men were enduring there such
And such things, in wire tangled, to shatters blown.
Courage kept, but ready to vanish at first touch.
Fear, but just held. Poets were luckier once
In the hot fray swallowed and some magnificence.

Written between 1922 and 1925, published 1982

Isaac Rosenberg (1890–1918)

Rosenberg hated war: he had no wish to fight or kill. "I never joined the army for patriotic reasons," he once said, "I thought if I'd join there would be the separation allowance for my mother." Until then, he followed an artistic and literary career, having trained as an engraver in London—a job he hated, but that allowed him the opportunity to read Blake, Shelley, and Keats, whose poetry he loved. In his early twenties he joined a group of young artists and writers in east London—Joseph Leftwich, Stephen Winsten, John Rodker, Mark Gertler, and David Bomberg—who (with Rosenberg) would become known as the Whitechapel Boys. He studied painting at the Slade, exhibited at the Whitechapel Gallery in 1914, and published two pamphlets of poetry. Bereft of prospects in October 1915, he enlisted in the army. It was amid the horrors of World War One that Rosenberg experienced the anti-Semitism of fellow soldiers and routine miseries of trench warfare. He composed poetry on wastepaper he scavenged, sending drafts home to his sister; she would type them and forward them to friends. It was as a war poet that Rosenberg came of age, composing what he described as "Simple *poetry*—that is where an interesting complexity of thought is kept in tone and right value to the dominating idea so that it is understandable and still ungraspable." Ordered to the front line just in time for the German offensive of spring 1918, he was killed at dawn near Fampoux, northeast of Arras, while on patrol, on April 1. He was twenty-seven. "Break of Day in the Trenches" is his most celebrated poem, praised by Siegfried Sassoon for its truthful portrayal of "sensuous frontline experience . . . hateful and repellent, unforgettable and inescapable."

Break of Day in the Trenches

The darkness crumbles away.
It is the same old druid Time as ever,

Only a live thing leaps my hand,
A queer sardonic rat,
As I pull the parapet's poppy
To stick behind my ear.
Droll rat, they would shoot you if they knew
Your cosmopolitan sympathies.
Now you have touched this English hand
You will do the same to a German
Soon, no doubt, if it be your pleasure
To cross the sleeping green between.
It seems you inwardly grin as you pass
Strong eyes, fine limbs, haughty athletes,
Less chanced than you for life,
Bonds to the whims of murder,
Sprawled in the bowels of the earth,
The torn fields of France.
What do you see in our eyes
At the shrieking iron and flame
Hurled through still heavens?
What quaver—what heart aghast?
Poppies whose roots are in man's veins
Drop, and are ever dropping;
But mine in my ear is safe,
Just a little white with the dust.

Written June 1916, published December 1916

Returning, We Hear the Larks

Somber the night is.
And though we have our lives, we know
What sinister threat lurks there.

Dragging these anguished limbs, we only know
This poison-blasted track opens on our camp—
On a little safe sleep.

But hark! joy—joy—strange joy.
Lo! heights of night ringing with unseen larks.
Music showering our upturned list'ning faces.

Death could drop from the dark
As easily as song—
But song only dropped,
Like a blind man's dreams on the sand
By dangerous tides,
Like a girl's dark hair for she dreams no ruin lies there,
Or her kisses where a serpent hides.

Written 1917, published 1922

Dead Man's Dump[1]

The plunging limbers[2] over the shattered track
Racketed with their rusty freight,
Stuck out like many crowns of thorns,
And the rusty stakes like sceptres old
To stay the flood of brutish men
Upon our brothers dear.

The wheels lurched over sprawled dead
But pained them not, though their bones crunched,
Their shut mouths made no moan,
They lie there huddled, friend and foeman,
Man born of man, and born of woman,
And shells go crying over them
From night till night and now.

---

1. Rosenberg regarded this as his most important work. It was "suggested by going out wiring, or rather carrying wire up the line on limbers [two-wheeled cart] and running over dead bodies lying about."
2. limbers] front of the gun carriage, consisting of two wheels, axle, pole, and ammunition box.

Earth has waited for them,
All the time of their growth
Fretting for their decay:
Now she has them at last!
In the strength of their strength
Suspended—stopped and held.

What fierce imaginings their dark souls lit
Earth! have they gone into you?
Somewhere they must have gone,
And flung on your hard back
Is their souls' sack,
Emptied of God-ancestralled essences.
Who hurled them out? Who hurled?

None saw their spirits' shadow shake the grass,
Or stood aside for the half-used life to pass
Out of those doomed nostrils and the doomed mouth,
When the swift iron burning bee
Drained the wild honey of their youth.

What of us who, flung on the shrieking pyre,
Walk, our usual thoughts untouched,
Our lucky limbs as on ichor fed,
Immortal seeming ever?
Perhaps when the flames beat loud on us,
A fear may choke in our veins
And the startled blood may stop.

The air is loud with death,
The dark air spurts with fire,
The explosions ceaseless are.
Timelessly now, some minutes past,
These dead strode time with vigorous life,
Till the shrapnel called "an end!"
But not to all. In bleeding pangs
Some borne on stretchers dreamed of home,
Dear things, war blotted from their hearts.

Maniac Earth! howling and flying, your bowel
Seared by the jagged fire, the iron love,
The impetuous storm of savage love.
Dark Earth! dark Heavens! swinging in chemic smoke,
What dead are born when you kiss each soundless soul
With lightning and thunder from your mined heart,
Which man's self dug, and his blind fingers loosed?

A man's brains splattered on
A stretcher bearer's face;
His shook shoulders slipped their load,
But when they bent to look again
The drowning soul was sunk too deep
For human tenderness.

They left this dead with the older dead,
Stretched at the crossroads.

Burned black by strange decay
Their sinister faces lie,
The lid over each eye,
The grass and coloured clay
More motion have than they,
Joined to the great sunk silences.

Here is one not long dead;
His dark hearing caught our far wheels,
And the choked soul stretched weak hands
To reach the living word the far wheels said,
The blood-dazed intelligence beating for light,
Crying through the suspense of the far torturing wheels
Swift for the end to break
Or the wheels to break,
Cried as the tide of the world broke over his sight.

Will they come? Will they ever come?
Even as the mixed hoofs of the mules,
The quivering-bellied mules,

And the rushing wheels all mixed
With his tortured upturned sight.
So we crashed round the bend,
We heard his weak scream,
We heard his very last sound,
And our wheels grazed his dead face.

Written by May 14, 1917, published 1922

Archibald MacLeish (1892–1982)

"I WAS SO sick of the First World War that I couldn't cleanse my mind of it," MacLeish once remarked—sentiments that must have chimed with those of other veterans. Born in Glencoe, Illinois, he was the son of a Scots dry goods merchant. After reading English at Yale and studying law at Harvard, he volunteered for service in the war, beginning as an ambulance driver with the Yale Mobile Hospital Unit, before commanding a battery of field artillery and rising to the rank of captain. MacLeish fought in the Second Battle of the Marne (July–August 1918), which led to hundreds of thousands of casualties on both sides, including twelve thousand dead or wounded Americans. The death in battle of his brother, Kenneth, affected him deeply, bringing about disillusionment with the war: "There was no reason for it except reasons of commercial competition. There were no moral reasons, humanitarian reasons, no humane reasons. Nothing. It killed millions of men. It slaughtered an entire generation. It's the most disgusting thing that has happened really in the history of the planet. Vietnam is just a smear beside it." MacLeish felt differently about the Spanish Civil War, which he saw as "a warm-up for a second world war. . . . I felt very strongly about it." American involvement in World War Two was something of which he was proud, describing it as "the noblest period of our history that I know anything about." Roosevelt made MacLeish Librarian of Congress, and drew on his organizational talent to found the Office of Strategic Services, precursor of the Central Intelligence Agency. During the postwar period, he remained a keen-sighted and principled commentator on current events through his poetry.

Memorial Rain[1]

For Kenneth MacLeish

Ambassador Puser the ambassador
Reminds himself in French, felicitous tongue,
What these (young men no longer) lie here for
In rows that once, and somewhere else, were young. . . .

All night in Brussels the wind had tugged at my door:
I had heard the wind at my door and the trees strung
Taut, and to me who had never been before
In that country it was a strange wind, blowing
Steadily, stiffening the walls, the floor,
The roof of my room. I had not slept for knowing
He too, dead, was a stranger in that land
And felt beneath the earth in the wind's flowing
A tightening of roots and would not understand,
Remembering lake winds in Illinois,
That strange wind. I had felt his bones in the sand
Listening.
          . . . Reflects that these enjoy
Their country's gratitude, that deep repose,
That peace no pain can break, no hurt destroy,
That rest, that sleep. . . .

At Ghent the wind rose.
There was a smell of rain and a heavy drag
Of wind in the hedges but not as the wind blows
Over fresh water when the waves lag
Foaming and the willows huddle and it will rain:
I felt him waiting.

       . . . Indicates the flag
Which (may he say) enisles in Flanders plain

---

1. This poem describes Macleish's visit to his brother's grave in Belgium on Memorial Day, 1924, when the American ambassador spoke.

This little field these happy, happy dead
Have made America. . . .

In the ripe grain
The wind coiled glistening, darted, fled,
Dragging its heavy body: at Waereghem
The wind coiled in the grass above his head:
Waiting—listening. . . .

. . . Dedicates to them
This earth their bones have hallowed, this last gift
A grateful country. . . .

Under the dry grass stem
The words are blurred, are thickened, the words sift
Confused by the rasp of the wind, by the thin grating
Of ants under the grass, the minute shift
And tumble of dusty sand separating
From dusty sand. The roots of the grass strain,
Tighten, the earth is rigid, waits—he is waiting—

And suddenly, and all at once, the rain!

Written c. May 30, 1924, published October 1925

The Silent Slain

For Kenneth MacLeish, 1894–1918

We too, we too, descending once again
The hills of our own land, we too have heard
Far off—Ah, que ce cor a longue haleine—
The horn of Roland in the passages of Spain,
The first, the second blast, the failing third,
And with the third turned back and climbed once more
The steep road southward, and heard faint the sound

Of swords, of horses, the disastrous war,
And crossed the dark defile at last, and found
At Roncevaux upon the darkening plain
The dead against the dead and on the silent ground
The silent slain—

Published 1926

Hugh MacDiarmid (C. M. Grieve) (1892–1978)

THE DAY AFTER Armistice Day, MacDiarmid commented: "I myself believe
that we have lost this war—in everything but actuality! When I see scores of
sheep go to a slaughterhouse I do not feel constrained to admire their resig-
nation." Before the First World War, he had been a journalist and teacher;
when war was declared in August 1914, MacDiarmid (a committed socialist)
saw it as a ploy to pit socialists against each other. All the same, he had been
a member of the Royal Army Medical Corps since 1908 and by 1915 was quar-
termaster sergeant of a company one thousand strong. From August 1916 to
May 1918 he served at the Allied refueling base at Salonica in Greece, where
the principal enemy was malaria, which MacDiarmid contracted three times
during his stay. Unlike many, he would survive, though the war changed him
(as he recalled, writing of himself in the third person): "He brought back to
civilization an ardor of revolt, a sharp bitterness, made up partly of hatred and
partly of pity. He saw with eyes different from those of other men's—clearer
or more blurred, anyhow not the same. His state of mind was grievous." Most
of all, war made him more politically determined; during its course he was
deeply moved by the Easter Rising in Dublin and the Bolshevik Revolution
in Russia. He would soon be one of Stalin's most fervent admirers (at a period
when such views were fashionable), while hatred of the English inclined him
to favor independence from the United Kingdom. During the Second World
War, MacDiarmid made artillery shells in a factory but was badly injured
by an accident, and later transferred as a deckhand to the merchant navy,
delivering mail and supplies to Allied ships in the Clyde estuary. *A Drunk
Man Looks at the Thistle* is his masterpiece; according to fellow poet Norman
MacCaig it is "the best poem written in Scots *ever*—and that includes the

auld Makars." This remarkable 2,685-line poem pushes the boundaries of the dramatic monologue to its limits, incorporating lyrics, nonsense verse, and vers libre, as well as translations from German, French, and Russian. It is a modernist masterpiece, ranking with *The Waste Land* and *Briggflatts*.

A Drunk Man Looks at the Thistle (**extract**)[1]

The function, as it seems to me,
O Poetry is to bring to be   *Of*
At lang, lang last that unity. . . .

But wae's me on the weary wheel!   *woe is*
Higgledy-piggledy in't we reel,
And little it cares hou we may feel.

Twenty-six thousand years 'tll tak
For it to threid the Zodiac   *thread*
—A single round o the wheel to mak!

Lately it turned—I saw mysel
In sic a company doomed to mell.   *mix*
I micht hae been in Dante's Hell.

It shows hou little the best o men
E'en o themsels at times can ken,
—I sune saw that when I gaed ben   *went in*

The lesser wheel[2] within the big
That moves as merry as a grig,   *lively child*
Wi mankind in its whirligig

And hasna turned ae circle yet   *one*
Tho as it turns we slide in it,
And needs maun tak the place we get,

---

1. Our extract is from the conclusion of MacDiarmid's poem, lines 2,584–2,685.
2. The lesser wheel] Scotland.

I felt it turn, and syne I saw
John Knox and Clavers[3] in my raw,   *row*
And Mary Queen o Scots anaa,   *as well*

And Rabbie Burns and Weelum Wallace,
And Carlyle lookan unco gallus,   *very reckless*
And Harry Lauder[4] (to enthrall us).

And as I looked I saw them aa,   *all*
Aa the Scots baith big and smaa,
That e'er the braith o life did draw.

"Mercy o Gode, I canna thole   *stand*
Wi sic an orra mob to roll."   *disreputable*
—"*Wheesht! It's for the guid o your soul.*"   *Hush!*

"But what's the meanin, what's the sense?"
—"*Men shift but by experience.*
Twixt Scots there is nae difference.

They canna learn, sae canna move,
But stick for aye to their auld groove
—The only race in History who've

Bidden in the same category
Frae stert to present o their story,
And deem their ignorance their glory.

The mair they differ, mair the same.
The wheel can whummle aa but them,   *overturn*
—They caa their obstinacy 'Hame,'   *call*

And 'Puir Auld Scotland' bleat wi pride,
And wi their minds made up to bide
A thorn in aa the wide world's side.

---

3. Clavers] John Graham of Claverhouse, first viscount Dundee (1648–1689), renowned
Jacobite who remained loyal to James II of England after he left England prior to the
Glorious Revolution of 1689.
4. Harry Lauder (1870–1950) was a music hall singer.

There hae been Scots wha hae haen thochts,
They're strewn through maist o the various lots
—Sic traitors are nae langer Scots!"

"But in this huge ineducable
Heterogeneous hotch and rabble,   *swarm*
Why am *I* condemned to squabble?"

"A Scottish poet maun assume
The burden o his people's doom,
And dee to brak their livan tomb.   *die*

Mony hae tried, but aa hae failed.
Their sacrifice has nocht availed.
Upon the thistle they're impaled.

You maun choose but gin ye'd see
Anither category ye
Maun tine your nationality."   *lose*

And I look at aa the random
Band the wheel leaves whaur it fand 'em.   *found*
        "Auch, to Hell,
I'll tak it to avizandum. . . ."   *under judicial advisement*

O wae's me on the weary wheel,   *woe is*
And fain I'd understand them!

And blessin on the weary wheel,
Whaurever it may land them! . . .

But aince Jean kens what I've been through   *once*
The nicht, I dinna doot it,   *tonight*
She'll ope her airms in welcome true,
And clack nae mair aboot it. . . .   *talk*

              *

The stars like thistle's roses flouer
The sterile growth o Space outour,   *across*

That clad in bitter blasts spreids out
Frae me, the sustenance o its root.

O fain I'd keep my hert entire,
Fain hain the licht o my desire,   *preserve*
But ech! the shinean streams ascend,   *shining*
And leave me empty at the end.

For aince it's toomed my hert and brain,   *has emptied*
The thistle needs maun faa again.   *has to fall*
—But aa its growth 'll never fill
The hole it's turned my life intill! . . .   *into*

Yet hae I Silence left, the croun o aa.

No her, wha on the hills langsyne I saw   *long ago*
Liftan a foreheid o perpetual snaw.

No her, wha in the how-dumb-deid o nicht   *midnight*
Kyths, like Eternity in Time's despite.   *Appears*

No her, withouten shape, whas name is Daith,
No Him, unkennable abies to faith   *except*

—God whom, gin e'er He saw a man, wad be
E'en mair dumfounerd at the sicht than he.

—But Him, whom nocht in man or Deity,
Or Daith or Dreid or Laneliness can touch,
Wha's deed owre often and has seen owre much.   *died too*

O I hae Silence left
              —"And weel ye micht,"
Sae Jean'll say, "efter sic a nicht!"

Written by August 28, 1926, published November 22, 1926

May Wedderburn Cannan (1893–1973)

CANNAN WOULD HAVE trained as an actress had it not been for the First World War. As daughter of the dean of Trinity College in Oxford, she had an excellent education, publishing her first poetry at the age of twelve. At eighteen, she trained as a nurse with the Oxford Voluntary Aid Detachment and, with the onset of World War I, worked as an auxiliary nurse. In 1915 she spent four weeks in Rouen, France, a British supply base for the war effort, where she ran a canteen that catered to as many as two thousand soldiers at a time. That brought her into contact with many combatants, allowing her to witness the impact of war; even in the comparative safety of the café, conditions were difficult, as she later recalled: "One was hot or horrid cold, harried, dirty, and one's feet ached with the stone floors." When she returned to Oxford, she helped produce propaganda at the University Press and went on to work for British intelligence (MI5). She was in Paris when the Armistice was declared. She later remarked: "I did not believe the dead had died for nothing, nor that we should have 'kept out of the war'—the dead had kept faith, and so, if we did not grudge it, had we." In December 1918 she was engaged to Major Bevil Quiller-Couch (son of Sir Arthur Quiller-Couch) who survived the war only to die during the influenza pandemic in 1919. Grief inspired one of the most poignant elegies of the period, "When the Vision dies."

Rouen

26 April–25 May 1915

Early morning over Rouen, hopeful, high, courageous morning,
And the laughter of adventure and the steepness of the stair,
And the dawn across the river, and the wind across the bridges,
And the empty littered station, and the tired people there.

Can you recall those mornings and the hurry of awakening,
And the long-forgotten wonder if we should miss the way,
And the unfamiliar faces, and the coming of provisions,
And the freshness and the glory of the labour of the day?

Hot noontide over Rouen, and the sun upon the city,
Sun and dust unceasing, and the glare of cloudless skies,
And the voices of the Indians and the endless stream of soldiers,
And the clicking of the tatties,[1] and the buzzing of the flies.

Can you recall those noontides and the reek of steam and coffee,
Heavy-laden noontides with the evening's peace to win,
And the little piles of woodbines, and the sticky soda bottles,
And the crushes in the "Parlour," and the letters coming in?

Quiet nighttime over Rouen, and the station full of soldiers,
All the youth and pride of England from the ends of all the earth;
And the rifles piled together, and the creaking of the sword-belts,
And the faces bent above them, and the gay, heart-breaking mirth.

Can I forget the passage from the cool white-bedded Aid Post
Past the long sun-blistered coaches of the khaki Red Cross train
To the truck train full of wounded, and the weariness and laughter,
And "Good-bye, and thank you, Sister," and the empty yards again?

Can you recall the parcels that we made them for the railroad,
Crammed and bulging parcels held together by their string,
And the voices of the sergeants who called the Drafts together,
And the agony and splendor when they stood to save the King?

Can you forget their passing, the cheering and the waving,
The little group of people at the doorway of the shed,
The sudden awful silence when the last train swung to darkness,
And the lonely desolation, and the mocking stars o'erhead?

---

1. tatties] damp screens placed over doors and windows, used to cool and freshen the early summer air.

Can you recall the midnights, and the footsteps of night watchers,
Men who came from darkness and went back to dark again,
And the shadows on the rail lines and the all-inglorious labour,
And the promise of the daylight firing blue the windowpane?

Can you recall the passing through the kitchen door to morning,
Morning very still and solemn breaking slowly on the town,
And the early coastways engines that had met the ships at daybreak,
And the Drafts just out from England, and the day shift coming
    down?

Can you forget returning slowly, stumbling on the cobbles,
And the white-decked Red Cross barges dropping seawards for the
    tide,
And the search for English papers, and the blessed cool of water,
And the peace of half-closed shutters that shut out the world outside?

Can I forget the evenings and the sunsets on the island,
And the tall black ships at anchor far below our balcony,
And the distant call of bugles, and the white wine in the glasses,
And the long line of the street lamps, stretching eastward to the sea?

. . . When the world slips slow to darkness, when the office fire burns
    lower,
My heart goes out to Rouen, Rouen all the world away;
When other men remember I remember our adventure
And the trains that go from Rouen at the ending of the day.

Written November 1915, published 1917

When the Vision Dies

When the Vision dies in the dust of the marketplace,
    When the light is dim,
When you lift up your eyes and cannot behold his face,
    When your heart is far from him,

Know this is your War; in this loneliest hour you ride
    Down the roads he knew;
Though he comes no more at night he will kneel at your side,
    For comfort to dream with you.

Published 1919

Sylvia Townsend Warner (1893–1978)

UNTIL THE FIRST World War, Warner believed herself bound to a musical career. She was tutored by various masters at Harrow, including her father and the distinguished musician Percy Buck (with whom she had an affair lasting seventeen years). Excited by new developments in music, most notably those arising from serialism, she planned to study with Arnold Schoenberg in Berlin, but the outbreak of war put an end to that. Instead, she remained in England, supporting efforts to settle Belgian refugees in Harrow and working as a shell machinist in a munitions factory. (Her recollections of the war were published as a series of short stories, *Scenes of Childhood* (1981).) From 1932 she was the devoted partner of Mary Kathleen ("Valentine") Ackland, and remained so until Ackland's death in 1969. They moved to East Chaldon, Dorset, in 1930, where Warner helped found the local Left Book Club and worked as secretary to the Dorset Peace Council. She and Ackland attempted also to politicize farm laborers. They became interested in Communism, joining the party in 1935, and as a result came under surveillance by military intelligence. In September 1936 they visited Barcelona to assist the British Medical Aid Committee during the Spanish Civil War, and were thrilled by its revolutionary buzz; Warner described it as "the nearest thing I shall ever see to the early days of the USSR." The following year they returned to Barcelona as delegates to the Second Congress of the International Association of Writers for the Defence of Culture. When the Congress traveled to Madrid, they witnessed shelling by Franco's artillery, and admired the "expression of indomitable concentrated rage" on its residents. The Hotel Victoria, where they stayed, had already been hit, and gunfire was audible from outside. When air raids started at 5 a.m., everyone went down to the foyer and was overcome by a "strange amorousness"—including (according to Ackland) Warner.

> I remember detaching Sylvia from a West Indian negro who was weeping on her breast but who seemed perfectly contented to be moved gently onto a next-door French woman who herself had been making very sophisticated love to a tall, large Swedish woman next to her. And then, to make all things totally mad, two English journalists burst in through the front door shouting, "The Hospital is on fire—who wants to come and see—" . . .

Visiting the front line near the Pass of Guadarrama, where fighting was particularly intense, Warner joked about the propaganda value were she to be killed by a stray bullet. During the Second World War, she joined the Women's Voluntary Service, helping to organize rest centers for evacuees. She was intensely saddened by the fall of Paris on June 14, 1940: to her and many others, it seemed that Germany might successfully invade Britain. In that mood she composed two of her finest poems, of which her editor, Claire Harman, comments: " 'Road, 1940' is an extraordinary depiction of the disintegration of human sympathy as soon as individual survival is threatened, while 'Recognition' concludes that there can be no special case made for one's own casualties in war."

Road, 1940

Who do I carry, she said,
This child that is no child of mine?
Through the heat of the day it did nothing but fidget and whine,
Now it snuffles under the dew and the cold star-shine,
And lies across my heart as heavy as lead,
Heavy as the dead.

Why did I lift it, she said,
Out of its cradle in the wheel-tracks?
On the dusty road burdens have melted like wax,
Soldiers have thrown down their rifles, misers slipped their packs:

Yes, and the woman who left it there has sped
With a lighter tread.

Though I should save it, she said,
What have I saved for the world's use?
If it grow to hero it will die or let loose
Death, or to hireling, nature is already too profuse
Of such, who hope and are disinherited,
Plough and are not fed.

But since I've carried it, she said,
So far I might as well carry it still.
If we ever should come to kindness someone will
Pity me perhaps as the mother of a child so ill,
Grant me even to lie down on a bed;
Give me at least bread.

Written c. June 1940, published 1944

Recognition

But this child was not of wax.
Life was under the mute skin
And still showed red through the cracks.
It is well known that the children of Spain

Were carved cheaply out of wood,
The children of China but yellow leaves on the wind:
This was an English child that lay in the road.
They told me to weep once more, but I found

No tears, and though the mourners then
Threw stones at me in grief's and God's name
I had no blood to quicken for God or man.
For I remembered how to my childhood had come

Hearsay of Justice. Now, overhead,
Rang the inflexible music of her sword;
Blindfold she went over with sure tread.
I knew, and acknowledged her, and adored.

Published December 20, 1941

David Jones (1895–1974)

FEW WRITERS HAD a more arduous war than Jones, even though he was to survive it. From 1910 to 1914, he studied at the Camberwell School of Arts and Crafts; through his teacher, Archibald Hartick (who had known Gauguin and Van Gogh), he met Walter Sickert, who had just founded the Camden Town Group. Caught up in the patriotic fervor of war, Jones enlisted enthusiastically with the newly formed 15th Battalion of the Royal Welch Fusiliers, raised from Welshmen living in London, as well as native Londoners (Jones's father was Welsh, his mother English and Italian). Shipped to France in December 1915, he went straight to the Western Front at La Bassée, before marching southward to the Somme in mid-June 1916. Battle commenced there on July 1, when nineteen thousand British soldiers were killed in no-man's-land, still the worst death toll for the army on a single day of combat. On July 10, Jones was involved in the attack on German-held Mametz Wood and wounded in the leg, one of over five thousand casualties in his division alone. It felt, he later recalled, "as if a great baulk of timber or a heavy bar of some sort had struck me sideways, in fact I thought a ponderous branch of one of the trees of the wood had been severed by shrapnel and fallen across my leg." After convalescing, he was sent to the north flank of the British front in the Boesinghe, north of the Ypres Salient; eleven months later he was moved to the south of Armentières to participate in the opening stages of the Passchendaele Offensive. Years later, he recalled the "heavy mortars operating from behind each stark ridge." In February 1918, Jones came down with trench fever (a debilitating illness transmitted by rats) and was evacuated back to England. After demobilization, he returned to art, first at the Westminster School of Art and then with Eric Gill. His work came to be highly regarded and in 1928 he was elected to the Five and Seven Society where he exhibited alongside Henry Moore, Barbara Hepworth, and John Piper. In that year he also began *In Parenthesis*, which recalls life on the front line.

In Parenthesis

PART 3: STARLIGHT ORDER (EXTRACT)

At intervals lights elegantly curved above his lines, but the sheet-rain made little of their radiance. He heard, his ears incredulous, the nostalgic puffing of a locomotive, far off, across forbidden fields; and once upon the wind, from over his left shoulder, the nearer clank of trucks, ration-laden by Mogg's Hole.

    And the rain slacks at the wind veer

           and she half breaks her cloud cover.

    He puts up a sufficient light dead over the Neb; and in its moments hanging, star still, shedding a singular filament of peace, for these fantastic undulations.

    He angled rigid; head and shoulders free; his body's inclination at the extreme thrust of the sap head; outward towards them, like the calm breasts of her, silent above the cutwater,

foremost towards them

and outmost of us, and

brother-keeper, and ward-watcher;

his messmates sleeping like long-barrow sleepers, their

dark arms at reach.

Spell-sleepers, thrown about anyhow under the night.

And this one's bright brow turned against your boot leather, tranquil as a fer sídhe sleeper, under fairy tumuli, fair as Mac Og sleeping.

    Who cocks an open eye when you stamp your numbed feet on the fire step slats,

who tells you to stow it,

to put a sock in it,

to let a man sleep o' nights

—and redistributes his cramped limbs, and draws closer over his woollen comforter.

You shift on the boards a little to beat your toes against the revetment where this other one sits upright, wakeful and less fastidious, at an angle of the bay; who speaks without turning his head to you, his eyes set on the hollow night beyond the parados, he nursing his rifle, the bayonet's flat to his cheekbone; his syntax of the high hills—and the sharp inflection:

Starving night indeed—important to maintain the circulation—there's starving for you—important to keep the circulation.

Yes corporal.

Can you see anything, sentry.

Nothing corporal.

'o1 Ball is it, no.

Yes corporal.

Keep a sharp outlook sentry—it is the most elementary disciplines—sights at 350.

Yes corporal.

300 p'r'aps.

Yes corporal.

Starving as brass monkeys—as the Arctic bear's arse—Diawl!—starved as Pen Nant Govid, on the confines of hell.

Unwise it is to disturb the sentinel.

*

And the deepened stillness as a calm, cast over us—a potent influence over us and him—dead-calm for this Sargasso dank, and for the creeping things.

You can hear the silence of it:
you can hear the rat of no-man's-land
rut-out intricacies,
weasel-out his patient workings,
scrut, scrut, sscrut,
harrow-out earthly, trowel his cunning paw;
redeem the time of our uncharity, to sap his own amphibious paradise.

You can hear his carrying-parties rustle our corruptions through the night-weeds—contest the choicest morsels in his tiny conduits, bead-eyed feast on us; by a rule of his nature, at night feast on the broken of us.

Those broad pinioned;

blue-burnished, or brinded-back;
whose proud eyes watched
                            the broken emblems
droop and drag dust,
suffer with us this metamorphosis.
    These too have shed their fine feathers; these too have slimed
their dark-bright coats; these too have condescended to dig in.
    The white-tailed eagle at the battle ebb,
                                where the sea wars against the river
the speckled kite of Maldon
and the crow
have naturally selected to be un-winged;
to go on the belly, to
sap   sap   sap
with festered spines, arched under the moon; furrit with whiskered
snouts the secret parts of us.
    When it's all quiet you can hear them:
scrut scrut scrut
when it's as quiet as this is.
    It's so very still.
    Your body fits the crevice of the bay in the most comfortable
fashion imaginable.
    It's cushy enough.

    The relief elbows him on the fire-step: All quiet china?—bugger
all to report?—kipping mate?—christ, mate—you'll 'ave 'em all over.

Published 1937

Edmund Blunden (1896–1974)

TOWARD THE END of his life, Blunden wrote: "My experiences in the First World War have haunted me all my life and for many days I have, it seemed, lived in that world rather than this." He was born to schoolteachers in London, the eldest of nine children. He left his studies at Oxford to volunteer for the British army in 1915, joining the 11th Royal Sussex Regiment. Like David Jones, he went straight to the Western Front at La Bassée where he saw many comrades shot or blown to pieces. Years later Blunden described a soldier "collapsing like a sack of potatoes, spouting blood at twenty places," and a young lance corporal hit by a shell while making tea: never would he forget "the gobbets of blackening flesh, the earth wall sotted with blood, with flesh, the eye under the duckboard, the pulpy bone." Blunden arrived at the Somme shortly after the initial offensive on July 1, where he was exposed to more horrors, as he told his mother: "Some of the dugouts where some Germans were killed with bombs are indescribable." He was awarded the Military Cross for his part in a reconnaissance mission in 1916 before being moved to Ypres, where he fought at the Third Battle (Passchendaele), making frequent sorties into no-man's-land, sniper fire a constant danger. He survived three gas attacks, proving a soldier of extraordinary courage and stamina. For more detail the reader should turn to his memoir, *Undertones of War*, one of the best prose accounts of World War One. Not surprisingly for someone who had seen so much, he suffered post-traumatic stress disorder, though it was not diagnosed as such during his lifetime. "I know, now I am an old man," he wrote in 1968, "I take with me something that will never yield to the restoratives of time."

Preparations for Victory[1]

My soul, dread not the pestilence that hags
The valley; flinch not you, my body young.
At these great shouting smokes and snarling jags
Of fiery iron; as yet may not be flung
The dice that claims you. Manly move among
These ruins, and what you must do, do well;
Look, here are gardens, there mossed boughs are hung
With apples who bright cheeks none might excel,
And there's a house as yet unshattered by a shell.

"I'll do my best," the soul makes sad reply,
"And I will mark the yet unmurdered tree,
The relics of dear homes that court the eye,
And yet I see them not as I would see.
Hovering between, a ghostly enemy
Sickens the light, and poisoned, withered, wan,
The least defiled turns desperate to me."
The body, poor unpitied Caliban,
Parches and sweats and grunts to win the name of Man.

Days or eternities like swelling waves
Surge on, and still we drudge in this dark maze;
The bombs and coils and cans by strings of slaves
Are borne to serve the coming day of days;
Pale sleep in slimy cellars scarce allays
With its brief blank the burden. Look, we lose;
The sky is gone, the lightless drenching haze
Of rainstorms chills the bone; earth, air are foes,
The black fiend leaps brick red as life's last picture goes.

Written September 1916, published 1925

---

1. This ironically named poem concerns the attack on German-held Beaumont Ridge of September 3, 1916, in the Somme, in which Blunden was involved. His job was to carry buckets of bombs to the forward trenches, running through the thick green smoke that gave momentary protection from the chunks of shrapnel that filled the air. The result of the attack was an advance of twenty yards at a cost of many casualties on the British side.

Festubert, 1916

Tired with dull grief, grown old before my day,
I sit in solitude and only hear
Long silent laughters, murmurings of dismay,
The lost intensities of hope and fear;
In those old marshes yet the rifles lie,
On the thin breastwork flutter the gray rags,
The very books I read are there—and I
Dead as the men I loved, wait while life drags

Its wounded length from those sad streets of war
Into green places here, that were my own;
But now what once was mine is mine no more,
I seek such neighbors here and I find none.
With such strong gentleness and tireless will
Those ruined houses seared themselves in me,
Passionate I look for their dumb story still,
And the charred stub outspeaks the living tree.

I rise up at the singing of a bird
And scarcely knowing slink along the lane,
I dare not give a soul a look or word
Where all have homes and none's at home in vain:
Deep red the rose burned in the grim redoubt,   *stronghold*
The self-sown wheat around was like a flood,
In the hot path the lizard lolled time out,
The saints in broken shrines were bright as blood.

Sweet Mary's shrine between the sycamores!
There we would go, my friend of friends and I,
And snatch long moments from the grudging wars;
Whose dark made light intense to see them by. . . .
Shrewd bit the morning fog, the whining shots
Spun from the wrangling wire: then in warm swoon
The sun hushed all but the cool orchard plots,
We crept in the tall grass and slept till noon.

Written 1921, published 1922

Premature Rejoicing[1]

What's that over there?

                Thiepval Wood.

Take a steady look at it; it'll do you good.

Here, these glasses will help you. See any flowers?

There sleeps Titania (correct—the Wood is ours);

There sleeps Titania in a deep dugout,

Waking, she wonders what all the din's about,

And smiles through her tears, and looks ahead ten years,

And sees the Wood again, and her usual Grenadiers,

           All in green,

           Music in the moon;

      The burned rubbish you've just seen

      Won't beat the Fairy Queen;

           All the same, it's a shade too soon

           For you to scribble rhymes

           In your army book

           About those times;

           Take another look;

That's where the difficulty is, over there.

Published 1930

---

1. This poem recalls the same action during the Battle of the Somme as "Preparations for Victory." The Germans had held Thiepval Ridge since September 1914, from which in 1916 they rained down bombs and incendiary devices onto unfortunate Tommies, trapped in vulnerable and exposed trenches, on the far side of the river. Blunden's poem recalls the nightmarish no-man's-land between the trenches and the river, in which many men were to die.

Basil Bunting (1900–1985)

BORN TO A Quaker family in Northumberland and educated at Quaker schools, Bunting remained faithful to its tenets, refusing to serve in World War One, regarding it as tainted by imperialist ambition. He was arrested and spent nearly eighteen months in prison. Between the wars, he became the friend and colleague of Ford Madox Ford, Ezra Pound, W. B. Yeats, James Joyce, and Louis Zukovsky. By the time of the Second World War, his stance had changed; he knew fascism had to be stopped. Despite poor eyesight he enlisted in the Royal Air Force, and in 1942 was stationed in Iran as an interpreter. "I planned operations," he told Zukovsky in 1944, "interpreted orders from above, ruled everything without official authority or backing. I even started and regulated a civilian market (not black but stripy), caught and punished thieves, instituted liaison with an Italian regiment." Bunting also worked in espionage and took responsibility for tracing enemy spies. After the war he was Vice Consul at the British Embassy in Iran, becoming chief of political intelligence in 1946. In this position, as one contemporary observer noted, he was "known for the wisdom of his political judgments," having "quelled a German-aided revolt of the Bakhtiari tribesmen almost single-handed." He became a *Times* correspondent in Iran in 1950 but was expelled by its prime minister the following year. He remained unknown as a poet until "discovered" by Tom Pickard, the poet and publisher who issued Bunting's masterpiece, *Briggflatts*, in 1965. It was, Bunting observed, autobiography "but not a record of fact. . . . The truth of the poem is of another kind." Briggflatts is a small hamlet close to the Cumbrian town of Sedbergh. The passage we have extracted from Bunting's poem begins at the side of the River Rawthey, close to the Quaker meetinghouse which has its own burial ground.

Briggflatts (extract)

Brag, sweet tenor bull,
descant on Rawthey's[1] madrigal,
each pebble its part
for the fells' late spring.
Dance tiptoe, bull,
black against may.
Ridiculous and lovely
chase hurdling shadows
morning into noon.
May on the bull's hide
and through the dale
furrows fill with may,
paving the slowworm's way.

A mason times his mallet
to a lark's twitter,
listening while the marble rests,
lays his rule
at a letter's edge,
fingertips checking,
till the stone spells a name
naming none,
a man abolished.
Painful lark, labouring to rise!
The solemn mallet says:
In the grave's slot
he lies. We rot.

Decay thrusts the blade,
wheat stands in excrement
trembling. Rawthey trembles.
Tongue stumbles, ears err
for fear of spring.
Rub the stone with sand,

---

1. Rawthey's] The River Rawthey flows close to the Quaker meetinghouse at Briggflatts, Cumbria.

wet sandstone rending
roughness away. Fingers
ache on the rubbing stone.
The mason says: Rocks
happen by chance.
No one here bolts the door,
love is so sore.

Stone smooth as skin,
cold as the dead they load
on a low lorry by night.
The moon sits on the fell   *hill*
but it will rain.
Under sacks on the stone
two children lie,
hear the horse stale,
the mason whistle,
harness mutter to shaft,
felloe to axle squeak,
rut thud the rim,
crushed grit.

Stocking to stocking, jersey to jersey,
head to a hard arm,
they kiss under the rain,
bruised by their marble bed.
In Garsdale, dawn;
at Hawes, tea from the can.
Rain stops, sacks
steam in the sun, they sit up.
Copper-wire moustache,
sea-reflecting eyes
and Baltic plainsong speech
declare: By such rocks
men killed Bloodaxe.[2]

---

2. Erik Bloodaxe (d. 954) was a Viking warrior chieftain and King of Northumbria (c. 947–948 and 952–954).

Fierce blood throbs in his tongue,
lean words.
Skulls cropped for steel caps
huddle round Stainmore.
Their becks ring on limestone,   *streams*
whisper to peat.
The clogged cart pushes the horse downhill.
In such soft air
they trudge and sing,
laying the tune frankly on the air.
All sounds fall still,
fellside bleat,
hide-and-seek peewit.

Her pulse their pace,
palm countering palm,
till a trench is filled,
stone white as cheese
jeers at the dale.
Knotty wood, hard to rive,   *split*
smoulders to ash;
smell of October apples.
The road again,
at a trot.
Wetter, warmed, they watch
the mason meditate
on name and date.

Rain rinses the road,
the bull streams and laments.
Sour rye porridge from the hob
with cream and black tea,
meat, crust and crumb.
Her parents in bed
the children dry their clothes.
He has untied the tape
of her striped flannel drawers
before the range. Naked

on the pricked rag mat
his fingers comb
thatch of his manhood's home.

Gentle generous voices weave
over bare night
words to confirm and delight
till bird dawn.
Rainwater from the butt
she fetches and flannel
to wash him inch by inch,
kissing the pebbles.
Shining slowworm part of the marvel.
The mason stirs:
Words!
Pens are too light.
Take a chisel to write.

Every birth a crime,
every sentence life.
Wiped of mould and mites
would the ball run true?
No hope of going back.
Hounds falter and stray,
shame deflects the pen.
Love murdered neither bleeds nor stifles
but jogs the draftsman's elbow.
What can he, changed, tell
her, changed, perhaps dead?
Delight dwindles. Blame
stays the same.

Brief words are hard to find,
shapes to carve and discard:
Bloodaxe, king of York,
king of Dublin, king of Orkney.
Take no notice of tears;
letter the stone to stand

over love laid aside lest
insufferable happiness impede
flight to Stainmore,
to trace
lark, mallet,
becks, flocks   *streams*
and axe knocks.

Dung will not soil the slowworm's
mosaic. Breathless lark
drops to nest in sodden trash;
Rawthey truculent, dingy.
Drudge at the mallet, the may is down,
fog on fells. Guilty of spring
and spring's ending
amputated years ache after
the bull is beef, love a convenience.
It is easier to die than to remember.
Name and date
split in soft slate
a few months obliterate.

Published 1965

Karl Shapiro (1913–2000)

SHAPIRO WAS, BY his own admission, changed forever by the Second World War: "war seems to be a permanent tattoo, or scar, on those who have been in it," he once said. He was training to be a librarian when, a year before America entered the war, he was drafted into the Medical Corps. While stationed in the South Pacific (Australia, the Trobriand Islands, New Guinea, the Dutch East Indies), he had access to a typewriter as the company clerk—though, as he recalled, "I carried a .45 and a carbine like everyone else." During the war he was surprisingly productive, writing four volumes of poetry. His remarkable "Essay on Rime," a 2,072-line blank-verse meditation that discussed poetry in the modern world, was written on active service, though it was *V-Letter and Other Poems* (1944) that won him the Pulitzer Prize. That volume was conceived in March 1943 in New Guinea, where Shapiro was constantly under fire, whether from Japanese snipers or air raids. (Its title alludes to a new form of postal system begun in June 1942 whereby letters to and from servicemen were microfilmed.) For a few weeks in 1944, Shapiro was a member of a mobile hospital unit that accompanied marines and infantry, performing surgery as the troops attempted to recapture islands from the Japanese. "I can't write when the bullets whistle," he commented of this period.

> The dead and wounded were carried into the little galley and sometimes carried out again after a word from one of the doctors, all four of whom were operating elbow to elbow. After an operation, even an amputation, the patient was carried out on deck to make room. A few times the just-operated-upon-man would be struck again by flying shrapnel or a bullet, and would be brought back in.

Shapiro declared he could never write poetry about this "night of death." In subsequent years, he found himself in the position of social and political dissident, prone to write essays on such topics as, for instance, the desirability of abolishing children. He declined membership of the American Academy and Institute of Arts and Letters for "no particular reason, except I didn't see what it was for"; described American poetry "as all jagged glass and rusty nails"; and was the sole member of the Bollingen Prize committee to object publicly to the award granted to Ezra Pound for *The Pisan Cantos*. It was with pride he characterized himself as "a kind of guerilla fighter and sniper," at best a "mad guest" in English departments.

Troop Train

It stops the town we come through. Workers raise
Their oily arms in good salute and grin.
Kids scream as at a circus. Business men
Glance hopefully and go their measured way.
And women standing at their dumbstruck door
More slowly wave and seem to warn us back,

As if a tear blinding the course of war
Might once dissolve our iron in their sweet wish.

Fruit of the world, oh clustered on ourselves
We hang as from a cornucopia
In total friendliness, with faces bunched
To spray the streets with catcalls and with leers.
A bottle smashes on the moving ties
And eyes fixed on a lady smiling pink
Stretch like a rubber-band and snap and sting
The mouth that wants the drink-of-water kiss.

And on through crummy continents and days,
Deliberate, grimy, slightly drunk we crawl,
The good-bad boys of circumstance and chance,
Whose bucket-helmets bang the empty wall
Where twist the murdered bodies of our packs
Next to the guns that only seem themselves.
And distance like a strap adjusted shrinks,
Tightens across the shoulder and holds firm.

Here is a deck of cards; out of this hand
Dealer, deal me my luck, a pair of bulls,
The right draw to a flush, the one-eyed jack.
Diamonds and hearts are red but spades are black,
And spades are spades and clubs are clovers—black.
But deal me winners, souvenirs of peace.
This stands to reason and arithmetic,
Luck also travels and not all come back.

Trains lead to ships and ships to death or trains,
And trains to death or trucks, and trucks to death,
Or trucks lead to the march, the march to death,
Or that survival which is all our hope;
And death leads back to trucks and trains and ships,
But life leads to the march, oh flag! at last
The place of life found after trains and death—
Nightfall of nations brilliant after war.

Published August 23, 1943

Sunday: New Guinea

The bugle sounds the measured call to prayers,
The band starts bravely with a clarion hymn,
From every side, singly, in groups, in pairs,
Each to his kind of service comes to worship Him.

Our faces washed, our hearts in the right place,
We kneel or stand or listen from our tents;
Half-naked natives with their kind of grace
Move down the road with balanced staffs like mendicants.

And over the hill the guns bang like a door
And planes repeat their mission in the heights.
The jungle outmaneuvers creeping war
And crawls within the circle of our sacred rites.

I long for our disheveled Sundays home,
Breakfast, the comics, news of latest crimes,
Talk without reference, and palindromes,
Sleep and the Philharmonic and the ponderous *Times*.

I long for lounging in the afternoons
Of clean intelligent warmth, my brother's mind,
Books and thin plates and flowers and shining spoons,
And your love's presence, snowy, beautiful, and kind.

Written 1943, published November 1943

On Reading Keats in Wartime

As one long lost in no-man's-land of war
Dreams of a cup of pure forgetful wine,
Dark waters deeper than the ancient Rhine
Where Saturnalian maidens swam before
The age of knowledge, and all your golden lore
Held in the splendor of a castle's shine

At sunset on a crag of somber pine—
But wakes to death and thirst and cannon's roar;

So I have come upon your book and drunk
Even to the dregs of melancholy bliss
Your poetry, Keats, and smoothing down your page,
Thought how a soldier leaner than a monk
Still loves, though time without the lover's kiss
Pours out its viscous hemlock on our age.

Published August 1944

The Conscientious Objector

The gates clanged and they walked you into jail
More tense than felons but relieved to find
The hostile world shut out, the flags that dripped
From every mother's windowpane, obscene
The bloodlust sweating from the public heart,·
The dog authority slavering at your throat.
A sense of quiet, of pulling down the blind
Possessed you. Punishment you felt was clean.

The decks, the catwalks, and the narrow light
Composed a ship. This was a mutinous crew
Troubling the captains for plain decencies,
A Mayflower brim with pilgrims headed out
To establish new theocracies to west,
A Noah's ark coasting the topmost seas
Ten miles above the sodomites and fish.
These inmates loved the only living doves.

Like all men hunted from the world you made
A good community, voyaging the storm
To no safe Plymouth or green Ararat;
Trouble or calm, the men with Bibles prayed,
The gaunt politicals construed our hate.

The opposite of all armies, you were best
Opposing uniformity and yourselves;
Prison and personality were your fate.

You suffered not so physically but knew
Maltreatment, hunger, ennui of the mind.
Well might the soldier kissing the hot beach
Erupting in his face damn all your kind.
Yet you who saved neither yourselves nor us
Are equally with those who shed the blood
The heroes of our cause. Your conscience is
What we come back to in the armistice.

Published summer 1946

John Cornford (1913–1936)

THE LIFE OF John Cornford seems to exemplify that of those idealists who in the early twentieth century were willing to die for a more just society. His father was professor of ancient philosophy at Cambridge University, and through his mother he was Charles Darwin's great-grandson. As a Young Communist League member he worked to realize Marx's vision in England, becoming a party member in 1935. He won an exhibition to Trinity College, Cambridge, where his academic record was distinguished—he achieved first-class marks in both parts of the history tripos and was awarded a scholarship to study the Elizabethans. But when the Spanish Civil War was declared he disappeared, without a word to his family, becoming the first Englishman to enlist in the war against Franco. By his third day in Spain he was on his way to the front line in Aragon, to fight with the POUM militia, where he soon came under fire: "suddenly bullets began to whistle very close—zip—zip—zip." During these weeks he composed the poems included here. Cornford took part in the battle for Madrid in November 1936, where he was involved in concentrated fighting during a siege that would continue until March 1939 (when the city fell to Franco). By the time he wrote to Margot Heinemann on November 21, he had been "three times heavily and accurately bombarded by artillery." "Continuous fighting, heavy losses, many of them simply due to inexperience," he wrote home, "but we've been on the whole successful." He was embroiled in the Battle of Lopera, December 27–29, 1936; at a severe disadvantage, his unit had no telephone communications, little training, and no air or artillery support. Such was the chaos that at one point Cornford and his company were under fire from their own side. They were decimated by the superior firepower of Franco's fascists, losing eight hundred men out of a force of three thousand. Cornford was among those killed—how and when is disputed; if, as some claim, it was on December 27, he died on his twenty-first birthday. His body was never recovered.

A Letter From Aragon

This is a quiet sector of a quiet front.

We buried Ruiz in a new pine coffin,
But the shroud was too small and his washed feet stuck out.
The stink of his corpse came through the clean pine boards
And some of the bearers wrapped handkerchiefs round their faces.
Death was not dignified.
We hacked a ragged grave in the unfriendly earth
And fired a ragged volley over the grave.

You could tell from our listlessness, no one much missed him.

This is a quiet sector of a quiet front.
There is no poison gas and no H.E.[1]

But when they shelled the other end of the village
And the streets were choked with dust
Women came screaming out of the crumbling houses,
Clutched under one arm the naked rump of an infant.
I thought: how ugly fear is.

---

1. H.E.] high explosives.

This is a quiet sector of a quiet front.
Our nerves are steady; we all sleep soundly.

In the clean hospital bed, my eyes were so heavy
Sleep easily blotted out one ugly picture,
A wounded militiaman moaning on a stretcher,
Now out of danger, but still crying for water,
Strong against death, but unprepared for such pain.

This on a quiet front.

But when I shook hands to leave, an Anarchist worker
Said: "Tell the workers of England
This was a war not of our own making
We did not seek it.
But if ever the Fascists again rule Barcelona
It will be as a heap of ruins with us workers beneath it."

Written August 1936, published November 1936

Full Moon at Tierz: Before the Storming of Huesca[1]

1
The past, a glacier, gripped the mountain wall,
And time was inches, dark was all.
But here it scales the end of the range,
The dialectic's point of change,
Crashes in light and minutes to its fall.

Time present is a cataract whose force
Breaks down the banks even at its source
And history forming in our hand's
Not plasticine but roaring sands,
Yet we must swing it to its final course.

---

1. Huesca was a Nationalist stronghold during the Spanish Civil War. The Republican offensive took place June 12–19, 1937.

The intersecting lines that cross both ways,
Time future, has no image in space,
Crooked as the road that we must tread,
Straight as our bullets fly ahead.
We are the future. The last fight let us face.

2

Where, in the fields by Huesca, the full moon
Throws shadows clear as daylight's, soon
The innocence of this quiet plain
Will fade in sweat and blood, in pain,
As our decisive hold is lost or won.

All round the barren hills of Aragon
Announce our testing has begun.
Here what the Seventh Congress said,[2]
If true, if false, is live or dead,
Speaks in the Oviedo Mausers'[3] tone.

Three years ago Dimitrov fought alone
And we stood taller when he won.[4]
But now the Leipzig dragon's teeth
Sprout strong and handsome against death
And here an army fights where there was one.

We studied well how to begin this fight,
Our Maurice Thorez[5] held the light.

---

2. what the Seventh Congress said] In August 1935, Georgi Dimitrov (1882–1949), the Bulgarian communist, argued, at the seventh (and last) Congress of the Communist International, that non-Communist organizations should unite in the battle against facism.

3. Oviedo Mausers'] Mauser rifle made at the Fabrica de Armas arsenal in Oviedo, Spain.

4. Three years . . . when he won] Cornford refers to Georgi Dimitrov, the Bulgarian Communist accused by the Nazis of having set fire to the Reichstag. In court in Leipzig, Dimitrov denounced Goering and Goebbels: he was acquitted on December 23, 1933. It should be added that Dimitrov was not quite alone; his co-accused, the Dutch anarchist Marinus van der Lubbe (1909–1934), was executed for his part in the fire.

5. Maurice Thorez (1900–1964) was the leader of the French Communist Party from 1930 until his death.

But now by Monte Aragon
We plunge into the dark alone,
Earth's newest planet wheeling through the night.

3
Though Communism was my waking time,
Always before the lights of home
Shone clear and steady and full in view—
Here, if you fall, there's help for you—
Now, with my Party, I stand quite alone.

Then let my private battle with my nerves,
The fear of pain whose pain survives,
The love that tears me by the roots,
The loneliness that claws my guts,
Fuse in the welded front our fight preserves.

Oh be invincible as the strong sun,
Hard as the metal of my gun,
Oh let the mounting tempo of the train
Sweep where my footsteps slipped in vain,
October in the rhythm of its run.

4
Now the same night falls over Germany
And the impartial beauty of the stars
Lights from the unfeeling sky
Oranienburg[6] and freedom's crooked scars.
We can do nothing to ease that pain
But prove that agony was not in vain.

England is silent under the same moon,
From Clydeside to the gutted pits of Wales.
The innocent mask conceals that soon

---

6. Oranienburg] near Berlin, site of a concentration camp renowned for its brutality, established by the SA (stormtroopers) in March 1933. It was used to confine Communists. It was closed by 1935.

Here, too, our freedom's swaying in the scales.
Oh understand before too late
Freedom was never held without a fight.

Freedom is an easily spoken word
But facts are stubborn things. Here, too, in Spain
Our fight's not won till the workers of all the world
Stand by our guard on Huesca's plain,
Swear that our dead fought not in vain,
Raise the red flag triumphantly
For Communism and for liberty.

Written August 1936, published March 1937

To Margot Heinemann[1]

Heart of the heartless world,
Dear heart, the thought of you
Is the pain at my side,
The shadow that chills my view.

The wind rises in the evening,
Reminds that autumn's near.
I am afraid to lose you,
I am afraid of my fear.

On the last mile to Huesca,
The last fence for our pride,
Think so kindly, dear, that I
Sense you at my side.

And if bad luck should lay my strength
Into the shallow grave,

---

1. Margot Heinemann (1923–1992) was a fellow Communist who Cornford met in 1935. In later years she became a highly respected Shakespeare scholar.

Remember all the good you can;
Don't forget my love.

Written August 1936, published autumn 1937

William Stafford (1914–1993)

"I THOUGHT ALL right-thinking people would behave that way," Stafford once responded when asked why he had been a conscientious objector during the Second World War. "In those days, the 1930s, the peace movement was strong in America. In fact, Franklin Roosevelt, to get elected, had to promise no war. The other people changed, and I was surprised. I thought a commitment was a commitment. There were peace people everywhere, in all countries, and I was not about to break ranks with that worldwide fellowship." When America entered the war, Stafford was a graduate student working for his master's at the University of Kansas. On being drafted he registered as a conscientious objector, and over the next four years worked in four different Civilian Public Service camps in Arkansas, California, and Illinois, where he was paid $2.50 per month for assigned duties such as fire fighting, soil conservation, and building and maintaining roads and trails. It had a profound impact on him, as he recalled: "My four years of 'alternative service under civilian direction' turned my life sharply into that independent channel of the second river—a course hereafter distinguished from any unexamined life, from the way it might have been in any of my hometowns." His stand took courage, for it earned nothing but hostility from his countrymen. He later recalled how he and two companions had gone into a town together to write poetry, only for their presence to inflame its citizens to the point at which an angry mob formed, ready to lynch them: they had to be rescued by an understanding sheriff. Stafford later described this period as being "out in the cold, for four crucial years." In its midst, the writing of poetry each morning was "maintenance work or repair work on my integrity." These experiences provided the foundation for the vision that sustained his creative work for the rest of his life; it is articulated in his prose memoir, *Down in My Heart*, and throughout his verse.

At the Bomb Testing Site

At noon in the desert a panting lizard
waited for history, its elbows tense,
watching the curve of a particular road
as if something might happen.

It was looking at something farther off
than people could see, an important scene
acted in stone for little selves
at the flute end of consequences.

There was just a continent without much on it
under a sky that never cared less.
Ready for a change, the elbows waited.
The hands gripped hard on the desert.

Published 1960

Traveling Through the Dark

Traveling through the dark I found a deer
dead on the edge of the Wilson River road.
It is usually best to roll them into the canyon:
that road is narrow; to swerve might make more dead.

By glow of the taillight I stumbled back of the car
and stood by the heap, a doe, a recent killing;
she had stiffened already, almost cold.
I dragged her off; she was large in the belly.

My fingers touching her side brought me the reason—
her side was warm; her fawn lay there waiting,
alive, still, never to be born.
Beside that mountain road I hesitated.

The car aimed ahead its lowered parking lights;
under the hood purred the steady engine.
I stood in the glare of the warm exhaust turning red;
around our group I could hear the wilderness listen.

I thought hard for us all—my only swerving—,
then pushed her over the edge into the river.

Published 1962

At the Un-National Monument Along the Canadian Border

This is the field where the battle did not happen,
where the unknown soldier did not die.
This is the field where grass joined hands,
where no monument stands,
and the only heroic thing is the sky.

Birds fly here without any sound,
unfolding their wings across the open.
No people killed—or were killed—on this ground
hallowed by neglect and an air so tame
that people celebrate it by forgetting its name.

Published 1977

1940

It is August. Your father is walking you
to the train for camp and then the War
and on out of his life, but you don't know.

Little lights along the path glow under their hoods
and your shoes go brown, brown in the brightness
till the next interval, when they disappear in the shadow.

You know they are down there, by the crunch of stone
and a rustle when they touch a fern. Somewhere above,
cicadas arch their gauze of sound all over town.

Shivers of summer wind follow across the park
and then turn back. You walk on toward
September, the depot, the dark, the light, the dark.

Published 1987

William Meredith (1919–2007)

THE ROLE OF dissident, Meredith once observed, "is the most *urgent* role at a time like ours. . . . The time is always *a time like ours*." As an undergraduate at Princeton, he wrote his senior thesis on Robert Frost, who he met in New England. After graduation he worked briefly at *The New York Times* before America entered the war. Having enlisted in the army, he transferred to the navy, serving as naval pilot on aircraft carriers in the Pacific Theater, first in the Aleutian Islands and then in Hawaii. During this period, he became a published poet, his first collection, *Love Letter from an Impossible Land*, appearing in 1944. He went on to teach literature at Princeton and the University of Hawaii in Honolulu, and reenlisted at the outbreak of the Korean War, earning two Air Medals during his two years of service. Meredith was a friend of Robert Lowell and John Berryman, but it was the critic Edward Hirsch who noted Meredith's "powerful impulse to move beyond their doubts, misgivings and grievances" toward "a complex and committed optimism." Meredith himself said he wanted to be "useful": "I am a useful poet because I write to ordinary people, not intellectuals. Intellectuals don't care anyhow."

Airman's Virtue

After Herbert

High plane for whom the winds incline,
Who own but to your own recall,
There is a flaw in your design,
For you must fall.

High cloud whose proud and angry stuff
Rose up in heat against earth's thrall,
The nodding law has time enough
To wait your fall.

High sky, full of high shapes and vapors,
Against whose vault nothing is tall,
It is written that your torch and tapers
Headlong shall fall.

Only an outward-aching soul
Can hold in high disdain these ties,
And fixing on a farther pole,
Will sheerly rise.

Published January 1943

Navy Field

Limped out of the hot sky a hurt plane,
Held off, held off, whirring pretty pigeon,
Hit then and scuttled to a crooked stop.
The stranger pilot who emerged—this was the seashore,
War came suddenly here—talked to the still mechanics
Who nodded gravely. Flak had done it, he said,
From an enemy ship attacked.
            They wheeled it with love

Into the dark hangar's mouth and tended it.
Coffee and cake for the pilot then who sat alone
In the restaurant, reading the numbered sheets
That tell about weather.
    After, toward dusk,
Mended the stranger plane went back to the sky.
His curly-headed picture, and mother's and medal's pictures
Were all we knew of him after he rose again,
Those few electric jewels against the moth and shining sky.

Published January 1943

For Air Heroes

I sing them spiraling in flame,
Them gliding, all fuel spent,
Checked by no opening silk plume:
The dedicated and the dead,
Themselves quite lost,
Articulate at last;

Sing them telling what they meant,
No small repeated dream,
As public and grandiose their want
As their last lowering scene:
Burning, dropping host,
Articulate at last;

And sing them making purchases
Beyond our furthest means,
Themselves the greatly valued pledges;
Oh let the contract somehow be redeemed!
They speak for most,
Articulate at last.

Published 1944

Notes for an Elegy

The alternative to flying is cowardice,
And what is said against it excuses, excuses;
Its want was always heavy in those men's bodies
Who foresaw it in some detail; and failing that,
The rest were shown through its skyey heats and eases
In sleep, awoke uncertain whether their waking cry
Had been falling fear only, or love and falling fear.
When the sudden way was shown, its possibility
In terms of the familiar at last shown,
(How absurdly simple the principle after all!)
Any tyrant should have sensed it was controversial:
Instrument of freedom; rights, not Wrights;
Danger should never be given out publicly.
The men could easily have been disposed of,
They and their fragile vehicle. Then the sky
Would perhaps have darkened, earth shaken, nothing more.
In practice the martyrdom has been quiet, statistical,
A fair price. This is what airmen believe.

The transition to battle was smooth from here.
Who resents one bond resents another,
And who has unshouldered earth-restraining hand
Is not likely to hear out more reasonable tyrannies.

The woods where he died were dark even at sunup,
Oak and long-needle pine that had come together
Earlier, and waited for the event at the field's edge.
At sunset when the sky behind was gay
One had seen the lugubrious shapes of the trees,
Bronze and terrible, but had never known the reason,
Never thought they were waiting for someone in particular.
They took him at night, when they were at their darkest.

How they at last convinced him is not known:
The crafty engine would not fall for their softness,
(Oh, where were you then, six hundred cunning horses?)

In the end it had torn hungrily through the brush
To lie alone in the desired clearing. Nor the wings;
(And you, with your wide silver margin of safety?)
They were for the field, surely, where they so often
Had eased their load to ground. No, the invitation
Must have been sent to the aviator in person:
Perhaps a sly suggestion of carelessness,
A whispered invitation perhaps to death.

He was not badly disfigured compared to some,
But even a little stream of blood where death is
Will whimper across a forest floor,
Run through that whole forest shouting.

Him now unpersoned, warm, and quite informal,
Dead as alive, raise softly sober interns;
Lift gently, God, this wholly airborne one.
Leads out all his life to this violent wood.

Note that he had not fought one public battle,
Met any fascist with his skill, but died
As it were in bed, the waste conspicuous;
This is a costly wreck and costly to happen on:
Praise and humility sound through its siren shrieks,
And dedication follows in car.

The morning came up foolish with pink clouds
To say that God counts ours a cunning time,
Our losses part of an old secret, somehow no loss.

Published 1944

Keith Douglas (1920–1944)

"HELL CANNOT BE let loose twice," Douglas wrote. "It was let loose in the Great War and it is the same old hell now." Douglas is the preeminent English poet of the Second World War, responsible in "Vergissmeinnicht" and "How to Kill" for the two most unflinching poems of that conflict. As an undergraduate at Merton College, Oxford, his tutor was Edmund Blunden (see p. 569), with whose accounts of an earlier war his are sometimes compared. He enlisted with the Nottinghamshire Sherwood Rangers yeomanry, a tank regiment stationed in North Africa, and was active in the Western Desert Campaign, in Egypt and Tunisia. "Thank heavens I can't see what is going to happen to us all as clearly as you must be able to," he wrote to Blunden. Some of his most accomplished verse was written when he was hospitalized from January to August 1943, suffering from injuries sustained in an explosion. On June 6, 1944, Douglas commanded a tank troop in the D-Day assault on the beaches of Normandy; three days later he was killed by an exploding mortar outside the village of St. Pierre, and buried in the war cemetery at Tilly-sur-Seulles. He was twenty-four. His *Collected Poems* appeared in 1951 and made no impact; only with publication of his *Selected Poems* (1964) was he given his due. Honesty characterizes his vision, something emphasized in one of his letters home. "I don't know if you have come across the word Bullshit," he writes. "It is an army word and signifies humbug and unnecessary detail. It symbolizes what I think must be got rid of—the mass of irrelevancies, of 'attitudes,' 'approaches,' propaganda, ivory towers, etc., that stands between us and our problems and what we have to do about them. To write on the themes which have been concerning me lately in lyrical and abstract forms, would be immense bullshitting."

Vergissmeinnicht[1]

Three weeks gone and the combatants gone
returning over the nightmare ground
we found the place again, and found
the soldier sprawling in the sun.

The frowning barrel of his gun
overshadowing. As we came on
that day, he hit my tank with one
like the entry of a demon.

Look. Here in the gunpit spoil
the dishonoured picture of his girl
who has put: *Steffi. Vergissmeinnicht*
in a copybook gothic script.

We see him almost with content,
abased, and seeming to have paid
and mocked at by his own equipment
that's hard and good when he's decayed.

But she would weep to see today
how on his skin the swart flies move;
the dust upon the paper eye
and the burst stomach like a cave.

For here the lover and killer are mingled
who had one body and one heart.
And death who had the soldier singled
has done the lover mortal hurt.

TUNISIA, MAY–JUNE 1943

Published 1946

---

1. Vergissmeinnicht] Forget me not.

How to Kill

Under the parabola of a ball,
a child turning into a man,
I looked into the air too long.
The ball fell in my hand, it sang
in the closed fist: *Open Open
Behold a gift designed to kill.*

Now in my dial of glass appears
the soldier who is going to die.
He smiles, and moves about in ways
his mother knows, habits of his.
The wires touch his face: I cry
NOW. Death, like a familiar, hears

and look, has made a man of dust
of a man of flesh. This sorcery
I do. Being damned, I am amused
to see the center of love diffused
and the waves of love travel into vacancy.
How easy it is to make a ghost.

The weightless mosquito touches
her tiny shadow on the stone,
and with how like, how infinite
a lightness, man and shadow meet.
They fuse. A shadow is a man
when the mosquito death approaches.

Written 1943, published 1946

Hayden Carruth (1921–2008)

BETWEEN COMPLETION OF his studies at the University of North Carolina (Chapel Hill) and graduate work at the University of Chicago, Carruth served in the Second World War. He trained as a cryptographer in the signal branch of the Army Air Corps but was later moved to the 455th Heavy Bombardment Group, operating out of Cerignola in southern Italy. During that period he took part in a campaign that incurred nearly seven hundred thousand casualties on both sides, working principally in public relations, writing newspaper articles and recording radio interviews for consumption at home. "The loneliness of my life was acute," he later recalled of the war, "I suffered constantly from psychosomatic disorders, including recurrent attacks of 'fake appendicitis.' Extreme insomnia was the rule." After the war, Carruth funded his master's studies on the G.I. Bill, during which he edited *Poetry* magazine and worked at the University of Chicago Press. In 1953, he suffered a breakdown triggered in part by struggles with alcoholism. Diagnosed as suffering from acute and chronic anxiety psychoneurosis with phobic dimensions, he was treated with electroconvulsive therapy at a private psychiatric hospital and emerged "in worse shape" than he went in. For the rest of his life, he suffered from "chronic psychiatric disorders that were acute during my thirties and have been slowly and painfully—and imperfectly—overcome in the years since then." Doctors told him he "would never lead anything like a normal life." For the next five years he lived in an attic in his parents' house, unable to face other human beings, before moving to rural Vermont, where he found stability as a farm laborer and mechanic; though he continued to write poetry and work as a copy editor, he was always short of money, at times being compelled to steal cattle feed to survive. For years, Carruth seemed to live in a state of intermittent crisis that culminated in a suicide attempt: "Early in the morning of February 24, 1988, I intentionally and massively overdosed myself with every pill I possessed." Yet despite these obstacles, he was intensely productive, the author of more than thirty books, one of which won a Pulitzer Prize in 1996. He disliked parties, religions, and societies, preferring the free-wheeling manner of the jazz clarinetist.

Three Sonnets on the Necessity of Narrowly Escaping Death

DEFENSE

Collapsible, selfwilled and jealousjelled,
My self once gave me screech pale sob white pain.
Thereafter, handicapped, I joined the rain
And only seldom stretched an arm that swelled
With water, like a bag. My toes were held
By webs, my face grew flat. Across a plain,
Down then a straight ravine, dragging my brain,
I came, I sank, I was at last hardshelled.

The great anemones with stately grace
Waved over my castle; tides brought shifting hulks;
And retinues of luminous eyes would pace
Before my door, then go with slow rolling bulks.
But I and other mollusks held our peace,
Hardshelled, unargumentative, obese.

RESTRICTION

The shells that men secrete are made of words,
And even those undignified by print
Are hard and multiple. Through cracks, asquint,
We twist for prismed glimpses of the birds
That flash and wheel and cry, the hundred herds
Whose thundering hooves roar over the earth in sprint.
We ache for motion, now and then by dint
Of impulse move a nerve and think in surds.

Motion is meaning, meaning knowledge. Locked
In shells of words, the mollusks know not things,
Nor even selves, the crimped and cramped, unblocked,
Unwatched and unexpressed. The radio sings,
We think with archness of the Pleistocene,
And fuel our flaccid hearts with gasoline.

ESCAPE

The earth immediately was torn apart.
I found a friendly piece, fell in and caught

My ear against the noise that raged. I thought:
I knew this coming, no cry now. But tart
And sharp, all fear sprang out aquiver, heart
Stammered and leapt, teeth were cold and taut.
I jumped, and terror smashed our juggernaut;
And I could move, my arm a robust upstart.

And when I rose and walked, the bits of shell
Crunched underfoot, as on a windy beach.
The clean and rainless wind blew off the swell
And stung my rounded face and tore my speech.
I felt my wounds, I watched the shrinking flood,
I dipped my separate fingers in my blood.

Published February 1948

Emergency Haying

Coming home with the last load I ride standing
on the wagon tongue, behind the tractor
in hot exhaust, lank with sweat,

my arms strung
awkwardly along the hayrack, cruciform.
Almost 500 bales we've put up

this afternoon, Marshall and I.
And of course I think of another who hung
like this on another cross. My hands are torn

by baling twine, not nails, and my side is pierced
by my ulcer, not a lance. The acid in my throat
is only hayseed. Yet exhaustion and the way

my body hangs from twisted shoulders, suspended
on two points of pain in the rising
monoxide, recall that greater suffering.

Well, I change grip and the image
fades. It's been an unlucky summer. Heavy rains
brought on the grass tremendously, a monster crop,

but wet, always wet. Haying was long delayed.
Now is our last chance to bring in
the winter's feed, and Marshall needs help.

We mow, rake, bale, and draw the bales
to the barn, these late, half-green,
improperly cured bales; some weigh 150 pounds

or more, yet must be lugged by the twine
across the field, tossed on the load, and then
at the barn unloaded on the conveyor

and distributed in the loft. I help—
I, the desk-servant, word-worker—
and hold up my end pretty well too; but God,

the close of day, how I fall down then. My hands
are sore, they flinch when I light my pipe.
I think of those who have done slave labor,

less able and less well prepared than I.
Rose Marie in the rye fields of Saxony,
her father in the camps of Moldavia

and the Crimea, all clerks and housekeepers
herded to the gaunt fields of torture. Hands
too bloodied cannot bear

even the touch of air, even
the touch of love. I have a friend
whose grandmother cut cane with a machete

and cut and cut, until one day
she snicked her hand off and took it
and threw it grandly at the sky. Now

in September our New England mountains
under a clear sky for which we're thankful at last
begin to glow, maples, beeches, birches

in their first color. I look
beyond our famous hayfields to our famous hills,
to the notch where the sunset is beginning,

then in the other direction, eastward,
where a full new-risen moon like a pale
medallion hangs in a lavender cloud

beyond the barn. My eyes
sting with sweat and loveliness. And who
is the Christ now, who

if not I? It must be so. My strength
is legion. And I stand up high
on the wagon tongue in my whole bones to say

woe to you, watch out
you sons of bitches who would drive men and women
to the fields where they can only die.

Published spring 1969

Samuel Menashe (1925–2011)

WRITING IN 1971, Stephen Spender commented of Menashe: "nothing seems more remarkable about him than that his poetry goes so little remarked. Here is a poet who compresses thoughts and sensations into language intense and clear as diamonds." The son of Russian immigrants, Menashe enrolled in Queens College, City University of New York, but left in 1943 for the army. He fought with the 87th Infantry Division (Golden Acorn), and was one of those who, at the end of December 1944, crossed the Saar Valley in time to take part in the Battle of the Bulge. In the midst of snow, sleet, and biting cold, Menashe and his comrades found themselves in the center of the battle zone, ordered to recapture villages and towns taken by the Germans; they succeeded, and managed to sever German supply lines. It was a turning point in the battle on the Western Front, though at great cost. On a single day, all but 29 of his company of 190 were either killed, wounded, or captured. The experience changed him forever: "if I hadn't been in the infantry and lucky enough to survive physically unharmed, I might have had a much more conventional life. I remember I used to hear people, when I came home from the war, talking about what they intended to do 'next summer,' and I was amazed by their certainty that they would be alive 'next summer.' I always thought that each day was the last day for the first few years. And then it changed: not each day as the *last* day, but each day as the *only* day. It's more hopeful in a way." At first, he had no intention of writing verse—"I had never met a poet and never dreamed of being a poet. Poets were dead immortals"—indeed, his major was in biochemistry. He went to Paris and took his doctoral degree at the Sorbonne, but one night in February 1949 found a line of verse in his head: "All my life when I woke up at night." He spent the rest of his life in a fifth-floor, three-room walk-up in Greenwich Village, living in monkish self-denial. British writers such as Kathleen Raine and Stephen Spender were the first to recognize his genius, long before his first American volume appeared in 1971; his achievement was acknowledged when in 2004 the Poetry Foundation awarded him its Neglected Masters Award. Our selection contains five poems inspired by war: "Winter," "Warrior Wisdom," "Cargo," "Beachhead," and "All my friends are homeless." "At a Standstill" is a late meditation on the trauma of war and the way it changed him: "Usually, I could give the day its due, live in the present, but I had no foresight for the future. Perhaps it is why I am still in the flat to which I moved when I was thirty-one years old."

Warrior Wisdom

Do not scrutinize
A secret wound—
Avert your eyes—
Nothing's to be done

Where darkness lies
No light can come

Published 1961

Winter

I am entrenched
Against the snow,
Visor lowered
To blunt its blow

I am where I go

Published March 7, 1970

Cargo

Old wounds leave good hollows
Where one who goes can hold
Himself in ghostly embraces
Of former powers and graces
Whose domain no strife mars—
I am made whole by my scars
For whatever now displaces
Follows all that once was
And without loss stows
Me into my own spaces

Published 1971

All my friends are homeless

All my friends are homeless
They do not even have tents
Were I to seek a safe place
I would run nights lost
Ice pelting my face
Sent the wrong way
Whenever I ask—
Afraid to run back,
Each escape the last

Lie down below trees
Be your own guest
Give yourself up . . .
Under this attentive pine
Take your time at noon
The planes will drone by soon

Published May 31, 1973

At a Standstill

That statue, that cast
Of my solitude
Has found its niche
In this kitchen
Where I do not eat
Where the bathtub stands
Upon cat feet—
I did not advance
I cannot retreat

Published 1980

Beachhead

The tide ebbs
From a helmet
Wet sand embeds

Published 1986

W. D. Snodgrass (1926–2009)

SNODGRASS WAS "THE most gifted of all American young poets now alive," in the opinion of James Wright. He was about to enter the Julliard School of Music, his timpani playing having won him a place there, when drafted to serve in the U.S. Navy in the Second World War. He was a brig guard, 1944–1946, detaining American soldiers in holding cells for disciplinary infractions. "Being a brig guard," he once remarked, "is not one of those things that you can be very proud of." Asked whether he felt he should have refused to do some of the things he had been ordered to do, Snodgrass replied, "I should have, but I didn't have the courage." Nor did he ever forget how, while being trained, he had been taught how to blind a man with his bare hands "and then . . . rip off his face." Although he saw little action, his wartime experience caused long-term trauma, leading him to register as a conscientious objector during the Korean War. After demobilization, he enrolled in the Iowa Writers' Workshop where his mentor and teacher was Robert Lowell, who remarked of him: "He flowered in the most sterile of sterile places: a post war, cold war midwestern university's workshop for graduate student poets." His first book, *Heart's Needle* (1959), which won the Pulitzer Prize, led to his being regarded as a confessional poet, a label he later disowned. Snodgrass's war experiences ultimately led him to write *The Führer Bunker* (1995), a volume that absorbed twenty-five years of his life and consisted of monologues by Hitler and his circle during the final days of the Third Reich. His research included an interview with Albert Speer. "By talking about how evil other people are, you talk about how evil we all are," Sndograss once remarked. "We pretty much share the same good and bad possibilities."

The Führer Bunker (extract)
Magda Goebbels—30 April 1945

AFTER DR. HAASE GAVE THEM SHOTS OF MORPHINE, MAGDA GAVE EACH
CHILD AN AMPULE OF POTASSIUM CYANIDE FROM A SPOON.

This is the needle that we give
Soldiers and children when they live
Near the front in primitive
    Conditions or real dangers;
This is the spoon we use to feed
Men trapped in trouble or in need,
When weakness or bad luck might lead
    Them to the hands of strangers.

This is the room where you can sleep
Your sleep out, curled up under deep
Layers of covering that will keep
    You safe till all harm's past.
This is the bed where you can rest
In perfect silence, undistressed
By noise or nightmares, as my breast
    Once held you soft but fast.

This is the Doctor who has brought
Your needle with your special shot
To quiet you; you won't get caught
    Off guard or unprepared.
I am your nurse who'll comfort you;
I nursed you, fed you till you grew
Too big to feed; now you're all through
    Fretting or feeling scared.

This is the glass tube that contains
Calm that will spread down through your veins
To free you finally from all pains
    Of going on in error.
This tiny pinprick sets the germ

Inside you that fills out its term
Till you can feel yourself grow firm
   Against all doubt, all terror.

Into this spoon I break the pill
That stiffens the unsteady will
And hardens you against the chill
   Voice of a world of lies.
This amber medicine implants
Steadfastness in your blood; this grants
Immunity from greed and chance,
   And from all compromise.

This is the serum that can cure
Weak hearts; these pure, clear drops insure
You'll face what comes and can endure
   The test; you'll never falter.
This is the potion that preserves
You in a faith that never swerves;
This sets the pattern of your nerves
   Too firm for you to alter.

I set this spoon between your tight
Teeth, as I gave you your first bite;
This satisfies your appetite
   For other nourishment.
Take this on your tongue; this do
Remembering your mother who
So loved her Leader she stayed true
   When all the others went,

When every friend proved false, in the
Delirium of treachery
On every hand, when even He
   Had turned His face aside.
He shut himself in with His whore;
Then, though I screamed outside His door,
Said He'd not see me anymore.
   They both took cyanide.

Open wide, now, little bird;
I who sang you your first word
Soothe away every sound you've heard
   Except your Leader's voice.
Close your eyes, now; take your death.
Once we slapped you to take breath.
Vengeance is mine, the Lord God saith
   And cancels each last choice.

Once, my first words marked out your mind;
Just as our Leader's phrases bind
All hearts to Him, building a blind
   Loyalty through the nation,
We shape you into a pure form.
Trapped, our best soldiers tricked the storm,
The Reds: those last hours, they felt warm
   Who stood fast to their station.

You needn't fear what your life meant;
You won't curse how your hours were spent;
You'll grow like your own monument
   To all things sure and good,
Fixed like a frieze in high relief
Of granite figures that our Chief
Accepts into His true belief,
   His true blood-brotherhood.

You'll never bite the hand that fed you,
Won't turn away from those that bred you,
Comforted your nights and led you
   Into the thought of virtue;
You won't be turned from your own bed;
Won't turn into that thing you dread;
No new betrayal lies ahead;
   Now no one else can hurt you.

Published 1987

Robert Creeley (1926–2005)

IN 1944 CREELEY was asked to withdraw from Harvard during his freshman year, having been arrested while trying to find liquor. Instead he joined the American Field Service for which he drove a three-ton Chevrolet ambulance in the India-Burma Theater of World War Two (as he had a glass eye, he could not be deployed in the front line). He tended those wounded during the attempt to retake Rangoon in the spring of 1945, including a soldier with his entire side blown off, for whom there was little to be done. He saw how the Ghurkas refused to pass out while being operated on, despite anesthetic—on one occasion watching as a man in his sixties, shot three times by .45 caliber bullets (twice in the solar plexus), walked calmly from the operating theater. He admired the Japanese most of all: they would shoot at their captors even while being taken; one, riddled with bullets, jerked upright on the operating table and knifed the surgeon. Though Creeley saw little action, it was traumatic work, and he drank rye or smoked marijuana whenever he could, later admitting he was "out of my head those days, with or without stimulus." On return to America, he returned to Harvard where he was attracted to Communism, but dropped out in his final semester, disillusioned with what he felt to be the unimaginativeness of his teachers. His first published poem, "Return," written under the influence of marijuana, concerns the alienation he felt on returning home after witnessing the horrors of war.

Return

Quiet as is proper for such places;
The street, subdued, half-snow, half-rain,
Endless, but ending in the darkened doors.
Inside, they who will be there always,
Quiet as is proper for such people—

Enough for now to be here, and
To know my door is one of these.

Written winter 1945, published spring 1946

Men

Here, on the wall
of this hotel in
Singapore, there's a

picture, of a woman,
big breasted, walking,
blue coated, with

smaller person—both
followed by a house men
are carrying. It's a day

in the life of the world.
It tells you, somehow,
what you ought to know.

*

Getting fainter, in the world,
fearing something's fading,
deadened, tentative responses—
go hours without eating,
scared without someone to be
with me. These empty days.

*

Growth, trees, out window's
reminiscent of other days,

other places, years ago,
a kid in Burma, war,

fascinated, in jungle,
happily not shot at,

hauling the dead and dying
along those impossible roads

to nothing much could help.
Dreaming, of home, the girl

left behind, getting drunk,
getting laid, getting beaten

out of whorehouse one night.
So where am I now.

*

Patience gets
you the next place.

So they say.

*

Some huge clock
somewhere said it was
something like sixteen

or twenty hours later
or earlier there, going
around and around.

Written 1976, published 1978

Thom Gunn (1929–2004)

By 1983, when gay men began to hear about AIDS, Thom Gunn was a well-established poet with seven collections of poetry behind him. Brought up in England, he had been alienated from his father even as a boy, though close to his mother, who committed suicide when he was fifteen. He discovered his homosexuality while an undergraduate at Trinity College, Cambridge, after two years' national service (which he later described as "drudgery and boredom"). Asked about the prevalence of soldier figures in his early poetry, Gunn once remarked: "I was ten at the beginning of World War Two and sixteen when it ended, so my visual landscape was full of soldiers. Of course, I became a soldier for two years of national service and so that was another kind of soldier." In 1954 he was awarded a creative writing fellowship at Stanford University, where he studied with Yvor Winters, under whose influence he flourished, four years later becoming an instructor at the University of California at Berkeley, where he would remain until 1999. The experience of nursing a close friend dying of AIDS led to composition of a series of fifty poems about the disease. They were epigrammatic, modeled on the poetry of Ben Jonson, geared to restrained elegy. "What most of these poems have in common as a subject is the way people face death," he once remarked. By the time he published *The Man with Night Sweats* in 1992, Gunn could tell an interviewer, in direct contradiction to those who doubted its existence, "AIDS is something real. It is a fact. It is a past fact too, and a present fact. Most of my friends have been killed by AIDS, most of my friends." We regard Gunn as an activist, in that he drew popular attention to the disease at a time when it was either denied or regarded as the preserve of homosexuals. *The Man with Night Sweats* succeeded not merely in memorializing those who perished, but in bringing to wider attention a threat with which everyone would have to contend.

The Man With Night Sweats

I wake up cold, I who
Prospered through dreams of heat
Wake to their residue,
Sweat, and a clinging sheet.

My flesh was its own shield:
Where it was gashed, it healed.

I grew as I explored
The body I could trust
Even while I adored
The risk that made robust,

A world of wonders in
Each challenge to the skin.

I cannot but be sorry
The given shield was cracked,
My mind reduced to hurry,
My flesh reduced and wrecked.

I have to change the bed,
But catch myself instead

Stopped upright where I am
Hugging my body to me
As if to shield it from
The pains that will go through me,

As if hands were enough
To hold an avalanche off.

Published 1992

Henry Dumas (1934–1968)

HENRY DUMAS'S LIFE was cut short at the age of thirty-four by a police-man's bullet, when he was killed in a subway station at 125th Street and Lenox Avenue in New York City on May 23, 1968—a case of "mistaken identity." His wrongful death, emblematic of the position African Americans occupied in the 1960s, ended a promising career in poetry almost before it began: the vast majority of his work was gathered and submitted for publication post-humously by his friend and colleague, Eugene Redmond. Having grown up in racially segregated Arkansas, where he witnessed firsthand the oppressive effects of Jim Crow laws, Dumas absorbed from his earliest years the folk and religious traditions of the black South. He went on to join the U.S. Air Force, and was stationed in San Antonio, Texas, as well as Saudi Arabia, where he studied Arab culture and religion. After discharge, he took a job with IBM and in his spare time played an active role in civil rights efforts, transporting food and clothing to protesters in tent cities in Tennessee and Mississippi. In 1967 he took a teaching job at Southern Illinois University, where he met Eugene Redmond; it was while visiting New York City that he was gunned down by a transit policeman in Harlem. Amiri Baraka has hailed Dumas as "an underground deity"; Toni Morrison who (as senior editor at Random House in the 1970s) saw some of Dumas's earliest volumes into print, observes he "was able to penetrate, almost like an archeologist, those areas that com-prise the extraordinary, varied experiences of black people of all ages."

Son of Msippi

Up
from Msippi I grew.
(Bare walk and cane stalk
make a hungry belly talk.)

Up
from the river of death.
(Walk bare and stalk cane
make a hungry belly talk.)

Up
from Msippi I grew.
Up
from the river of pain.

Out of the long red earth dipping, rising,
spreading out in deltas and plains,
out of the strong black earth turning
over by the iron plough,

out of the swamp green earth dripping
with moss and snakes,

out of the loins of the leveed lands
muscling its American vein:
the great Father of Waters,
I grew
up,
beside the prickly boll of white,
beside the bone-filled Mississippi
rolling on and on,
breaking over,
cutting off,
ignoring my bleeding fingers.

Bare stalk and sun walk
I hear a boll weevil talk
cause I grew
up
beside the ox and the bow,
beside the rock church and the shack row,
beside the fox and the crow,
beside the melons and maize,

beside the hound dog,
  beside the pink hog,
flea-hunting,
mud-grunting,
cat-fishing,
dog pissing
in the Mississippi
rolling on and on,
ignoring the colored coat I spun
of cotton fibers.

Cane-sweat riverboat
nigger-bone floating.

Up from Msippi
I grew,
wailing a song with every strain.

Woman gone woe man too
baby cry rent-pause daddy flew.

Published 1970

Agha Shahid Ali (1949–2001)

"I WISH ALL this had not happened," Ali once said, "this dividing of the country, the divisions between people—Hindu, Muslim, Muslim, Hindu—you can't imagine how much I hate it. It makes me sick." Born in New Delhi to a Shiite Muslim family less than two years after the partition of India, Ali grew up in Srinagar, in the Vale of Kashmir—a majority Muslim state invaded by Pakistan in 1947, divided under a 1949 ceasefire, and thereafter a flashpoint both for indigenous liberation struggles and tensions between India and Pakistan. As a boy he attended an Irish Catholic school and learned three languages—Urdu, Kashmiri, and English. "It was culturally a very rich atmosphere," he recalled. "There was never a hint of any kind of parochialism in the home." He wrote his first poems at the age of twelve, and would continue writing for the rest of his life. He already had a master's in English from the University of Delhi when in 1976 he moved to the United States to earn his doctoral degree at Penn State that led to the publication of *T. S. Eliot as Editor* in 1986. Ali remained in America until his death, but was deeply troubled as the political situation in Kashmir deteriorated, something he witnessed firsthand on occasional return visits; it dominates his last two books, *The Country Without a Post Office* (1997) and *Rooms Are Never Finished* (2001). "I think of people who because of historical forces have lost so much," he once said. "I mean, these things are in my way of looking at the world. I'm in one way or another obsessed with all that."

At the Museum

But in 2500 B.C. Harappa,
who cast in bronze a servant girl?

No one keeps records
of soldiers and slaves.

The sculptor knew this,
polishing the ache

off her fingers stiff
from washing the walls

and scrubbing the floors,
from stirring the meat

and the crushed asafoetida
in the bitter gourd.

But I'm grateful she smiled
at the sculptor,

as she smiles at me
in bronze,

a child who had to play woman
to her lord

when the warm June rains
came to Harappa.

Published April 1990

I See Chile in My Rearview Mirror

> By dark the world is once again intact,
> Or so the mirrors, wiped clean, try to reason . . .
>
> —JAMES MERRILL

This dream of water—what does it harbor?
I see Argentina and Paraguay
under a curfew of glass, their colors
breaking, like oil. The night in Uruguay

is black salt. I'm driving toward Utah,
keeping the entire hemisphere in view—
Colombia vermilion, Brazil blue tar,
some countries wiped clean of color: Peru

is titanium white. And always oceans
that hide in mirrors: when beveled edges
arrest tides or this world's destinations
forsake ships. There's Sedona, Nogales

far behind. Once I went through a mirror—
from there too the world, so intact, resembled
only itself. When I returned I tore
the skin off the glass. The sea was unsealed

by dark, and I saw ships sink off the coast
of a wounded republic. Now from a blur
of tanks in Santiago, a white horse
gallops, riderless, chased by drunk soldiers

in a jeep; they're firing into the moon.
And as I keep driving in the desert,
someone is running to catch the last bus, men
hanging on to its sides. And he's missed it.

He is running again; crescents of steel
fall from the sky. And here the rocks
are under fog, the cedars a temple,
Sedona carved by the wind into gods—

each shadow their worshiper. The siren
empties Santiago; he watches
—from a hush of windows—blindfolded men
blurred in gleaming vans. The horse vanishes

into a dream. I'm passing skeletal
figures carved in 700 B.C.
Whoever deciphers these canyon walls
remains forsaken, alone with history,

no harbor for his dream. And what else will
this mirror now reason, filled with water?
I see Peru without rain, Brazil
without forests—and here in Utah a dagger

of sunlight: it's splitting—it's the summer
solstice—the quartz center of a spiral.
Did the Anasazi know the darker
answer also—given now in crystal

by the mirrored continent? The solstice,
but of winter? A beam stabs the window,
diamonds him, a funeral in his eyes.
In the lit stadium of Santiago,

this is the shortest day. He's taken there.
Those about to die are looking at him,
his eyes the ledger of the disappeared.
What will the mirror try now? I'm driving,

still north, always followed by that country,
its floors ice, its citizens so lovesick
that the ground—sheer glass—of every city
is torn up. They demand the republic

give back, jeweled, their every reflection.
They dig till dawn but find only corpses.
He has returned to this dream for his bones.
The waters darken. The continent vanishes.

Published 1991

The Floating Post Office

THE POST BOAT WAS LIKE A GONDOLA THAT CALLED AT
EACH HOUSEBOAT. IT CARRIED A CLERK, WEIGHING SCALES,
AND A BELL TO ANNOUNCE ARRIVALS.

Has he been kept from us? Portents
of rain, rumors, ambushed letters . . .
Curtained palanquin, fetch our word,
bring us word: Who has died? Who'll live?
Has the order gone out to close
the waterways . . . the one open road?

And then we saw the boat being rowed
through the fog of death, the sentence
passed on our city. It came close
to reveal smudged black-ink letters
which the postman—he *was* alive—
gave us, like signs, without a word,

and we took them, without a word.
From our deck we'd seen the hill road
bringing a jade rain, near olive,
down from the temple, some penitent's
cymbaled prayer? He took our letters,
and held them, like a lover, close

to his heart. And the rain drew close.
Was there, we asked, a new password—
blood, blood shaken into letters,
cruel primitive script that would erode
our saffron link to the past? Tense
with autumn, the leaves, drenched olive,

fell on graveyards, crying "O live!"
What future would the rain disclose?
O Rain, abandon all pretense,
now drown the world, give us your word,
ring, sweet assassin of the road,
the temple bell! For if letters

come, I will answer those letters
and my year will be tense, alive
with love! The temple receives the road:
there, the rain has come to a close.
Here the waters rise; our each word
in the fog awaits a sentence:

His hand on the scales, he gives his word:
Our letters will be rowed through olive
canals, tense waters no one can close.

Published 1997

Land

For Christopher Merrill

Swear by the olive in the God-kissed land—
There is no sugar in the promised land.

Why must the bars turn neon now when, Love,
I'm already drunk in your capitalist land?

If home is found on both sides of the globe,
home is of course here—and always a missed land.

The hour's come to redeem the pledge (not wholly?)
in Fate's "Long years ago we made a tryst" land.

Clearly, these men were here only to destroy,
a mosque now the dust of a prejudiced land.

Will the Doomsayers die, bitten with envy,
when springtime returns to our dismissed land?

The prisons fill with the cries of children.
Then how do you subsist, how do you persist, Land?

"Is my love nothing for I've borne no children?"
I'm with you, Sappho, in that anarchist land.

A hurricane is born when the wings flutter . . .
Where will the butterfly, on my wrist, land?

You made me wait for one who wasn't even there
though summer had finished in that tourist land.

Do the blind hold temples close to their eyes
when we steal their gods for our atheist land?

Abandoned bride, Night throws down her jewels
so Rome—on our descent—is an amethyst land.

At the moment the heart turns terrorist,
are Shahid's arms broken, O Promised Land?

Published July 2001

Permissions Acknowledgments

Grateful acknowledgment is made to the following editors, authors, heirs, publishers, and agents for their permission to reprint poems in *Poetry of Witness: The Tradition in English, 1500–2001*.

Agha Shahid Ali, "At the Museum" and "The Floating Post Office." Copyright © 1997 by Agha Shahid Ali. "I See Chile in My Rearview Mirror." Copyright © 1991 by Agha Shahid Ali. "Land." Copyright © 2003 by Agha Shahid Ali Literary Trust. From *The Veiled Suite: The Collected Poems* by Agha Shahid Ali. Reprinted by permission of W. W. Norton & Company, Inc.

Edmund Blunden, "Preparations for Victory," "Festubert, 1916," and "Premature Rejoicing" from *Selected Poems* edited by Robyn Marsack. Copyright © 1986 by Carcanet Press. Reprinted by permission of the Carcanet Press.

Basil Bunting, *Briggflatts* (extract) from *Complete Poems* edited by Richard Caddel. Copyright © 2000 by Bloodaxe Books. Reprinted by permission of Bloodaxe Books.

Hayden Carruth, "Emergency Haying" from *From Snow and Rock, From Chaos* by Hayden Carruth. Copyright © 1973 by New Directions Publishing Corp. Reprinted by permission of New Directions Publishing Corp. "Three Sonnets on the Necessity of Narrowly Escaping Death" from *Poetry* magazine, vol. 71, no. 5 (February 1948), pp. 244–45. Copyright © 1948 by Hayden Carruth. Reprinted by permission of Joe Anne McLaughlin Carruth.

John Clare, "I dreaded walking where there was no path," from *Northborough Sonnets* edited by Eric Robinson. Copyright © 1995 by the Carcanet Press. Reprinted by permission of the Carcanet Press. *The Village Minstrel* (extract) and "The Moors," from *A Champion for the Poor* edited by P. M. S. Dawson, Eric Robinson and David Powell. Copyright © 2000 by the Carcanet Press. Reprinted by permission of the Carcanet Press.

John Cornford, "To Margot Heinemann," "A Letter from Aragon," and "Full Moon at Tierz: Before the Storming of Huesca" from *Collected Writings* edited by Jonathan Galassi. Copyright © 1989 by the Carcanet Press. Reprinted by permission of the Carcanet Press.

Index

Harry Mattison

Carolyn Forché, poet and translator, is the author of four volumes of poetry: *Gathering the Tribes*, *The Country Between Us*, *The Angel of History*, and *Blue Hour*. The recipient of the Yale Series of Younger Poets Award, a Lannan Literary Award, the *Los Angeles Times* Book Prize, and, most recently, the Academy of American Poets Fellowship, she is also the editor of the anthology *Against Forgetting*, a companion volume to *Poetry of Witness*.

Duncan Wu, biographer and scholar, is a professor of English Literature at Georgetown University, where he specializes in British Romanticism. His numerous publications include *William Hazlitt: The First Modern Man*, *Wordsworth: An Inner Life*, and *Romanticism: An Anthology*.